Essentials of
Life Insurance Products

Financial Advisor Series

C. Bruce Worsham, Editor

Forthcoming Titles in the Series

Sales Skills Techniques

Techniques for Marketing Financial Services Products

Techniques for Meeting Client Needs

Techniques for Building a Financial Services Career

Product Essentials

Essentials of Annuities

Essentials of Disability Income Insurance

Essentials of Life Insurance Products

Essentials of Life Insurance Law

Essentials of Employee Benefits

Planning Foundations

Foundations of Senior Planning

Foundations of Estate Planning

Foundations of Retirement Planning

Foundations of Financial Planning: An Overview

Foundations of Financial Planning: The Environment

Financial Advisor Series: Product Essentials

Essentials of
Life Insurance Products

Burke A. Christensen, JD, CLU and
Glenn E. Stevick, Jr., CLU, ChFC, LUTCF, Editors

THE
AMERICAN
COLLEGE
THE LEADER IN FINANCIAL SERVICES EDUCATION

ISBN 1-57996-090-1

Contents

Preface vii
Acknowledgments ix
About the Editors xi
Special Notes to Advisors xiii
About the Financial Advisor Series xv
Overview of the Book xvii

1. Economic Basics of Life Insurance
Overview and Learning Objectives 1-1
Basic Principles 1-3
Human Life Value 1-17
Chapter One Review 1-39

2. Term and Whole Life Insurance
Overview and Learning Objectives 2-1
Term Insurance 2-3
Whole Life Insurance 2-19
Chapter Two Review 2-29

3. Variations of Whole Life Insurance
Overview and Learning Objectives 3-1
Whole Life Variations 3-3
Chapter Three Review 3-39

4. Personal, Family, and Business Uses of Life Insurance
Overview and Learning Objectives 4-1
Personal and Family Uses of Life Insurance 4-3
Business Uses of Life Insurance 4-19
Chapter Four Review 4-65

5. Comparing Costs and Policy Illustrations
Overview and Learning Objectives 5-1
Methods of Comparing Life Insurance Policy Costs 5-3
Policy Illustrations 5-17
Chapter Five Review 5-41
Tables 5-47

6. Selection and Classification of Risks

    Overview and Learning Objectives..6-1

    Selection of Risks 6-3

    Classification of Risks 6-21

    Chapter Six Review 6-39

7. Policy Provisions

    Overview and Learning Objectives 7-1

    Policy Provisions 7-3

    Chapter Seven Review 7-41

8. Settlement Agreements and Ethical Issues of Classifying Risks

    Overview and Learning Objectives 8-1

    Settlement Agreements 8-3

    Ethical Issues of Classifying Risk..8-29

    Chapter Eight Review 8-47

Glossary...G-1

Answers to Questions A-1

Index Index-1

Preface

The mission of this book is to develop your professionalism as a financial advisor counseling prospects and clients about the need for life insurance. We intend to do this by teaching you about the benefits of life insurance in shaping your performance as a successful advisor. By gaining a deeper understanding of the life insurance contract and the economic needs it satisfies, you will become a better financial advisor. The text will also analyze the technical aspects of life insurance policies and study ways of comparing them. It will review the selection and classification of risks process and examine the life insurance policy provisions. It is our hope that this book has the right blend technical knowledge and practical information to accomplish this mission.

While much of the text material will be new to you, some will, no doubt, refresh knowledge you acquired in the past. In either case, all of the text material is both valuable and necessary if you aspire to be successful in the life insurance marketplace. The benefits you gain from studying the text material will be directly proportional to the effort you expend. So read each chapter carefully and answer both the essay and multiple choice review questions for the chapter (preferably before looking in the back of the book for the answers); to do less would be to deprive yourself of a unique opportunity to become familiar with life insurance and to learn more about selling it.

The book includes numerous educational features designed to help you focus your study of life insurance. Among the features found in each chapter of the book are

- an overview and learning objectives
- a chapter outline
- examples, figures, and lists
- key terms and concepts
- review questions (essay format)
- self-test questions (multiple choice format)

The back of the book includes a glossary, answers to the questions, and an index.

Finally, all of the individuals noted on the acknowledgments page made this a better book, and we are grateful. However, in spite of the help of all of these fine individuals, some errors have undoubtedly eluded us. For these we are solely responsible. At the same time, however, we accept full credit for giving those of you who find these errors the exhilarating intellectual experience produced by such discovery.

Acknowledgments

This book was edited by Glenn Stevick, Jr., LUTC author/editor at The American College. The manuscript was adapted by Burke A. Christensen, JD, CLU, from *McGill's Life Insurance*, 4th edition, Edward E. Graves, Editor.

For their valuable contribution to the development of this book, appreciation is extended to senior editor Todd Denton for editing the manuscript, and to Charlene McNulty and Evelyn Rice for production assistance.

Very special thanks to Burton T. Beam, Jr. associate professor of insurance at The American College, and Edward E. Graves, associate professor of insurance and Chairholder of the Charles J. Zimmerman Chair in Life Insurance Education at The American College, for their generous help and expertise in creating this book.

To all of these individuals, without whom this book would not have been possible, the College expresses its sincere appreciation and gratitude.

      C. Bruce Worsham
      Associate Vice President and Director
      Educational Development
      The American College

About the Editors

Burke A. Christensen, JD, CLU, has 25 years of experience as an insurance, tax, and estate planning lawyer. He was awarded the Chartered Life Underwriter designation in 1987. In April 1995, he became a life insurance agent and was appointed vice president of A.W. Ormiston & Co., a 64-year-old insurance brokerage agency, which specializes in providing life and health insurance to large law firms throughout the United States. From 1984 to 1995, Mr. Christensen was vice president and general counsel for the American Society of CLU & ChFC (now called the Society of Financial Service Professionals) in Bryn Mawr, Pennsylvania. He has served on the drafting committees for the American Society's Life Insurance Illustration Questionnaire and the policy Replacement Questionnaire (RQ). He is a frequent author and lecturer on insurance and estate planning. Since 1979, his column, "Law & Life Insurance," has appeared monthly in *Trusts & Estates* magazine. He was a contributing author for the 1994 edition of *McGill's Life Insurance,* and he has written other articles for the *Journal of Insurance Regulation, Trusts & Estates, Probate & Property,* and the *National Law Journal.* Since 1985, he has been the author of the Society's column on business and professional ethics, "Strictly Speaking," which is published in the *Journal of the Financial Service Professionals.* Mr. Christensen is a graduate of Utah State University and the University of Utah College of Law. He is a member of the Pennsylvania and American Bar Associations, and he is admitted to practice before the United States Supreme Court.

Glenn E. Stevick, Jr., MA, CLU, ChFC, LUTCF, is an author/editor at The American College. His responsibilities at the College include writing and preparing text materials for the LUTC *Meeting Client Needs, Long-Term Care* and *Essentials of Business Insurance* courses. He writes articles for *Advisor Today,* the national magazine distributed to members of NAIFA. He also currently teaches the Insurance and Financial Planning course at the American College.

Before joining the College, Mr. Stevick worked for New York Life as a training supervisor for 15 years in its South Jersey office. He also served as an agent with New York Life for more than 2 years. Prior to his insurance industry experience, Mr. Stevick taught psychology at the college level and worked in various educational and mental health programs. Mr. Stevick earned his BA degree from Villanova University and his MA degree from Duquesne University.

Special Notes to Advisors

Text Materials Disclaimer

This publication is designed to provide accurate and authoritative information about the subject covered. While every precaution has been taken in the preparation of this material to insure that it is both accurate and up-to-date, it is still possible that some errors eluded detection. Moreover, some material may become inaccurate and/or outdated either because it is time sensitive or because new legislation will make it so. Still other material may be viewed as inaccurate because your company's products and procedures are different from those described in the book. Therefore, the authors and The American College assume no liability for damages resulting from the use of the information contained in this book. The American College is not engaged in rendering legal, accounting, or other professional advice. If legal or other expert advice is required, the services of an appropriate professional should be sought.

Caution Regarding Use of Illustrations

The illustrations, sales ideas and approaches in this book are not to be used with the public unless you have obtained approval from your company. Your company's general support of The American College's programs for training and educational purposes does not constitute blanket approval of the sales ideas and approaches presented in this book, unless so communicated in writing by your company.

Use of the Terms *Financial Advisor* or *Advisor*

Use of the term *financial advisor* as it appears in this book is intended as the generic reference to professional members of our reading audience. It is used interchangeably with the term *advisor* to avoid unnecessary redundancy. *Financial advisor* takes the place of the following terms:

Account Executive
Agent
Associate
Broker (stock or insurance)
Financial Consultant
Financial Planner
Financial Planning Professional
Financial Services Professional
Health Underwriter
Insurance Professional

Life Insurance Agent
Life Underwriter
Planner
Practitioner
Producer
Property & Casualty Agent
Registered Investment Advisor
Registered Representative
Senior Advisor

Answers to the Questions in the Book

The answers to all essay and multiple-choice questions in this book are based on the text materials as written.

About the Financial Advisor Series

The mission of The American College is to raise the level of professionalism of its students and, by extension, the financial services industry as a whole. As an educational product of the College, the Financial Advisor Series shares in this mission. Because knowledge is the key to professionalism, a thorough and comprehensive reading of each book in the Series will help the practitioner advisor to better service his or her clients. A task made all the more difficult because the typical client is becoming ever more financially sophisticated with each passing day and demands that his or her financial advisor be knowledgeable about the latest products and planning methodologies. By providing practitioner advisors in the financial services industry with up-to-date, authoritative information about various marketing and sales techniques, product knowledge, and planning considerations, the books of the Financial Advisor Series will enable many practitioner advisors to continue their studies so as to develop and maintain a high level of professional competence.

When all books in the Financial Advisor Series are completed, the Series will encompass 15 titles spread across three separate subseries, each with a special focus. The first subseries, *Sales Skills Techniques,* will focus on enhancing the practitioner advisor's marketing and sales skills, but will also cover some product knowledge and planning considerations. The second subseries, *Product Essentials,* will focus on product knowledge, but will also delve into marketing and sales skills as well as planning considerations in many of its books. The third subseries, *Planning Foundations,* will focus on various planning considerations and processes that form the foundation for a successful career as a financial services professional. When appropriate, product knowledge and sales and marketing skills will also be touched upon in many of its books.

When all 15 titles in the Series are completed, they will be divided among the three subseries as follows:

Sales Skills Techniques
- *Techniques for Marketing Financial Services Products*
- *Techniques for Meeting Client Needs*
- *Techniques for Building a Financial Services Career*

Product Essentials
- *Essentials of Annuities*
- *Essentials of Long-Term Care Insurance*
- *Essentials of Business Insurance*
- *Essentials of Disability Income Insurance*

- *Essentials of Life Insurance Products*
- *Essentials of Life Insurance Law*
- *Essentials of Employee Benefits*

Planning Foundations
- *Foundations of Senior Planning*
- *Foundations of Estate Planning*
- *Foundations of Retirement Planning*
- *Foundations of Financial Planning: An Overview*
- *Foundations of Financial Planning: The Environment*

This book, *Essentials of Life Insurance Products,* is the third in the Series. Other books in the Series will be forthcoming over the ensuing months and years.

Overview of the Book

Essentials of Life Insurance Products is an adaptation and selection of topics from *McGill's Life Insurance*.

This book examines the fundamentals of the life insurance product. It begins with the basics of life insurance, including insurance principles, product design and the economic value of a human life. The course covers the two most basic forms of life insurance, term and whole life, then expands into the variations of whole life insurance, which represent the great array of products sold in today's markets. Additional topics include the personal, family, and business uses of life insurance, comparing costs between policies, policy illustrations, the selection and classification of risks, policy provisions and surrender options, and settlement options and the ethical issues facing the financial advisor.

To accomplish this, the text covers in Chapter 1 the economic basics of life insurance, with emphasis on the human life value approach and the economic justifications for its use. The concepts covered include risk pooling, how the premium is determined, personal life insurance needs, and how to determine the amount of life insurance needed by an individual. Chapter 2 provides an in-depth look at the term and whole life insurance policies, explaining how they work and the uses for each. Chapter 3 examines the variations of whole life insurance in great detail. Chapter 4 expands on the personal needs for life insurance, and provides a detailed and comprehensive review of the needs and uses for life insurance in business situations. Chapter 5 reviews the methods of fairly comparing policy costs and some critical components of policy illustrations of which most of the public and even some advisors are unaware or simply overlook. Chapter 6 examines the selection and risk classification process in life insurance underwriting, bringing to life the factors of risk selection that a financial advisor should know. Chapter 7 studies the policy provisions that define the life insurance contract and how it operates.   Lastly, Chapter 8 covers the topic of settlement agreements and reviews ethical principles for a professional financial advisor.

Essentials of
Life Insurance Products

1

Economic Basics of Life Insurance

Overview and Learning Objectives

Chapter 1 explores the concept of risk pooling and the principles of life insurance. It then discusses the concept of human life value and the economic basis for the economic basis for the need for life insurance. It then focuses on the specific needs for life insurance and techniques that can be used for determining these needs.

By reading this chapter and answering the questions, you should be able to

1-1. Explain the concept of risk pooling.

1-2. Explain how the premium for yearly renewable term is determined.

1-3. Describe why the period for renewability for term insurance is limited.

1-4. Describe how the level premium insurance concept works.

1-5. Explain the concept of human life value and how it relates to the need for life insurance.

1-6. Apply the five-step process for estimating a person's economic value to the family.

1-7. List and explain the life insurance needs used by needs analysis to determine the need for life insurance.

1-8. Explain the process of providing for the post-death financial needs of survivors.

Chapter Outline

Basic Principles   1-3
    Risk Pooling   1-3
    Level Premium Plan   1-8
Human Life Value   1-17
    The Concept of Human Life Value   1-17
    Source of the Economic Value of the Human Life   1-18
    Measurement of Monetary Value   1-20
    Diminishing Nature of the Economic Value   1-25
    Bases for Insurance   1-26
    Needs Analysis   1-27
Chapter Review   1-39

Basic Principles

Insurance has been defined in many different ways and from different institutional points of view. From an economic viewpoint, insurance is a system for reducing financial risk by transferring it from a policyowner to an insurer. The social aspect of insurance involves the collective bearing of losses through contributions by all members of a group to pay for losses suffered by some group members.

Insurance substitutes certainty for uncertainty through the pooling of hazards to which groups of people are exposed. Uncertain risks of individuals are combined, making the possible loss more certain, providing a financial solution to the problems created by the loss. Small, periodic contributions by the individuals provide a fund from which those who suffer loss may be reimbursed. Insurance thus manages the uncertainty of one party through the transfer of particular risks to another party who offers a restoration, at least in part, of economic losses suffered by the insured individual.

From a business viewpoint, insurance achieves the sharing of risk by transferring risks from individuals and businesses to financial institutions specializing in risk. Lastly, from a legal standpoint, an insurance contract or policy transfers a risk (for a premium) from one party, known as the insured or policyowner, to another party known as the insurer. By virtue of a legally binding contract, the possibility of an unknown large financial loss is exchanged for a comparatively small certain payment. This contract is not a guarantee against a loss occurring, but a method of ensuring that payment will be received for a loss that does occur.

Risk Pooling

Underlying all of these definitions is the concept of *risk pooling*, or group sharing, of losses. That is, persons exposed to loss from a particular source combine their risks and agree to share losses on some equitable basis. The risks may be combined under an arrangement whereby the participants mutually insure each other, a plan that is appropriately designated "mutual insurance," or they may be transferred to an organization that, for a consideration called the "premium," is willing to assume the risks and pay the resulting losses. In life insurance, such an organization is a stock life insurance company. While several elements must be present in any sound insurance plan, the essence of the arrangement is the pooling of risks and losses.

Illustration of the Risk Pooling Concept

The simplest illustration of risk pooling involves insurance for one year, with all members of the group the same age and possessing roughly similar prospects for longevity. The members of this group might mutually agree that a specified sum, such as $100,000, will be paid to the designated beneficiaries of those members who die during the year, the cost of the payments being borne equally by the members of the group. In its simplest form, this arrangement might involve an assessment upon each member in the appropriate amount as each death occurs. In a group of 1,000 persons, each death would produce an assessment of $100 per member. Among a group of 10,000 males aged 35, 21 of them could be expected to die within a year, according to the *Commissioners 1980 Standard Ordinary Mortality Table (1980 CSO Table)*; if expenses of operation are ignored, cumulative assessments of $210 per person would provide the funds for payment of $100,000 to the beneficiary of each of the 21 deceased persons. Larger death payments would produce proportionately larger assessments based on the rate of $2.10 per $1,000 of benefit.

The CSO Mortality Table is used to calculate reserves and minimum cash values for state regulatory purposes. A new table, the 2001 CSO Mortality Table is currently being introduced and approved for use in the various states.

Example:	10,000 males aged 35 contribute to a life insurance pool. Twenty-one of the 10,000 are expected to die while aged 35 (based on 1980 CSO mortality table). If each of the 10,000 contributes $210 to fund death benefits (ignoring costs of operation), a death benefit of $100,000 could be paid for each of the 21 expected deaths.

The 1980 CSO mortality table lists different rates at each age for men and women. The rate per $1,000 of benefit for women aged 35 is $1.65 in the 1980 CSO table. Most large insurance companies base their rates on their own statistics rather than 1980 CSO. The companies that issue policies only to the healthiest applicants will have rates significantly lower than those of the CSO tables used for reserving purposes by the regulators. Even insurance companies issuing policies to applicants in average health usually experience rates lower than CSO rates.

We will first examine how the premium for a *Yearly Renewable Term (YRT)* insurance policy is calculated. YRT is the simplest form of insurance offered by regular life insurance companies. It provides insurance for a period of 1 year only but permits the policyowner to renew the policy for successive periods of one year each without the necessity of furnishing *evidence of insurability*. This means the policyowner can renew the policy without submitting to a medical examination or providing other evidence of good health, simply by paying the renewal premium.

Determining the Premium

The premium for yearly renewable term insurance is determined by the death rate for the attained age of the individual involved. (This ignores expenses of operation and interest earned on invested prepaid premiums, but the principle involved is still valid.) This is attributable to the fact that each premium purchases only one year of insurance protection. Moreover, each group of policy owners of a given age is considered to be a separate class for premium purposes; each group must pay its own death claims, the burden borne pro rata by the members of the group.

Because the death rate increases with age, the premium for yearly renewable term insurance increases each year.

Example: In a group of 100,000 women aged 25
- Mortality rate for females aged 25: 1.16 per 1,000
- Expected deaths from group: —116
- $1,000 death benefit per deceased=$116,000 in claims
- Each woman could contribute $1.16 and cover the death benefit amount (ignoring costs of operation)

To illustrate, the female death rate at age 25, according to the 1980 CSO Table, is 1.16 per 1,000. If an insurance company should insure a group of 100,000 women aged 25 for $1,000 each for one year, it could expect 116 death claims, aggregating $116,000. Because premiums are paid to the life insurance company in advance, the cost of the anticipated death claims would be distributed pro rata over the 100,000 policy owners, and a premium of $1.16 would be exacted from each policyowner. Note that:

- the premium is precisely the same as the death rate applicable to those insured
- those policyowners who, according to the mortality projection, will die during the year contribute on the same basis as those who will survive

The implication of the latter is that each policyowner pays a share of his or her own death claim. This is a principle that underlies all life insurance contracts. The proportion, however, varies with the type of contract, age at issue, and duration of the protection. The implications of the former are made clear in the following paragraphs.

If the 99,884 survivors of the original group of 100,000 policy owners should be insured for another year, they would be exposed to the death rate for persons aged 26, or 1.19 per 1,000, which would theoretically produce 119 deaths and claims totaling $119,000. That sum divided equally among the 99,884 participants would yield a share, or premium, of $1.19 per person. If the 99,765 women who survived the first and second year should desire insurance for another year, provision would have to be made for $122,000 in death claims, necessitating a premium of $1.22 per person.

For the first several years, the premium would continue to increase slowly, being only $1.35 at age 30, $1.65 at age 35, and $2.42 at age 40. Thereafter, however, the premium would rise sharply, reaching $3.56 at age 45, $4.96 at 50, $7.09 at 55, $9.47 at 60, and $14.59 at 65. If the insurance should be continued beyond age 65, the cost would soon become prohibitive, soaring to $22.11 per $1,000 at age 70, $38.24 at 75, $65.99 at 80, and $116.10 at 85. The premium at 90 would be $190.75 per $1,000; at 95, $317.32. Finally, if a woman aged 99 should want $1,000 of insurance on the yearly renewable term basis, she would have to pay a premium of $1,000, since the 1980 CSO Table assumes that the limit of life is 100 years and that a person aged 99 will die within the year.

Limiting the Period of Renewability

If the surviving members of the aforementioned group should continue to renew their insurance year after year, the steadily increasing premiums would cause many to question the advisability of continuing the insurance. After a point, there would be a tendency for the healthy individuals to give up their protection, while those in poor health would continue to renew their policies, regardless of cost. This is *adverse selection* against the insurance company.

The withdrawal of the healthy members would accelerate the increase in the death rate among the continuing members and, unless ample margins were provided in the insurance company's premium rates, could produce death claims in excess of premium income. In this event, the loss would be borne by the company, because the rates at which the policy can be renewed are guaranteed for the entire period of *renewability*. It is for this reason that companies offering yearly renewable term insurance on an individual basis often place a limit on the period during which the insurance can be renewed.

Even without restrictions on the period during which the insurance can be renewed, yearly renewable term insurance is not usually feasible for long-term protection. Dissatisfaction with increasing premiums causes many policyowners to discontinue their insurance, often at a time when, because of physical condition or other circumstances, they cannot obtain other insurance. They are also likely to resent that after years of premium payments at increasing financial sacrifice, the insurance protection is lost, with no tangible benefits for the sacrifice involved.

More important, however, is the fact that few, if any, individuals are able and willing to continue their insurance into the advanced ages where death is most likely to occur. Yet the great majority of individuals need insurance that can be continued until death, at whatever age it might occur. This need led to the development of level premium insurance.

Level Premium Plan

Level premium insurance is just what the name implies—a plan of insurance under which premiums do not increase from year to year but, instead, remain constant throughout the premium-paying period. It does not imply that the insured must pay premiums as long as he or she has insurance protection, only that all premiums required will be of equal size. (In modified life policies, the premium for the first few years of the contract is lower than that required for the remainder of the premium-paying period. There are also graded premium policies with increasing premiums over a period up to 20 years that are followed by level premiums thereafter.)

It must be apparent that if premiums that have a natural tendency to increase with each passing year are leveled out, the premiums paid in the early years of the contract will be more than sufficient to meet current death claims, while those paid in the later years will be less than adequate to meet incurred claims. This is a simple concept, but it has manifold ramifications and far-reaching significance.

With the level premium technique the redundant premiums in the early years of the contract create an accumulation that is held by the insurance company for the benefit and to the credit of the policyowners. (This is not a trust fund in the legal sense, which would require the insurance company to establish separate investment accounts for each policyowner and render periodic accountings.) This accumulation is called a *reserve,* which is not merely a restriction on surplus as in the ordinary accounting sense, but an amount that must be accumulated and maintained by the insurance company in order to meet definite future obligations.

Because the manner in which the fund is to be accumulated and invested is strictly regulated by law, the reserve is usually referred to in official literature as the *legal reserve.* Technically the reserve is a composite liability account of the insurance company, not susceptible to allocation to individual policies, but for present purposes it may be viewed as an aggregate of individual accounts established to the credit of the various policyowners. In practice each policy is credited with a cash value or surrender value, which is not the same as the reserve but has its basis in the redundant premiums of the early years.

Term Policies

From the standpoint of an individual policy, the excess portions of the premiums paid in the early years of the contract are accumulated at compound interest and subsequently used to supplement the inadequate premiums of the later years. This process can be explained most simply in connection with a contract that provides protection for only a temporary period, as opposed to one that provides insurance for the policyowner's whole of life.

Figure 1-1 shows the level premium mechanism in connection with a term policy issued at age 25, to run to age 65. The level premiums to age 65 are based on the 1980 CSO Female Table and an interest assumption of 4.5 percent. In other words, it is assumed, with respect to the level premium calculations, that the reserves are invested at 4.5 percent, and with respect to the yearly renewable term premiums, that each premium earns 4.5 percent for one year before being disbursed in the form of death benefits.

In this example no allowance is made for expenses, which makes it easier to understand. It also conforms to the legislative and regulatory approach of setting reserves strictly on the basis of interest and mortality without consideration of other operating costs.

In figure 1-1 the curve *AB* represents the premiums at successive ages that would be required to provide $1,000 of insurance from age 25 to age 65 on the yearly renewable term basis. The premium ranges from $1.16 at age 25 to $14.59 at age 65. The line *CD* represents the level premium that would be required to provide $1,000 of insurance from age 25 to age 65 on the *level term* basis. The amount of this level premium that would be paid each year through age 64 is $2.99. This exceeds the premiums that would be payable on the yearly renewable term basis prior to age 44 but is smaller than those payable thereafter.

The area *AXC* represents the excess portions of the level premiums paid prior to age 43; the area *BXD* represents the deficiency in premiums after that age. It is apparent that the second area is much larger than the first. The disparity in the size of the two areas is attributable to the fact that the sums represented by the area *AXC,* which constitute the reserve under the contract, are invested at compound interest, and the interest earnings are subsequently used along with the principal sum to supplement the inadequate premiums of the later years.

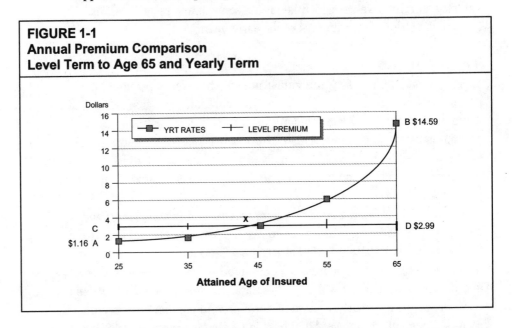

FIGURE 1-1
Annual Premium Comparison
Level Term to Age 65 and Yearly Term

Dollars

Attained Age of Insured

The reserve is completely exhausted at age 65 (the expiration of coverage), having been used to pay the policy's share of death claims submitted under other policies. In other words the reserve, including the investment earnings derived therefrom, is gradually used up after age 44 in the process of supplementing the then-deficient level premium. The reserve under this particular contract—term to 65, issued at age 25—reaches its maximum size at age 53, diminishing thereafter at an accelerating rate until exhausted at the expiration of the policy.

Ordinary Life Policies

The functioning of the level premium plan is even more striking—though more difficult to grasp—when applied to a policy providing insurance for the whole of life. A comparison of the level premium required under an *ordinary life policy* with that required on the yearly renewable term basis is presented in figure 1-2. An ordinary life policy is a type of whole life insurance for which level premiums are based on the assumption that they will be paid until the insured's death or the policy termination date of age 100, whichever comes first.

As in the case of figure 1-1, the age of issue is 25, and the premiums are based on the 1980 CSO Female Table and 4.5 percent interest, with no allowance for expenses. In this case, an annual level premium of $6.09 per $1,000 paid as long as the insured lives would be the mathematical equivalent of a series of premiums on the yearly renewable term basis, ranging from $1.16 per $1,000 at age 25 to $956.94 at age 99.

The 1980 CSO Female Table assumes that everyone who survives to age 99 will die during the year, producing a net premium on the yearly renewable term basis equal to the face of the policy, less the interest that will be earned on the premium during the year. In figure 1-2 line *CD* bisects the curve *AB* between the ages of 53 and 54.

Yearly-Term versus level Premium for life for Female Aged 25

- Annual level premium of $6.09 per $1,000 of coverage
- Exceeds yearly term cost of $1.16 per $1,000 coverage at age 25
- Level premium will exceed the yearly term premium until the insured reaches her mid-50's
- Beyond age 55, the level premium of $6.09 per $1,000 of coverage will be less than the cost of yearly term coverage per $1,000
- By age 99, the yearly term premium of $956.94 per $1,000 of coverage greatly exceeds the $6.09 cost per $1,000

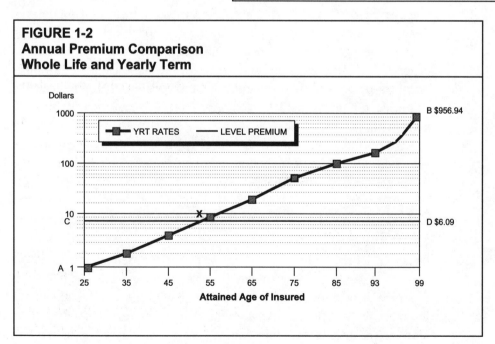

FIGURE 1-2
Annual Premium Comparison
Whole Life and Yearly Term

The disparity between the areas bounded by *AXC* and *BXD* is very much greater in this case than in figure 1-1. Even more amazing, however, is the fact that the excess premiums (area *AXC)* in the early years of an ordinary life contract (or, for that matter, any type of insurance contract except term) will not only offset the deficiency in the premiums of the later years when the term premium is in the hundreds of dollars, but with the aid of compound interest will also accumulate a reserve equal to the face of the policy by the time the insured reaches the terminal age in the mortality table.

This is in contrast to the level premium term contract, under which the reserve is completely used up at the expiration of the contract. The difference is because the risk (probability of occurrence) under a contract providing protection for the whole of life is one "converging into a certainty," while the risk under a term policy is a mere contingency—one that may or may not occur. Under a whole life contract, provision must be made for a death claim that is certain to occur, the only uncertainty being the time it will occur.

By the time an insured has reached 99, the reserve under his or her policy must have accumulated to an amount that, supplemented by the final annual premium and interest on the combined sums for the last 12 months of the contract, will equal the face amount of the policy. This must be the case if each class of policyowners is to be self-supporting, since there are no other funds for the payment of the claims of the last members to die. In effect, such policyowners pay off their own death claims, in addition to paying their share of the death claims of all other members of the group. It should not be surprising, therefore, that the aggregate premiums paid by long-lived persons can exceed the face amount of the policy.

The manner in which the level premium arrangement makes provision for a risk converging into a certainty is explained more thoroughly in the next section.

Effect of Level Premium Technique on Cost of Insurance

Under a level premium type of contract, the accumulated reserve becomes a part of the face amount payable upon the death of the insured. From the standpoint of the insurance company, the effective amount of insurance is the difference between the face amount of the policy and the reserve. Technically speaking, this is the *amount at risk*. As the reserve increases, the amount at risk decreases. The significance of this relationship under discussion is that as the death rate increases, the amount at risk (the effective amount of insurance) decreases, producing a *cost of insurance* within practicable limits.

The cost of insurance is an actuarial term referring to the sum obtained by multiplying the death rate at the insured's attained age by the net amount at risk. This is the amount a policyowner must pay for protection. It is the sum that each policyowner must contribute as his or her pro rata share of death claims in any particular year. This process is illustrated in table 1-1.

As stated earlier, the net level premium for an ordinary life contract on a female issued at age 25, calculated on the basis of the 1980 CSO Table and 4.5 percent interest, is $6.09. Since the death rate at age 25 is 1.16 per 1,000, about $5 of the first premium is excess and goes into the policy reserve. If the policyowner should die during the first year, the company would use the $5 in settling the claim and would have to draw only $995 from the premiums contributed by the other policyowners in the age and policy classification of the deceased. This would mean that each member's pro rata share of death claims in the first year would be only $1.15 (1.16 x 0.995), instead of $1.16, the yearly renewable term premium for $1,000 of insurance at age 25 (with no allowance for interest).

By the end of the 5th year, the reserve, or accumulation of excess payments, will have increased to $22 per $1,000, which sum would be available for settlement of a death claim under the policy. The net amount at risk would have decreased to $978, which would necessitate a contribution from the other policyowners (and the deceased) of only $1.27, instead of the yearly renewable term premium of $1.30. The reserve will have grown to $139 per $1,000 by the end of the 20th year, which would reduce the cost per $1,000 from $3.32 to $2.86. By the time the insured has reached 65, the reserve under the policy will have accumulated to $397, and the actual amount of protection will have shrunk to $603.

A death claim in the 40th year of the contract would be settled by payment of the $397 in the reserve and $603 from the current year's premium payments (of all the policyowners). The pro rata share of each policyowner for all death claims during the year would be only $7.99, as compared to $13.25 if no reserve had been available. The influence of the reserve on the cost of insurance is even more striking at the advanced ages.

TABLE 1-1
Influence of the Reserve on Cost of Insurance, Ordinary Life Contract for $1,000 Issued at Age 25; 1980 CSO Female Table and 4.5 Percent Interest

Year	Attained Age at Beginning of Year	Reserve End of Year Even Dollars	Net Amount at Risk	Death Rate per 1,000	Cost of Insurance
1	25	$ 5	$995	1.16	$1.15
5	29	22	978	1.30	1.27
10	34	55	945	1.58	1.49
20	44	139	861	3.32	2.86
30	54	252	748	6.61	4.94
40	64	397	603	13.25	7.99

The true nature of level premium insurance should now be apparent. Under the level premium plan, a $1,000 policy does not provide $1,000 of insurance. The company is never at risk for the face amount of the policy—even in the first year. The amount of actual insurance is always the face amount, less the policyowner's own accumulated excess payments. The accumulation is the reserve for insurance company purposes but the cash value (slightly less in early years) for policyowner purposes. Because the excess payments may be withdrawn by the policyowner at any time through the cash surrender or loan privilege, they may be regarded as a savings or accumulation account. Thus, a level premium policy does not provide pure insurance but a combination of decreasing insurance and increasing cash values, the two amounts computed so that in any year their sum is equal to the face amount of the policy. This is illustrated in figure 1-3 for an ordinary life policy of $1,000 issued at age 25. The calculations are based on the 1980 CSO Female Table and 4.5 percent interest.

The area below the curve represents the reserve under the contract or, as mentioned above, the policyowner's equity in the contract. The area above the curve represents the company's net amount at risk and the policyowner's amount of protection. As the reserve increases, the amount of protection decreases. At any given age, however, the two combined will equal the face amount of the policy. By age 95 the protection element of the contract has become relatively minor, and by age 100—the end of the contract—it has completely disappeared. At age

100, the policyowner will receive $1,000, composed entirely of the cash value element.

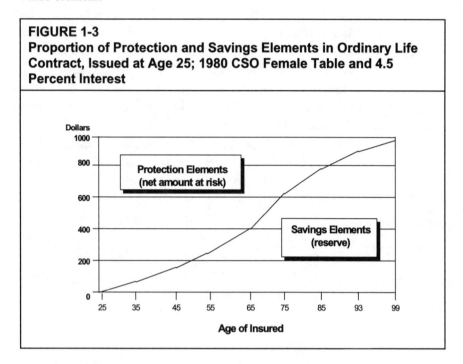

FIGURE 1-3
Proportion of Protection and Savings Elements in Ordinary Life Contract, Issued at Age 25; 1980 CSO Female Table and 4.5 Percent Interest

This combination of protection and accumulated cash values is characteristic of all level premium plans with the exception of most term contracts. Fundamentally, one contract differs from another only in the proportion in which the two elements are combined. This basic truth should be kept in mind as the study of contract forms is undertaken.

Yearly term insurance is all protection and has no cash value, while single premium life insurance is at the other end of the spectrum with the highest cash values and lowest proportion at risk. Accumulated cash values should be thought of as some degree of prefunding. Single-premium policies are fully prefunded, and lower-premium policies that develop cash values are only partially prefunded. The shorter the premium-paying period, the higher the relative proportion of cash value to death benefit.

Further Significance of Level Premium Plan

The impact of the level premium plan is felt by nearly all operations of a life insurance company. It accounts for a major portion of the composite assets of the United States life insurance companies that exceed $3.1

trillion and are increasing at more than $100 billion per year. The other main contributor to this asset growth is the reserve component for annuities and pension plans. The investment of these funds has presented the life insurance institution with one of its most challenging problems but, at the same time, has enabled the institution to contribute in a most material way to the dynamic expansion of the American economy.

The level premium plan underlies the system of cash values and other surrender options that has made the life insurance contract one of the most flexible and valuable contracts in existence. It has caused the life insurance contract to be regarded as one of the most acceptable forms of collateral for credit purposes. Despite these positive contributions—and the complications introduced into company operations—the greatest significance of the plan lies in the fact that it is the only arrangement under which it is possible to provide insurance protection to the uppermost limits of the human life span without the possibility that the cost will become prohibitive.

Major Contributions to Life Insurer Assets from level Contributions

- Cash values of life insurance
- Annuities
- Pensions and other qualified plans

Human Life Value

The economic values of a human life are the basis for the need for life insurance, and help determine the amount of life insurance needed by an individual or a family. Life insurance is concerned with the economic values of a human life, derived from that person's earning capacity and the financial dependence of others on that earning capacity. A human life has an economic value only if some person(s) or organization depends upon or expects to receive some monetary benefit through that life. The following discussion explains how the *human life value* is determined, the specific needs for life insurance, and the methods used to calculate the amount of life insurance needed by individuals and families.

The Concept of Human Life Value

A human life possesses many values, most of them irreplaceable and not easily measured. These values are founded on religious, moral, and social relationships. From a religious standpoint, for example, human life is regarded as immortal and endowed with a value beyond the comprehension of mortal man. In a person's relationship with other human beings, a set of emotional and sentimental attachments is created that cannot be measured in monetary terms or supplanted by material things. A human life may be capable of artistic achievements that contribute in a unique way to the culture of a society.

Such values, however, are not the foundation of life insurance. Although not oblivious to these values—in fact, the life insurance transaction has strong moral and social overtones—life insurance is concerned with the economic value of a human life, which is derived from its earning capacity and the financial dependence of other lives on that earning capacity. Because the economic value may arise out of either a family or a business relationship, it seems advisable to discuss the functions of life insurance under two headings: family purposes and business purposes.

Source of the Economic Value of the Human Life

In terms of its physical composition, the human body is worth only a few dollars. In terms of earning capacity, however, it may be worth millions of dollars. Yet earning power alone does not create an economic value that can logically serve as the basis of life insurance. A human life has an economic value only if some other person or organization can expect to derive an economic advantage through its existence.

If an individual is without dependents and no other person or organization stands to profit through his or her living either now or in the future, then that life, for all practical purposes, has no monetary value that needs to be perpetuated. Such an individual is rare. Most income producers either have dependents or can expect to acquire them in the normal course of events. Even those income earners with no family dependents often provide financial support to charitable organizations. In either case, a basis exists for life insurance.

Preservation of Family's Economic Security

In many cases an income producer's family is completely dependent on his or her personal earnings for subsistence and the amenities of life. In other words, the "potential" estate is far more substantial than the existing estate—the savings that the family has been able to accumulate. The family's economic security lies in the earning capacity of each income earner, which is represented by his or her "character and health, training and experience, personality and power of industry, judgment and power of initiative, and driving force to put across in tangible form the economic images of his mind," said S. S. Huebner in 1950.

Over a period of time, these economic forces are gradually converted into income, a portion of which is devoted to self-maintenance, a portion to support of dependents, and if the income is large enough, a portion to savings to meet future needs and contingencies. If the individual lives and stays in good health, the total income potential will eventually be realized, all to the benefit of the family and others who derive financial gain from his or her efforts. If an income earner dies or becomes permanently and totally disabled, the unrealized portion of his or her total earnings potential will be lost, and in the absence of other measures, the family will soon find itself destitute or reduced to a lower income than it previously enjoyed.

This need not happen, however, since there are contracts that can create a fund at death at least to partially, and possibly to fully, offset the lost income of the insured. Those contracts, of course, are life insurance. By means of life insurance, an individual can assure that the family will receive the monetary value of those income-producing qualities that lie within his or her physical being, regardless of when death occurs. By capitalizing (creating a fund large enough to generate investment income approximating the salary or wages of the individual) this life value, an income earner can leave the family in the same economic position that they would have enjoyed had he or she lived.

The Moral Obligation to Provide Protection

Most people assume major responsibility for the support and maintenance of their dependent children during their lifetime. In fact, they consider it one of the rewarding experiences of life. In any case, the law attaches a legal obligation to the support of a spouse and children. Thus if there is a divorce or a legal separation, the court will normally decree support payments for dependent children and possibly alimony for the dependent spouse. In some cases such payments, including alimony, are to continue beyond the provider's death, if the children are still dependent or if the alimony recipient has not remarried. In such event, the parent and ex-spouse are required to provide life insurance or to set funds aside in trust.

Nevertheless, it takes a high order of responsibility for a parent to voluntarily provide for continuation of income to dependents after his or her own death. It virtually always involves a reduction in the individual's own standard of living. Yet few would deny that any person with a dependent spouse, children, or parents has a moral obligation to provide them with the protection afforded by life insurance, as far as his or her financial means permit.

In his book Life Insurance, Dr. S. S. Huebner said the following concerning the obligation to insure:

> From the family standpoint, life insurance is a necessary business proposition that may be expected of every person with dependents as a matter of course, just like any other necessary business transaction which ordinary decency requires him to meet. The care of his family is man's first and most important business. The family should be established and run on a sound business basis. It should be protected against needless

bankruptcy. The death or disability of the head of this business should not involve its impairment or dissolution any more than the death of the head of a bank, railroad, or store. Every corporation and firm represents capitalized earning capacity and goodwill. Why then, when men and women are about to organize the business called a family should there not be a capitalization in the form of a life insurance policy of the only real value and goodwill behind that business? Why is it not fully as reasonable to have a life insurance policy accompany a marriage certificate as it is to have a marine insurance certificate invariably attached to a foreign bill of exchange? The voyage in the first instance is, on the average, much longer, subject to much greater risk, and in case of wreck, the loss is of infinitely greater consequence.

The growth of life insurance implies an increasing development of the sense of responsibility. The idea of providing only for the present must give way to recognition of the fact that a person's responsibility to his family is not limited to the years of survival. Emphasis should be laid on the "crime of not insuring," and the finger of scorn should be pointed at any man who, although he has provided well while he was alive, has not seen fit to discount the uncertain future for the benefit of a dependent household . . . Life insurance is a sure means of changing uncertainty into certainty and is the opposite of gambling. He who does not insure gambles with the greatest of all chances and, if he loses, makes those dearest to him pay the forfeit.

Measurement of Monetary Value

It seems agreed that an individual should protect his or her earning capacity for the benefit of dependents by carrying life insurance in an appropriate amount. The question logically arises at this point as to how much is an "appropriate" amount.

One method of determining how much life insurance a person should carry is called the *human life value approach*. It is based on the proposition that a person should carry life insurance in an amount equal to the *capitalized value* of his or her net earnings. Under this theory, a person should capitalize this economic value at an amount large enough to yield, at a reasonable rate of interest, an income equal to the family's share of those earnings.

In an attempt to obtain the same general result, others have recommended that a person capitalize this value at a figure large enough to yield an annual income equal to a specified percentage, such as 50 percent, of those personal earnings at the time of the provider's death. In response to the significant inflation in recent decades, some suggest capitalizing the worker's full income (or more) so that the income portion that would otherwise have gone to income taxes and the insured's self-maintenance can be used to offset general price inflation.

All of these approaches are based on the assumption that the income from personal efforts will not end. All would preserve the capitalized value of a portion of those earnings into perpetuity. Such an assumption is theoretically invalid. Personal earnings are subject to termination at any time by the producer's death or disability and, in any case, will generally not continue beyond the date of retirement. Therefore, in capitalizing the earnings of an individual, their terminable nature can be taken into account.

The technically accurate method of computing the monetary value of a person is too complex for general use. It involves an estimate of the individual's personal earnings for each year from his or her present age to the date of retirement, taking into account the normal trend of earnings and inflation. From each year's income the cost of self-maintenance, life insurance premiums, and personal income taxes is deducted. The residual income for each year is then discounted at an assumed rate of interest and against the possibility of its not being earned. In the latter calculation, the three contingencies of death, disability, and unemployment have to be considered. The sum of the discounted values for each year of potential income is the *present value* of future earnings or the monetary value of the life in question. *Present value* is equivalent to the given sum to be received in the future, discounted (reduced) by an interest rate representing what could be earned on that money if it was received today instead of in the future.

When determining the economic value of a human life for purposes of insuring that value against loss by death, one should consider the projected flow of income to the family rather than the probability of the provider's death. The objective is to determine the present value of the income flow to the family if the family provider survives to the end of his or her income-producing period since ideally insurance will be sufficient to permit the family to enjoy the same standard of living that it would have enjoyed had the provider(s) not died.

Five-step Procedure for Estimating Economic Value

A reasonably accurate estimate of a person's economic value for purposes of life insurance can be derived by a simple-to-understand method that can be used by anyone with access to a computer, a financial calculator, or compound-interest discount tables. There are five steps in this procedure:

1. Estimate the individual's average annual earnings from personal efforts over the remaining years of his or her income-producing lifetime.
2. Deduct federal and state income taxes, life insurance premiums, and the cost of self-maintenance.
3. Determine the number of years between the individual's present age and the contemplated age of retirement.
4. Select a reasonable rate of interest at which future earnings will be discounted.
5. Multiply (1) minus (2) by the present value of $1 per annum for the period determined in (3), discounted at the rate of interest selected in (4).

In the first step an effort should be made to anticipate the pattern of future earnings. In the majority of cases, particularly among semiskilled and clerical workers, earnings will reach their maximum at a fairly early age, perhaps around 40, and will remain at that level (except for inflation adjustments) until retirement. The earnings of professional people continue to increase until about age 55, after which they level off or decline somewhat unless they are adjusted for inflation. The earnings of still other groups may continue to rise until shortly before retirement. It is difficult to estimate accurately the average annual income that can be expected. Inflation, technological change, and increased global competition are accelerating the rate of change and our society's economic volatility.

The costs in the second step are also difficult to estimate, but income taxes and the cost of self-maintenance can be approximated within a reasonably close margin of error unless Congress makes a drastic change in the future tax rates. The purpose of step (2) is to discount the funds that serve purposes other than supporting one's dependents and to arrive at the family's share of the breadwinner's personal earnings. The determination of the income tax liability, life insurance premiums, and the cost of self-maintenance can be dispensed with if the individual can estimate what portion of personal earnings currently goes to the support of the family. In the typical case it is probably relatively accurate to assume that about half of the provider's gross personal earnings is devoted to the support of the family. In the low-income brackets, the percentage is undoubtedly a little higher but in no event more than two-thirds; in the higher-income brackets, the percentage might be lower than one-half.

The purpose of step (3) is to determine how long the family can expect to receive the income projected in step (2), ignoring, for reasons indicated above, the probability that the individual may die before reaching normal retirement age.

The rate of interest selected in step (4) should be in line with the rate generally payable on proceeds left with the insurance company since it is usually a conservative estimate of conditions over the relevant future period. Another acceptable interest rate estimate is the rate used by the Pension Benefit Guaranty Corporation (PBGC is a federal agency located in Washington, DC) for valuing defined-benefit pension liabilities.

> **Elements of Economic Value Estimates**
>
> - Average annual earnings estimate
> - Taxes, self-maintenance costs, life insurance premiums
> - Remaining years in workforce before retirement
> - Estimated interest rate applicable to future working years

Calculating Present Value

The *present value of $1 per annum*, the only new element involved in step (5), is obtained directly from a financial calculator or a computer using financial software. Alternatively it can be derived from a compound-discount table that shows the present value of a series of future income payments—specifically, $1 per annum—for various periods of time and at various rates of interest.

The entire process of computing the monetary value of a human life can be illustrated with the following example:

Diminishing Nature of the Economic Value

The economic value of an income earner tends to diminish with the passage of time. His or her earning level may continue to increase for a certain period or indefinitely, but with each passing year, the remaining period of productivity becomes shorter. Each year of income that is realized means that there is less that remains to be earned. Because an individual's economic value is nothing more than the unrealized earning capacity represented by native ability and acquired skills, his or her value must diminish as potential income is converted into actual income. This principle is illustrated by the diagram in figure 1–4.

The chord (a straight line joining two points on a curve) *AB* represents the lifetime of an individual born at point *A* and dying at point *B*. The chord *AB* also represents the cost of maintenance and, during his or her productive years, the individual's income tax liability. The arc *CD* represents earning capacity. During the period *A to C*, there are no earnings, but there are costs of maintenance represented by the triangle *AEC*. Earnings commence at *C*. The area of arc *CD* that extends above arc *AB* represents earnings in excess of taxes and the cost of self-maintenance. Point *D* marks the age of retirement, and the area *DFB* symbolizes the second major period in the individual's life, during which the cost of self-maintenance exceeds his or her income.

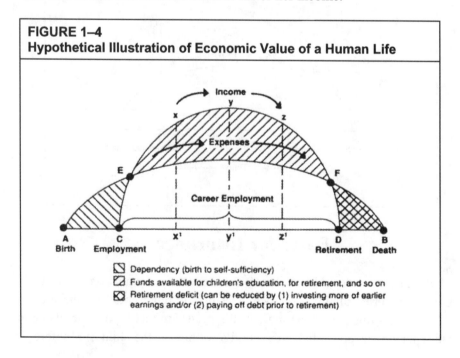

FIGURE 1–4
Hypothetical Illustration of Economic Value of a Human Life

In figure 1–4 the monetary value of the individual is at its peak at point E since net earnings are just commencing. At the point where xx^1 intersects the arcs, the earnings rate has increased, but potential future earnings have declined. The earnings potential shows further decreases at yy^1 and zz^1; at point F, it has shrunk to zero.

Figure 1–4 is diagrammatic and obviously unrealistic. Neither earnings nor maintenance expenses follow a symmetrical curve. For example, the childhood period starts with a highly unsymmetrical outlay for maternity costs. Income is also likely to commence earlier than at point C, particularly among lower-income groups, and under no circumstances is it likely to decline so gradually to the age of retirement. In most occupations people reach their maximum earnings in their 40s, and earnings decline only slightly to retirement, when they terminate abruptly. Figure 1–5 shows a fairly typical pattern of earnings among clerical and professional groups.

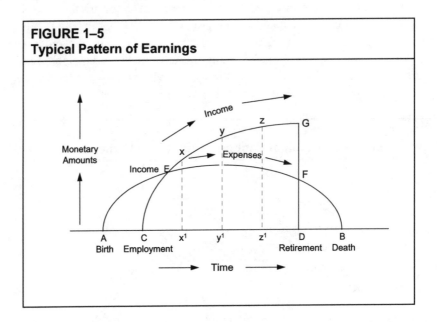

FIGURE 1–5
Typical Pattern of Earnings

Bases for Insurance

These diagrams roughly illustrate the economic foundation of three broad categories of life insurance. The first is represented by the area AEC. During this period the individual's needs are met by the parents or other persons responsible for the child's welfare. If the child dies before becoming a producer, the investment in nurturing, maintenance, and education is sacrificed. This can be a sizable sum, especially if the child has been educated at private schools. Various studies have shown that the cost of rearing a child to age 18 ranges from 1.5 times to 3.25 times the parents' average annual income. At today's prices the cost may be even higher. While most parents regard these expenditures as one of the duties and privileges of parenthood and justifiably shrink from labeling them as an investment to be recovered in the event of the child's death, such costs do create a substantial insurable value. This value can logically serve as one of the bases for juvenile insurance—a strong segment of the life insurance business.

The second category of insurance is portrayed by the area EGF. The surplus earnings represented by this area are the source of support for the individual's dependents and a broad measure of the economic loss to the family if the producer(s) should die. A portion of these earnings will go toward insurance premiums, and another portion should be set aside for both spouses' old-age needs, but the share that is destined for the care and maintenance of the family should be capitalized and preserved for the family through the medium of life insurance. This is family insurance in the purest sense.

Finally, the individual's retirement needs are represented by the area *DFB*. Although the income vacuum may be partially filled by federal OASDI (Old Age, Survivors, and Disability Income)—Social Security—benefits, pension plans and other tax-qualified plans (such as profit sharing, income deferral, and thrift or savings), and individual investments, the most realistic source of funds to cover any income shortage is through investment income, life insurance and annuities. This remaining need can be satisfied with group life insurance through employment and/or a personal insurance program. For long-term planning purposes, however, individuals should not rely on group life insurance for any more than the funds that can—and will—be kept in force after an unforeseen job loss. Individuals should check their employer's plan to find out how much of the group life insurance they can convert to individual insurance after termination of employment.

Needs Analysis

The human life value approach produces a present value for a person at a given point in time. This method may not fully anticipate other needs that arise with the death of a person. An estimate of these additional concerns is obtained through a *needs analysis approach* to the question: How much life insurance is enough? The needs analysis approach is a way of determining how much life insurance a person should carry by analyzing the various needs a family or other dependents would experience if the income producer died.

It would be difficult, if not impossible, to prepare a list of all needs that might possibly arise after the death of the income producer. Family circumstances differ, and a list of needs that would be appropriate for one family might be quite unsuitable for another. Moreover, within any particular family, the needs picture changes from time to time. The most that can be attempted in this section is to outline the general categories of needs that are likely to be found in any family situation. These categories are discussed in the order in which they arise, which in most cases is also the order of importance.

Cleanup Fund

The death of an insured family member usually terminates an income stream that the family has relied upon. The costs of daily living for survivors, final expenses for the deceased insured, and emergencies, repairs and replacements associated with events surrounding the family member's death, death taxes, and the cost of estate administration (including executor's or administrator's fee, appraisers' fees, and legal fees) create an immediate need for funds. Mortgages might well be included in the list, but in view of their size and the special problems frequently encountered in their connection, they are usually treated as a separate need.

One of the goals of proper planning is to make sure the emergency fund is adequate to meet the survivors' needs until life insurance proceeds and other potential sources of funds become available.

Families having an adequate source of emergency funds in liquid holdings, such as money market funds, mutual funds, bank balances, cash management accounts, life insurance cash values, and so forth, may easily meet any need for immediate cash following the death. However, the need for additional funds becomes urgent if the family does not have an emergency fund or has depleted it prior to the death.

Readjustment Income

Few individuals are able to leave an estate, including life insurance, substantial enough to provide their dependents with an income as large as they enjoyed while the income earner was alive. This means that an adjustment will generally have to be made in the family's standard of living. To cushion the economic and emotional shock, however, it is desirable to postpone that adjustment for a period following the income producer's death. The length of the period depends largely on the magnitude of the change that the family will have to make in living standards. If the surviving spouse must refresh or acquire skills to gain employment, a longer period may be needed. Whatever the duration, the income during this readjustment period should be approximately equivalent to the family's share of the producer's earnings at the time of his or her death.

Income During Dependency Period

After the expiration of the readjustment period, income should be provided in a reduced amount until the children, if any, are able to support themselves. Two concepts are involved: how much income should be provided and for how long.

As a minimum, there should be enough income that the family can remain intact and the surviving spouse can devote adequate time to the care and guidance of the children during their formative years.

The most important determinants of the income's duration are the present ages of the insured's children and the type of education they will receive. In any case, income should continue until the youngest child is 18. If there are several children, the income can be reduced somewhat as each reaches the age of self-sufficiency. If the children are to receive a college education, income will have to continue for a longer period. For planning purposes, the immediate death of the income producer is assumed. The projected income is then presumed to be needed for a period equal to the difference between the present age of the youngest child and the age at which the child is expected to become self-supporting.

Life Income for Surviving Dependent Spouse

After the children have become self-supporting, the widow(er) will still have needs as an individual and will require an income from some source.

If the surviving spouse is a full-time homemaker until the children finish at least part of their education, he or she may subsequently be able to obtain employment, but the earning power for people entering the workforce at that age will have declined substantially. After the birth of children, for example, a wife sometimes gives up her job or the opportunity to become self-supporting. As the years pass, whatever occupational skills she may have possessed may have diminished and she will most likely have to return to the labor market as a middle-aged woman with deficient skills. Under such circumstances, employment opportunities are limited. Many individuals feel a moral obligation, therefore, to provide their spouses with incomes that will continue throughout the remaining years of their lives. The income may be modest, but it can be the difference between complete dependency on welfare services and reasonable self-sufficiency.

Special Needs

There are certain needs that are not found in every family situation and, even when they are found, are not likely to enjoy as high a priority as those previously discussed. Three of the most prominent of these are mortgage redemption, educational, and emergency needs.

Mortgage Redemption Needs—Home ownership is usually burdened with a mortgage and it is highly probable that a balance will still be outstanding upon the death of a person with dependent children. In some cases, of course, the widow(er) may want to sell the house and move into a smaller one or into an apartment, and it would not be essential to provide funds for the liquidation of the mortgage. In many cases, however, it is contemplated that the survivors will continue to occupy the family residence, and funds to pay off the mortgage may be needed. If the family can occupy the home free of a monthly mortgage payment, it will greatly reduce the amount of income that they would otherwise require.

Elements of Needs Analysis

- Cleanup fund
- Readjustment income
- Income during dependency period
- Life income for surviving dependent spouse
- Special needs
- Mortgage redemption needs
- Educational needs
- Emergency needs

Educational Needs—The income provided for a surviving spouse during the period when the children are dependent should normally be adequate for secondary school expenses, as well as for general maintenance. If a college education for one or more of the children is envisioned, however, additional income will be needed. There is no question that a college or professional education is beyond the means of many dependent children who lose an income-earning parent.

Emergency Needs—From time to time in the life of a family, unforeseen needs for money arise because of illness, surgery, major dental work, home repairs, or many other reasons. It is unrealistic for the family income providers to leave enough income for the family to subsist on only if everything goes well and no unusual expenditures are incurred. Therefore, a liquid fund should be set up from which additional income can be provided if and when it is needed. Some financial planners suggest that the emergency fund often warrants a higher priority than income for dependents. The actual setting of priorities is properly the responsibility of the income earner(s).

Retirement Needs—Retirement planning is a contingency that the financial planner and estate planner must anticipate. This contingency determines the type of insurance the worker should purchase. If the family needs are met with cash value life insurance (assuming adequate funds for premiums), the cash values under this insurance can supplement other retirement income sources to take care of the postretirement needs of the insured and the spouse, if still living.

Monetary Evaluation of the Cash and Income Needs

It is interesting to compare the monetary value of the above needs with the economic value of the human life computed earlier. For purposes of comparison, assume—as in the earlier illustration—that the family head is a male aged 35, has gross annual earnings of $40,000, and devotes $20,000 per year to his family. Assume further that he has a wife aged 30 and two children, ages 2 and 5, and that an income of $1,700 per month is to be provided during the first 2 years, $1,460 per month during the next 14 years, and $971 per month thereafter for the life of the surviving spouse.

In computing the present value of the foregoing series of income payments (*income needs*), it is advisable to treat them as a life income of $971 per month payable from the surviving spouse's age 30 with an additional income of $240 per month for 16 years and another $50 per month for 2 years. On the basis of the 1983 Individual Annuity Table and 4-percent interest, a life income of $971 per month for a female aged 30, with payments guaranteed for 20 years, has a present value of approximately $220,000. Provision must be made for guaranteed payments during the children's dependency, since in the event of the widow's early death, the income to the children will be reduced from $971 per month to $489 ($729 per month during the first 2 years). Guaranteed installments are available only in multiples of 5 years (up to 20 years), and at age 30, a 20-year guarantee can be obtained at a sacrifice of only 1 cent per $1,000 of principal sum, compared to the cost of a 15-year guarantee that would be one year short of the 16-year dependency period. The present value on a 4-percent interest basis of $489 per month for 16 years is $69,263, and the present value of $240 per month for 2 years is $5,526. The present value of the family's income needs when the figures are rounded to the nearest hundred dollars is $294,800.

The total increases when the *cash needs* (cleanup fund and mortgage redemption fund, educational needs, and emergency needs) are added. Even if no provision is made for the children's college education, a cleanup fund of $20,000, a mortgage redemption fund of $80,000, and an emergency fund of $30,000 will increase the total to $424,800. If $80,000 is provided to each of the children for a college education, the total income requirements reach $584,800.

Example:	Married male aged 35, spouse aged 30, children ages 2 and 5	
	Income needed first 2 year	$ 1,700 per month
	Income needed next 14 years	$ 1,460 per month
	Income thereafter for surviving spouse	$971 per month
	Assumed interest rate	4.0 percent
	Cleanup fund	$ 20,000
	Mortgage redemption fund	$ 80,000
	Emergency fund	$ 30,000
	Education fund for children	$ 160,000
	Combined needs (rounding to nearest $100)	$ 584,800

It is not likely that these needs will have to be met entirely through personal life insurance. If the individual in the example is covered under the federal OASDI program (Social Security) with benefits approaching the maximum—which, in view of his earnings, is very probable—nearly two-thirds of the income needed until the youngest child is 18 will be provided by the federal government (assuming the widow will not remarry and both children survive the period). This would reduce the personal insurance requirements by approximately $170,000.

If the husband had attained "fully" insured status for Social Security at the time of his death—also a reasonable assumption—the widow at age 62 would become entitled to a life income of $800 per month, which would reduce the personal insurance requirements by another $29,600. The individual may also be covered by group life insurance, with benefits of possibly $150,000 or more. Therefore, it is not beyond the realm of possibility that all the needs, including those requiring lump-sum payments, may be met in full with the purchase of $235,000 of additional life insurance.

The retirement needs of the husband do not impose additional quantitative requirements. If the husband purchases $300,000 of life insurance (roughly the equivalent of the income needs computed earlier) on the ordinary life plan (the lowest premium type of permanent insurance) before age 35, it will have accumulated at least $125,000 in cash values by age 65. This will provide him with a life income, with payments guaranteed for 10 years, of more than $1,012 per month. If his wife is also alive and in need of old-age protection, the accumulated sum could be converted into a joint-and-last-survivor annuity, which would provide a lower (a 7.5 percent to 14 percent reduction) income per month as long as either the husband or the wife survives.

Such an income, supplemented by federal OASDI benefits and possibly retirement benefits from an employer pension plan, should meet their old-age needs with ample margins. (If the insured keeps premium outlays down through a liberal use of term insurance, the cash values available at age 65 will be reduced accordingly.)

Amount of Insurance Needed

Ideally, the life of each productive member of society should be insured for an amount equal to his or her full economic value, as measured by contributions to those who depend on that income. Upon the death of the income producer, the insured sum should then be liquidated in a manner consistent with the purposes for which it was created, meeting the various needs in the order of their importance. If the insured lives to retirement, the sums accumulated through premium payments may be used, with the exception of amounts required for cleanup and other necessary purposes, to satisfy the postretirement needs of the insured and his or her spouse.

As a practical matter, attaining this ideal is difficult, even when death benefits available under the federal OASDI program and employer benefit plans are taken into account. The basic obstacle is that when both the economic value and the needs are at their maximum—at younger ages—the funds available for premium payments are at their minimum. In the lower income groups, the bulk of the family income is spent on the necessities of life; very little is saved. As the family income rises, aggregate expenditures for consumer goods increase, but they constitute a smaller percentage of total income. Thus, more money is available for insurance premiums and other forms of savings. By that time, however, the need for insurance may have declined somewhat.

Various formulas have been developed in an attempt to establish the proper relationship between family income and the amount of insurance to carry. A rule of thumb that has gained some acceptance is that 10 percent of gross family income should be devoted to life insurance premiums. Although this ratio is probably unrealistic at lower income levels, it becomes attainable as the income level increases. Another rule states that the typical wage earner should carry insurance equal to some specified multiple of annual gross income, while persons in the higher income brackets should capitalize a higher multiple of annual earnings. Such rules of thumb are too simplistic because they do not take into consideration either (1) accumulated assets or (2) family composition and objectives.

An attempt to determine life insurance needs that does not rely upon a fair amount of client information is of questionable worth. The rule-of-thumb approach ignores information about the specific needs of the client's dependents, how much the client has already accumulated, and any existing external sources of finance such as trusts and inheritances. The simplistic rule-of-thumb approach can err in either direction; that is, it can either overinsure or underinsure the client.

Simplistic rules of thumb may perform a positive function if they are the only approach or logic that motivates the client to purchase needed insurance. Sometimes clients do resist providing the information necessary for an appropriate and thorough analysis of their needs.

Amount of Insurance Needed

- Estimated economic value or amount needed to fund desires
- Less amounts already available (Social Security, investments, existing benefits and so on)
- Equals the unfunded amount that can be made up with life insurance

---

Shortcoming of Rules of Thumb

- They do not recognize accumulated assets.
- They do not recognize individual family circumstances or family objectives.

In this chapter it is assumed that clients are serious about their financial future and that the financial services professional has established enough trust for the information-gathering and analysis process to proceed. Problem solving in this arena requires complete and accurate information about current income, potential future income, accumulated assets, investments, pensions, and other qualified plan holdings. In addition, it is important to develop a profile of the client's priorities and goals or objectives. A fair amount of time and energy is often spent in gathering the necessary information before any steps can even be taken toward analysis and recommendation.

The conceptual approach to determining needs is very easily explained. The client's desires must be translated into estimated costs, and then those costs must be evaluated to determine how much of the funding is already in place. Any deficit between the intended goals and objectives and current financial sources usually creates a candidate for life insurance. Life insurance provides a means of completing the financing of family goals and objectives that individuals work toward during their lifetime. In essence, life insurance can be a personally arranged and collectively financed means of replacing lost income, and in some ways it is analogous to trusts and inheritances in wealthy families.

Deriving Components of Need

Post-death Financial Needs—Post-death financial needs are conveniently separated into two main categories:

1. cash (lump sum) needs at death
2. ongoing income

The amounts associated with each of these categories vary widely from one individual to another and from one family to another. Reliance on general guidelines rather than on individual evaluation increases the likelihood that important and potentially costly needs may be overlooked or ignored.

Because the purpose of life insurance is to fund the unfunded portion of these objectives, it is important to consider any and all existing funds that can provide part or all of these needs. For simplicity and efficiency, most planners suggest using some target percentage of the insured's current income as the target income level rather than calculating a composite of each individual anticipated need component. It is often suggested that the survivor(s) will need about 70 percent of the predeath income to carry on after death.

Projecting future cash flow and deducting the existing sources of income are the first steps in determining the income deficit. The next step is to find the present value of all those future income needs. This calculation can be done in many different ways and with many different levels of specificity. Often it is broken up into component segments so that the income deficit will be the same throughout that particular component period. If the calculation is done that way, the final calculation of the total income need is the sum of the present values of each of the separate, individually calculated segments.

Most financial advisors suggest that these components be kept at a minimum and that simplifying assumptions be made whenever possible or appropriate in order to keep this estimation process from becoming too cumbersome and time consuming. It is important to remember that this is still an estimation process intended to simulate unknown future occurrences. The estimates are made without the benefit of knowing what future inflation rates and investment returns will be. Financial advisors and insurance agents are no more omniscient than economists are when it comes to estimating future investment income and inflation rates.

In fact, some advisors suggest that all values should be done in current dollar amounts and with no discounting applied to future income periods. They maintain that such discounting merely complicates an imprecise estimation process and that ignoring inflation as well will probably make the estimates somewhere near what will ultimately happen. There is much merit in these suggestions. An inordinate amount of time and resources can be spent trying to estimate to the penny future income flows. Computers make it possible to estimate every last detail in fractions of a cent. However, just because a computer spits out numbers with four-decimal-place accuracy or more does not mean that those numbers will actually unfold in the future.

After future income needs have been estimated and combined into a total, there is another important step that must be completed to translate this need into a stated funding objective. Future income

---

Liquidating Approach

- All investment income is distributed
- Part of the investment capital is being distributed with each payment
- Intent is to nearly exhaust the investment fund at the end of recipient's life
- Requires estimation of the remaining lifetime

---

payments can be comprised solely of investment earnings on a capital sum, or they can be a combination of investment earnings and liquidation of part of the capital sum. The advantage of using investment earnings only to supply such income streams is that the capital sum is not being depleted, and consequently a termination date on the income stream is not necessary. This means that individuals relying upon the income will not outlive their income stream. The disadvantage of this strategy is that it takes more money in the capital fund to fully fund this approach than it takes to fund a program that relies on liquidation of part of the principal.

A serious shortcoming of the liquidating approach is that the fund will eventually be totally dissipated. The strategy requires estimating the insured's likely maximum age at death and planning liquidation for that date or later. Any liquidation planning predicated on the beneficiary's death at an early age runs a high risk of liquidating the proceeds while the beneficiary is still dependent on them. As one famous agent likes to put it, they run out of money before they run out of time. Financial advisors are well advised to plan for a liquidation in such a way that the beneficiary is likely to run out of time before he or she runs out of money.

There are essentially two ways of eliminating this potential problem associated with liquidating the principal sum over the beneficiary's lifetime. One approach is to use policy proceeds at death to provide a life income through policy settlement options or separate annuity contracts. These arrangements guarantee lifelong income payments regardless of how long the recipient lives. The other approach (nonliquidating) is the previously mentioned capitalization at a high enough level that all the income benefits can be provided from the investment income only.

Nonliquidating Approach (Capital Needs)

- Benefit payments are completely derived from investment income
- Investment fund is not diminished
- Benefits can be paid as long as needed
- Requires larger investment fund than that for a liquidating approach
- Much simpler to calculate

Within the life insurance industry the liquidating approach is often referred to as the *financial needs analysis*, and a nonliquidating approach is often referred to as the *capital needs analysis*.

Another advantage of the nonliquidating approach is the simplicity of calculating the needed capital fund. The desired income level is easily capitalized by dividing that income amount by the applicable interest rate representing the after-tax investment return anticipated on the capital sum. For example, if $100,000 per year is desired, and the capital sum generating those income payments can realistically expect to generate a 5 percent return after taxes, a $2 million fund is sufficient. This is

---

determined by taking the desired income amount and dividing into that the realistic estimate of the after-tax investment return rate. In our example it was .05, or 5 percent. That division yields the $2 million capital fund amount needed. Obviously, the lower the after-tax investment return rate, the higher the capital fund needed to throw off the same amount of income. Similarly, higher marginal tax rates will lower the after-tax return rate and increase the size of the fund needed to generate the income.

Chapter One Review

Key terms and concepts are explained in the glossary. Answers to the review questions and the self-test questions follow the Glossary.

Key Terms and Concepts

risk pooling

1980 CSO Table

yearly renewable term insurance

evidence of insurability

adverse selection

renewability

level premium insurance

reserve

legal reserve

level (premium) term

ordinary life policy

amount at risk

costs of insurance

human life value

human life value approach

capitalized value

present value

present value of $1 per annum

needs analysis approach

cleanup fund

readjustment income

dependency period

income needs

cash needs

financial needs analysis

capital needs analysis

Review Questions

1-1.   Explain the concept of risk pooling and how it relates to life insurance.

1-2.   Explain how the premium for Yearly Renewable Term (YRT) is determined.

1-3.   Explain why the period for renewal is limited in term policies.

1-4.   Explain how the level premium insurance concept works.

1-5.   Explain the concept of human life value and how is relates to life insurance.

1-6.   Explain the five-step process for estimating a person's economic value for purposes of life insurance.

1-7.   List and explain the six life insurance needs used to determine the amount of life insurance a person should carry.

1-8.   Explain the process of providing for the post-death financial needs of survivors using financial needs analysis and capital needs analysis.

Self-Test Questions

Instructions: Read the chapter first, then answer the following 10 questions to test your knowledge. Circle the correct answer, then check your answers in the answer key in the back of the book.

1-1.   When planning for post-death income needs, the liquidating approach, using both principal and interest from life insurance proceeds, is known as the:

   (A)   capital needs analysis approach
   (B)   financial needs analysis approach
   (C)   human life value approach
   (D)   capital conservation approach

1-2.   The human life value approach is based on

   (A   a person's eligibility for social security income
   (B)   the amount of life insurance he or she owns
   (C)   the standard of living he or she wishes to have
   (D)   the capitalized present value of potential lifetime earnings

1-3.   In a level premium ordinary life policy, the net amount at risk

   (A)   increases each year
   (B)   decreases each year
   (C)   remains the same over time
   (D)   could increase or decrease based on investment returns

1-4. Which of the following is a characteristic of an ordinary life policy?

(A) It is the most expensive form of cash value insurance.
(B) It matures at age 65.
(C) It has an increasing cash value and decreasing risk amount.
(D) Both the cash value and amount at risk increase annually.

1-5. Which of the following statements concerning yearly renewable term is correct?

(A) The insurance company may experience some adverse selection at renewal time.
(B) The premiums do not increase from year to year.
(C) Evidence of insurability must be furnished at the time of each renewal.
(D) The insured can renew the policy each year by completing a medical exam.

1-6. The tendency for healthy individuals to give up their insurance as its costs increase while those in poor health to continue to renew it regardless of its cost is referred to as

(A) risk pooling
(B) risk tolerance
(C) adverse selection
(D) yearly renewable term

1-7. Which of the following statements concerning the capital needs analysis approach to calculating the insurance need on the family income earner is (are) correct?

I. Divide the income amount by the applicable interest rate representing the after-tax investment return anticipated on the capital sum.
II. The lower the after-tax investment return rate, the higher the capital fund needed to provide the same amount of income.

(A) I only
(B) II only
(C) Both I and II
(D) Neither I nor II

1-8. Which of the following statements concerning the readjustment period for survivors after a wage earner's death is (are) correct?

I. The length of the period should be less than one year.
II. The income during this period should be approximately equivalent to the insured's earnings at the time of death.

(A) I only
(B) II only
(C) Both I and II
(D) Neither I nor II

1-9. All of the following statements concerning yearly renewable term insurance are correct EXCEPT

(A) The premium is determined by the death rate at the insured's attained age.
(B) The policyowner must furnish evidence of insurability to renew coverage.
(C) The right to renew coverage may be limited to a specified age or a specified period.
(D) The face amount of the coverage is paid to the beneficiaries at the death of the insured.

1-10. All of the following statements concerning risk pooling are correct EXCEPT

(A) It involves combing risks by persons exposed to loss from a particular source.
(B) It involved sharing losses on some equitable basis.
(C) It is one important element that must be present in any sound insurance plan.
(D) It is used only when the insurance is issued by a mutual company.

2

Term and Whole Life Insurance

Overview and Learning Objectives

Chapter 2 reviews the features of the life insurance policy and contract. The focus is on the two major types of products, term insurance and whole life insurance. It then briefly introduces a few of the main variations of these basic policy designs, which will be the topic of Chapter 3.

By reading this chapter and answering the questions, you should be able to

2.1. Describe the nature and features of term life insurance.

2.2. Explain the renewability and conversion provisions.

2.3. Compare term insurance variations and their usefulness.

2.4. Describe the features of whole life insurance policies.

2.5. Explain how joint life policies work and compare them with single life policies.

2.6. Compare the differences between limited-payment policies and ordinary life policies

Chapter Outline

Term Insurance   2-3
    Nature of Term Insurance   2-3
    Critiques Of Term Insurance   2-12
Whole Life Insurance   2-19
    Principal Types of Whole Life Insurance   2-19
    Joint Life Insurance   2-26
    Functions of Whole Life Insurance   2-28
Chapter Two Review   2-29

Term Insurance

There are five basic types of life insurance contracts: term, whole life, universal life, endowment, and annuity. The function of the first four is to create a principal sum or estate, either through the death of the insured or through the accumulation of funds set aside for investment purposes. The function of the annuity, on the other hand, is to liquidate a principal sum in a scientific manner, regardless of how that sum was created. This dissimilarity in the basic functions of life insurance and annuities has caused some to question the propriety of classifying annuities as a type of life insurance contract, but there appear to be enough similarities to justify the practice. This section discusses term insurance contracts.

Note: Endowment life insurance policies are still viable and popular in other countries, but United States tax law changes have nearly eliminated endowment sales in this country.

Nature of Term Insurance

Term insurance provides life insurance protection for a limited period only. The face amount of the policy is payable if the insured dies during the specified period, and nothing is paid if the insured survives. The period may be as short as one year, or it may run to age 65 or above. The customary terms are one, 5, 10, 15, and 20 years. Such policies may insure for the agreed term only, or they may give the insured the option of renewing the protection for successive terms without evidence of insurability. Applications for term insurance are carefully underwritten; various restrictions may be imposed on the amount of insurance, the age before which it must be obtained, the age beyond which it cannot be renewed, and the like.

Term insurance may be regarded as temporary insurance and, in principle, is more nearly comparable to property and casualty insurance contracts than any of the other life insurance contracts in use. If a person insures his or her life under a 5-year term contract, no obligation is incurred by the insurance company unless the death of the insured occurs within the term. All premiums paid for the term protection are considered to be fully earned by the company by the end of the term, whether or not a loss has occurred, and the policy has no further value. This is similar to auto and homeowners insurance.

The premium for term insurance is initially relatively low, despite the fact that it contains a relatively high expense loading and an allowance for adverse selection. The reason premiums can be low is that most term contracts do not cover the period of old age when death is most likely to occur and when the cost of insurance is high. In other words, a term policy, because its term may end prior to the insured's death, insures against a contingency, and not a certainty as do other kinds of policies.

Renewability

Many term insurance contracts contain an option to renew for a limited number of additional periods of term insurance, usually of the same length. The simplest policy of this type is the yearly renewable term policy, which is a one-year term contract renewable for successive periods of one year each. Longer-term contracts, such as the 10-year term, may also be renewable. The following is a typical renewal provision:

> **Renewal Privilege.** The insured may renew this policy for further periods of 10 years each without medical examination, provided there has been no lapse in the payment of premiums, by written notice to the company at its home office before the expiration of any period of the insurance hereunder and by the payment in each year, on the dates above specified, of the premium for the age attained by the insured at the beginning of any such renewal period in accordance with the table of rates contained herein.

The key to the *renewable* feature is the right to renew the contract without a medical examination or other evidence of insurability. Where the term policy contains no renewal privilege, or where it can be renewed only upon evidence of insurability satisfactory to the company, the insured may find that coverage cannot be continued as long as needed. Because of poor health, a hazardous occupation, or some other reason, the insured might be unable to secure a renewal of the contract or to obtain any other form of life insurance protection. The renewal feature prevents this situation. Its chief function is to protect the insurability of the named insured.

Under a term insurance contract the premium increases with each renewal, based on the attained age of the insured at the time of the renewal. The term insurance premium for a person aged 50 or above, for example, is higher than the premium for a whole life contract acquired before age 35. Within the contract period, however, the premium is level. Over a long period of time, punctuated by several renewals, the premium will consist of a series of level premiums, each series higher than the previous one. Moreover, the rate will continue to increase with each renewal. The scale of rates at which the insurance can be renewed is published in the original contract and cannot be changed by the company as long as the contract remains in force. Evidence of renewal is usually provided in the form of a certificate to be attached to the original contract, although some insurance companies issue a new contract with each renewal.

Insurers have mixed feelings about renewable term insurance. There is no question that properly used it fills a real need. However, it presents certain problems to the company that writes it. Whether the policy is on the yearly renewable term plan or a longer-term basis, there is likely to be strong selection against the company at time of renewal, and this adverse selection will become greater as the age of the insured—and hence, the renewal premium—increases.

Resistance to increasing premiums will amuse many of those who remain in good health to fail to renew each time a premium increase takes effect, while those in poor health will tend to take advantage of the right of renewal. As time goes on, the mortality experience among the surviving policyowners will become increasingly unfavorable. While dividend adjustment can provide for adverse mortality experience, it requires substantial margins in the premium rates. As a result, each dollar of protection on the term basis tends to cost middle-aged or older policyowners more than under any other type of contract.

Renewability Features
• Can renew without medical or other evaluation
• Premiums change upon renewal
• Some insurers prohibit renewals beyond a specified age

As a further safeguard against adverse selection, companies generally do not permit renewals to carry the coverage beyond a specified age such as 65, 70, or 75 (although some insurers guarantee renewability to age 95 or 99). In addition, limitations on yearly renewable term are usually more stringent; coverage is frequently restricted to 10 or 15 years or, occasionally, to age 65, whichever is earlier. Renewable term insurance, therefore, is satisfactory for individual coverage to both the policyowner and the company when coverage does not extend into the higher ages.

Convertibility

In addition to the renewable privilege, a term policy may contain a *convertibility* provision that permits the policyowner to exchange the term contract for a contract on a permanent plan, likewise without evidence of insurability. In other words, a term insurance policy may be both renewable and convertible. The convertible feature serves the needs of those who want permanent insurance but are temporarily unable to afford the higher premiums required for whole life and other types of cash value life insurance. Convertibility is also useful when the policyowner desires to postpone the final decision as to the type of permanent insurance to be purchased until a later date when, for some reason, it may be possible to make a wiser choice. Thus, convertible term insurance provides a way to obtain temporary insurance and an option on permanent insurance in the same policy.

Insurability is protected by the convertible feature in an even more valuable manner than under the renewable feature because convertibility guarantees access to permanent insurance—not just continuation of temporary protection. The two features together afford complete protection against loss of insurability.

The conversion may be effective as of the date of the exchange or as of the original date of the term policy. If the term policy is converted as of the current date, conversion is usually referred to as the *attained age* method since the current age determines the premium level. A conversion using the original date of the term policy for the conversion is referred to as the *original age* method or a *retroactive conversion*.

Retroactive Conversion—Some insurers allow a policy to be converted retroactively within the first few years after issue. When the conversion is effective as of the original date, the premium rate for the permanent contract is that which would have been paid had the new contract been taken out originally, and the policy form is that which would have been issued originally. It is these two features that motivate the insured to convert retroactively in most instances. The advantage of the lower premium is obvious, but in many cases, the contract being issued at the original date contains actuarial assumptions or other features more favorable than those being incorporated in current policies.

Offsetting these advantages, however, is the fact that a financial adjustment—involving a payment by the insured to the company—is required, which may be quite substantial if the term policy has been in force for several years. This adjustment may be computed on a variety of bases, but a great number of companies specify that the payment will be the larger of (1) the difference in the reserves (in some companies, the cash surrender values) under the policies being exchanged or (2) the difference in the premiums paid on the term policy and those that would have been paid on the permanent plan, with interest on the difference at a stipulated rate. Under the second type of financial adjustment, an allowance is frequently made for any larger dividends that would have been payable under the permanent form. Some companies require a payment equal to the difference in reserves, plus a charge of up to 8 percent to provide the previously forgone investment return.

The purpose of the financial adjustment, regardless of how it is computed, is to place the insurance company in the same financial position it would have enjoyed had the permanent contract been issued in the first place. Therefore, apart from the possibility of obtaining more favorable actuarial assumptions, there does not seem to be any financial advantage to the insured to convert retroactively. The insured will admittedly pay a smaller premium but—by making up the deficiency in the term premium—will, in effect, pay it over a longer period of time; actuarially, the two sets of premiums are equivalent. Some people are under the mistaken impression that by making the financial adjustment required for conversion as of the original date, they are investing money retroactively and being credited with retroactive interest. The fact is, however, that the insured pays the company

---

Retroactive Conversion

- Premiums after conversion based on earlier (original) age
- Must pay an adjustment to insurer
- Converts term policy to cash value type policy
- Provides level or flexible premiums thereafter
- Conversion must be made before limiting age

---

the interest it would have earned had the larger premium been paid from the beginning.

The insured should consider many factors in making a choice between the two bases of conversion, one of the most important being the state of his or her health. The insured would be ill advised to convert retroactively—and pay a substantial sum of money to the insurance company—if his or her health were impaired. The sum the insured pays would immediately become a part of the reserve under the contract and would not increase the amount of death benefits in the event of the insured's early demise—or ever, for that matter. The payment would simply reduce the effective amount of insurance.

In most cases, if the insured has surplus funds to invest in insurance, he or she should consider purchasing additional insurance or perhaps prepaying premiums on existing policies, including the newly converted one. Subject to certain limitations, most companies permit the insured to prepay fixed premiums, either in the form of so-called premium deposits or through discounting of future premiums. The two procedures are very similar. The principal difference is that under the discount method, credit is taken in advance for the interest to be earned on the funds deposited. Under both arrangements, the funds deposited with the company are credited with interest at a stipulated rate and, in some instances, are credited with the interest earned by the company in excess of the stipulated rate. In the event of the insured's death, the balance of any such deposits is returned to the insured's estate or designated beneficiaries in addition to the death benefit of the policy. Some companies permit withdrawal of premium deposits at any time, in which case a lower rate of interest may be credited, while others limit withdrawals to anniversary or premium due dates. A few companies permit withdrawals only in case of surrender or death. Some companies credit no interest or otherwise penalize the insured if the funds are withdrawn.

Time Limit for Conversion—As previously noted, a retroactive conversion must take place within a specified number of years after issue. If the term of the policy is no longer than 10 years, a conversion as of a current date can usually be accomplished throughout the full term. If the term is longer than 10 years, the policy may stipulate that the conversion privilege must be exercised, if at all, before the expiration of a period shorter than the term of the policy. For example, a 15-year term policy must usually be converted, if at all, within 12 years from date of issue, a 20-year term policy within 15 years.

The purpose of a time limit is to minimize adverse selection. There is always a substantial degree of adverse selection in the conversion process. Those policyowners in poor health as the time for conversion approaches are more likely to convert and pay the higher premiums than those who believe themselves to be in good health. If the decision to convert must be made some years before the expiration of the term policy, a higher percentage of healthy policyowners, uncertain of their health some years hence, will elect to convert. Even so, experience has shown that the death rate among those who convert is higher than normal. This accounts for the fact that premium rates for convertible term insurance are somewhat higher than those for term policies not containing the conversion privilege.

If the policy is renewable, the only time limitation may be that it is converted before age 60 or 65. In other cases, the contract will state that the policy must be converted within a certain period before the expiration of the last term for which it can be renewed. In all cases, conversion may be permitted beyond the time limit, but within the policy term, upon evidence of insurability.

Some companies issue term policies that are automatically converted at the expiration of the term to a specified plan of permanent insurance. It is doubtful that this procedure is effective in reducing adverse selection since healthy individuals may fail to continue the permanent insurance.

Re-entry Term (Select and Ultimate Term Insurance)

The life insurance industry has developed a term insurance policy intended to charge higher premiums to those in poorer health when they renew their term insurance, thereby reducing the degree of adverse selection. The product is commonly called *re-entry term insurance*. It is really a policy subject to two different premium schedules. The lower premium rate is based on select mortality (that applicable to an insured who has recently given evidence that he or she is in good health). The select rates are available as long as the insured is able to provide new evidence of insurability at each renewal date and at other dates specified by the insurer.

The higher premium schedule is based on ultimate mortality rates (that applicable to insureds at least 15 or 20 years after they last provided evidence of insurability). The insureds that cannot provide evidence of insurability acceptable to the insurance company when requested or required must pay the higher premium schedule rates to renew their coverage. They are known to be in poorer health and have to pay for the increased risk now and probably for each subsequent renewal, unless they experience an improvement in their health.

It is hard to argue with the logic or concept of equity in this approach. In order to get the lower premiums while healthy, the individual should be willing to pay the higher premium when his or her health deteriorates. However, it is questionable whether the policyowner knows or realizes the full import of a decision to buy re-entry term insurance. Young people in good health believe they are immortal and will never have to pay the higher rates. Few of them stop to consider that they may actually end up paying the ultimate rates and that when that happens they will usually be precluded from buying coverage from another insurer. The single premium schedule term insurance they could have bought instead of re-entry term might have been a significant bargain. Unfortunately, when that realization sinks in, it is too late to select that option.

Re-entry term is economical for those who remain healthy into their retirement years, but it may end up being very costly for anyone whose health deteriorates at about the same rate as that of the general population. On average, people start to experience declining health between the ages of 45 and 55. If they reach their life expectancy (at least 50 percent should), they can live 40 to 50 years in an impaired physical condition—paying the higher term rates for many more years than they enjoyed lower term rates.

| *Example:* | Mary purchased a re-entry term policy 3 years ago. She saved 10 percent based on the premiums that would have been required for a traditional renewable term policy that guarantees future premium rates. Mary suffered a severe heart attack just before she was required to have her health reassessed for the re-entry term. Her new premium is more than double what the renewal premium would have been under the traditional renewable term policy. That difference may get even larger in the future. |

It is suggested that the decision to purchase re-entry term insurance should involve comparison of the high rates of competing insurers for similar coverage. If the insured cannot provide satisfactory evidence of insurability, the lower premium schedule is irrelevant. Helpful in making such comparisons are pro forma cash flow simulations of the premiums (both high and low rates) for each policy being considered at a range of premium increase dates. Another important point for evaluation is whether or not the insurer considers the policy a new contract with a new contestable period after the insured fails a re-entry test. Some insurers treat the new premium as an adjustment on continuing coverage, but others impose a new contestable period.

Guarding Against Contestability

In general it is a good idea to keep existing coverage in force until after the intended replacement coverage has actually been issued and the policy delivered. It is important for the policyowner to realize that new policies remain contestable for at least one year (and often for 2 years). If the insured dies while the policy remains contestable, the claim will be investigated much more thoroughly and take longer to settle than one for a policy that is already incontestable.

Long-Term Contracts

While most term contracts provide protection for a relatively short period, subject to renewal for successive periods of the same duration, some term contracts are designed to provide long-period protection in the first instance. These policies often give prospective policyowners the option to purchase waiver-of-premium and accidental death benefits.

A term-to-65 contract, for example, provides protection on a level premium basis from the age of issue to age 65. It is not to be confused with yearly renewable or other forms of term insurance that can be renewed until the insured reaches age 65. The period covered by this contract is normally somewhat shorter than the life expectancy, but its termination date coincides with the age generally regarded as the normal retirement age. Hence it probably comes closest to limiting its protection to the years when the insured's income is derived from personal efforts. Because the term is shorter than that of whole life contracts, the premium will be smaller. It is customary to provide for cash and other surrender values. A conversion privilege may be offered, but if so, it must usually be exercised some time before the expiration of the policy. A typical form requires conversion prior to age 60.

Nonlevel Term Insurance

The preceding discussion has presumed that the amount of insurance is level or uniform throughout the term of the policy. This is not necessarily the case since the amount of insurance may increase or decrease throughout the term. As a matter of fact, a substantial—if not predominant—portion of term insurance provides systematic decreases in the amount of insurance from year to year. This type of term insurance, appropriately called *decreasing term insurance,* may be written in the form of a separate contract, a rider to a new or existing contract, or as an integral part of a combination contract. Mortgage redemption insurance is probably the most familiar form of decreasing term insurance.

Increasing term insurance in the form of a return-of-premium provision has been around for a long time, but in recent years the concept has enjoyed a much wider application in connection with various arrangements, specifically split-dollar plans, which may contemplate borrowing or encumbering the cash value of an underlying policy. In order to provide a uniform death benefit to the insured's personal beneficiaries, contracts developed for these uses frequently make provision for the automatic purchase of an additional amount of term insurance each year in the exact or approximate amount that the cash value increases. Increasing term insurance may be provided on a year-to-year basis through the operation of the so-called fifth-dividend option.

Renewable Term Characteristics

- Coverage for a stated period
- Premium based on age at beginning of each new period
- Premiums increase with age
- Rate of premium increases accelerates after age 40
- Can be renewed for a new period without health assessment (up to limiting age specified in policy)
- Additional charges for adverse selection included in premium at advanced ages
- Does not provide living benefits such as cash values, policy loans, and so on

---

Critiques Of Term Insurance

Term insurance has long been a controversial type of insurance. Many people, not familiar with or perhaps not sympathetic to the principle of level premium insurance, advocate the use of term insurance in all situations to the virtual exclusion of permanent insurance. There are certain insurance "consultants" who, when they find permanent plans in an insurance program, will advise their surrender for cash and replacement with term insurance. On the other hand, the insurance companies, mindful of the limitations of term insurance and fearful of possible adverse public reaction, tend to discourage its indiscriminate use. This has given rise to a widespread impression that insurance companies are opposed to term insurance, preferring the higher-premium forms that add more to income and assets. It might be helpful therefore to point out the areas that can legitimately be served by term insurance and to analyze briefly some of the fallacious arguments that have been advanced in favor of term insurance.

Areas of Usefulness

Term insurance is suitable when either (1) the need for protection is purely temporary, or (2) the need for protection is permanent, but the insured temporarily cannot afford the premiums for permanent insurance. In the first case, term insurance is the complete answer, but it should be renewable in the event that the temporary need should extend over a longer period than was originally anticipated. Theoretically the policy need not be convertible, but since relatively few people carry an adequate amount of permanent insurance and since the loss of insurability is a constant threat, it is advisable to obtain a policy with the conversion privilege.

The second broad use of term insurance requires that the policy be convertible. The conversion privilege is the bridge that spans the gap between the need for permanent insurance and the financial ability to meet the need. In this case, since the insured's financial situation might persist longer than anticipated, the policy should be renewable as well as convertible. Thus, the renewable and convertible features serve quite different functions and, ideally, should be incorporated in all term policies.

Temporary Need for Protection—Examples of temporary needs that can—and should—be met through term insurance are encountered daily. One of the most obvious is the need to hedge a loan. A term policy in the amount of the loan payable to the lender not only protects the lender against possible loss of principal but also relieves the insured's estate of the burden of repaying the loan if the insured dies. A mortgage redemption policy serves the same purpose. An individual who has invested heavily in a speculative business venture should protect his or her estate and family by obtaining term insurance in the amount of the investment.

If a business firm is spending a considerable sum in an experimental project, the success of which depends on the talents and abilities of one individual or a few individuals, term insurance on the appropriate person or persons will protect the investment. A parent with young children is likely to need more insurance while the children are dependent than he or she will need when they have grown up and become self-sufficient. The additional insurance during the child-raising period can be—and usually is—provided through term insurance. Frequently, decreasing term insurance is superimposed on a plan of permanent insurance.

> *Example:* Tom and Marsha have two very young children and need more life insurance to protect them. However, Marsha will become the recipient of a large trust in 8 years. At that time, they will have a diminished need for life insurance. Term insurance is appropriate for the temporary need.

Lack of Finances for Permanent Insurance—The second function of term insurance is particularly important to young people who expect substantial improvement in their financial situation as the years go by. Young professionals who have made a considerable investment in their education and training, but whose practices must be built up gradually, are likely prospects for term insurance. Young business executives are also good prospects.

Danger of Relying Solely on Group Term Insurance

In these times of fierce competition and corporate downsizing, it can be precarious to rely heavily on employer-provided group life insurance to satisfy all or most of a family's death benefit needs. Individuals should find out how much of the employer group coverage can be converted after an involuntary termination of employment—for example, mandatory early retirement, workforce reduction, plant closing, reorganization after a merger or acquisition, employer bankruptcy, statutory banning of a product (freon, for instance), or chronic health impairment resulting from accident or disease. Individual term insurance may be appropriate to cover the potential net reduction in coverage after post-employment conversion of the existing coverage. The safest way for the individual to cover this risk is to purchase an individual policy while he or she is still employed. The cost of such risk aversion is the amount spent on premiums for coverage in excess of the individual's current needs between policy formation and a premature employment termination.

Fallacious Arguments in Favor of Term Insurance

Some of the fallacious arguments in favor of term insurance can just as aptly be described as criticisms of level premium insurance. Upon analysis, most of the arguments can be merged into two sweeping allegations: (1) Level premium insurance overcharges the policyowner, and (2) the accumulation and protection elements should be separated.

The basis for the first allegation is the indisputable fact that if a policyowner dies in the early years of the contract, premium outlay under the level premium plan is considerably larger than it would have been under a term plan. It follows, then, according to the term advocates, that the policyowner paid a larger premium than was necessary. Term advocates question whether it is wise for the insured to pay in advance for something he or she may never need or live to enjoy. They argue that it is better "to pay as you go and get what you pay for."

There is no question that insureds would be far better off financially with term insurance if they could be sure that they would die within a relatively short time. On the other hand, they would be far worse off if they guessed wrong and lived to a ripe old age. Although no one knows whether he or she will die young or live to an excessively old age, the chances of living to an age where the total term premiums exceed the total premiums paid under a level premium plan are relatively high.

The level premium plan protects the insured against the consequences of living too long and having to pay prohibitive premiums for insurance protection. In effect, it shifts a portion of the premium burden of those who live beyond their life expectancy to those who die young and produce an exceedingly large return on their premium outlay. Because at the outset no one can know which group he or she will be in, payment of the level premium by all is a fair and satisfactory arrangement.

Those who argue that level premium insurance overcharges policyowners sometimes assert that the reserve under permanent forms of insurance is forfeited to the company in the event of the insured's death. To correct this "inequity," they contend the normal death benefit should be increased by the amount of the reserve.

It should be apparent that this argument strikes at the very heart of the level premium plan. As stated before, the essence of this plan is a gradual reduction in the net amount at risk as the reserve increases. If the reserve is to be paid in addition to the face amount of the policy, this reduction in the amount at risk does not occur, and premiums that were calculated on the assumption of a decreasing risk will clearly be inadequate. Some companies offer a contract that promises to return the reserve in addition to the face amount of the policy, but the premium is increased accordingly.

The second allegation—that the savings and protection elements of the contract should be separated—is based on the proposition that an individual can invest his or her surplus funds more wisely and with a greater return than the life insurance company can. Those who believe this recommend that individuals buy term insurance and then place the difference between the term premium and the premium they would have paid for level premium insurance in a separate investment program. Some suggest investing this difference in premiums in government bonds, others recommend investment trusts or mutual funds, while others advocate an individual investment program in common stocks. This argument needs to be analyzed in terms of the objectives of any investment program.

Investment Program Objectives

The principal investment program objectives are safety of principal, yield, and liquidity.

Regarding safety of principal, the life insurance industry has compiled a solvency record over the years that is unmatched by any other type of business organization. It has survived wars, depressions, and inflation; composite losses to policyowners have been relatively rare. Even the few companies seized by the regulators in recent years have been able to rescue most of their policyowners' contracts.

This excellent record has been achieved through quality investments and concentration on government bonds (federal, state, and local), high-grade corporate bonds, and real estate mortgages, and through emphasis on diversification. Investments are diversified by industry, geographical distribution, maturity, and size. Many of the larger companies have from 100,000 to 200,000 different units of investment. The individual policyowner's reserve or investment is commingled with all other policyowners' reserves. The insurance company has invested in assets to offset these liabilities (reserves). In effect therefore each policyowner owns a pro rata share of each investment unit in the company's portfolio. The insured may have as little as one cent invested in some units. Such diversification—which is the keystone of safety—is obviously beyond the reach of the individual investor. Only by investing exclusively in federal and state government bonds, with the consequent interest rate risk and sacrifice of yield, could the individual investor hope to match the safety of principal that his or her funds would enjoy with a reputable life insurance company.

Life insurance companies unquestionably obtain the highest possible yield commensurate with the standard of safety that they have set for themselves. As a group, life insurance companies in the United States earned over 9.0 percent of their mean ledger assets during the 1980's and into the 1990's, reaching 9.87 percent in 1985. This figure represents the net investment income on aggregates of all U.S. life insurance companies (but does not reflect capital gains and losses) after deducting all expenses allocable to investment operations but before deducting federal income taxes. It is the highest during the 20th century for the United States life insurance industry. In 2002 life insurers net rate of return on total assets dropped to 5.38 percent from 6.31 percent a year earlier. Excluding separate accounts, the portfolio net rate of return on general account assets was 6.64 percent in 2002, down from 7.13 percent in 2001 (ACLI's *Life Insurers Fact Book 2003*, American Council of Life Insurers, 101 Constitution Ave. NW, Washington, D.C. 20001-2133).

Net rates have been declining since 1985 as general investment returns have sagged for all sectors of the economy. Many individuals therefore may be able to secure a higher yield than that provided by a life insurance company by investing in common stocks or other equity investments, especially if unrealized capital appreciation is taken into account, and some exceptional investors will be able to do it under virtually any circumstances. It is highly questionable, however, that the typical life insurance policyowner can, over a long period, earn a consistently higher yield than a life insurance company, regardless of the type of investment program he or she pursues. Moreover, it should be noted that the annual increases in cash values are not subject to federal income taxes as they accrue, while the earnings from a separate investment program would be taxed as ordinary income. (Except in the case of death, most of the earnings on the reserve of a life insurance contract are eventually taxed to the insured, but usually at a time when he or she is in a much lower tax bracket.)

With respect to the third objective of an investment program, the liquidity of a life insurance contract is unsurpassed. The policyowner's investment can be withdrawn at any time with no loss of principal. This can be accomplished through surrender for cash or through policy loans. The insured never faces the possibility of liquidating his or her assets in an unfavorable market; nor can the insured's policy loans be called because of inadequate collateral. Certain types of investments' approach the liquidity of life insurance cash values, but no investment whose value depends on the market can match the liquidity of the demand obligation represented by the life insurance contract.

Principal Investment Program Objectives
• Safety of principal
• Yield
• Liquidity

More important perhaps than any of the preceding factors is the question of whether savings under a separate investment program would have been accomplished in the first place. Life insurance that develops cash values is a form of "forced" saving. Not only do its periodic premiums provide a simple and systematic mechanism for saving, but when the savings feature is combined with the protection feature, there is also far more incentive for the insured to save than there would otherwise be. An individual who is voluntarily purchasing a bond a month or setting aside a certain amount per month in some other type of savings account may skip a month or two if some other disposition of money is more appealing. If, however, failure to set aside the predetermined contribution to a savings account would result in loss of highly prized insurance protection that might be irreplaceable, he or she will be far more likely to make the savings effort. The insured saves because it is the only way of preserving his or her protection.

The foregoing is not to disparage other forms of investment. All have their place in an individual's financial program. Level premium life insurance, however, should be the foundation of any lifelong financial program.

Whole Life Insurance

In contrast with term insurance, which pays benefits only if the insured dies during a specified period of years, whole life insurance provides for the payment of the policy's face amount upon the death of the insured, regardless of when death occurs. It is this characteristic—protection for the whole of life—that gives the insurance its name. The expression has no reference to the manner in which the premiums are paid, only to the duration of the protection. If the premiums are to be paid throughout the insured's lifetime, the insurance is known as *ordinary whole life;* if premiums are to be paid only during a specified period, the insurance is designated *limited-payment whole life.*

Principal Types of Whole Life Insurance

Ordinary Life Insurance

Ordinary life insurance is a type of whole life insurance for which premiums are based on the assumption that they will be paid until the insured's death. It is desirable to define ordinary life insurance this way since, in an increasing number of cases, life insurance is purchased with no intention on the policyowner's part to pay premiums as long as the insured lives. In many cases the insurance is purchased as part of a program that anticipates the use of dividends to pay up the insurance by the end of a period shorter than the life expectancy of the insured. In other cases the plan may be to eventually surrender insurance for an annuity or for a reduced amount of insurance. The point is that ordinary life should not be envisioned as a type of insurance on which the policyowner is irrevocably committed to pay premiums as long as the insured lives or even into the insured's extreme old age. Rather, it should be viewed as a type of policy that provides permanent protection for the lowest total premium outlay and some degree of flexibility to meet changing needs and circumstances for both long-lived persons and those with average-duration lifetimes. Ordinary life insurance is an appropriate foundation for any insurance program, and in an adequate amount it could well serve as the entire program. Its distinctive features are discussed below.

Permanent Protection—The protection afforded by the ordinary life contract is *permanent*—the term never expires, and the policy never has to be renewed or converted. If insureds continue to pay premiums or pay up their policy, they have protection for as long as they live, regardless of their health; eventually, the face amount of the policy will be paid. This is a valuable right because virtually all people need some insurance as long as they live, if for nothing more than to pay last-illness and funeral expenses. In most cases the need is much greater than that.

In one sense ordinary life can be regarded as an endowment. An *endowment insurance* contract pays the face amount of the policy, whether the insured dies prior to the endowment maturity date or survives to the end of the period. If age 100 is considered to be the end of the endowment period—as well as the end of the mortality table—then an ordinary life policy is equivalent to an endowment contract that pays the face amount as a death claim if the insured dies before age 100 or as a matured endowment if he or she survives to age 100.

Lowest Premium Outlay—The net single premium for a whole life policy is computed without reference to the manner in which the periodic premiums will be paid and, at any particular age, is the same for ordinary life insurance and any form of limited-payment life insurance. Naturally, the longer the period over which the single-sum payment is spread, the lower each periodic payment will be.

The gross annual premiums per $1,000 charged by two life insurance companies for the same two contracts at ages 25 and 35 are shown in table 2-1, below. The gross premium is the premium actually paid by the policyowner. It is the net premium increased by an allowance for the insurer's expenses and contingencies.

TABLE 2-1
Sample Gross Annual Premiums per $1,000

| Issue Age | Ordinary Whole Life | | 20-Pay Whole Life | |
	Company A	Company B	Company A	Company B
25	$ 9.28	$11.90	$13.28	$17.70
35	$ 13.21	$16.90	$19.26	$22.50

Essentials of Life Insurance Products

Limited-payment insurance contracts provide benefits that justify the higher premium rates. If, however, the insured's objective is to secure the maximum amount of permanent insurance protection per dollar of annual premium outlay, then his or her purposes will be best served by the ordinary life contract.

Cash Value or Accumulation Element—As level premium permanent insurance, ordinary life accumulates a reserve that gradually reaches a substantial level and eventually equals the face amount of the policy. As is to be expected, however, the reserve at all durations is lower than that of the other forms of permanent insurance. In other words, the protection element tends to be relatively high. Nevertheless, it is the opinion of many that the ordinary life contract offers the optimal combination of protection and savings. The contract emphasizes protection, but it also accumulates a cash value that can be used to accomplish a variety of purposes.

The cash values that accumulate under an ordinary life contract can be utilized as surrender values, paid-up insurance, or extended term insurance. Cash values are not generally available during the first year or two of the insurance because of the cost to the company of putting the business on the books. Common exceptions are single-premium policies and some durations of limited-payment whole life policies whose first-year premiums are large enough to exceed all first-year expenses incurred to create the policy and maintain policy reserves.

Policy Loans. All level premium life insurance policies that develop cash values (for example, whole life, universal life, adjustable life, variable life, variable universal life, and current assumption whole life) have provisions for policy loans. These *policy loans* give the policyowner access to the cash value that accumulates inside the policy without having to terminate the policy.

The policyowner merely requests a loan and the life insurer will lend the funds confidentially. The loan provisions in the policy specify what portion of the cash value is available for loans and how interest will be determined on the loan. In most policies over 90 percent of the cash value is available for loans—some policies may restrict the amount of loanable funds to 92 percent of the cash value in recognition of an 8-percent policy loan interest rate—and any portion of the cash value can be borrowed. Policyowners indicate in their requests the amount desired, and they can take out more than one policy loan as long as the aggregate amount of all outstanding loans and accrued interest applicable to those loans does not exceed the policy cash value.

Policy loans do involve interest charged on the borrowed funds. There are two different approaches to setting the policy loan interest rate. The policy will stipulate either (1) a fixed rate as specified in the policy (commonly 5, 6, or 8 percent) or (2) a variable interest rate tied by formula to some specified index. One variable approach is to use Moody's composite yield on seasoned corporate bonds or some index that is regularly published in the financial press, such as *The Wall Street Journal* or *The Journal of Commerce.* Another index may be the interest rate being credited to the cash value plus a specified spread.

State laws impose changing upper limits on variable policy loan interest rates. These laws require that the rate charged be lowered whenever the upper limit drops to more than half of 1 percent below the rate being charged. The rate charged can be changed up to four times each year.

The policyowner has the option of paying the policy loan interest in cash or having the unpaid interest charge added to the balance of the outstanding loan(s). The latter choice can be expensive because future interest charges will be applied to the unpaid interest amount as well as the initial policy loan. The policyowner may choose to pay any part of the principal or interest charge he or she desires since there is no repayment schedule or requirement.

If the policy loan and accrued interest are not paid in cash, the life insurer can recover the outstanding balance of the loans and accrued interest from the death benefits if the insured dies, or from the cash surrender value if the policy is terminated. In fact, the policy will automatically terminate if the policy loan balance plus unpaid interest ever exceeds the policy cash value.

Some whole life policies give policyowners an automatic premium loan option. When this option is selected, a delinquent premium will be paid automatically by a new policy loan. This will keep the policy in force as long as there is adequate cash value to cover each delinquent premium. However, the policy will terminate if the cash value is exhausted.

The automatic premium loan provision does not apply to flexible premium policies because the insurer usually deducts mortality charges and other expenses directly from the cash value. Hence no interest charges are incurred for skipped premium payments.

Policy loans result in the life insurer's release of funds it would otherwise invest to earn investment income. If the rate of investment return on the insurer's portfolio is greater than the rate being applied to the policy loan, the insurer experiences a reduction in earnings. Therefore the insurance company usually takes steps to offset such loan-induced losses in order to preserve a rough equity between policyowners who leave their cash values invested and those who prevent the insurer from reaping the higher yield.

In traditional participating whole life policies, policyowner dividends were not affected by policy loans, but most participating whole life policies being sold today use what is called *direct recognition* to reduce dividends on policies with outstanding loans. This not only adjusts for the differential in earnings but also discourages policy loans.

For universal life policies and other non-participating designs, there are no dividends to adjust; insurers may compensate for lost earnings by reducing the earnings rate being credited directly to the cash value. If there are no policy loans, the insurer credits its normal crediting rate to the full cash value. However, if there are policy loans, the insurer can credit the normal rate to the unloaned portion of the cash value and a lower rate (often 2 percent or 200 basis points lower) to the portion of the cash value equal to the loan indebtedness. When the loan is repaid, the insurer resumes crediting the higher rate to the full cash value. There is no retroactive payment to eliminate the past differential.

The creation of a policy loan does have negative consequences on the policy. The death benefit payable to the beneficiary is reduced by the full amount of outstanding policy loans and accrued interest under most types of policies. Therefore, an irrevocable beneficiary's consent may be required to obtain a policy loan. A policy loan is really an advance against the death benefit; thus the death benefit is adjusted to reflect the prior disbursement.

Outstanding policy loans also reduce the nonforfeiture benefits. The net cash value available to provide either extended term insurance or reduced paid-up insurance is lessened by the loan indebtedness. In the case of extended term insurance, the amount of term

---

Policy Loan Features

- Available on demand of policyowner
- Interest charges apply
- Depending on the specific contract, interest rates are either fixed or variable
- Variable interest rates tied to a published index
- Unpaid interest charges added to loan balance
- Repayment of loans is at discretion of policyowner
- Outstanding policy loans plus unpaid interest is recovered from either death benefit or surrender value
- Policy terminates if loans plus unpaid interest ever exceed the policy cash value

---

insurance is reduced from the original amount of coverage by the amount of loan indebtedness as well. State statutes allow life insurers to delay lending funds for up to 6 months after requested, and is known as the *delay clause*. This is a form of emergency protection for the insurance company in case policyowners' demand for loans accelerates to the point that the insurer is forced to liquidate other assets at significant losses to satisfy the loan demands. In actuality, delaying access to funds is an indication of financial weakness or lack of policyowner confidence that insurers wish to avoid. Those life insurers that have failed in recent years chose not to invoke their right to delay policy loan disbursements. Quick access to cash values was terminated only after the insurance commissioner seized control of the company.

Limited-Payment Life Insurance

Limited-payment life insurance is a type of whole life insurance for which premiums are limited by contract to a specified number of years.

The limitation in limited-payment policies may be expressed in terms of the number of annual premiums or of the age beyond which premiums will not be required. Policies whose premiums are limited by number usually stipulate 1, 5, 7, 10, 15, 20, 25, or 30 annual payments, although some companies are willing to issue policies calling for any desired number of premiums. The greater the number of premiums payable, naturally, the more closely the contract approaches the ordinary life design. For those who prefer to limit their premium payments to a period measured by a terminal age, companies make policies available that are paid up at a specified age—typically, 60, 65, or 70. The objective is to enable the insured to pay for the policy during his or her working lifetime. Many companies issue contracts for which premiums are payable to an advanced age, such as 85, but for all practical purposes, these contracts can be regarded as the equivalent of ordinary life contracts.

Because the value of a limited-payment whole life contract at the date of issue is precisely the same as that of a contract purchased on the ordinary life basis, and because it is presumed that there will be fewer premium payments under the limited-payment policy, it follows that each premium must be larger than the comparable premium under an ordinary life contract. Moreover, the fewer the guaranteed premiums specified or the shorter the premium-paying period, the higher each premium will be. However, the higher premiums are offset by greater cash and other surrender values.

Thus the limited-payment policy will provide a larger fund for use in an emergency and will accumulate a larger fund for retirement purposes than will an ordinary life contract issued at the same age. On the other hand, if death takes place within the first several years after issue of the contract, the total premiums paid under the limited-payment policy will exceed those payable under an ordinary life policy. The comparatively long-lived policyowner, however, will pay considerably less in premiums under the limited-payment plan than on the ordinary life basis. This is because a greater portion of the insurance costs will be paid by investment earnings.

There is no presumptive financial advantage between policy forms (types of contracts and the state-mandated standard provisions that must be included). The choice depends on circumstances and personal preference. The limited-payment policy offers the assurance that premium payments will be confined to the insured's productive years, while the ordinary life contract provides maximum permanent protection for any given annual outlay. The limited-payment policy contains the same surrender options, dividend options, settlement options, and other features that make for significant flexibility.

Single-Premium Life Insurance—An extreme form of limited-payment contract is the *single-premium life* insurance policy. Under this plan the number of premiums is limited to one. The effective amount of insurance protection (i.e., the at-risk portion of the death benefit) is, of course, substantially less than the face amount of the policy, and the investment element is correspondingly greater. Such contracts therefore are purchased largely for accumulation purposes. They offer a high degree of security, a satisfactory interest yield, and ready convertibility into cash on a basis guaranteed by the insurer for the entire duration of the contract. Since the single premium represents a substantial amount of money and since it is computed on the basis that there will be no return of any part of it in the event of the insured's early death, it has only limited appeal for protection purposes.

The limited-payment principle is applicable to any type of contract and is frequently used in connection with endowment contracts. However, it is important to differentiate between a limited-payment policy (in which paid-up status is guaranteed at the end of the premium-paying period) and a premiums-paid-by-dividend approach (which uses policyowner dividends to pay all of the premiums after they are adequate to do so). Premiums-paid-by-dividend approaches have sometimes been sold using the misnomer of *vanishing premium*. The notable difference between the two is that under the misnamed vanishing-premium approach dividends are not guaranteed and may decline in the future. If dividends turn out to be inadequate to pay the premiums, the policyowner will have to resume actual premium payments out of pocket or let the policy lapse. There is no guarantee that so-called vanishing premiums will actually vanish, or that if they do vanish they will never reappear. This concept created many sales, as well as many disappointed consumers and class-action law suits when interest rates plummeted in the 1990's.

Joint Life Insurance

The typical life insurance contract is written on the life of one person and is technically known as *single-life insurance*. A contract can be written on more than one life, however, in which event it is known as a joint life contract, also called a *first-to-die joint life policy*. Strictly speaking, a joint life contract is one written on the lives of two or more persons and payable upon the death of the first person to die. If the face amount is payable upon the death of the last of two or more lives insured under a single contract, it is called either a *survivorship policy or a second-to-die policy*. Such policies have become quite popular as a means of funding federal estate taxes of wealthy couples whose wills make maximum use of tax deferral at the first death. Joint life policies are fairly common for funding business buy-sell agreements.

The joint life policy may cover from two to 12 lives, but because of expense and other practical obstacles, most companies limit the number to three or four lives. (Theoretically there is no limit on the number of lives that can be insured under a joint contract. A few insurers will issue policies on more than 12 lives if they all have related business interests.) The contract is most often written on the whole life plan, either ordinary life, limited-payment or universal life. It is seldom written on the term plan since separate term policies on each life for the same amount would cost little more than a joint policy and would offer the advantage of continued protection to the survivor or survivors.

The premium for a joint life policy is somewhat greater than the combined premiums on separate policies providing an equivalent amount of insurance. In other words, the premium for a $200,000 joint life policy covering two lives is larger than the sum of the premiums on two separate contracts providing $100,000 each. This is because only

$100,000 is payable upon the death of the first of the two insureds to die with separate policies, while $200,000 is payable under a joint life policy. Moreover, since two lives are covered, the cost of insurance is relatively high, and cash values are relatively low. However, a joint life policy costs less than two separate policies providing $200,000 each.

The provisions of the joint life contract closely follow those of the single-life contract. The clause allowing conversion to other policy forms differs in that it allows conversion policies on separate lives as follows:

1. conversion to single-life policies on the same plan as that of the joint policies upon divorce or dissolution of business
2. division of the amount of insurance among the insured lives either equally or unequally
3. dating of the new policies as of the original date of issue of the joint policy

Business partners sometimes take out a joint policy covering the lives of all partners and written for an amount equal to the largest interest involved. Upon the death of the first partner, the surviving partners receive funds with which to purchase the deceased's partnership interest. Stockholders in a closely held corporation may follow the same practice. Because the insurance usually terminates upon the first death of the partners or stockholders, the remaining members of the firm will not only be without insurance but—of greater consequence—may also be uninsurable.

Some life insurers have introduced joint life policies designed specifically for business buy-sell funding. Some of them offer a short period of extended coverage for the surviving partners or shareholders and guarantee their insurability under a new joint life policy similar to the previous one. A few insurers have even introduced joint life policies that allow allocations of unequal amounts of death proceeds to match actual unequal ownership interests.

Joint Life Features

- Insure more than one life with one policy
- Pay only one death benefit
- First-to-die policies pay death benefit when the first death of the insureds occurs
- Survivorship or second-to-die policies pay death benefit when the second insured person dies (no benefit at first death)
- Survivorship policies often used to prefund federal estate taxes of husband and wife
- May be converted to single-life policies if insureds divorce or dissolve their business relationship

---

A joint life policy may be suitable for a husband and wife when the death of either will create a need for funds, as would be true if death taxes were involved. Even here, dissatisfaction sometimes arises when the survivor faces the fact that he or she no longer has any coverage under the contract.

Functions of Whole Life Insurance

At this point, the purposes served by whole life insurance should be clear. In summary, the whole life policy

- provides protection against long-range or permanent needs
- accumulates a savings fund that can be used for general purposes or to meet specific objectives

The protection function is particularly applicable to a surviving spouse's need for a life income, last-illness and funeral expenses, expenses of estate administration, death taxes, philanthropic bequests, and the needs of dependent relatives other than the surviving spouse. The general savings feature of the whole life policy is useful in a financial emergency or as a source of funds to take advantage of an unusual business or investment opportunity. The policyowner may use the policy for the specific purpose of accumulating funds for his or her children's college education, to set a child up in business, to pay for a child's wedding, or to supplement the insured's retirement income.

Chapter Two Review

Key terms and concepts are explained in the glossary. Answers to the review questions and the self-test questions are found in the back of the book, following the Glossary.

Key Terms and Concepts

renewability

convertibility

attained age

original age

retroactive conversion

re-entry term

decreasing term insurance

increasing term insurance

select and ultimate term insurance

ordinary whole life insurance

limited payment whole life

permanent insurance

endowment insurance

policy loan

direction recognition

delay clause

single life insurance

joint life policy (first-to die)

Review Questions

2-1.   Describe the basic nature of term insurance.

2-2.   Describe the available variations of term insurance.

2-3.   Describe the protection provided by renewability provisions in term life insurance contracts.

2-4.   Compare the attained-age method of converting term insurance with the retroactive conversion method.

2-5.   Explain why there are time limitations on conversion rights for term insurance, and describe some forms of such limits.

2-6.   Explain how select and ultimate term (re-entry term) differ from traditional forms of term insurance.

2-7.   How do term-to-65 policies differ from shorter-duration term life insurance contracts?

2-8.   Describe the most common situations for which term insurance is suitable and useful.

2-9.   List the fallacious arguments against level premium ordinary permanent (whole life) insurance, in favor of term insurance.

2-10.   Describe the general features of whole life insurance policies.

2-11.   Describe how limited-payment life insurance differs from ordinary life insurance.

2-12.   Describe the two types of joint life insurance policies and indicate their common uses.

2-13.   Explain how a policy loan changes the rights of (1) the beneficiary and (2) the policyowner.

2-14.   Explain the functions of whole life insurance.

Self-Test Questions

Instructions: Read Chapter 2 first, then answer the following questions to test your knowledge. There are 10 questions; circle the correct answer, then check your answers with the answer key in the back of the book.

2-1.   Policy loans require the policyowner to

    (A)   have collateral
    (B)   be charged interest on the loan
    (C)   agree to a repayment schedule
    (D)   complete a form disclosing the reason for the loan

2-2.   An unpaid loan against the cash value of an ordinary life policy will

    (A)   cancel the death benefit
    (B)   increase the death benefit
    (C)   decrease the death benefit
    (D)   not change the death benefit

2-3.   At maturity, the face amount of an ordinary life insurance policy will

    (A)   be paid to the policy owner
    (B)   be paid to the beneficiary
    (C)   pay the cash value plus mortality adjustments
    (D)   remain in trust until death occurs, but premiums will stop

2-4. Term insurance policies always provide

(A)   a benefit only at the end of the term
(B)   only temporary life insurance protection
(C)   a small cash payment at expiration
(D)   convertibility within the term to another plan of insurance

2-5. Re-entry term insurance allows insureds to keep a select premium rate after the initial period if:

(A)   they meet underwriting standards
(B)   they are under the age of 40 at initial application
(C)   mortality tables do not increase more rapidly than 10 percent per annum
(D)   the company still issues insurance in that policy series at subsequent 5-year intervals.

2-6. The type of life insurance policy that provides insurance on two lives, with nothing payable upon the first death, is often called

(A)   estate insurance
(B)   first-to-die insurance
(C)   joint survivor insurance
(D)   survivorship life insurance

2-7. Which of the following statements concerning limited-pay whole life insurance is (are) correct?

I. The limitation on the number of premiums to be paid may be expressed as either a number of years or an age beyond which premiums are not payable.
II. If the insured dies during the premium-paying period, the total premiums paid will exceed those paid for an ordinary life policy of the same face amount issued at the same age.

(A) I only
(B) II only
(C) Both I and II
(D) Neither I nor II

2-8. Which of the following statements concerning re-entry term insurance is (are) correct?

I. The initial premium is based on an ultimate mortality table if the insured's health is better than average.
II. Future premiums will be based on a select mortality table if satisfactory evidence of insurability is periodically provided as required by the insurer.

(A) I only
(B) II only
(C) Both I and II
(D) Neither I nor II

2-9. All of the following statements concerning term insurance are correct EXCEPT

(A) Term insurance is comparable to property insurance in that both provide coverage for a limited time.
(B) Term insurance policies provide protection from a certainty (death).
(C) The chief function of the renewable feature in term insurance is to protect the insurability of the insured.
(D) There is an adverse selection opportunity against the insurer at each renewal.

2-10. All of the following statements are correct concerning whole life insurance EXCEPT

(A) A whole life policy surrendered for its cash value cannot usually be reinstated unless the insured provides new evidence of insurability.
(B) Limited-payment life insurance policies will have higher cash values than ordinary life policies for the same face amount issued at the same age in the same year.
(C) Vanishing premium policy designs are really just limited payment life insurance policies.
(D) A whole life policy can be regarded as an endowment at age 100.

3

Variations of Whole Life Insurance

Overview and Learning Objectives

Chapter 3 explores the many variations of permanent life insurance, most which have evolved over the last 25 years or so. Creative market forces and client needs have merged to enable companies to design products that allow advisors to tailor their solutions to the specific needs, goals and circumstances of their clients.

By reading this chapter and answering the questions, you should be able to

3-1. Understand the concept of endowment life insurance and be aware that many endowment policies are still in force.

3-2. Understand the adjustable life policy design.

3-3. Describe the features of variable life and understand its dual regulation status.

3-4. Be aware of the variable adjustable life policy and its features.

3-5. Describe the universal life policy and explain how its features differ from whole life policies.

3-6. Describe and understand the current assumption variations of life insurance.

3-7. Describe and understand variable universal life insurance policies.

Chapter Outline

Whole Life Variations   3-3
    Endowment Policies   3-3
    Adjustable Life Insurance   3-7
    Variable Life Insurance   3-8
    Variable Adjustable Life Insurance   3-14
    Universal Life Insurance   3-15
    Current Assumption Whole Life   3-27
    Variable Universal Life   3-32
Chapter Three Review   3-39

Whole Life Variations

Endowment Policies

As mentioned previously, level premium term insurance to age 100 is identical to whole life insurance in the use of the level premium technique. There is also another type of life insurance that is identical to whole life insurance—endowment at age 100. However, the majority of endowment contracts mature at ages less than 100. At earlier maturity dates they are not identical to whole life policies.

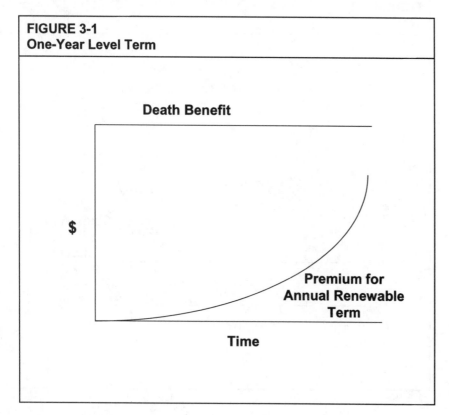

FIGURE 3-1
One-Year Level Term

Death Benefit

$

Premium for
Annual Renewable
Term

Time

Endowment life insurance policies are a variation of whole life insurance. They provide level death benefits and cash values that increase with duration so that a policy's cash value equals its death benefit at maturity. They also allow the purchaser to specify the policy's maturity date.

A whole life contract provides a survivorship benefit at maturity (i.e., age 100) that is equal to the death benefit that would have been payable prior to the insured's age 100 (see figure 3-2). Endowment contracts merely make the same full survivorship benefit payable at younger ages. Endowment policies are available for a set number of years or to a specified age.

The endowment contract was designed to provide a death benefit during an accumulation period that is equal to the target accumulation amount. Purchasing an endowment policy with a face amount equal to the desired accumulation amount assures that the funds will be available regardless of whether the insured survives the target date.

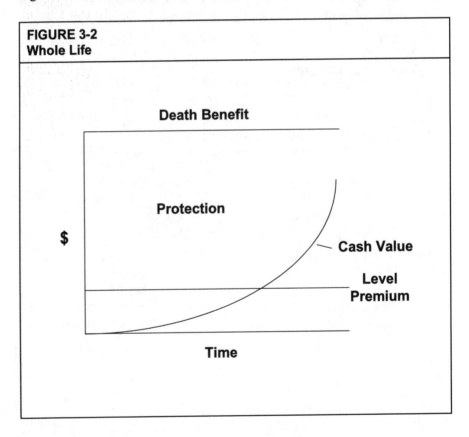

FIGURE 3-2
Whole Life

Sales of endowment contracts were declining in the United States even before the federal income tax law was changed in 1984 to take away the tax-free buildup of flexible-premium endowment policies' cash value. Congress was concerned that life insurance policies (especially endowment and universal life) with high cash values relative to their death benefit amounts were being used as a tax-advantaged accumulation vehicle by the wealthy. Congress enacted a test for flexible-premium life insurance in *IRC Sec. 101(f)* that eliminated the tax preference that flexible premium endowments previously enjoyed, although it retained the preference for policies in force before 1985. Subsequently, *IRC Sec. 7702* extended the test to all life insurance policies, including fixed-premium endowments, entered into after October 22, 1986. IRC Sec. 7702 defines the two tests—the cash value accumulation test and the guideline premium and corridor test—that must be met in order for the death proceeds of life insurance contracts to be fully excludible from the beneficiaries' income. These tests were introduced to control the amount of premium that may be paid into a life insurance contract and still maintain the tax benefits of the Internal Revenue Code afforded to life insurance contracts.

Since 1984, sales of new endowment contracts have been very limited. While contracts are still available from a few insurers, most new sales are for policies used in tax-qualified plans where the tax treatment is controlled by other factors.

Outside of the United States, especially in countries with high savings rates, however, the endowment policy is still quite successful and widely used to accumulate funds for a variety of purposes. It is frequently purchased to fund retirement and sometimes to fund children's higher education.

It is interesting to note that endowment policies purchased in other countries are usually bought for the same reasons permanent life insurance policies are purchased in the United States. Regardless of the society or its tax laws, the primary factor motivating life insurance sales is an individual's concern about financial security for his or her children, spouse, parents, and/or business partners. The individual's particular needs tend to change in predictable ways over a normal life cycle.

TABLE 3–1
Corridor Test for Cash Value Life Insurance

Age	Death Benefit Must Exceed Cash Value by This Multiple	Cash Value May Not Exceed This % of Death Benefit
0 to 40	2.50	0.40
41	2.43	0.41
42	2.36	0.42
43	2.29	0.44
44	2.22	0.45
45	2.15	0.47
46	2.09	0.48
47	2.03	0.49
48	1.97	0.51
49	1.91	0.52
50	1.85	0.54
51	1.78	0.56
52	1.71	0.58
53	1.64	0.61
54	1.57	0.64
55	1.50	0.67
56	1.46	0.68
57	1.42	0.70
58	1.38	0.72
59	1.34	0.75
60	1.30	0.77
61	1.28	0.78
62	1.26	0.79
63	1.24	0.81
64	1.22	0.82
65	1.20	0.83
66	1.19	0.84
67	1.18	0.85
68	1.17	0.85
69	1.16	0.86
70	1.15	0.87
71	1.13	0.88
72	1.11	0.90
73	1.09	0.92
74	1.07	0.93
75 to 90	1.05	0.95
91	1.04	0.96
92	1.03	0.97
93	1.02	0.98
94	1.01	0.99
95	1.00	1.00

Source: IRC Sec. 7702(d)(2)

Adjustable Life Insurance

Families changing needs for life insurance over long durations prompted some insurers to introduce whole life insurance that can be adjusted when needed to accommodate life cycle shifts. The *adjustable life policy,* which can be configured anywhere along the spectrum from short duration term insurance through single premium whole life insurance, gives the policyowner the right to request and obtain a reconfiguration of the policy at specified intervals. It appeals to purchasers who want the ability to restructure their coverage without assuming any of the investment or mortality risks.

One important aspect of adjustable life is that it is a whole life policy with fixed premiums. Although premiums can be changed, such a change requires a formal adjustment agreed to by both insurer and policyowner before it can be made. The premium remains fixed and inflexible between formal adjustments. Adjustable life insurance policies offer all of the same guarantees regarding cash values, mortality, and expenses as traditional whole life policies do. The elements subject to change are the premium, face amount, and cash value (see figure 3-3). Most changes can be made without evidence of insurability, but the insurer can require such evidence if the proposed change increases the amount at risk.

Events that frequently prompt policy adjustments include dependent children starting college, the self-sufficiency of the youngest child, loss of employment, the start or failure of a business venture, change of career, or retirement. Some adjustments involve lowering the premium level to lessen the cash flow burden and some involve increasing the premium as the policy owner's discretionary income improves.

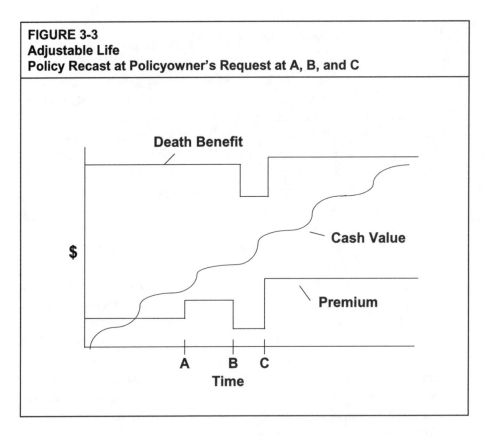

FIGURE 3-3
Adjustable Life
Policy Recast at Policyowner's Request at A, B, and C

This type of policy was introduced in the mid-1970s and had gained modest success with a few insurers before the advent of universal life policies. Interest in adjustable life waned after the success of universal life in the 1980s. Some of the insurers that maintained adjustable life as part of their product line, however, found that it had renewed acceptability after universal life lost its predominant share of new product sales in the low-interest environment of the early 1990s.

Variable Life Insurance

Variable life insurance was the first life insurance policy designed to shift the investment risk to policyowners. A *variable life insurance* policy provides no guarantees of either interest rate or minimum cash value. Theoretically, the cash value can go down to zero, and if so, the policy will terminate. In order for policyowners to gain the additional benefit of better-than-expected investment returns, they also have to assume all of the downside investment risk. Consequently, the SEC required variable life policies to be registered with the SEC and all sales to be subject to the requirements applicable to other registered securities. In other words, policy sales can be made only after the prospective purchaser has a chance to read the policy prospectus. The SEC also requires that the insurance company be registered as an investment company and that agents become registered representatives. Agents who sell variable life insurance policies must be licensed as both life insurance agents and securities agents.

SEC Objections to Variable Life

The first generation of variable life insurance products were fixed-premium products (see figure 3-4). The only real innovation was the variable investment aspect—that is, the policyowner was permitted to select among a limited number of investment portfolio choices, with the death benefit amount varying as a function of the portfolio's investment performance.

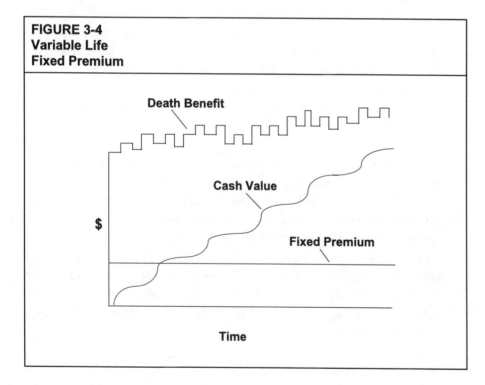

FIGURE 3-4
Variable Life
Fixed Premium

Death Benefit

Cash Value

Fixed Premium

$

Time

Investment Choices

Generally, the first generation of variable life insurance policies gave the purchaser three investment options into which the funds could be directed. There was usually a minimum requirement of at least 5 or 10 percent of incoming funds that had to be allocated to any investment option the policyowner selected. The purpose of this minimum requirement was to eliminate the possibility that administrative costs would exceed the amount of money being directed into a particular option.

Very often the options were a stock fund, a bond fund, and either a treasury fund or a money market fund. The funds were essentially mutual funds run by the insurance company and set aside as separate accounts (required by the SEC) that do not constitute part of the insurance company's general investment fund and put such assets beyond the claims of its general creditors.

Although the policyowner chooses among the offered funds, he or she has no control over the assets purchased and sold by the individual funds. That portion of the investment decision process is still within the hands of the insurance company's portfolio management team. However the policyowner plays a participative role in the selection of the investments that support the policy and consequently can benefit directly from better results or bear the brunt of poor investment performance. The results of the investment performance are credited directly to the policy cash values.

Ability to Tolerate Risk—Individuals who are already experienced in equity investments are quite comfortable with the variable life insurance policy. However, this policy is subject to daily portfolio fluctuations and can provoke great anxiety in individuals who are not used to or comfortable with such market value fluctuations.

A variable life policy is a market-driven phenomenon, and its popularity is influenced by general investment market conditions. The policy becomes more acceptable to consumers after a long period of market increases and falls out of favor when the market experiences a general decline in prices.

Insurance Charges—Variable life insurance contracts are not exclusively investments. They also sustain mortality charges for the death benefits they provide. Consequently, the pre-tax return on the invested funds within a variable life insurance contract will never equal that of a separate investment fund that does not provide death benefits but invests in assets of a similar type and quality.

Variable life insurance should not be purchased as a short-term investment vehicle. Although investment performance in equities tends to equal or exceed inflation in the economy over the long term, the correlation is not perfect in the short term. It is possible for inflation to exceed increases in the investment performance for short durations of time. In addition, the combination of sales load, mortality charges, and surrender charges will significantly reduce any potential gains in the policy's early years.

Increased Number of Investment Fund Options
Variable life insurance designs have not been static since their introduction in the mid-1970s. Life insurance companies are now offering many investment fund options. There are usually a variety of stock and bond funds. In addition, many insurance companies offer a managed fund as one of the portfolio choices. The policyowner can put all of the policy funds in a managed portfolio fund and have the investment allocation decisions made by a professional money manager working for the insurance company. This appeals to policyowners who do not want to spend a lot of time studying the market and making investment decisions. With a managed portfolio policyowners can reap all of the long-term advantages of a variable insurance contract without having to perform the investment allocation function themselves.

Some insurance companies have formed alliances with large mutual fund groups that make their entire range of mutual funds available. Such alliances make it possible for these life insurance companies to gain access to the administrative services already in place in these large mutual fund family groups.

Policy Cash Values
Policy premiums paid under variable life insurance contracts are often subject to an administrative charge; the balance of the premium payment goes into the cash value account. The actual value of the cash component is determined by the net asset value of the separate account funds that make up the policy portfolio. The cash value of a variable life policy fluctuates daily. Each day's net asset value is based on the closing price for the issues in the portfolio on that trading day. Cash value accounts are further diminished by mortality charges to support the death benefits.

As with traditional life insurance contracts, the policyowner has access to the cash value via policy loans. The earnings on the cash value are obviously affected by any outstanding policy loans. The policyowner accrues indebtedness at the applicable policy loan interest rate, and that is the yield applicable to the assets associated with the portion of the cash value offset by the outstanding loan. Whenever the policy loan interest rate is lower than the portfolio investment earnings rate, the insurance company experiences a lower effective investment return. The only time the insurance company experiences a financial gain from policy loans is when the policy loan interest rate exceeds that earned by the portfolio backing the policies.

Policy loans can be repaid at any time in part or in full, but there is no requirement that policy loans be repaid in cash at any time during the existence of the life insurance contract. For any portion of the loan not repaid, interest accrues on a compound basis. Outstanding policy loans under a variable life insurance policy reduce the death benefit payable. The policy loan is always fully secured by the remaining cash value in the policy. Whenever the outstanding loans plus accrued interest equal the remaining cash value, the net cash value becomes zero and the policy terminates.

The net cash value in the contract is also closely related to the nonforfeiture options available under the policy. Variable life insurance contracts provide the same range of nonforfeiture options as do traditional whole life policies.

Variable life insurance policies also contain the usual form of reinstatement provisions, including a specific prohibition on reinstatements if the policy has been surrendered for its cash value. Contracts also have the standard waiver-of-premium option since premiums are fixed and the policy will lapse if they are not paid.

The Prospectus

Variable life insurance policies cannot be sold without an accompanying *prospectus*. The variable life prospectus mandated by the SEC is similar in many respects to the prospectus required of new stock issues. The prospectus provides thorough and accurate information to the prospective purchaser concerning the company issuing the life insurance contract as well as a full disclosure of all the provisions of the contract, including

---

Primary Focus of Prospectus Disclosure

- Operating expenses
- Marketing expenses
- Taxes and fees
- Cost of insurance charge
- Surrender charges
- Investment charges
- Investment performance

---

expenses, investment options, benefit provisions, past performance of the investment options, and policyowner rights under that contract. It is a lengthy and detailed document.

Expense Information—The prospectus explains all of the expense charges levied by the insurance company against variable life insurance contracts. This includes commissions paid to soliciting agents, state premium taxes, administrative charges, collection charges, and possibly fees for specific future transactions. The prospectus also indicates whether or not there is any maximum guarantee on those administrative fees over the duration of the contract.

In addition, the prospectus sets forth the manner in which charges are made against the asset account to cover the cost of insurance under the contract. The prospectus specifies what rate will be used to determine *cost-of-insurance* charges and if there is any maximum rate above the intended rate. It also explains the manner in which charges are levied against the separate account itself; these are the fees associated with managing the various types of mutual fund accounts from which the policyowner can choose.

Surrender Charges—The charges applicable to policy surrenders are usually set forth in a tabular form, giving the policy year and the applicable percentage for the surrender charge in that year. Surrender charges are commonly levied during the first 10 to 15 years of the contract. The actual number of years and specific rates are always set forth in the prospectus.

Investment Portfolio Information—The prospectus sets forth the investment objectives of each of the available investment funds and a record of their historical performance. It includes detailed information on the current holdings of each of the available portfolios, usually supplemented by information about purchases and sales of individual equities or debt instruments by the fund over the previous 12 months. Further information is given about earnings during that same period of time, and usually for longer intervals of prior performance if those portfolio funds have been in existence long enough to give investment results for trades over 5 or 10 years. Any investment restrictions applicable to these portfolios are fully disclosed.

There are also projections of future performance under the contract if portfolio funds generate a fixed level of investment earnings over the projected interval. Under SEC regulations the permissible rates of return that can be projected are the gross annual rates after tax charges but before any other deductions at 0, 4, 6, 8, 10, or 12 percent. The insurance company can decide which of those permissible rates it chooses to project.

Risks the Policyowner Assumes

Fixed-premium variable life insurance contracts are very similar to whole life insurance contracts, except that the policyowner assumes the investment risk. The fixed-premium provision does not allow the policyowner to increase or decrease the death benefit by negotiated adjustment. Favorable results automatically translate into increased death benefit amounts.

One unique benefit of a variable life policy is that it does guarantee a minimum death benefit equal to the original face amount of the contract, regardless of how badly the investment performance turns out to be. If all of the required premiums are paid, the insurance company guarantees that the death benefit equal to the original face amount of the policy will be paid even if the investment funds are otherwise inadequate to support the policy. Therefore, the variable feature of this contract can provide additional coverage if investment experience warrants, but the policyowner will never be required to pay more or permitted to pay less than the guaranteed premium.

A fixed-premium variable life insurance policy provides more guarantees to the policyowner than universal life and variable universal life.

Variable Adjustable Life Insurance

Variable adjustable life is a policy that can be negotiated to change the death benefit level up or down, or to increase or decrease premium amounts to a new fixed level (which can shorten or lengthen the premium-paying period). It also offers the policyowner the ability to choose the investment portfolio, within limits. This contract overcomes one of the shortcomings of the fixed-premium variable life contract by allowing the policyowner to negotiate with the insurance company a changed policy configuration that more closely fits the policyowner's changed circumstances.

The policyowner does not have the unilateral right to skip premium payments or vary the amount of any premium payment at will without prior negotiation with the insurance company. As with the first generation of variable life insurance contracts, the death benefit is tied to investment performance but guaranteed never to be less than the original amount of coverage under the policy.

Most of the insurance companies offering variable adjustable life coverage chose not to enter the universal life market. If fact, they introduced *variable adjustable life insurance* as a defensive move to compete with universal life, after the marketing success of its flexible-premium design.

Universal Life Insurance

Universal life insurance was introduced in 1979 as a revolutionary new product. It was the first variation of whole life insurance to offer truly flexible premiums. It also included adjustment provisions similar to those contained in the adjustable life contract. These policies shifted some of the investment risk to the policyowner because the premium was based on interest rates in excess of the guaranteed interest rate, but they did not give the policyowner any option to direct the investment portfolio. Two other features initiated with universal life policies are: (1) the policyowner's ability to withdraw part of the cash value without having the withdrawal treated as a policy loan and (2) the choice of either a level death benefit design or an increasing death benefit design.

Flexible Premiums

The true innovation of universal life insurance was the introduction of completely flexible premiums after the first policy year, the only time a minimum level of premium payments for a universal life policy is rigidly required. As usual, the first year's premium can be arranged on a monthly, quarterly, semiannual, or annual basis. The insurance company requires only that a minimum specified level of first-year premium payments be equaled or exceeded. After the first policy year, it is completely up to the policyowner as to how much premium to pay and even whether or not to pay premiums.

Nevertheless, the aggregate premiums paid, regardless of their timing, must be adequate to cover the costs of maintaining the policy. If the policy cash value is allowed to drop too low (for example, the cash value is inadequate to cover the next 60 days of expense and mortality charges), the policy will lapse. If an additional premium payment is made soon enough, the policy may be restarted without a formal reinstatement process. However, if an injection of additional funds comes after the end of the grace period, the insurance company may force the policyowner to request a formal reinstatement before accepting any further premium payments.

Prefunding

Prefunding a universal life policy means putting more money into the policy than is currently needed to cover the costs of keeping the policy in force. The higher the amount or proportion of prefunding, the more investment earnings will be utilized to cover policy expenses. This brings us to the legendary adage that there are two sources of money: people at work and money at work. By putting money into the policy early, the money starts earning money and therefore reduces the amount of premium payments needed from people at work at later policy durations. The ultimate extreme of prefunding is the single premium approach, where an adequate fund is created at the inception of the policy to cover all future costs. The more common approach is a level-premium structure in which partial prefunding creates an ever-increasing cash value that in turn generates increasing investment returns to offset mortality and administrative costs.

All premium suggestions are based on some assumed level of investment earnings and the policyowner bears the risk that actual investment earnings will be less than that necessary to support the suggested premium. Even though investment earnings cannot go below the guaranteed rate, a long-term shortfall may necessitate either an increase in premiums or a reduction in coverage at some future point.

At the other end of the spectrum is the minimum-premium approach, which is virtually synonymous with annual renewal term insurance. There is minimal, if any, prefunding, and premium payments barely cover the current mortality and expense charges. Under this approach the premiums must increase as the insured ages since mortality rates increase with the age of the insured. Premiums increase rapidly at advanced ages because there is still a maximum amount at risk (the cash value is very low, and the mortality rate must be applied to nearly the full death benefit amount). Under the partial prefunding approach, however, cash value increases make the amount at risk decrease (amount at risk equals the policy's face amount minus its cash value) as the insured ages, and the increasing mortality rate is applied to a smaller at-risk amount.

Under traditional whole life insurance policies insurance companies designed a wide range of level premium contracts, each with a different level of fixed premiums. Contracts with a higher level premium tended to develop larger cash values at earlier policy durations. Once the policy cash value was adequate to prefund the policy totally, the policy could be converted to a guaranteed paid-up status. Under participating designs, dividends could exceed the premiums after the policy had developed a large enough cash value to prefund all future policy elements.

Under the traditional contracts with cash values, the only mechanism for returning any policy overfunding in the early years was policyowner dividends. With universal life policies, however, the accumulations from prefunding are credited to the policy's cash value and are quite visible to the policyowner. The earnings rates applied to those accumulations are also clearly visible as they fluctuate with current economic conditions.

Withdrawal Feature

Another new feature introduced with universal life policies is the policyowner's ability to make partial withdrawals from the policy's cash value without incurring any debt. Money can be taken out of the universal life policy cash value just like a withdrawal from a savings account, and there is no obligation to repay those funds; nor is there any incurring interest on the amount withdrawn. Withdrawals do affect the policy's future earnings because the policy's cash value (which is the source of future earnings) is reduced by the amount of the withdrawal. Its effect on the death benefit depends on the type of death benefit in force.

Target Premium Amount

Nearly every universal life policy is issued with a target premium amount. The *target premium* amount is the suggested premium to be paid on a level basis throughout the contract's duration. This amount is merely a suggestion and carries no liability if it is inadequate to maintain the contract to any duration, much less to the end of life.

In some insurance companies that target premium is actually sufficient to keep the policy in force (under relatively conservative investment return assumptions) through age 95 or 100 and to pay the cash value equivalent to the death benefit amount if the insured survives to either age 95 or 100. On the other hand, some companies with a more aggressive marketing stance have chosen lower target premiums, which are not adequate to carry the policy in force to advanced ages, even under more generous assumptions of higher investment returns over future policy years.

If the actual investment return credited to the policy cash value falls short of the amounts assumed in deriving the target premium, the policyowner will be faced with two options: (1) to increase the premium level or (2) to reduce the death benefit amount.

Some insurance companies have introduced a secondary guarantee associated with their target premium. These companies have pledged contractually to keep the policy in force for, say, 15 or 20 years and to pay the full death benefit as long as the premium has been paid in an amount equal to or greater than the target premium amount at each suggested premium-payment interval. Even these guarantees do not extend to age 95 or 100, but they are at least a guarantee that the premium suggested as a target will be adequate to provide the coverage at least as long as the guarantee period. Probably the best indication of whether or not the target premium is adequate to keep the policy in force up through age 95 or 100 is to compare it with premiums for a traditional whole life policy of a similar face amount and issue age. Universal life policy target premiums less than premiums for a comparable whole life policy should be suspect; they may be intentionally low by design because the insurance company does not expect the policy to remain in force until the very end of life in the majority of cases. The only people who will ever really find out whether or not their policy target premiums are adequate are those who pay the premiums religiously throughout the duration of the contract and live to be an age that is old enough to test the target premium.

Example: Bert is now 70 years old. He has paid the target premium on his universal life policy for the last 15 years. He was not told, and he did not realize, that the target premium was only intended to keep coverage in force to age 65. Bert wants to keep his coverage, but the target premium he is paying is not adequate to support it. He will have to increase premium payments by more than 20 percent to keep the same amount of coverage, or else he will have to reduce the amount of coverage to a level where the target premium is adequate to support the reduced coverage.

Additional Premium Payments—The flexible features of universal life premiums allow policyowners to make additional premium payments above any target premium amount at any time the policyowner desires without prior negotiation or agreement with the insurance company. The only limitation on paying excess premiums is associated with the income tax definition of life insurance (IRC SEC. 7702). However, the insurance company reserves the right to refuse additional premium payments under a universal life policy if the policy's cash value is large enough to encroach upon the upper limit for cash values relative to the level of death benefit granted in the policy.

Death Benefit Type

Universal life insurance gives policyowners a choice between level death benefits and increasing death benefits. The level death benefit design is much like the traditional whole life design (see figures 3-5 and 3-6). When the death benefit stays constant and the cash value increases over the duration of the contract, the amount at risk or the protection element decreases.

The one new aspect of a level death benefit designed under universal life policies is not really a function of universal life itself but a function of a tax law definition of life insurance that was added to the Code shortly after the introduction of universal life insurance policies, requiring that a specified proportion of the death benefit is derived from the amount at risk. This is IRC Sec. 7702 referred to earlier in this chapter. Whenever the cash value in the contract gets high enough that this proportion is no longer satisfied, the universal life policy starts increasing the death benefit (corridor test) even though the contract is called a level death benefit contract. This phenomenon typically does not occur until ages beyond normal retirement, and it is not a significant aspect of this design.

The increasing death benefit design is a modification that was introduced with universal life policies (see figures 3-7 and 3-8). Under this approach there is always a constant amount at risk that is superimposed over the policy's cash value, whatever it may be. As the cash value increases, so does the total death benefit payable under the contract. A reduction in the cash value will reduce the death benefit. This design pays both the policy's stated face amount and its cash value as benefits at the insured's death. Policies with an increasing death benefit design overcome the criticism of whole life policies that the death benefit is partially made up of the contract's cash value portion. By selecting the increasing death benefit option under a universal life policy the policyowner is ensuring that the death benefit will be composed of the cash value and an at-risk portion equal to the original face value of the contract.

Death Benefit Type Mortality Charges

- Mortality charges for level death benefit type apply to a decreasing amount at risk.
- Mortality charges for increasing death benefit type apply to a constant amount at risk.

There is nothing magical about this larger death benefit amount. As is often said, there is no free lunch. A higher portion of the premium is needed for the larger amount at risk under this design.

There are similarities between the increasing death benefit design for universal life and the paid-up additions option under a participating whole life policy. Under a whole life policy, dividends are used to purchase single-premium additions to the base policy. In both types of policies the excess investment earnings are used to increase the cash value and the death benefit.

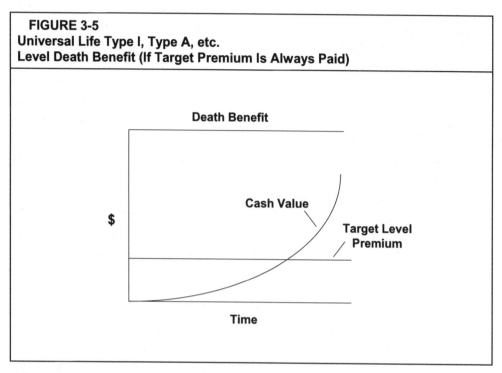

FIGURE 3-5
Universal Life Type I, Type A, etc.
Level Death Benefit (If Target Premium Is Always Paid)

Death Benefit

Cash Value

Target Level
Premium

$

Time

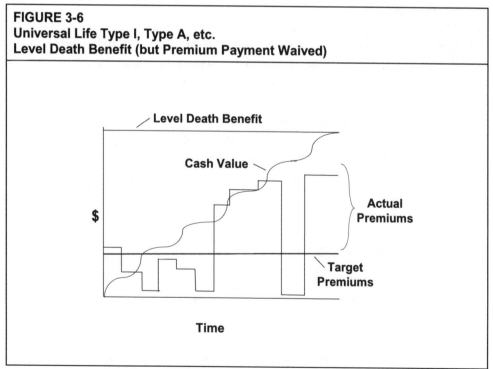

FIGURE 3-6
Universal Life Type I, Type A, etc.
Level Death Benefit (but Premium Payment Waived)

Level Death Benefit

Cash Value

Actual
Premiums

$

Target
Premiums

Time

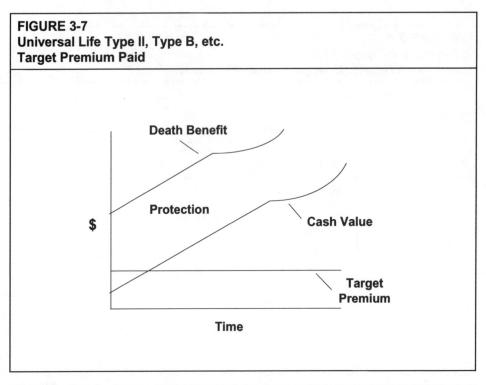

FIGURE 3-7
Universal Life Type II, Type B, etc.
Target Premium Paid

Death Benefit

Protection

Cash Value

$

Target
Premium

Time

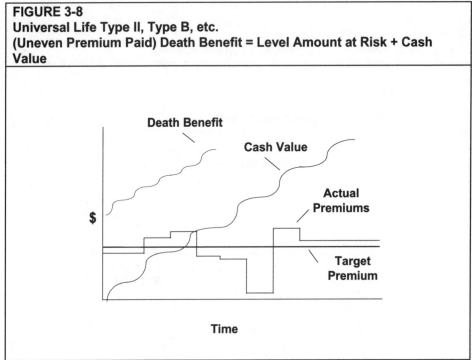

FIGURE 3-8
Universal Life Type II, Type B, etc.
(Uneven Premium Paid) Death Benefit = Level Amount at Risk + Cash Value

Death Benefit

Cash Value

Actual
Premiums

$

Target
Premium

Time

Because the mechanics of the two death benefit designs and the universal life policies are slightly different, the effect of partial withdrawals on the death benefit amount differs. Partial withdrawals do not reduce the death benefit amount under the level death benefit design. They do, however, decrease the amount of the policy's cash value and correspondingly increase the amount at risk. As a result, the mortality charge will increase after the partial withdrawal to pay the mortality risk applicable to the greater amount at risk.

Partial withdrawals under the increasing death benefit design will in fact reduce the death benefit payable because the withdrawal decreases the cash value that constitutes part of the death benefit amount. However, such withdrawals will not reduce the mortality charges for the amount at risk because that at-risk amount remains constant. Reducing the cash value by the amount of the partial withdrawal does, however, have a negative impact on the amount of investment earnings credited to the cash value.

Effect of Policy Loans

Another aspect of policy design ushered in with universal life policies is the differential crediting rate on the cash value, depending on whether there are policy loans outstanding. Most universal life policies credit current interest rates on the cash value as long as there are no outstanding policy loans. Once the policyowner borrows funds from the cash value, the insurance company usually credits a lower interest rate or earnings rate to the portion of the cash value associated with the policy loan. This is another effort to curb disintermediation.

Outstanding policy loans at the time the insured dies will reduce the death benefit by the amount of the loan plus any unpaid interest on the loan. This is the same for universal life policies as it is for any life insurance policy that has policy loans.

Universal life policies sold today generally credit the cash value with the current rate for nonborrowed funds and a lower rate, which is often 2 percent (200 basis points) lower than the current rate, for borrowed funds.

Internal Funds Flow

Although universal life insurance policies are still relatively young in the overall realm of life insurance products, some policies are already in their fifth or sixth generation of policy series from the company that introduced them. As with all products, the individual policy designs constantly evolve in response to the economy, competitive pressures, tax code changes and innovative zeal. Most of the first generation of universal life policies were heavily front-end-loaded products. They took a significant proportion of each premium dollar as administrative expenses, and the remaining portion was then credited to the policy cash value account.

After the funds had reached the policy cash value account, they were subject to charges for current death benefits in the form of a mortality charge based on the amount at risk. In most insurance companies the mortality rate actually charged was often in the neighborhood of 50 percent of the guaranteed maximum mortality rate set forth in the policy contract for each attained age of the insured. The difference in the mortality rate actually being charged and the maximum permitted mortality rate published in the policy represents the safety margin the life insurance company is holding in reserve. If the future mortality costs for the block of policies turn out to be more expensive than initially assumed, the insurance company can increase the mortality rate as long as it does not exceed guaranteed maximum rates specified in the contract itself.

After deductions for expenses and mortality, the universal life cash value account is then increased at the current crediting rate to reflect investment earnings on that cash value. These are the dollars at work for the policyowner to help reduce his or her current and future out-of-pocket premium expenses. The actual rate credited is a discretionary decision on the part of the insurance company, and it tends to fluctuate freely, reflecting current economic conditions.

There have been times when some insurers were reluctant to credit the current interest rate to the policy's cash value. As interest rates were dropping gradually and steadily over the last decade, many insurance companies were hesitant to allow their current interest crediting rate to drop below 10 percent, and interest crediting rates seemed to stick around that point. Eventually, the economic folly of crediting interest rates in excess of actual earnings on the invested assets became apparent, and single-digit interest rates replaced double-digit rates in the crediting formula.

Interest crediting rates have been the focal point of most of the competition among companies selling universal life policies. There has been very little emphasis on the mortality rates charged or the expense charges levied against incoming premiums. In reality all three concepts constitute the total cost of insurance. Interest rates can be (and have been) intentionally elevated to a level above what the investment portfolio actually supported, but they are still viable because of compensating higher levels of mortality charges and expense deductions. When consumers choose to focus only on one of the three elements, it is not surprising that the marketing efforts zero in on that element. The assessment of overall policy efficiency requires that all factors be considered in concert.

As the universal life insurance policies evolved, more of them moved to a back-end loading design. In other words, they lowered or eliminated the up-front charge levied against incoming premium amounts and instead imposed new or increased surrender charges applicable to the cash value of a policy surrendered during the contract's first 7 to 15 years. Surrender charges are usually highest during the first policy year and decrease on a straight-line basis over the remaining years until the year in which the insurance company expects to have amortized all excess first-year expenses. At that point the surrender charge is reduced to zero and will not be applicable at later policy durations. The actual surrender charge itself can be based on either the cash value amount or on the target premium level. Some insurers have developed a hybrid that depends on both approaches to generate the full surrender charge. The surrender charge usually decreases by the same percentage on each policy anniversary until the applicable charge reaches zero. The net amount payable for a surrendered policy is determined by deducting any applicable surrender charge from the policy cash value minus any unpaid policy loans and interest.

Companies with the highest surrender charges tend to have little or no front-end expenses charged against premiums. Some companies have policies that combine moderate front-end loading and moderate surrender charges. There seems to be a discernible preference for higher surrender charges and little or no front-end loading in most universal life policies being marketed today.

The actual component of the front-end loading can be a flat annual charge per policy plus a small percentage of premium dollars actually received, and a charge of a few cents per each $1,000 of coverage in force under the policy. The charges applicable to the premiums and the amount of coverage are usually deducted monthly from the policy cash value account. Similarly, the current interest crediting rate is also usually applied monthly. These are the deposits and withdrawals from our gas tank.

Some companies have actually eliminated charges based on the amount of coverage in force. Competitive pressures have also caused many insurance companies to minimize front-end loading in order to emphasize that nearly all premium dollars go directly into the cash value account. The actual expenses are still being exacted internally, but the manner in which they are handled is not easily discernible by the consuming public. For example, expenses can be embedded in the spread between actual mortality costs and actual mortality charges or in the spread between investment earnings and the interest rate credited to the cash value accounts.

It is important to realize that no insurance company is able to operate without generating legitimate costs of operations above the amount needed to pay death benefits only. These expenses must be covered somehow, and the method of allocating them is nothing more or less than a cost-accounting approach. The exact allocation formula is always arbitrary and to some extent guided by the philosophy of the insurance company management team. It must address such issues as equity among short-term and long-term policyowners, the appropriate duration for amortizing excess first-year expenses, and how much investment and operations gains to retain for company growth and safety margins and how much to distribute to policyowners.

Flexibility to Last a Lifetime

The astonishing flexibility of premiums under universal life policies and the ability to adjust death benefits upward and downward have created life insurance policies that can literally keep pace with the policyowner's needs. The policy can be aggressively funded when the premium dollars are available, and premium payments can be intentionally suspended during tight budget periods, such as the formation of a new business or while children are attending college. The policy death benefit can be increased (sometimes requiring evidence of insurability) if the need exists, and after any temporary needs have expired the policy can be adjusted downward to provide lower death benefits if that is what the policyowner wants. The ability of a universal life contract to fit constantly changing policyowner needs and conditions has led some companies to label this coverage irreplaceable life insurance. Some see it as the only policy ever needed because its versatility will allow it to compensate for any necessary changes.

Probably the most serious drawback to universal life policies is the competitive forces insurance marketers use to try to convince the prospect that their own version of universal life is better than anyone else's. In reality all universal life policies are similar, and only future investment performance will really determine which one turns out to be slightly more efficient than its competitors. Consumers will be better off seeking a policy that does well over the long haul than looking for a policy that wins every short-term contest, because no policy can be best in all facets at every duration. Sometimes focusing on a single competitive advantage prompts insurance companies to make short-term adjustments that are not necessarily in their own or the policyowner's best interest in the long-term scenario.

Current Assumption Whole Life

Current assumption whole life is a variation of traditional whole life that lies somewhere between adjustable life and universal life. Its cash value development is more like that of universal life than any other policy. It has a redetermination feature that essentially recasts the premium amount, and in some instances the death benefit, in reaction to the most recent interval of experience. That interval varies from one company to another but is frequently 5 years, although it can be as short as 2 years or as long as 7 years. The main feature that differentiates current assumption whole life from universal life is the absence of total premium flexibility in the renewal years (see figure 3-9).

Current assumption whole life is sometimes described as universal life with fixed premiums. This is an oversimplification because premiums can and will be restructured at specified policy anniversary dates. However, the analogy is probably useful in getting a mental image of this type of policy and how it differs from the traditional whole life policy, the adjustable life policy, and the universal life policy. It is just another example of refinements in policy design that fill in some of the missing points along a continuum of possibilities between both extremes—all fixed components and guarantees at one end and all flexible and nonguaranteed components at the other.

There are still quite a few guaranteed elements in current assumption whole life policies. There is a guaranteed death benefit and a minimum guaranteed interest rate to be credited on policy cash values. Some companies guarantee the mortality charge and the expense charges. When mortality and expense charges are guaranteed, the policy is often referred to as an *interest-sensitive whole life* policy because excess interest (credited interest minus guaranteed interest) credited to the cash value becomes the only nonguaranteed element in the contract. However, the bulk of the current assumption whole life policies have some degree of flexibility in the expense elements. Because many of these designs periodically recast the premium amount based on recognition of the most recent interval of experience, some of these policies are referred to as *indeterminate premium whole life* policies. The idea is that there is a guaranteed maximum possible premium that could be charged, but the actual mortality, interest, and expenses give rise to lower premium amounts actually being assessed as a result of favorable experience under the policy.

Current assumption whole life policies are nonparticipating policies that have some after-the-fact adjustment mechanisms without actually creating explicit policyowner cash dividends. These adjustment mechanisms allow the insurer to constantly fine-tune its policy and keep it competitive in the marketplace, based on actual company experience underlying the particular blocks of policies. From a company standpoint one of the big advantages of this policy design is its ability to eliminate the need for any deficiency reserve for the block of policies. Policy reserves can be calculated on the basis of the maximum chargeable premium and the minimum interest rate guarantee. Reserves will always be based on these factors, even though the premiums actually collected are lower than the premium assumption underlying the reserve and, more importantly, are less than the guideline premium for reserve valuation.

For competitive purposes in the marketplace, current assumption whole life gives the insurance company a product with a mechanism for sharing favorable investment returns with policyowners. These policies take away the advantage that participating whole life policies had over nonparticipating whole life policies. They are not so rigid that a change in market conditions automatically renders them obsolete, as was the unfortunate case with nonparticipating whole life policies before 1980.

Most current assumption whole life policies base their maximum possible mortality rate on 1980 Commissioners Standard Ordinary (CSO) Table rates. Because most insurance companies experience mortality significantly less costly than indicated by the CSO rates, the differential provides a very large safety margin for the insurer if it is later necessary to increase mortality rates and possibly even increase premiums on policy anniversaries when redetermination occurs.

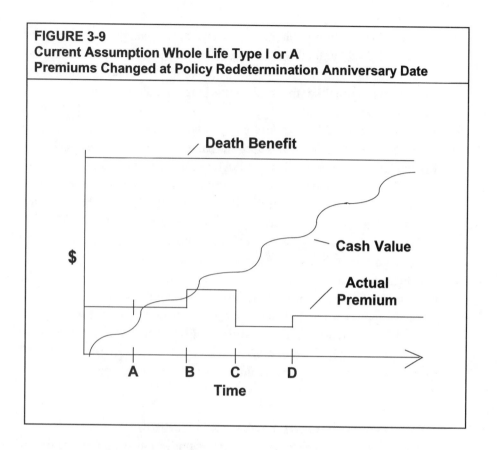

FIGURE 3-9
Current Assumption Whole Life Type I or A
Premiums Changed at Policy Redetermination Anniversary Date

Death Benefit

$

Cash Value

Actual
Premium

A   B   C   D

Time

Cash Value Illustrations

There are some variations in the way insurance companies approach the illustration of current assumption whole life policies. Nevertheless, it is possible to classify these variations into two basic categories.

The first basic category has a guaranteed cash value column and a separate column for excess accumulations (or some other descriptive title indicating that these values supplement the guaranteed cash value amounts). The total cash value for the policy is the sum of the guaranteed cash value and the accumulation supplements. The most complete representation tends to have three different columns for cash values—one for the guaranteed amount, one for the excess accumulations, and one representing the total of the two components. Any insurance company has wide discretion in how it depicts this approach in its illustrations. For example, illustrations often depict only the total cash value column and may or may not explicitly indicate that the cash value depends on projections of nonguaranteed amounts.

The second basic category merely has a single column titled "Enhanced Cash Value" (or an equivalent thereof). There is rarely any inclusion of the guaranteed cash value amount. This approach makes the policy look more like the cash value accumulation account reported under most universal life policies: premiums are shown as an incoming item that is reduced by expense charges before being added to the cash value account. Interest on the account balance is usually credited before any mortality charges are deducted. After mortality charges are deducted, the end-of-year fund balance is derived. The significant difference between the accumulation accounts in current assumption whole life and universal life is that universal life policies tend to charge off both expenses and mortality before crediting investment earnings. Current assumption whole life policies tend to deduct expenses from premiums but then credit that amount to the cash value and reflect a credit for investment earnings before deducting a mortality charge.

This approach has led many people to describe current assumption whole life as a hybrid of universal life and traditional whole life because it has cash value accumulations of excess interest crediting but still maintains a rigid level premium structure that can be changed on redetermination anniversaries.

Low Premium/High Premium Designs

The proportion of excess accumulations under these policy designs is highly dependent on the premium level in the base design.

Some insurance companies use a relatively low-premium current assumption whole life design. Adjustments on redetermination dates are more likely to involve an adjustment of the death benefit to make the policy compatible with the premium level being paid. However, sometimes adjustments are to the premium (up or down), which may or may not change the death benefit.

At the other end of the spectrum some insurers utilize a high-premium design of current assumption whole life, where the premium paid is usually more than adequate and normally does not require an upward adjustment on a redetermination date. The high-premium design is more likely to involve projections of how long premiums may be needed until the policy is expected to be self-supporting without further contributions from the policyowner. It is a form of misnamed vanishing premium design.

The caution, however, is that excess accumulations are not guaranteed; nor is the projected period of premium payments guaranteed to make the policy fully paid up at the end of that period. The policy will be paid up only if the future experience under the policy from that date forward is such that the interest credited and the accumulated account generate enough funds to meet all mortality charges and expenses over the entire remainder of the contract. There are no guarantees that this accumulation account might not have to be supplemented at some point if mortality charges and expenses cost more than the accumulation account can provide.

On the optimistic side, the policy could continue to exceed expectations even after it reaches paid-up status. If the investment returns on the accumulated fund keep the balance in that account more than adequate to pay all mortality charges and expenses, the policy could continue to enhance the benefits on each redetermination date. This would most likely involve an increase in death benefits since there are no further premiums to reduce at that point.

Redetermination

The level of premiums influences the frequency of *redetermination*. The lower the premium design, the more frequent the policy's redetermination dates. In some of the more recent policy designs redetermination can be every year; more often the redetermination frequency is every 2 years or every 5 years. On policy anniversaries when it is applicable, the insurance company looks at its actual experience for the block of policies since the previous redetermination date and decides what adjustments, if any, are necessary, based on the assumption that past experiences are indicative of what to expect in the period before the next redetermination.

Policyowner Options—The policyowner generally selects the method he or she prefers to adjust the policy from an available group of options when redetermination occurs. For example, if the redetermination results in a potentially lower premium, the policyowner usually has the option of continuing the past level of premiums and having the favorable results applied to enhance the policy's cash value or increase the death benefit (assuming the insured can provide satisfactory evidence of insurability), or the policyowner may choose to pay the lower policy premium amount.

When past experience is less favorable than expectations, the policyowner again has a range of options, including lowering the death benefit, increasing the premium amount, or maintaining the status quo and allowing the policy accumulation account to decrease as the mortality and expense charges exceed the investment earnings on the accumulated fund. This last choice, if available, may have restrictions on its use.

Uses of Current Assumption Whole Life

In a current assumption whole life policy current interest rates are used to enhance the accumulation account, but the policy does not provide the premium flexibility of a universal life policy. Current assumption whole life is an appropriate policy choice for individuals who need the discipline imposed by its fixed-premium design but want to participate at least in part in the positive investment returns beyond the guaranteed interest rate in the policy. Under this type of policy, the policyowner assumes some of the investment risk and a limited portion of the mortality risk. If actual experience turns out to be poor, the policy may be periodically downgraded on each redetermination date. If actual experience is positive, the policyowner participates in the upside as the quid pro quo for assuming those risks or a portion thereof. Costs in the long run may turn out to be much less than the original projections if experience is favorable enough over the duration of the contract. The real challenge with this and many other life insurance products in which policyowners assume some of the risk is to make sure policyowners understand the nature and extent of the risk being assumed.

Variable Universal Life

Variable universal life insurance incorporates all of the premium flexibility and policy adjustment features of the universal life policy with the policyowner-directed investment aspects of variable life insurance. Obviously this design discards the fixed-premium features of the variable life insurance contract (see Figures 3-10 and 3-11).

One of the most interesting aspects of *variable universal life insurance* is that it eliminates the direct connection between investment performance above or below some stated target level and the corresponding formula-directed adjustment in death benefits. Instead variable universal life insurance adopts the death benefit designs applicable to universal life policies, namely, either a level death benefit or an increasing death benefit design where a constant amount of risk is paid in addition to the cash accumulation account. Under the first of those options, the death benefit doesn't change, regardless of how positive or negative the investment performance under the contract turns out to be. If the policyowner wants to have the death benefit vary with the performance of the investments under the contract, he or she must choose the increasing death benefit design. All of the increase or decrease is a direct result of the accumulation account balance, rather than the result of purchasing paid-up additions (or some form of modified premium addition) as is the case under fixed-premium life insurance.

Variable universal life policies offer the policyowner a choice among a specified group of mutual fund types of separate accounts that are created and maintained by the insurance company itself or by selected investment management firms.

Like variable life insurance, variable universal life insurance policies are securities and are subject to the same licensure and registration regulation (including a prospectus requirement) by the SEC and by the state insurance commissioners.

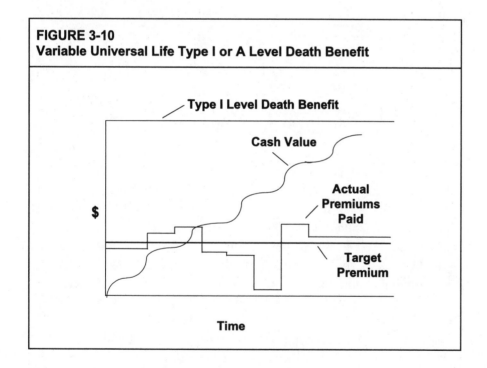

FIGURE 3-10
Variable Universal Life Type I or A Level Death Benefit

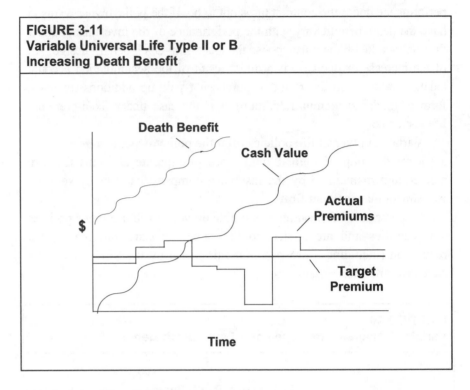

FIGURE 3-11
Variable Universal Life Type II or B
Increasing Death Benefit

Death Benefit

Cash Value

Actual Premiums

$

Target Premium

Time

Ultimate Flexibility

Probably the easiest way to describe variable universal life insurance is to say that it is a universal life insurance policy with the added feature that the policyowner gets to choose the investments, as under fixed-premium variable life insurance contracts. Variable universal life offers the ultimate in both the flexibility afforded to the policyowner and the amount of risk shifted to the policyowner. There are no interest rate or cash value guarantees and very limited guarantees on the maximum mortality rates applicable. Policyowners have wide-open premium flexibility under this contract and can choose to fund it at whatever level they desire as long as it is at least high enough to create coverage similar to yearly renewal term and not in excess of the amount that would drive the cash accumulation account above the maximum threshold set forth in I.R.C. Sec. 7702. Policyowners do not need to negotiate with the insurance company or inform the insurer in advance of any premium modification or cessation.

These contracts permit partial withdrawals that work just like those under universal life policies. Early partial withdrawals may be subject to surrender charges, and surrender charges are applicable to total surrenders in the policy's early years when the insurance company is still recovering excess first-year acquisition costs. The surrender charges vanish at a specified policy duration.

Variable universal life can be aggressively prefunded so that the policy can completely support itself from its cash value. If adequate premiums are contributed to the contract, this can be accomplished in a relatively short number of years. As with universal life and current assumption whole life, variable universal life policies have no guarantee that once the cash value is large enough to carry the policy it will always be able to do so. The policyowner assumes the risk of investment return and, to a limited extent, some of the risk of mortality rate charges. Consequently, the policyowner has to make adjustments and either pay more premiums or reduce the death benefit at some future time if in fact the cash value subsequently dips below the level needed to totally prefund the remaining contract years.

By choosing the increasing death benefit option under this contract policyowners are afforded an automatic hedge against inflation. This inflation protection is general in nature and subject to a timing mismatch in that investment experience may not keep pace with short-term bursts of inflation. Over the long haul, however, the investment-induced increases in coverage should equal, if not exceed, general increases in price levels.

As with variable life, the policyowner is able to switch investment funds from one of the available choices to any other single fund or combination thereof whenever desired. Some insurance companies put a limit on how many fund changes can be made without incurring explicit costs for those changes. Some companies allow one change of funds per year at no cost, others allow one change per open fund per year with no explicit charges, and others specify in the prospectus a given number of fund changes that can be accomplished during any given time interval (usually annually but sometimes other intervals such as quarterly or monthly) without incurring additional charges. Switching investment funds is accomplished without any internal or external taxation of inherent gains in the funds. The internal buildup of the cash value is tax deferred at least as long as the policy stays in force and will be tax free if the policy matures as a death claim.

Variable universal life insurance policies are still primarily life insurance contracts that generate cash value as part of the prefunding level premium mechanism. They are not strictly investment contracts and should not be viewed as such. Philosophically there seems to be a conflict when policyowners manage variable life or variable universal life policies for maximum aggressive growth when in fact the reason for the contracts is to provide a financial safety net for beneficiaries. If the primary coverage is for its death benefits, it seems more appropriate that the investment allocations not pursue the most aggressive growth objectives. A more conservative growth approach is suggested.

On the other hand, if the primary objective for acquiring the contract is for its cash value and the policyowner intends to use the policy's cash values prior to the insured's death, perhaps the more aggressive growth stance is acceptable. In this case the policyowner is likely to be the beneficiary and the risk bearer.

Income Tax Burdens for Early Depletion

Variable universal life policies should not be utilized as short-term investment vehicles. There are two potential traps for policyowners who significantly deplete the policy's cash values at various intervals during the first 15 policy years. These income tax burdens are in addition to any surrender charges that may be applicable within the policy itself.

One potential trap is the modified endowment contract provisions of the Tax Code, which treat all cash value distributions as taxable income until all investment returns have been taxed, and before the remainder of the distribution is treated as a recovery of capital. Such treatment is possible whenever material policy changes are made and the policy fails the seven-pay test (reaching the cash value amount for a policy paid up after 7 years). If the policy fails the seven-pay test, not only will the distributed amounts be subject to income tax (up to the extent of the gain); there may also be a 10-percent penalty tax applicable to those taxable gains if the policyowner is younger than 59 1/2 years of age. High cash value/high premium configuration variable universal life policies are the most likely candidates for this tax trap. Making sure that the cash value before and after any material change is lower than what it would be if the policy were fully paid up after 7 years will, in most cases, avoid this potential problem.

The other potential trap again deals with high levels of cash value approaching the upper limits permitted under the Tax Code. If a reduction in the death benefit level forces a distribution of the cash value in order to retain life insurance status under the Code, those distributions may be taxable income to the extent that they represent gain in the policy. The most stringent constraints apply to such "forced out" withdrawals during the first 5 years of the policy's existence. Slightly less binding constraints are applicable for policy years 6 through 15. Any policyowner contemplating a switch from the increasing death benefit design to the level benefit design during the policy's first 15 years should consider these rules before making the switch. As long as there is no forced distribution or concurrent request by the policyowner for a discretionary distribution of cash value funds, there will be no problem. Conversely, if the increasing death benefit form of the contract is already prefunded near the maximum limitations, there is the possibility that some cash value will be forced out to maintain compliance with the Tax Code limitations on life insurance policies.

Neither of these tax traps has any consequence if there are no gains in the contract (premiums paid exceed cash value) when distributions are made. Also, under Modified Endowment Contract (MEC) provisions the taxation will be applicable only if there are distributions of the cash value. If the funds are left in the contract and allowed to remain part of the cash value, there will be no taxation even though the potential still exists for any distribution once the policy has become classified as a MEC.

Variable universal life contracts are not desirable for policyowners who do not wish to assume the investment risk under the contract. Potential policyowners who say they want to assume the investment risk but become extremely anxious over any short-term fall in the value of the selected investment portfolio funds should also be cautioned.

Chapter Three Review

Key terms and concepts are explained in the glossary. Answers to the review questions and the self-test questions follow the Glossary.

Key Terms and Concepts

endowment life insurance	universal life insurance
IRC Se. 7702	target premium
adjustable life insurance	current assumption whole life
variable life insurance	interest-sensitive whole life
prospectus	indeterminate premium whole life
cost-of-insurance charge	redetermination
variable adjustable life insurance	variable universal life insurance

Review Questions

3-1.   Explain how endowment life insurance differs from whole life insurance and why endowment policies have nearly disappeared from new policy sales.

3-2.   Explain why variable life insurance policies are subject to Securities and Exchange Commission (SEC) regulation, and describe the requirements that regulation imposes on the insurers, agents, and policies.

3-3.   Describe the link between investment performance and death benefits under variable life insurance policies.

3-4.   Explain how investment options have changed under many variable life policies over the past two decades.

3-5.   Explain how the cash value of a variable life policy differs from that of a whole life policy.

3-6.   Describe the type of information in a variable life insurance prospectus.

3-7.   Describe the risks the policyowner assumes under a variable life policy.

3-8. Compare variable adjustable life insurance with adjustable life insurance.

3-9. Describe universal life insurance and explain why it was so successful in the 1980s.

3-10. Describe universal life insurance's flexible premium feature.

3-11. Explain how partial withdrawals of cash value from a universal life policy differ from a policy loan from that policy.

3-12. Explain the target premium concept applicable to universal life insurance.

3-13. Describe both of the death benefit options commonly available to universal life insurance purchasers.

3-14. Explain how policy loans affect universal life insurance's cash value and death benefit.

3-15. Describe the explicit loading charges and surrender charges in universal life insurance policies.

3-16. Describe current assumption whole life insurance, and explain why some of its variations have different names in the marketplace.

3-17. Describe the redetermination concept as it applies to current assumption whole life insurance.

3-18. Describe variable universal life insurance and explain how it differs from
   a. universal life
   b. variable life

Self-Test Questions

Instructions: Read the chapter first, then answer the following 10 questions to test your knowledge. Circle the correct answer, then check your answers in the answer key in the back of the book.

3-1. Which of the following statements concerning variable adjustable life insurance is correct?

   (A) The policyowner has the unilateral right to skip premium payments.
   (B) Most companies marketing this coverage also market universal life.
   (C) The death benefit can be less than the original amount of coverage if investment performance is lower than originally projected.
   (D) The policyowner has a limited ability to choose the investment portfolio.

3-2. Which of the following statements concerning current assumption whole life is correct?

(A) It has a redetermination feature that reconfigures the premium amount in light of recent experience.
(B) It is a variation of traditional whole life that provides no guarantees for the policyowner.
(C) Its cash value development is more like that of variable life than any other policy.
(D) It is participating insurance that has several unique dividend features.

3-3. Which of the following statements concerning universal life is correct?

(A) The level death benefit option pays the constant amount at risk plus the cash value as a death benefit.
(B) If the universal life policy is underfunded, the policyowner has the choice to either (a) increase the premium or (b) reduce the face amount.
(C) Universal life policies require premium payments after the first policy year even if the policy's cash value is adequate to cover the next 60 days of expenses and mortality charges.
(D) Money can be withdrawn for a universal life policy, but it must be paid back with interest.

3-4. The target premium in a universal life policy is

(A) the suggested premium to be paid on a level basis throughout the contract's duration
(B) the amount that must be paid on a universal life policy or it will lapse
(C) the maximum amount that is allowed to paid on a universal life policy under Sec. 7702 guidelines
(D) The amount of premium that will guarantee that the policy will stay in force until age 95

3-5. Which of the following statements concerning adjustable life insurance is (are) correct?

I. The adjustable life policy gives the policyowner the right to request and obtain a reconfiguration of the policy at specified intervals.

II. The adjustable life policy offers all of the same guarantees regarding cash values, mortality, and expenses as traditional whole life policies do.

(A) I only
(B) II only
(C) Both I and II
(D) Neither I nor II

3-6. Which of the following statements concerning universal life insurance premium payment is (are) correct?

I. At no time is there a required minimum level of premium payment.

II. Nearly every policy is issued with a target premium amount.

(A) I only
(B) II only
(C) Both I and II
(D) Neither I nor II

3-7. Which of the following statements concerning current assumption whole life is (are) correct?

I. Current assumption whole life has the same premium flexibility as universal life.

II. The cash value of current assumption whole life includes both guaranteed and nonguaranteed elements.

(A) I only
(B) II only
(C) Both I and II
(D) Neither I nor II

3-8. All of the following statements concerning universal life insurance policies are correct EXCEPT

(A) Under the increasing death benefit option the total death benefit equals the stated face amount plus the amount at risk.
(B) Most policies credit current interest rates on the cash value as long as there are no outstanding policy loans.
(C) Withdrawals effect future earnings because the fund still intact to earn interest is reduced by the amount of the withdrawal.
(D) The target premium amount is merely a suggestion and carries no liability if it is inadequate to maintain the contract to any duration.

3.9. All of the following statements regarding variable universal life are correct EXCEPT

(A) The policies do not permit the policyowner to direct the investment portfolio.
(B) The policies treat all cash value withdrawals as policy loans.
(C) The policies shift some of the investment risk to the policyowner.
(D) The policies have either a level death benefit or an increasing death benefit.

3-10. All of the following statements concerning variable life insurance are correct EXCEPT

(A) Advisors who sell variable life products must be licensed with both life insurance and securities licenses.
(B) Variable life policies can be sold only after a prospectus have given to the prospective buyer.
(C) Variable life policies become more acceptable to consumers after a long period of market increases.
(D) Variable life policies provide guarantees of both the interest rate and a minimum cash value

4

Personal, Family, and Business Uses of Life Insurance

Overview and Learning Objectives

Chapter 4 defines the personal and family needs for life insurance, then turns to a thorough examination of the needs and uses for life insurance that are presented through a business. The discussion of business life insurance needs addresses employee benefit plans, executive compensation plans and business insurance plans that can take advantage of tax provisions established in the Internal Revenue Code.

An understanding of the material in this chapter should enable the student to

4-1. Identify and explain the expenses commonly associated with death and settling the deceased's estate.

4-2. List and explain the ongoing income needs of family survivors.

4-3. Identify and explain the potential sources of retirement income.

4-4. Describe how life insurance can be used to fund charitable donations and bequests.

4-5. Explain how life insurance can enhance a business's credit.

4-6. Discuss briefly how life insurance is used in employee benefit planning, including group term life insurance and executive bonus (Sec. 162) plans.

4-7. Explain the basic concepts of split-dollar life insurance plans and the two tax regimes applied to these plans under Revenue Ruling 2003-105.

4-8 Explain the major concepts of deferred compensation and how life insurance can be used in these executive compensation plans.

4-9.   Discuss how life insurance is used for key employee protection for a business.

4-10.   Explain the basic concepts of buy-sell agreements and how life insurance is used in this type of planning.

Chapter Outline

Personal and Family Uses of Life Insurance   4-3
    Sources of Immediate Funds   4-3
    Income to Family Survivors   4-8
    Funds to Repay Debt   4-11
    Funds to Pay Death Taxes   4-12
    Funds for Dependents' Education   4-13
    Funding Trusts at Death   4-14
    Charitable Donations   4-15
    Funding for Gifts to Individuals   4-16
    Supplementing Retirement Income   4-17
    Funding Home Health Care or Nursing Home Care   4-17
Business Uses of Life Insurance   4-19
    Group Term Life Insurance (IRC Sec. 79) Plans   4-21
    Executive Bonus (Sec. 162) Life Insurance Plans   4-23
    Split-Dollar Life Insurance Plans   4-25
    Other Tax and Regulatory Issues   4-37
    Reverse Split-Dollar   4-39
    Combining Split-Dollar Plans with Nonqualified Deferred
        Compensation   4-40
    Life Insurance in Deferred-Compensation Plans   4-43
    Life Insurance in Qualified Plans, IRAs, and 403(b) Plans   4-43
    Life Insurance in Nonqualified Deferred-Compensation Plans   4-47
    Key Person Protection   4-50
    Funding Buy-Sell Agreements with Life Insurance   4-53
Chapter Four Review   4-65

Personal and Family Uses of Life Insurance

This chapter addresses the various situations that give rise to a need for funds that life insurance can supply. Some of the situations apply to almost all families, while others may be relatively complicated and apply only to special circumstances. Nevertheless there are many planned and unplanned needs for funds that can be satisfied with life insurance policies. Policies with cash values can provide funds during the insured's lifetime and benefits after the insured's death. Death benefits can be paid within a few days of the claim filing and are, therefore, an excellent source of immediate cash to the surviving family members. Life insurance makes the funds available upon death to meet any of the beneficiary's subsequent needs, unless the contract intentionally directs the funds to a restricted use or availability.

Sources of Immediate Funds

The death of an insured family member usually terminates an income stream that the family has relied upon. The costs of daily living for survivors, final expenses for the deceased insured, and emergencies, repairs and replacements associated with events surrounding the family member's death create an immediate need for funds. Families having an adequate source of emergency funds in liquid holdings, such as money market funds, mutual funds, bank balances, cash management accounts, life insurance cash values, and so forth, may easily meet any need for immediate cash following the death. However, the need for additional funds becomes urgent if the family does not have an emergency fund or has depleted it immediately prior to the death.

One of the goals of proper planning is to make sure the emergency fund is adequate to meet the survivors' needs until life insurance proceeds and other potential sources of funds become available. Life insurance proceeds often provide a significant portion of the emergency fund itself. This reliance on the immediate availability of death benefits should not be associated with policies that are still contestable—in force less than 2 years. There could be some delay in settling claims of contestable life insurance polices. After a policy becomes incontestable, however, it is reasonable to count on quick availability of death benefits.

Cash to Meet Daily Living Needs

Surviving family members will be faced with the financial demands of maintaining the household and meeting the needs of household members. There will be continuing costs for food, transportation, and utilities. Mortgage payments may have to be continued and, even if they are insured, will have to be paid temporarily. It will take a while for the survivors to ascertain whether or not there is current life insurance on the mortgage and to file a claim if coverage exists. In the absence of coverage, the surviving family members will have to continue making mortgage or rent payments.

The surviving family members often, at least temporarily, continue their established lifestyle and generate the same level of expense that they encountered before the death. This means a continuation of bills for cable TV services, magazine subscriptions, newspapers, club memberships, entertainment, and miscellaneous costs. If the surviving family members are aware of their financial situation and they have planned for the death contingency, they will know whether or not they can afford to maintain the same standard of living or if cost cutting will be necessary. Even if the household budget does have to be trimmed, it is unrealistic to expect the survivors to cut back on their expenses immediately after the death. Changes in a family's living standard are usually accomplished through a certain amount of trial-and-error adjustment over a period that often exceeds one year.

Private school tuition for the children is a good example of a cost that cannot necessarily be trimmed immediately. If at all possible, the children are often kept in the same school to complete the year in progress. This is much easier if the tuition has been paid in advance, but in the case of ongoing monthly tuition bills, the family may be forced to curtail other expenses in order to finance the school costs. At the end of the school year family members will have to decide what level of school costs they can afford over a longer period. This may mean a move to less-expensive private schools or enrollment in public schools. In some cases, the transition may require many years as the students gradually move to less expensive forms of schooling each year.

The emotional turmoil following the death of a close family member usually lasts about one year. As survivors cope with the emotions of anger, denial, depression, bargaining, and finally acceptance of the death, the grieving process often distracts them from concentrating on financial issues. They may forget to pay important bills, such as premiums on homeowner's and auto insurance that could worsen their financial position. Creditors insisting to be paid immediately can be an additional source of emotional stress at this time. Survivors who are able to convince these creditors that adequate life insurance will be available are usually not pressed for collection until proceeds have been received.

So far the focus has been on routine living expenses. Quite frequently a family death sets off a chain of events that generate additional costs, such as transportation for children, parents, and other family members to the funeral. These expenses can be significant if the family members live far away. Feeding and housing these temporary guests can also be expensive.

Cash to Pay Expenses Associated with Death

Burial or cremation expenses are by no means the only expenses associated with death. The final expenses depend very heavily on the individual circumstances of each death. Some people undergo a lengthy period of hospital treatment and incur large medical bills. Their medical care costs not covered by insurance could accumulate to a big debt. Home care or convalescent care is rarely covered by private insurance and has limited coverage under Medicare for those over 65. Prolonged medical care and rehabilitative treatment will often leave the family's finances devastated even before death occurs. Following death there are usually substantial; they include funeral expenses, transportation expenses, and cemetery or mausoleum charges.

Many of the expenses associated with a death are incurred after the funeral. The costs of settling financial and property matters in closing the deceased's estate are examples. Also included are court fees related to the appointment of an executor or administrator to manage and settle the estate, fees charged by the executor or administrator, and attorneys' fees in addition to the court costs for probate.

Managing the estate prior to final property disposition may be extremely complex. This may require the services of specialized investment managers and/or real estate managers to safeguard the property until it can be sold or distributed. The provisions of the will and the nature of the property involved may necessitate a long period of estate management before the estate can be closed. Some assets may be hard to sell in the economic conditions following death. The terms of the will may require the establishment of trusts and other legal work that is also very time consuming. Even the task of locating heirs or other beneficiaries of the estate may require a lengthy search to obtain death certificates for potential recipients who predeceased the insured. The longer this process takes and the more complex it is, the more it will cost.

The administrator or executor has responsibility for settling all the outstanding debts and closing out all the financial affairs of the deceased. This includes filing tax returns and paying tax liabilities. This process is much more easily addressed when there is adequate cash available through life insurance policy proceeds. It is usually not advisable to have such proceeds payable directly to the estate. Rather, they should be paid to a trust or to an individual with an interest in the estate. Cash can then be made available to the estate by cash purchases of assets from the estate or loans to the estate.

The size of the estate and the nature of the assets it contains heavily influence the optimal planning strategies for minimizing taxes and accomplishing individual objectives. Paying policy proceeds directly to the estate is less of a problem for small estates with no federal estate or gift tax liability than it is for large estates. The most important point is that any planning must be done in the appropriate manner prior to death to achieve best results. For sizable estates where there are transfers of life insurance policy ownership, it is better if the planning is done at least 3 years prior to the death. Tax treatment will be governed by policy ownership, beneficiary designations, and trusts in effect at the time of death. The estate may be subject to much higher taxes than would have been payable if there has not been appropriate preparation before death. Even if an administrator or executor knows how to minimize taxes, his or her hands will be tied unless assets have been properly positioned and the necessary documentation, trusts, and other instruments are in place before the insured's death.

Funds for Emergencies, Repairs, or Replacements

Although accidents and natural disasters account for only 5 percent of deaths in the United States, people who die from accidents may leave survivors with serious property damage that needs to be corrected immediately. Surviving family members may have to deal with salvaging, repairing, or replacing such damaged property. Just about any personal or real property can be damaged or destroyed by the same events that cause death. Examples include autos involved in traffic accidents, homes and their contents destroyed by a wind storm or other natural disaster, utility lines damaged by an earthquake or lightning strike, water wells polluted by flooding, and any number of other potential losses.

The important point is that surviving family members may be faced with an immediate need for cash in order to cope with the property damage coincident with the death. For example, they may have to purchase a replacement auto or rent alternative temporary housing. Even if the property loss is insured, the family may have to spend a significant amount of cash before a property insurance settlement is available. A homeowner's policy, for example, requires that damaged structures be temporarily repaired or protected in order to prevent additional damage from water, wind, theft, and many other sources. Failure to take such measures could drastically reduce the amount of the eventual property insurance claim settlement.

Some property damage is not insurable at all, such as flood damage to a residence. The family auto may not be covered for the physical damage to the vehicle caused by the fatal collision. Death benefits from the life insurance policy, however, are usually available very quickly. If the death and the property destruction occur at the same time and the claims are filed for each on the same day, the claim for the death benefit will probably be settled much sooner than the claim for the property damage. Consequently it is more likely that the life insurance proceeds will provide an immediate source of emergency funds following a death associated with property damage than will the property insurance. Moreover, the cash value of a life insurance policy can provide emergency funds for property loss in cases where there is no death in conjunction with the damage. For example, a policy loan may be the quickest way to obtain the cash needed to buy plywood and tarps to seal up a damaged house after a storm or fire.

Income to Family Survivors

Dependents

The financial needs of family survivors do not terminate at the closing of the deceased's estate. Minor children and other dependents may need support for a lifetime or at least for many years until they become self-supporting. Life insurance and other accumulated assets can provide that necessary financial support. With proper planning, a surviving spouse should be supported during this dependency period as well, rather than being forced to enter the labor market. In some cases whether or not the spouse works is not a discretionary planning option because the spouse may be disabled or may otherwise be unable to enter the work force.

When planning the income needs of family survivors it is important to include all persons who depend on the income of the person to be insured. Such planning is important for each member providing income to the family unit. This often includes both husband and wife, and it could include children living at home who contribute income to support the family.

Example: The death of a non income-earning spouse can greatly increase the costs of the surviving household. A single parent has to pay for essential services such as childcare, transportation, and domestic chores that were previously performed by the deceased spouse and cannot be done by the survivor.

Children—In today's world of frequent marriages and divorces it is common to have more than one group of minor children to be supported. The husband and wife may have children from previous marriages in addition to the children of the current marriage. This situation could involve the finances of three or more separate households, or all the children could live together with the husband and wife. The other sources of support available to children of previous marriages obviously affect the children's financial needs. The income needs of the youngest children—usually the children of the current marriage and those with the longest period of dependency—should be given top priority.

Other children who may need lifelong financial support are children with physical disabilities or mental impairments that will prevent them from ever becoming self-supporting. Their dependency can continue many years beyond the death of both parents. Planning for the financial support of these children can be very complex. Severely handicapped children may require institutional care, which can be extremely expensive in private facilities and is available through public institutions only if the family withdraws financial support so the child can qualify for welfare programs. Any asset or trust established for these children's support must be very carefully structured. The rendering of public institutional support often gives the government the right to take possession of assets that are for the benefit of the child receiving the institutional care. In some cases the government has even been able to invade trusts.

Parents caring for permanently dependent children have to consider the long-term need for finances to support themselves and the impaired child. Some degenerative diseases shorten life expectancy predictably, and parents can plan for their financial dependents with the knowledge that their impaired child is less likely to survive them. But other permanently dependent children have normal or unknown life expectancies. Planning for such a child's support may have to extend beyond the parents' lives.

Parents and Other Dependents—Another group of family dependents who may have a relatively short and predictable period of dependency are the husband's and wife's parents. The financial demands of providing parental support can be minimal—providing room and board in the home for example. At the other end of the spectrum, support of a parent in an institution can be very expensive. Care for an elderly parent in an upscale institution often costs more than two times the median family income.

Example:	Elderly parents can instantly loose their independence and self-sufficiency by means of an accident or sudden change in health. They may be hospitalized after a fall or a stroke and never be able to live by themselves again. Adult children are often overwhelmed by the demands of seeking care for a parent awaiting discharge from a hospital.

The voluntary assumption of financial support for another individual often implies a willingness to provide that support as long as it is needed. That need may extend beyond the death of the supporter. Careful planning and adequate amounts of life insurance can assure extended parental support even if the supporting child predeceases that parent. Otherwise the supporting child's death may force the parent to drastically change living arrangements and lower his or her standard of life.

Financial dependence is not restricted to children, spouses, and parents. In some cases distant relatives and current or ex-in-laws may have to be supported for one reason or another. Some take in foster children and develop emotional bonds that are as strong as those between natural parents and children. Many of these foster parents extend financial support above and beyond that required by the foster parent program.

Non-dependents

Many people make a regular, discretionary payments to their adult children to enhance their standard of living although there is clearly no parental obligation to make these gifts and the children are not dependent on the payments for necessities. Nevertheless, many parents in these circumstances have a strong desire to continue such enhancement payments at least until the grandchildren become self-supporting, even if the period of payments extends beyond the grandparent's life.

Payments to enhance someone's lifestyle, however, are not necessarily restricted to children or other family members. Payments are sometimes extended to lifelong domestic helpers and care givers as an informal pension, perhaps for the recipient's remaining lifetime. Life insurance can fund these payments if the benefactor dies first.

Level of Support

Any sort of plan to provide ongoing income payments to dependents or others after death requires the provider to make decisions about the amount of the payments and their duration. A starting point is to decide whether the income payments constitute partial support, full support, or full support plus an enhancement element. Another factor to consider is whether the payments are intended to be level or to change over time. In some cases there may be intent to phase out these income payments by decreasing them over a given interval in the expectation that the recipient will achieve financial independence. Conversely, when the intent is to provide full support, income payments may have to be increased to compensate for the effects of inflation.

The duration of support payments can vary widely, depending on the provider's objectives. Payments may go to a very specific and predictable date, such as age 21 of the grandchild, age 35 of a child, age

90 of a spouse or other dependent, or to a specified calendar year. Alternatively, payments may be designed to continue for an unknown length of time, such as the remaining lifetime of the recipient, until the recipient remarries, or until the birth of a child. Income payments can even be designed to be perpetual so that the capital sum supporting the income payments is not reduced or depleted. By using a perpetual-funding approach for lifetime incomes, the capital sum is a transferable asset after the income objectives are satisfied. A common application is the *qualified terminal interest property trust (QTIP)* used for estate planning purposes. In such a trust a lifetime income is paid to the surviving spouse, and the trust corpus is then distributed to children (or others) after the spouse dies.

Funds to Repay Debt

Many personal debt agreements have a clause specifying that the full remaining balance will become due and payable upon the death of the debtor. This separate clause may be present whether or not there is any credit life insurance covering the loan agreement. Although lending institutions regularly offer credit life insurance at the time the loan is initially created, such coverage is not mandatory and is often refused by the borrower. When credit life insurance is in force, the remaining loan balance will be repaid to the lender by the credit life insurance company as long as a death claim is filed so that the insurer can extinguish the debt. However, there is always the possibility that credit life insurance benefits will not be collected if the survivors or the executor or administrator is not aware of the insurance. Credit insurance information, therefore, should always be noted in files pertaining to the insured's debt.

Credit life insurance is not the only way of repaying debts that become due and payable at death. All types of life insurance policies provide death benefits that are suitable for repayment of debts. A single large policy can provide enough funds to liquidate many or all outstanding debts. Moreover, the standard types of individual life insurance policies may be lower in costs than credit life policies. There are some debts that do not become due and payable at the death of the borrower. This is more likely to be the case when both husband and wife are liable for the debt. Adequate amounts of individual life insurance will give the survivor the option of either paying off the debt or continuing to repay it according to schedule. That option is not available under credit life insurance because benefits automatically cancel the debt once a claim has been filed.

Funds to Pay Death Taxes

Individuals who acquire a sizable net worth during their lifetime may be subjected to taxes on that net worth at their death. There is a federal estate tax applicable to very large estates. The tax is progressive in nature with a lower rate (such as 38 percent) applicable to smaller estates, increasing to 55 percent for large estates. The Economic Growth and Tax Relief Reconciliation Act of 2001 (EGTRRA) phases out the federal estate tax through 2009 and repeals it in 2010. EGTRRA expires, however, in 2011, so the estate tax will be restored in 2011 unless Congress acts. The main elements of the phase-out are a cap on the top estate tax rate and an increase in the exemption amount.

Federal taxes must usually be paid within 9 months of the owner's death. This presents a real problem for individuals or families whose most important and largest assets are illiquid forms of investment, such as family-owned businesses and investment real estate. These assets cannot be quickly converted to cash without a significant decrease in value. In most cases the family would prefer to retain the asset and its future income-generating potential. Life insurance proceeds can provide the necessary cash to pay the tax liability and to preserve the assets being taxed for the benefit of family survivors.

Federal gift taxes can also be a sizable tax liability at death. The rates are the same as those for federal estate taxes. They apply to all nonexempt gifts on a cumulative basis. In other words, the aggregate amount of gifts made since 1932 is taken into consideration in determining the applicable gift tax rate for the gifts currently being taxed. For donors in the highest tax brackets the gift tax can equal 55 percent of the value of the gift itself.

The gift tax triggered by the donor's death often involves gifts that were completed by reason of that person's death. Examples include jointly owned property after one of the joint owners dies, and life insurance proceeds under some policy ownership and beneficiary designation situations. Settlement of the estate may also result in gift taxes due on gifts made shortly before death.

Some states impose death taxes in addition to the federal estate taxes. These taxes, like the federal taxes, are due within a relatively short period of time and must be paid with liquid funds. Careful planning is required to provide for these state and federal taxes, especially if life insurance is to be the funding mechanism. The policies themselves may in fact be subject to the tax and increase the tax liability being funded by the policy. Good tax counseling can save unnecessary taxes and provide the optimal tax-saving strategy for the family whose objectives and considerations preclude the usual steps to minimize taxes.

Funds for Dependents' Education

Minor children need uninterrupted support for their education—from their first day in the classroom to the realization of their educational objective. The funding requirements for educating children vary widely from one family to another. A public school education that terminates at high school has relatively modest costs compared to the costs of a private school education including preschool, prep school, private university, and professional school. The disparity in costs is a function of both each school's tuition and the duration of the schooling itself. The factors influencing parents' educational goals and decisions often involve a complex mixture of family history, family philosophy toward education, family income, and the abilities and personality of the child. Children are often encouraged to attain at least the same level of education as their parents. But planning on an ivy-league education, for example, will be for naught if the child does not have adequate financial support to enable him or her to attend a school of that caliber.

For very young children the planning horizon for education may exceed 20 years. Although primary school costs in the next few years may remain relatively similar to those today, adjustments for inflation must be made for educational costs to be incurred more than a decade into the future. Choosing the appropriate inflation factor involves some guessing, but it is safe to assume that the inflation rate will be greater than zero. Some authorities on the subject recommend a planning assumption of 7 percent to 8 percent annual inflation in taxation costs.

Permanently disabled children have special educational needs. Sometimes these children require lifelong training and education. Each family situation is likely to have its own unique set of needs and challenges, and each involves long-term planning.

Educational needs of the family are not restricted to the children. A surviving spouse may need further education to increase future income potential to help support the family. The spouse may need a modest refresher course or training to return to a prior occupation. On the other hand, the spouse's need may be extensive, such as preparing to enter the job market for the first time or trying to upgrade to a higher-paying career. There is even the possibility that a surviving spouse may need training for a less demanding career if he or she has become permanently disabled in some manner.

One very important consideration in providing education or training to the surviving spouse is whether the survivor will be able to earn any income while pursuing his or her education or training. Funding spousal education on a full-time basis usually requires prefunding family support while the spouse is a full-time student and prefunding the educational or training costs themselves.

In some cases the surviving spouse may be able to pursue the education on a part-time basis while he or she is employed in the workforce. This is a heavy emotional burden and a physically challenging avenue for a surviving spouse who becomes a single parent. Pursuing education on a part-time basis may greatly lengthen the period of time needed to complete the educational program. This will delay any significant increases in earned income for the surviving spouse and family members. If the potential increase in income because of further education is large enough, it may actually be less costly to prefund a full-time educational program. Obviously each situation must be evaluated on an individual basis.

Funding Trusts at Death

Trusts are contractual arrangements for the ownership and management of assets by a trustee according to the trust agreement. The trustee manages trust assets on behalf of and for the benefit of the trust beneficiaries. There are many different motivations for the establishment of a trust. One is to get professional management from a corporate entity, such as a trust company or a bank trust department, so that the trustee will not predecease any of the trust beneficiaries. Tax considerations sometimes justify the creation of a trust.

Life insurance is often an integral part of the trust funding. The trust itself often owns life insurance on the grantor, who names the trust as beneficiary of that insurance. Trusts can also be beneficiaries of insurance policies not owned by the trust. Those insurance proceeds provide the funds necessary for the trust to carry out its objectives. Some trusts are set up specifically for the purpose of funding life insurance premiums and receiving proceeds. If estate tax minimization is the objective of the trust, the trust is subject to more stringent requirements that can change many times during the existence of the trust.

Trusts have always been an important means of extending family financial management by the parents beyond their lifetime. In these arrangements the trust is often used to distribute funds periodically rather than in a lump sum. The objective is usually to protect a child from a propensity to spend funds frivolously. By spreading out the distribution, the child is unable to get access to and squander the entire sum immediately after the parents' death. Final distribution from such trusts is often predicated on the beneficiary's attainment of a specified age and is usually the parents' best guess as to when the child will be mature enough to handle the funds responsibly.

Trusts can be set up for the benefit of children with mental impairments or other problems that would preclude them from ever becoming capable of managing their own finances. The nature of the trust depends very heavily on the type of care being provided to such children, especially on whether the care is private or public.

> **Trusts**
> - Contractual agreement created by trustor
> - Managed by trustee
> - For benefit of trust beneficiaries, such as child or spouse
> - Can own and manage assets
> - Can be funded with life insurance
> - Can own life insurance policies

Trusts can also be an important tool for sequestering assets from a spouse to prevent the assets from being directed to a stepchild or to an unforeseen family member if the surviving spouse were to remarry after the insured's death.

Life insurance and trusts are often combined in creative ways to fund charitable gifts. Sometimes the entire arrangement is for the exclusive benefit of the charity. In other arrangements the trust is set up for a combination of family objectives and gifts to charitable institutions. Such arrangements usually involve a stream of income payments and subsequent distribution of the trust corpus. The charity or the family member can be the recipient of the income payments, the corpus, or both.

Charitable Donations

Life insurance policies are often used to increase the value of gifts to charities. This can be accomplished either by giving the policy itself to the charitable organization or by naming the charity as the beneficiary on the existing life insurance policies. Where federal estate tax considerations are important, a new life insurance policy may be purchased by the charity itself at the request of the donor, who would give the necessary permission and information to complete the policy application and would provide the funds for premium payments.

Most states have enacted specific statutes expressly stating that charitable organizations have an insurable interest in the life of the donor. The statutes were prompted by an IRS decision claiming that a charity lacked an insurable interest in the donor. In part that decision was based on a New York statute that has since been modified to recognize such insurable interest.

Life insurance can also be used for charitable giving even if the charity is not a beneficiary of the insurance policy. The donor can use adequate amounts of life insurance to fund all of the needs of surviving family members and thereby free up personal property and other assets for lifetime gifts to the charities.

Gift tax and estate tax considerations are often strong motives for making charitable gifts. Because tax laws can—and probably will—change, tax planning should be carefully coordinated by a knowledgeable tax adviser.

Funding for Gifts to Individuals

The use of life insurance is not limited to benefiting family members and related trusts and charities. Life insurance can easily be used to benefit anyone the donor specifies. The motivation could be friendship, long-term loyalty, respect for another's accomplishments, support of a common endeavor, or any other commitment about which the individual feels strongly. The intended recipient can be made beneficiary of a life insurance policy or a beneficiary of a trust funded by life insurance proceeds.

One of the strong factors favoring life insurance policies is that the proceeds do not generally go through probate and are not a matter of public record. The proceeds are payable quickly and directly to the beneficiary. Complications of settling or managing the estate have no bearing on nor do they delay the payment of proceeds under a life insurance policy unless the proceeds are payable directly to the insured's estate. In estates large enough to have a federal estate tax liability, therefore, it is generally not a good idea to have life insurance proceeds payable to the insured's estate.

Supplementing Retirement Income

Life insurance policies can be an important source of supplemental retirement income funds. The policy proceeds can obviously be an important source of funds for the surviving spouse. These funds can supplement any other source of retirement income available from corporate pensions, IRAs, other qualified plans, investments, and Social Security.

Life insurance can even provide supplemental retirement funds to the insured individual. This can be accomplished by utilizing the cash value of the life insurance prior to the insured's death. Some policies, such as universal life policies, allow partial withdrawals of cash value amounts without terminating the policy itself. Under any life insurance policy having a cash value, the policyowner can always gain access to the funds by either taking out a policy loan or surrendering the policy for the entire cash surrender value. (Surrendering the policy, of course, terminates any death benefit protection.)

Funding Home Health Care or Nursing Home Care

The cash values of life insurance policies can be used for home health care or nursing home care if that is deemed desirable or necessary. Access to the cash value is available through policy loans, partial withdrawals of the cash value, or outright surrender of the policy.

Long-term-care riders are available with some life insurance policies to provide for home health care or nursing home care needs. In some cases the rider is available without any additional charge; in other cases there is a nominal charge. In essence these riders make a portion of the death benefit, usually one or 2 percent of the face value of the policy, available each month that the insured qualifies for the benefit. The subsequent death benefit payable is reduced dollar-for-dollar for each accelerated benefit payment made under these riders. Their pre-death-benefit payments are usually subject to an aggregate limitation of 50 percent of the face value of the policy, although a few insurance companies have increased the aggregate limitation to 70 or 80 percent of the policy face value.

Long-term-care riders allow life insurance policies to do double duty. They make benefits available for both the insured's lifetime objectives and the survivors' objectives. This can create a complication, however, in that lifetime uses directly reduce the residual benefit payable upon death. It is important to recognize and evaluate the potential conflicts when planning for these needs.

Business Uses of Life Insurance

No well-run business entity can afford to operate without insurance covering its resources against loss. This is as true for the human resources of the business as it is for the buildings and equipment. Life insurance funds a wide variety of business needs. This chapter will briefly outline some of those uses.

Credit Enhancement

Life insurance can enhance a business concern's credit in two general ways: by improving its general credit rating and by making collateral available.

The first credit function of life insurance is closely allied to key person insurance. Anything that stabilizes a business concern's financial position improves its credit rating. Insuring the lives of key personnel not only assures banks and other prospective lenders that the business will have a financial cushion if a key person dies, it also improves the firm's liquidity through the accumulation of cash values that are available at all times. As a result, the firm is able to command more credit and obtain it on better terms.

A more specific use of life insurance for credit purposes is pledging it for collateral. The policy can serve two different purposes. It can protect the lender only against loss arising out of the death of a key person of the borrower, or it can provide protection against the borrower's unwillingness or inability to repay the loan.

An example of the first situation is a firm that has borrowed as much as is justified on the basis of conventional operating ratios but would like to borrow additional sums to take advantage of an unusual business opportunity. If the bank has confidence in the business and feels that the only contingency to fear is the death of the business head or other key person, it can safely extend the additional credit upon the borrower's assignment to the bank of a life insurance policy in an appropriate amount on the life of the proper official. The policy need not have cash values; therefore, term insurance may be used. The basic security behind the loan is the earning capacity of the business and the integrity of its officials. The policy provides protection only against the death of the person whose business acumen assures the loan's repayment. Such loans, secured only by the assignment of a term insurance policy on the borrower's life, are common in personal or non-business transactions—for example, an aspiring doctor who borrows money from a benefactor for medical school, repaying the funds after establishing a practice. In the interim, the benefactor is protected by a term insurance policy on the budding physician's life. This is a character loan, pure and simple; the only hazard to repayment is premature death.

A loan based on cash values is in a different category. The basic security lies in the policy values; the amount of the loan, therefore, is always less than the cash value under the policy assigned to the lender. If the borrower dies before the loan is repaid, the lender recovers funds from the death proceeds, with the difference paid to the insured's designated beneficiary. If the borrower lives but the loan is not paid at maturity, the lender can recover the funds by surrendering the policy for cash or by exercising the policy loan privilege. If the loan is repaid at maturity, the policy is reassigned to the borrower. Life insurance policies are widely used for this purpose in both business and personal situations. Policyowners frequently borrow from an insurance company through the policy loan privilege, rather than through assignment to a bank or other lender.

Life Insurance in Employee Benefit Planning

Designing the appropriate compensation package for the owners and employees of a business is a critical step in the business planning process. In small, closely held businesses, the businessowner's needs will often dictate both the size and form of compensation provided to the employees. In addition, non-owner key employees of closely held businesses must be compensated appropriately or the businesses could lose their services to competitors. Finally, larger, publicly held corporations must compete for the services of valued executives, and employee benefit packages represent a significant portion of the total compensation expense.

Employee benefit plans provide three broad types of benefits that can be financed through insurance: disability benefits, death benefits and pension benefits. The plans that provide such benefits are usually referred to, respectively, as group health insurance, group life insurance, and pensions.

The compensation package provided by an employer is usually divided into two portions—cash compensation and fringe benefits. The purpose of compensation planning is to design the compensation package to meet the needs of the owners and of the business. Some components of the compensation package will be dictated by the specific needs of the business owners. In other cases, the tax costs or benefits of providing such compensation will be balanced to maximize the overall compensation available to the owners.

The shareholder-employees of a closely held corporation have an advantage for the purposes of fringe benefit plans such as health insurance and group term life insurance. The corporation is permitted to fully deduct reasonable contributions for these benefit plans, including contributions made on behalf of owner-employees.

Group Term Life Insurance
(IRC Sec. 79) Plans

Group term life insurance is a benefit plan provided by an employer to a group of participating employees. Such plans, also known as IRC Sec. 79 plans, allow the employer a tax deduction for premium payments on behalf of a participant, unless the premium amounts cause the reasonable compensation limit to be exceeded (an unlikely event).

If the coverage provided by the plan is nondiscriminatory, the first $50,000 of coverage is provided tax free to all plan participants. If the plan discriminates in favor of key employees with respect to coverage or benefits, the actual premiums paid on behalf of such key employees are taxable as ordinary income. A key employee, as defined under the qualified plan rules, generally includes the shareholder-employees and officers of a closely held corporation.

The taxable amounts of coverage (amounts above $50,000) are taxed according to a rate schedule—the so-called Table I—provided by IRS regulations. The Table I rates are presented in Table 4-1.

Example: Suppose a retired executive has $150,000 of postretirement group term life coverage. Since $100,000 of this coverage is subject to tax, the executive would have to include $1,404 (12 x $1.17 x 100) in income annually at age 64. The annual taxable income incurred by the executive jumps to $2,520 at age 65, and $4,512 at age 70. (See Table 4-1.)

TABLE 4-1	
Cost per Month per $1,000	
5-Year Age Bracket	Table I Rates
Under 30	$0.08
30 to 34	0.09
35 to 39	0.11
40 to 44	0.17
45 to 49	0.29
50 to 54	0.48
55 to 59	0.75
60 to 64	1.17
65 to 69	2.10
70 and above	3.76

Requirements Under Sec. 79

Through a contract held directly or indirectly by the employer, coverage under a Sec. 79 plan must provide only death benefits excludible from income tax under Sec. 101(a) to a group of at least 10 *employees*, although special rules provide an exception for smaller groups. The insurance protection provided must prevent individual selection of the amount of coverage. The coverage can be based on formulas related to age, service, job classification, and compensation. For example, a plan that provides a death benefit five times the participant's annual salary precludes individual selection.

Nondiscrimination Rules Applicable to Sec. 79 Plans

Groups with 10 or More Members—The nondiscrimination requirements focus on both the coverage and the benefits provided by the plan. Under the *coverage* test the plan must meet one of the following requirements:

- cover at least 70 percent of all employees
- include no more than 15 percent of the participants from the key employee group
- benefit a reasonable classification of participants

For the purpose of this test, the corporation can exclude (1) employees with less than 3 years of service, (2) part-time or seasonal employees, and (3) employees subject to collective bargaining.

The *benefits* test requires that the benefits be either a flat amount or a uniform percentage of compensation (for example, 2.5 times current salary). The benefit restrictions permit voluntary purchase of additional coverage by the participant.

Groups with Fewer than 10 Members—The IRS regulations provide more stringent requirements for groups with fewer than 10 members. These groups must meet the following requirements or the favorable tax treatment will be lost:

- All full-time employees must be covered (a 6-month waiting period is permissible).
- Evidence of insurability may be tested only on the basis of a medical questionnaire.
- The benefits must be provided (1) on a uniform percentage of compensation or (2) in brackets where no bracket can be more than 2.5 times the next lowest bracket and the lowest bracket must be at least 10 percent of the highest.

Executive Bonus (Sec. 162) Life Insurance Plans

One type of employee compensation arrangement that is currently advantageous for shareholder-employees is the Sec. 162 life insurance plan. The primary advantage is the ability to avoid the nondiscrimination rules applicable to other fringe benefits.

In a Sec. 162 plan, shareholder-employees and executives who participate in the plan apply for, own, and name the beneficiary on permanent life insurance policies covering their lives. The premiums for such policies are provided through a bonus payment by the employer-corporation. The corporation either pays the premium directly to the insurer or gives the amount necessary to pay the premium as a bonus to the employee, who is then billed directly by the insurance company.

The income taxation of the plan is easy to illustrate to clients. The premium amount paid directly to the insurer (or to the employee, as a bonus) is treated as gross compensation income to the employee and is subject to the employee's normal individual income tax rate. If the bonus plus the employee's other compensation represents reasonable compensation, the corporation deducts the amount of the bonus as an ordinary business expense under Sec. 162(a)(1)—thus the origin of the name *Sec. 162 plans*. Although the tax burden of the plan is immediate to the executive, the bonus can be designed as a zero-tax bonus (making it large enough to pay the tax on the bonus) to reduce the executive's out-of-pocket costs.

The primary advantage of a closely held corporation's adoption of a Sec. 162 plan is its exemption from the federal nondiscrimination and administrative reporting rules applicable to most other types of fringe benefit plans. The board of directors of a closely held business or professional corporation can select the participants and limit the plan to those shareholder-employees who want individual life insurance coverage. In addition, there are no discrimination rules with respect to benefit limits.

However, the corporation should use caution in providing unlimited coverage since the corporate deduction for bonus payments to the plan is limited by the reasonable compensation rules. If the limit is exceeded, the corporate income tax deduction will be lost with respect to the amount of any bonuses to shareholder-employees that are deemed unreasonable, and the excess bonus will be treated as a dividend payment rather than as compensation. It is prudent for the corporation to adopt the Sec. 162 plan by board of directors' resolution and to provide evidence in the minutes of the corporate purpose for establishing the plan (for example, by indicating the need to retain or attract key executives by offering the Sec. 162 plan as a benefit).

Coordination of the Sec. 162 Plan with the Corporation's Group Term Life Insurance Plan—the Group Term Carve-out

Do the substantial individual insurance benefits available under a Sec. 162 plan render the Sec. 79 plan obsolete? Generally speaking, the group term life insurance plan concept should not be dropped simply because the employer adopts a Sec. 162 bonus plan. If they meet the nondiscrimination requirements, Sec. 79 plans still offer favorable tax treatment.

It is generally recommended that shareholders and other key employees for whom the corporation wishes to provide more substantial life insurance coverage participate in a Sec. 162 bonus life insurance plan to supplement a Sec. 79 plan. From the executive's standpoint, the Sec. 79 plan could still provide each key employee with the $50,000 of tax-free coverage. Additional group term coverage for these key employees would be taxable to the participants and could be deemed discriminatory, which would result in all benefits becoming taxable as income. This excess coverage could instead be "carved out" of the group term life insurance plan through a Sec. 162 bonus arrangement. Thus the executive bonus plan is also commonly referred to as a *Sec. 79 executive carve-out bonus plan*, or simply a *group term carve-out*.

The carved-out portion of coverage is actually superior to what could be provided under a Sec. 79 plan even if no nondiscrimination rules were applicable to group term coverage (see table 4-2). Key shareholder-employees participating in the plan receive permanent individual life insurance policies providing them with a tax-free cash surrender value build-up and other flexibilities associated with owning individual permanent life insurance.

TABLE 4-2
Comparison of Sec. 79 Plan and Carve-out Plan

	Sec. 79	Sec. 79 Carve-out
Coverage	Must meet the nondiscrimination test	Carve-out excess coverage on a discriminatory basis
Benefits	Flat amount or uniform percentage of compensation	Any amount of bonus for carve-out portion that can be justified as reasonable
Income Tax to Executive	Amounts above $50,000 taxed at Table I costs (all taxable to key employee if discriminatory) and cost rises with age	Amount of bonus taxable
Premium Deductibility	Fully deductible	Fully deductible

Split-Dollar Life Insurance Plans

Following the regulations announced on September 11, 2003 (Rev. Ruling 2003-105, T.D. 9092), the IRS predicts that split-dollar arrangements will no longer be the attractive vehicle to shelter compensation from taxes as they once were. The changes are so significant that even though the general thrust of split-dollar planning retains some of its traditional features, previous discussions of planning and taxation are now obsolete. These final regulations apply to any split-dollar arrangement entered into after September 17, 2003, and to existing arrangements that are materially modified after that date. This section will review split-dollar planning in its entirety, in light of the new IRS rules. Transitional or "grandfathering" provisions for existing plans are also discussed.

Split-dollar life insurance has been a frequently used arrangement of permanent life insurance to provide an executive compensation benefit. Although split-dollar arrangements are not limited to the employer-employee relationship—for example, as a gift or estate planning arrangement between a parent and child or in-law—this is their most common form.

Split-dollar life insurance plans have a long and varied history. The first IRS rulings on such arrangements were issued in the 1950s, but many new types of split-dollar arrangements have evolved since then to adapt to changing tax laws and to provide compensation for business executives. IRS has been placing increasing pressure on these plans in recent years, and these rulings by the Treasury and IRS represent the most recent and perhaps severest crackdown on split-dollar arrangements.

The following discussion summarizes several forms of split-dollar arrangements. However, it is important to note that there are numerous variations within each arrangement and that the general rule is almost the exception in actual practice.

Basic Concepts

Split-dollar life insurance plans split a life insurance policy's premium obligations and policy benefits between two individuals or entities, typically an employer and employee. The two parties share the premium costs while the policy is in effect, pursuant to a prearranged agreement. At the death of the insured or the termination of the agreement, the parties split the policy benefits or proceeds in accordance with their agreement. Plans must meet minimal reporting and disclosure compliance requirements. The insurer handles most of the administration.

Split-dollar plans are used as a fringe benefit option because the plans can be limited to a select group of shareholder-employees and other key personnel. The coverage amounts, and terms of a split-dollar arrangement are not subject to the nondiscrimination rules that apply to qualified pension plans and certain other benefit arrangements. The purpose of these plans is to provide a life insurance benefit at a low cost and low outlay to the executive. Executive needs include either or both (1) life insurance protection for the family and/or (2) estate liquidity.

Split-dollar plans are an alternative to other methods of providing death benefits (as a reward or incentive to selected executives), such as an insurance-financed. non-qualified deferred-compensation plan or life insurance in a qualified plan.

Split-dollar plans can also help provide business continuity, by providing funds for shareholder-employees to finance a buyout of stock under a cross purchase buy-sell agreement, or to make it possible for non-stockholding employees to effect a one-way stock purchase at an existing shareholder's death. This helps establish a market for what otherwise might be unmarketable stock while providing an incentive for employees to stay with the company.

Generally, the employer's cost for a split-dollar plan is fully secured by the insurance contract. At the employee's death or termination of employment, the employer is reimbursed from policy proceeds for its premium outlay. The employer receives no tax deduction for its payments, but because of the reimbursement the net cost to the employer for the plan is limited to the loss of the net after-tax income that could have been earned on the amount paid during the period the plan was in effect.

Normally to receive full benefit from a split-dollar plan, it must remain in effect for a reasonably long time—10 to 20 years—in order for policy cash values to rise to a level sufficient to maximize plan benefits. Nonetheless, the plan must generally be terminated at approximately age 65, since the employee's tax cost for the plan, the Table 2001 cost or equivalent, rises sharply at later ages.

A current issue, discussed further below, is that new tax rules discourage plans that provide the employee an interest in policy cash values (equity-type plans). These equity plans have in recent years become extremely popular as a means of providing savings, investment, and retirement benefits to executives. The market for split-dollar plans is apparently significantly diminished by this cutback on equity plans.

Policy Ownership

Common methods of arranging split-dollar policy ownership are discussed below.

Endorsement Method

- The employer owns the policy and is primarily responsible to the insurance company for paying the entire premium.

- The beneficiary designation provides for the employer to receive a portion of the death benefit equal to its premium outlay (or some alternative share), with the remainder of the death proceeds going to the employee's designated beneficiary.
- An endorsement to the policy is filed with the insurance company under which payment to the employee's beneficiary cannot be changed without consent of the employee (or, in some cases, a designated third person where the employee wishes to avoid incidents of ownership for estate tax purposes).

Advantages of the endorsement method are as follows:

- greater control by the employer over the policy
- simpler installation and administration; the only documentation required (except for possible ERISA requirements described below) is the policy and endorsement
- avoidance of any formal arrangement that might be deemed to constitute a "loan" for purposes of state and federal laws prohibiting corporate loans to officers and directors
- If the company owns an existing key employee policy on the employee, it can be used directly in the split-dollar plan without change of ownership. (Using an existing policy may be important if the employee has developed health problems since the policy was issued.)
- Under the new regulations (see below) the plan will be taxed under the economic benefit rules (participant reports income based on value of pure insurance coverage under Table 2001 or equivalent), which may be more advantageous than the alternative loan treatment.

Collateral Assignment Method—In the collateral assignment method of split-dollar policy ownership

- The employee (or a third party) is the owner of the policy and is responsible for premium payments.
- The employer then makes loans of the amount of the premium the employer has agreed to pay under the split-dollar plan.
- This arrangement is treated for tax purposes as a series of loans, unless the plan is a *nonequity plan* (see below).

- To secure the loans the policy is assigned as collateral to the employer.
- At the employee's death, the employer recovers its aggregate premium payments from the policy proceeds, as collateral assignee. The remainder of the policy proceeds is paid to the employee's designated beneficiary.
- If the plan terminates before the employee's death, the employer has the right to be reimbursed out of policy cash values; the employee continues as the owner of the policy.

Some advantages of the collateral assignment method are as follows:

- It arguably gives more protection to the employee and the employee's beneficiary.
- It is easier to implement using existing insurance policies owned by the employee.
- It is easier for the employee to keep the policy out of the estate for federal estate tax purposes. Typically this is done by having the policy owned from the outset by a third party chosen by the employee to funnel insurance proceeds to the desired beneficiary—for example, the employee's *irrevocable life insurance trust*.

Joint Ownership—Some split-dollar plans adopted in recent years have designated the employee and the employer organization as joint owners of the policy. As discussed below, the new regulations apparently would negate any advantages of this approach.

Premium Cost Split

There are four major categories of premium split. In designing the plan, these provide flexibility to meet the needs of the employee. However, the tax treatment under the new Regulations also must be considered, as discussed later.

- Under a *classic* or *standard* split-dollar plan, the employer pays a portion of the premiums equal to the increase in cash surrender value of the policy for the year, or the net premium due, if lower. The employee pays the remainder of the premium. This arrangement minimizes the employer's risk, since the policy's cash value is enough to fully reimburse the employer's cumulative payments even if the plan is terminated in the early years. However, the employee's outlay is very high in the initial years of the plan, when cash values increase slowly.

- Under a *Level premium* plan, the employee's premium share is leveled over an initial period of years, such as 5 or 10. This avoids the objection to the standard arrangement that the employee's initial premium share is too large. If the plan continues in effect long enough, the employee and employer eventually pay about the same total amount as under the standard arrangement. One disadvantage of the level premium plan is that if the plan is terminated in the early years, the policy cash value has not increased to a level that will fully reimburse the employer for its cumulative payments. In drafting the split-dollar agreement, some consideration should be given to providing the employer a remedy in this situation, although it is difficult to do this satisfactorily.

- With an *employer-pay-all* arrangement, the employer pays the entire premium. This arrangement is used when the employee's financial resources are limited. In an endorsement-type plan, the employee's reportable taxable income is the sum of cost of pure insurance coverage, plus any additional amount to reflect the employee's equity buildup, if any. (See Tax Treatment, below.) As with the level premium plan, if the plan is terminated early, the policy cash value will not fully reimburse the employer outlay; again, the agreement between the employer and employee should address this problem.

- Under an *offset* or *zero-tax* plan, the employee pays an amount equal to the term insurance cost for the coverage (or if less, the net premium due) each year. The employer pays the balance of the premium. The purpose of this arrangement is to *zero out* the employee's income tax cost for the plan, as discussed below. As a further refinement, the employer can reduce the employee's out-of-pocket cost for this arrangement by paying a tax-deductible *bonus* to the employee, equal to the employee's payment under the split-dollar plan. The employer might want to go a step further and pay an additional amount equal to the tax on the first bonus as a *double bonus*.

Cash Value and Death Proceeds Split

The first goal of the plan provision relating to the split of cash value or death proceeds is to reimburse the employer, in whole or in part, for its share of the premium outlay, if the employee dies or the plan is terminated. At the employee's death, any policy proceeds not used to reimburse the employer go to the employee's designated beneficiary. This provides a significant death benefit in the early years of the plan, one of the principal objectives of a split-dollar plan. If the plan provides cash value growth that is in excess of the employer's share and benefits the employee, it is regarded as an *equity split-dollar plan*, and the annual growth in the employee's equity may be taxed each year.

The New Split-Dollar Regulations

Revenue Ruling 2003-105, T.D. 9092, September, 2003

A. Definition of Split-Dollar—Under the new regulations, a split-dollar arrangement is "any arrangement between an owner and a nonowner of a life insurance contract" that satisfies three criteria: (1) Either party pays premiums, including a payment by means of a loan secured by the life insurance contract; (2) one of the parties can recover a portion of the premiums paid from the contract (or payment is secured by the contract); and (3) the arrangement is not part of a Sec. 79 group term life insurance plan.

The regulations provide that if (a) the plan is a *compensatory arrangement* (essentially one in which the beneficiary is one the employee "would reasonably be expected to designate as the beneficiary") and (b) the employer pays any part of the premium, then the plan is deemed a split-dollar plan, regardless of the criteria listed above. There is a similar provision for split-dollar plans for shareholders and corporations.

This is a broad definition and will cover most normal compensation-planning split-dollar arrangements between an employer and employee. It also covers the types of plans sometimes referred to as *private split-dollar* that are used among individuals for business continuation or estate planning purposes.

The following discussion focuses primarily on compensatory arrangements.

B. In General—Mutually Exclusive Regimes for Taxation—The regulations provide two "mutually exclusive regimes for taxing split-dollar life insurance arrangements." Ownership of the life insurance contract determines which regime applies. By designating one party or the other, the taxpayer decides whether to proceed under the economic benefit or loan regime.

1. Under the *economic benefit regime* "the owner of the life insurance contract is treated as providing economic benefits to the nonowner of the contract." This approach is similar to the old rules governing split-dollar plans, with some significant differences. That is, the value of the life insurance coverage or other benefit provided to an employee under a split-dollar plan is valued and taxed to the employee as additional taxable income. Under the regulations, the economic benefit regime essentially applies to two types of plans:

   a. an *endorsement-type* plan under which the employer is the owner of the life insurance contract and endorses a portion of the death benefit to the employee

   b. any split-dollar plan entered into in connection with the performance of services, where the employee or service provider is not the owner of the contract.

2. Under the *loan regime,* the nonowner of the life insurance contract is treated as loaning premium payments to the owner. The loan regime is the default treatment for split-dollar plans that do not meet the specified requirements for the economic benefit regime. Thus, loan treatment will apply to plans of the type that have been referred to as "collateral assignment plans," in which the employee or the employee's trust or beneficiary is the owner of the contract. It appears that loan treatment would not apply to a nonequity collateral assignment contract. (See below.)

C. Who is the Owner?
   1. General rules

      a. The person named as the policyowner is generally treated as the owner for purposes of the new regulations.

b. If two or more persons are named as owners and all named owners have all the incidents of ownership with respect to an undivided interest in the contract, each person is treated as owner of a separate contract.

c. If two or more persons are named as owners and each person does not have all incidents of ownership, the first-named owner is considered the owner for purposes of the new regulations.

D. Economic Benefit Treatment—Under the economic benefit regime, economic benefits must be fully and consistently accounted for by owner and nonowner. "The value of the economic benefits, reduced by any consideration paid by the nonowner to the owner, is treated as transferred from the owner to the nonowner." In the case of an employment relationship, this amount is treated as compensation. Other types of relationships result in a different tax treatment, accordingly.

If the plan is a nonequity arrangement (the economic benefit consists only of current life insurance protection), this economic benefit is to be valued in accordance with a table or method to be furnished in the future. For many years, the *"PS 58" table* was used for this purpose. This was a table based on 1940s mortality rates that provided relatively high insurance costs generally. A new transitional Table 2001 was adopted in Notices 2001-10 and 2002-8 (see Transitional Rules, below). The Table 2001 rates are much lower than the PS 58 rates.

Example: Employer R owns a $1,000,000 policy that is part of a split-dollar arrangement with Employee E. R pays all premiums and is entitled to receive the greater of its premiums or the cash surrender value of the contract when the arrangement terminates or E dies. In year 10 the cost of term insurance for E (under 2001 IRS table) is $1.00 per $1,000 of insurance and the cash surrender value of the contract is $200,000. In year 10, E must include in compensation income $800 ($1,000,000 – $200,000 payable to R, or $800,000, multiplied by .001 (E's premium rate factor). If E had paid $300 of the premium, E would include $500 in compensation income.

If the plan is an *equity-type* arrangement (a plan providing the nonowner something other than just current life insurance protection), then "any right in, or benefit of, a life insurance contract (including, but not limited to, an interest in the cash surrender value) provided during a taxable year to a nonowner . . . is an *economic benefit*."

In other words, current life insurance protection as well as any other benefit received by the employee during the year, presumably including any increase in the employee's vested interest in the policy's cash value, constitute taxable compensation income under these new regulations.

Rollout (Transfer of Contract). The 2003 regulations specifically provide that when a contract is transferred to a non-owner (transferee), the transferee has income equal to the fair market value of the contract over the sum of

- the amount paid by the transferee to the transferor and
- the amount that the transferee took into income as an economic benefit under an equity split-dollar arrangement, less (a) the economic benefit attributable to current life insurance protection and (b) any amount paid by the transferee for the pure equity element.

Fair market value for this purpose is the cash surrender value and the value of all other rights under the contract other than current life insurance protection. The possibility of an artificially low cash value (the "springing cash value" issue) is not alluded to in the new regulation.

Unlike prior rules for split-dollar plans, no amounts paid by the employee toward the premium are includible in the employee's basis. These amounts are included in the owner's (employer's) gross income and included in the owner's basis for the contract. This process discourages the use of contributory plans.

Policy Valuation at Rollout. Rollouts often involve the "springing cash value" issue. Insurance policies can be designed to specify very low cash values for a period of time, followed by a rapid increase in cash value. If rollout occurs when the cash value is low, the argument can be made that the tax consequence to the employee on distribution of the policy (or the cost for the employee to buy the policy) is low because of the low cash value at that time. However, the IRS position in general is that the tax consequences are based on the policy's *fair market value* and not the stated cash value alone. The fair market value is based on what the policy would be worth to a buyer or recipient in an arms-length transaction. Policy reserves used for purposes of insurance company income taxation can be used for this purpose.

Sec. 83. For a compensatory arrangement (employer-employee) the rules under this heading (Rollout) do not apply until the amount is taxable under Sec. 83 of the Code. That is, taxation to the employee could be delayed to a year later than the year of rollout if the contract is subject to a substantial risk of forfeiture. The amount would not be taxable until the year in which the contract is no longer subject to a risk of forfeiture (becomes substantially vested).

E. Loan Treatment—A payment under a split-dollar arrangement is treated as a loan for federal tax purposes if the arrangement is like the traditional *collateral assignment* arrangement, specifically if (1) the payment is made by the nonowner directly or indirectly to the owner or the insurance company; (2) the payment is a loan under general principles of federal tax law or if a reasonable person would expect the payment to be repaid in full to the nonowner; and (3) the payment is made from or secured by either the death benefit or the cash surrender value.

If the loan is an interest-free or below-market loan (as it generally would be), Sec. 7872 applies to determine the amount of resultant additional compensation that is taxed to the employee. Generally, except possibly where the employee is very old, Sec. 7872 will result in more income inclusion than the application of the economic benefit approach.

If the arrangement carries no stated interest rate and is considered a *demand loan*, it would be treated as follows:

- Employer is treated as if it paid additional compensation income to the employee equal to the "applicable federal rate." This amount is taxable to the employee and deductible by the employer.
- Employee is treated as if he or she paid this additional amount back to the employer. This amount is additional taxable income to the employer and is generally not deductible to the employee.

F. Transitional Rules from Notice 2002—The transitional rules from Notice 2002-8 are as follows:

- Arrangements entered into before the date of publication of final regulations will have no current tax on the equity buildup. However, the new regulations appear to provide for current taxation of equity buildup, as discussed previously.
- Arrangements entered into before the date of publication of final regulations will not be treated as terminated with a rollout and transfer of property as long as life insurance protection continues to be treated as an economic benefit to the employee.
- For arrangements entered into before the date of publication of final regulations, the parties will have the option of treating premium payments as loans under any reasonable effort to comply with Sec.7872 (the loan rules discussed above).
- For a split-dollar arrangement entered into before January 28, 2002, and which is terminated with a rollout before January 1, 2004, there will be no taxation of the rollout. This grandfathering provision is particularly welcome, since it recognizes that many of these arrangements have been sold to clients with representations that the rollout would not be a taxable event.

Notice 2002-8 retains new Table 2001, which replaces the PS 58 table for valuing economic benefit. This change is also accompanied with a series of transitional rules:

- Arrangements entered into before January 28, 2002, can continue to use the PS 58 table. Since the Table 2001 rates are lower than the PS 58 rates, this is useful only for limited purposes.
- Arrangements entered into "before the effective date of future guidance" can use Table 2001.
- Arrangements entered into before the effective date of the final regulations can use an insurer's lower term premium rate in lieu of PS 58 or Table 2001 rates. However, after December 31, 2003, the published insurer rates cannot be used "(i) unless the insurer generally makes the availability of such rates known to persons who apply for term insurance coverage from the insurer, and (ii) the insurer regularly sells term insurance at such rates to individuals who apply for term insurance coverage through the insurer's normal distribution channels."

G. Effective Date—The new regulations apply to arrangements entered into or materially modified after September 17, 2003. The new regulations provide that the transitional rules in Notice 2002-8 will continue to apply (see below) for arrangements entered into on or before September 18, 2003.

Other Tax and Regulatory Issues

Income Taxation of Death Benefits

Generally, the death benefits from a split-dollar plan are income tax free, including both the employer's share and the employee's beneficiary's share. The tax-free nature of the death proceeds is lost if the policy has been "transferred for value" in certain situations. This result should be avoided in designing split-dollar plans. The following transfers of insurance policies are exempt from the *transfer-for-value rules* (in other words, they will not destroy the tax exemption for death proceeds): (a) a transfer of the policy to the insured, (b) a transfer to a partner of the insured or to a partnership of which the insured is a partner, (c) a transfer to a corporation of which the insured is a shareholder or officer, and (d) a transfer in which the transferee's basis is determined in whole or in part by reference to the transferor's basis (that is, a *substituted* or *carryover basis*).

Estate Taxes

If the employee had no *incidents of ownership* in the policy, the death benefit is not includible in the employee's estate for federal estate tax purposes unless the policy proceeds are payable to the employee's estate. If an employee is potentially faced with a federal estate tax liability, all incidents of ownership in the policy should therefore be assigned irrevocably to a third party—a beneficiary or a trust. Proceeds generally should be payable to a named personal beneficiary and not to the employee's estate. If the employee is a controlling shareholder (more than 50 percent) in the employer corporation, the corporation's incidents of ownership in the policy will be attributed to the majority shareholder. The current IRS position is that even if the corporation has only the right to make policy loans against its share of the cash value, this is an incident of ownership that will be attributed to the controlling shareholder and cause estate tax inclusion of the policy death proceeds. For a majority shareholder, the only way to avoid estate tax inclusion is for not only the employee but also the employer to get rid of the incidents of ownership. The corporation can avoid such incidents by retaining no rights of ownership in the policy, including any policy contract provisions or riders relating to the split-dollar agreement. One method is for the employee's personal beneficiary to be the original purchaser of the policy, and the beneficiary to enter into the split-dollar agreement with the corporation on a collateral assignment basis. This is a common arrangement for split-dollar plans that primarily are intended to provide estate liquidity to a highly compensated executive.

Gift Taxes

The transfer of the policy from the employee to another party (such as a relative or the employee's irrevocable life insurance trust) is a gift subject to tax. In addition, there is a continuing annual gift if the employee pays premiums on the policy. There is also a continuing annual gift by the employee if the employer pays premiums, because this employer payment represents compensation earned by the employee that is indirectly transferred to the policyowner. Such potentially taxable gifts may avoid taxation if they qualify for the $11,000 (2002 and later) annual gift tax exclusion. Gifts made directly to beneficiaries generally qualify, while gifts to insurance trusts may be considered *future interests* that do not qualify for the $11,000 exclusion.

ERISA

A split-dollar plan is considered an *employee welfare benefit plan* and is subject to the ERISA rules applicable to such plans. A welfare plan can escape the ERISA reporting and disclosure requirements, including the Form 5500 filing and the summary plan description (SPD) requirement, if it is an *insured* plan maintained for "a select group of management or highly compensated employees." Most split-dollar plans qualify for this exception. If the plan covers more than a select group, it must provide SPDs to participants. (If the plan covers fewer than 100 participants, the SPD need not be filed with the Department of Labor (DOL). ERISA further requires a written document, a named fiduciary, and a formal claims procedure for split-dollar plans.

Sarbanes-Oxley Act

As part of the wave of corporate governance regulation arising out of the Enron collapse and similar events in 2001 and 2002, Congress enacted this law containing a range of corporate accountability provisions.

Included was a provision banning publicly traded corporations from making personal loans to any director or executive officer. The applicability of this provision to split-dollar plans is unclear. It could be argued that if applicable, it would apply only to split-dollar plans taxed under the loan regime under the 2003 new regulations discussed above. In any event, the law does not apply to split-dollar plans for employees who are not directors or officers, nor does it apply to any plan of a corporation that is not publicly traded.

Reverse Split-Dollar

A *reverse split-dollar* plan is one characterized as follows:

- The employee has the right to policy cash values up to the aggregate of his or her premium payments.
- The employer is beneficiary of the death proceeds in excess of the employee's share.

The benefits of reverse split-dollar are:

- It maximizes the investment benefit of the plan to the employee.
- Policy cash values provide a substantial investment return over the years as they build up (presumably free of tax under prior law). At retirement or when the plan terminates, the cash value is substantial and the policy is generally substantially funded.
- In the closely held corporation reverse split-dollar can be used to fund a stock redemption buy-sell agreement with the employee paying part of the cost with personal funds.

The disadvantage to the employee of a reverse split-dollar arrangement is that the death benefit for the employee's beneficiaries is very low in the early years, since the corporation, not the employee, is the beneficiary of the *amount at risk* (pure term life insurance element) of the arrangement. The premium is split so that the executive pays a share equal to the cash value build up, while the corporation pays the remainder of the premium.

Most tax planners have advised that the corporation should include something in income to reflect the economic benefit of the *amount at risk* or insurance coverage that will benefit the corporation if the employee dies. Prior to the 2003 new regulations, the practice was to use the old PS

58 rates, rather than the insurance company's lower term rates, since using the higher PS 58 rates reduces the employee's share of the premium.

Under the new regulations, the status of reverse split-dollar is uncertain; there is no specific provision for reverse plans in the new regulations. The new regulations would seem to mandate substantial ongoing taxation of the employee's equity-type benefits. Also, the IRS has ruled against the use of artificially high PS 58 rates in determining the employee premium share. The IRS has made it clear that they will not allow "gaming of the system" through valuation devices, artifices, or misuse of its tables.

In addition, if the employee is a majority shareholder, there is a risk of federal estate tax inclusion, as discussed above under "Other Tax and Regulatory Issues."

Combining Split-Dollar Plans with Nonqualified Deferred Compensation

Double-Duty Split-Dollar Plan

For executives and key employees who are compensated in the middle ranges, classic life insurance financing of deferred compensation may encounter some employer and employee objections. Employees may object to the fact that the preretirement death benefit is taxable to their beneficiaries even though life insurance is used (that is, the corporation, not the employee, benefits from the tax-free nature of the death proceeds). Employees with estate planning concerns may also object that the plan's death benefit cannot be excluded from their estates for federal estate tax purposes. In other words, during the employment period these employees essentially need a life insurance plan more than a retirement savings plan, while they still need some degree of supplemental retirement income.

From the corporate point of view, the degree of cost recovery may be an issue. The corporation's deduction for benefit payments is taken against a corporate tax rate that generally does not exceed 35 percent. Years ago, when corporate tax rates were higher, this deduction coupled with tax-free receipt of the death benefit provided more tax leverage than it does with the current 35-percent top rate. Therefore, the cost-recovery aspect of the traditional plan may not be particularly compelling to the corporation under current circumstances.

Combining a split-dollar life insurance plan with a deferred-compensation plan, using a single policy to finance both plans, may be an attractive approach in these situations. The split-dollar/deferred-compensation approach works as follows:

- The company provides two separate benefits for the covered executives—a split-dollar life insurance plan that operates only during the preretirement period, and a nonqualified deferred-compensation plan that applies only at retirement—a retirement-only salary continuation plan.

- The split-dollar insurance policy is typically owned by the employer under the endorsement method, so the employer has control of the cash values. The employee's share of the premium is negotiated; typically this involves little out-of-pocket cost for the employee.

- During the preretirement period, the employee pays taxes on the economic benefit of the pure insurance amount (the death benefit payable to his or her beneficiaries) less his or her share of the premium payments. In return for this small ongoing tax cost, however, if the employee dies during the preretirement period the death benefit is tax-free to his or her beneficiaries. For estate tax purposes, if the marital deduction is not available, the death benefit can be kept out of the employee's estate (if he or she is not a controlling shareholder) by making an irrevocable gift of his or her interest in the split-dollar plan to an irrevocable life insurance trust for the benefit of his or her heirs.

- At retirement, the split-dollar plan is terminated. The employer retains the full value of policy cash values at this point. The policy is used to finance the benefits under the nonqualified deferred-compensation plan. This is done either by currently making use of cash values to pay retirement benefits, or by paying retirement benefits out of current assets and holding the policy until the employee dies, thus receiving the death proceeds as cost recovery. The income tax deferral of the deferred-compensation benefits is unaffected—that is, tax is paid by the executive or beneficiary when benefits are received.

Reporting and Disclosure Requirements—Even though split-dollar plans are included in the category of welfare benefit plans, most of the ERISA requirements are not applicable. Split-dollar plans are exempt from the ERISA vesting, funding, and participation rules generally applicable to qualified plans. It is possible that the requirements of establishing an ERISA claims procedure and appointing a plan fiduciary can also be avoided, as discussed above.

Split-Dollar as an Executive Carve-out

As with executive bonus plans, a split-dollar carve-out arrangement can be designed to meet the corporation's objective of providing substantial levels of life insurance coverage for key executives in addition to coverage under the company's group term life insurance plan. Split-dollar plans are exempt from the Sec. 79 nondiscrimination requirements, along with most of the reporting and disclosure compliance applicable to many other types of fringe benefit arrangements. Furthermore, split-dollar arrangements allow corporate employers to discriminate freely in the class of employees participating (and in the level of benefits provided). The discrimination can eliminate all but shareholder-employees and other key executives from coverage. It has the dual advantages of giving select executives low-cost, permanent life insurance coverage and giving the employee an incentive to continue with the corporation.

Nondiscriminatory group term life coverage should still be adopted (or continued) if this coverage is otherwise desirable for the employer. Remember, Sec. 79 provides significant tax advantages to both the employer and employee. The split-dollar carve-out alternative is simply one method of providing excess (discriminatory) life insurance coverage to shareholder-employees and other key executives without running afoul of nondiscrimination rules. The individuals participating in the split-dollar carve-out should still be covered under the group term life insurance plan, but their coverage should be limited to $50,000, or permissible nondiscriminatory level of death benefits, if greater. If cost is a concern and the corporation does not need to provide life insurance to a broad class of employees, it should avoid the Sec. 79 plan.

Life Insurance in Deferred-Compensation Plans

Deferred-compensation plans are an important part of the employee compensation package. Under a deferred-compensation plan, part of the employee's compensation over the employee's service-providing years is deferred until a later period, such as the employee's retirement. This deferral meets two goals. First, the deferred compensation will provide income for the employee during his or her retirement. Second, the deferred-compensation plan can realize a tax-planning objective since taxation of properly designed deferred compensation is deferred until the income is received.

Deferred-compensation plans can be categorized as either *qualified* or *nonqualified*. Qualified plans must meet an overabundance of federal nondiscrimination and administrative compliance standards. These standards, of course, increase the cost of such plans since a broad base of employees must be included and significant administrative fees must be paid. However, the corporation gets an immediate income tax deduction for contributions to the plan while the employee's tax on plan benefits is deferred until the benefits are received. For the purpose of this discussion, qualified plans will include pension plans, IRAs, profit-sharing plans, and Sec. 403(b) plans.

Nonqualified plans provide a similar deferral of the employee's receipt of ordinary income. However, nonqualified plans also cause a deferral of the employer's tax deduction until such benefits are paid. Because closely held corporations often want to maximize the benefits for shareholder-employees, the goal of their retirement plans is to discriminate in favor of shareholder-employees and key executives to the fullest extent of the nondiscrimination rules. Since discrimination is permitted in nonqualified arrangements, these plans are often more favorable to the closely held corporation.

Life Insurance in Qualified Plans, IRAs, and 403(b) Plans

A qualified plan may provide a death benefit over and above the survivorship benefits required by law, even without using life insurance. In a defined-contribution plan, probably the most common form of death benefit is a provision that the participant's vested account balance will be paid to the participant's designated beneficiary if the participant dies before retirement or termination of employment. Defined-benefit plans, unless they use insurance as discussed below, usually do not provide an incidental death benefit; in such cases, the survivors receive no death benefit other than whatever survivor annuity provision the plan provides.

A qualified plan must generally purchase life insurance in order to provide any substantial pre-retirement death benefit. This gives the plan significant funds at a participant's death, which is particularly important in the early years of his or her employment when the amount contributed on the participant's behalf is still relatively small.

An insured pre-retirement death benefit can be provided in either a defined-benefit or defined-contribution plan. Contributions to the plan by the employer may be used to pay life insurance premiums as long as the amount qualifies under the tests for incidental benefits.

In general the IRS considers that non-retirement benefits—life, medical, or disability insurance, for example—in a qualified plan will be incidental and therefore permissible as long as the cost of providing these benefits is less than 25 percent of the cost of providing all the benefits under the plan. In applying this approach to life insurance benefits, the 25-percent rule is applied to the portion of any life insurance premium that is used to provide current life insurance protection. Any portion of the premium that is used to increase the cash value of the policy is considered to be a contribution to the plan fund that is available to pay retirement benefits, and it is not considered in the 25-percent limitation.

Fully Insured Pension Plans

A fully insured pension plan is one that is funded exclusively by life insurance or annuity contracts. There is no trusteed (uninsured) side fund. A plan is considered fully insured for the plan year if it meets the following requirements:

- The plan is funded exclusively by the purchase of insurance contracts. Under the regulations, such contracts can be either individual or group, and can be life insurance or annuity contracts, or a combination of both.
- The contracts provide for level annual (or more frequent) premiums extending to retirement age for each individual. However, the employer's cost need not be level since the

regulations permit the employer to experience gains and to use dividends to reduce premiums.

- Plan benefits are equal to the contract benefits and are guaranteed by a licensed insurance company.
- Premiums have been paid without lapse (or the policy has been reinstated after a lapse).
- No rights under the contracts have been subject to a security interest during the plan year.
- No policy loans are outstanding at any time during the plan year.

Fully insured funding can be used either with a new plan or an existing plan. The employer can be a corporation or an unincorporated business. Typically, a group type of contract is used, with individual accounts for each participant. All benefits are guaranteed by the insurance company. The premium is based on the guaranteed interest and annuity rates, which are typically conservative, resulting in larger initial annual deposits than in a typical uninsured plan. Excess earnings beyond the guaranteed level are used to reduce future premiums.

Using excess earnings to reduce future premiums results in a funding pattern that is the opposite of that found in a trusteed (uninsured) plan. In the insured plan for a given group of plan participants, the funding level is higher at the beginning of the plan and drops as participants move toward retirement. This maximizes the overall tax deduction by allowing more of it to be taken earlier. By comparison, a traditional trusteed plan starts with a relatively low level of funding, which increases as each participant nears retirement.

Coordination of Death Benefits

A lump-sum insured death benefit is often provided in a fully insured plan in addition to the pre-retirement survivor annuity required by law in most plans. If so, the total death benefit must not exceed the incidental limits. For example, if the lump-sum benefit is at the maximum limit, it can be reduced by the actuarial present value of the pre-retirement survivor annuity.

Survivorship Benefits

In addition to cash death benefits, death benefits can be provided in the form of annuity options with survivorship features—that is, annuities that continue partial or full payment to a beneficiary after the death of the participant. Survivorship annuities for the participant's spouse are required in certain cases. However, survivorship annuities for the spouse in a form somewhat different from the qualified joint-and-survivor annuity or survivorship annuities for beneficiaries other than the spouse can be included as benefit options in a qualified plan. These options must not exceed the plan's incidental limits for death benefits.

Designing Incidental Death Benefits

It is relatively uncommon for a qualified plan to provide term life insurance to participants because the tax treatment provides no advantage to the employee. It is more common, however, to use cash value life insurance as funding for the plan because the PS 58 rates or the insurance company's term rates may prove to be a relatively favorable way to provide life insurance.

The decision whether to include life insurance in a qualified plan depends on the plan's objective. The employer must first decide whether and to what extent it will provide death benefits to employees—under a group term or other plan or as an incidental benefit in a qualified plan. The death benefit should be designed to produce the lowest employer and employee cost for the benefit level desired. A death benefit should be included in the qualified plan only to the extent it is consistent with this objective.

Other Plans

A Keogh plan is a qualified plan available to a proprietor or one or more partners of an unincorporated business. Life insurance can be used to provide a death benefit for regular employees covered under the plan, and the rules discussed in this chapter apply. Life insurance can also be provided under the plan for a proprietor or partners, but the tax treatment for proprietors and partners is slightly less favorable.

Life insurance can also be used to provide an incidental benefit under a tax-deferred annuity plan on much the same basis as in a qualified profit-sharing plan. Covered employees will have PS 58 costs to report as taxable income, as in a regular qualified plan.

Life insurance contracts are not permissible investments for an individual retirement plan (IRA). In effect, this means that an IRA cannot provide an insured death benefit. Similarly, a SEP (simplified employee pension) plan cannot purchase life insurance since SEPs are funded with individual IRA contracts.

Life Insurance in Nonqualified Deferred-Compensation Plans

Advantages of Nonqualified Plans

A nonqualified deferred-compensation plan is an employer-provided retirement plan that does not meet the qualified plan rules. The nonqualified approach may be advantageous for a closely held corporation if it has the following objectives:

- to exceed the maximum benefit and contribution levels applicable to qualified plans for selected employees
- to provide a retirement plan for owners and other key employees without including rank-and-file employees in the plan
- to avoid the administrative compliance standards applicable to qualified plans
- to permit shareholder-employees or other key executives to temporarily defer taxes on income into a later tax year

Types of Nonqualified Deferred-Compensation Plans

Salary Reduction Arrangements—A salary reduction plan is an agreement between the employer and the participating employee either to reduce the employee's salary or to defer an anticipated bonus and provide that such amounts will be received in future tax years. These plans defer compensation that the employee would otherwise receive in cash, and they generally provide an investment return on the amounts deferred. One type of salary reduction plan, the top-hat plan, is a deferred-compensation plan for a select group of management or highly compensated employees in which the participant elects to defer current salary amounts to provide benefits at his or her retirement.

Salary Continuation Plans—Most nonqualified plans fit into the broad category of salary continuation plans. Salary continuation plans can be designed to provide deferred-compensation benefits at the participant's death, disability, and/or retirement. These arrangements have no current cash option available to the employee. The death or disability benefits are a percentage of the employee's compensation and are provided to the employee or his or her designated beneficiary.

Salary continuation plans designed to provide retirement benefits can be categorized as excess-benefit plans or supplemental executive retirement plans (SERPs). An excess-benefit plan is a retirement plan in which selected participants, generally shareholder-employees and key executives, will receive retirement benefits in excess of those possible under the qualified plan limitations. That is, these plans provide (1) benefits in excess of the 100-percent-of-salary or $130,000 ($160,000 limitation in defined-benefit plans in 2003 or (2) contributions in excess of the 25-percent-of-salary or $40,000 limitation in defined-contribution plans.

A SERP generally complements the qualified plan benefits for a selected group of participants. SERPs provide benefits for a corporation's key executives and, unlike excess-benefit plans, supplement the retirement benefits at levels both above and below the qualified plan limitations. These plans will meet the goal of providing discriminatory benefits to shareholder-employees and other key executives. A closely held business can use a salary continuation plan to provide a substantial retirement, disability, and death benefit to the owners without necessitating the costly inclusion of rank-and-file employees.

Death-Benefit-Only (DBO) Plans—DBO plans are nonqualified plans designed to provide death benefits to a participant's heirs. While DBO plans can provide a lump sum to the participant's survivors, they generally pay installment benefits at the participant's death. Since a DBO is a nonqualified plan, participation can be based on discriminatory factors. Survivor benefits are taxable as ordinary income to the recipient-survivor and are deductible by the corporation when paid to the survivors. The DBO plan benefits will be included in the participant's estate unless (1) the decedent participated in no other nonqualified deferred-compensation plan with the employer that provided living benefits and (2) the participant did not reserve the right to change the beneficiary initially designated. If estate inclusion is a problem, the employer and employee should consider a Sec. 162 bonus plan or a split-dollar agreement with the use of an irrevocable life insurance trust (ILIT).

Requirements for Income Tax Deferral in Nonqualified Deferred-Compensation Plans

The taxation of nonqualified deferred-compensation benefits links the timing of the corporation's deduction to the participant's receipt of benefits. The key to success is deferring the income tax liability until the receipt of the benefit. To avoid current taxation on the deferred benefit, the employee cannot (1) be in constructive receipt of the income or (2) receive a current economic benefit from the deferred amounts.

To avoid constructive receipt the employee's receipt of the income must be

- subject to substantial limitation or restriction. This requirement is met if the employee simply has to wait a certain time period (for example, until retirement) for the benefits.
- deferred by binding agreement prior to the time when the employee earns the compensation. The employee cannot have the choice of taking cash when the income is earned. In the salary reduction agreement the employee and employer make an agreement to defer the receipt of the salary or bonus before the related services are performed.

Any economic benefit currently received from the nonqualified plan is immediately taxable to the participant even if the benefit is not constructively received. The participant receives an economic benefit if funds are vested or set aside for the employee outside the claims of general corporate creditors. Under such circumstances the economic benefit exists because the employee has a cash equivalency in the form of a secured and funded promise. An economic benefit also exists if the funds are placed in an irrevocable trust on behalf of the participant. The corpus of the trust will be a cash equivalent because the employer has given up control of the assets in the plan.

To avoid an economic benefit, the plan assets must be subject to substantial risk of forfeiture. The assets can be set aside in (1) a reserve account held by the employer, (2) a revocable trust, or (3) a rabbi trust. A *rabbi trust* is a trust, usually irrevocable, established by a corporate employer to finance payment of deferred compensation benefits for an employee. The corporation places cash and other assets into the rabbi trust to finance its promise to pay benefits at the employee's retirement. The trust contains a provision, however, that trust assets are available to the claims of creditors of the corporation, which presents the necessary substantial risk of forfeiture to defer compensation. This also exposes the fund to the risk that it my not be paid, so this benefit is two-edged. Under a reserve account or revocable trust there is no economic benefit because all plan funds are subject to the employer's control. In a rabbi trust, because the assets are available to the general creditors of the corporation by the terms of the trust, no economic benefit exists. A rabbi trust is so named because the first trust of this kind ruled on by the IRS was established for a rabbi.

Financing the Employer's Obligation in Nonqualified Deferred-Compensation Plan with Life Insurance

The employer can finance its obligation in a nonqualified plan through corporate-owned life insurance. This type of financing is attractive since life insurance as a corporate asset is a good match for the type of liabilities created by the various nonqualified arrangements. The accumulation in an ordinary life insurance policy or the benefits of an annuity policy can be useful in the participant's retirement years to provide for any salary continuation benefits offered by the plan. Of course, the primary benefit of the life insurance financing is its ability to meet the employer's death benefit obligation should the participant die prematurely.

Nonqualified plan policies are owned by and payable to the employer. As such, they avoid the constructive-receipt or economic-benefit problems because the general creditors have access to the funding policies. The premiums are, of course, nondeductible; however, the cash surrender value builds up tax free, and the proceeds will be nontaxable when received. The corporation receives a deduction when the benefits are actually paid to the participant.

Key Person Protection

Key Person Indemnification

The most direct application of the principles of family insurance to the business world is key person insurance. Its purpose is to indemnify a business concern for the loss of earnings caused by the death of a key officer or employee. In many business concerns, there is one person whose capital, technical knowledge, experience, or business connections make him or her a valuable asset of the organization and a necessity to its successful operation. This is more likely to be true of a small organization, but innumerable examples can also be found in large organizations. A manufacturing or mining enterprise may depend on one or a few individuals whose engineering talents are vital to the concern. An employee with unusual administrative ability or the ability to develop and motivate a superior sales organization may also be a key person. An educational institution or other organization that depends partly on charitable giving may regard a highly successful fund-raiser as a key person.

It is difficult to estimate the economic loss that the organization would suffer in the event of the key person's death. In most cases the loss is measured in terms of earnings, but occasionally it is based on the additional compensation that would have to be paid to replace the key employee. In some cases, the reduction in earnings is assumed to be temporary (5 years, for example), while in other cases, a permanent impairment of earning power is envisioned.

Elements of Key Person Valuation

- Profits directly attributable to person's efforts
- Additional compensation necessary to replace the person
- Recruiting and training costs to find or create a replacement
- Lost revenue anticipated

The first step in handling this risk is to identify the key employees. Key employees have several characteristics distinguishing them from other employees, including the following:

- A key employee might have a specialized skill critical to the success of the particular closely held business. Potential replacements may possess this skill, but replacement employees might have to be recruited at higher salary levels.
- The employee has a significant customer or client base and is responsible for attracting significant amounts of business.
- The key employee might be a source of capital if his or her loss would damage the closely held business's credit rating.

Valuing the Key Employee

Determining the key employee's value to the closely held business is even more speculative than the valuation of the business itself. The actual valuation method depends on the characteristic of the employee that creates the key employee status. Determining the value of the key employee who attracts substantial business might be relatively easy. The net income resulting from the business he or she produces in excess of the amount of net income that could be expected from a similarly situated but less-effective employee could be capitalized in some manner. Or if business goodwill is attributed to one key employee, the income level above the amount expected for a similar business can be attributed to that employee. This income attributed to goodwill can be capitalized to arrive at a current value for the employee.

Example: A business currently has $500,000 of tangible assets and generates $100,000 a year in net income. Similarly situated businesses have a rate of return on tangible assets of 10 percent. In this case $50,000 of income can be attributed to capital, and $50,000 can be attributed to goodwill and the management skill of the key employee. Using business valuation capitalization methods, we can capitalize the $50,000 of earnings at the 10-percent expected-return rate and reach a value for the key employee. The capitalization factor in this case is 10 (100 ÷ 10).

$$\begin{array}{ccc} \text{Net income attritubed} \\ \text{to goodwill} \end{array} \text{ x } \begin{array}{c} \text{Capitalization} \\ \text{factor} \end{array} = \begin{array}{c} \text{Value of goodwill resulting} \\ \text{from employee} \end{array}$$

$$\$50,000 \times 10 = \$50,000$$

In this case the key employee's value to the business is $500,000

The value of a key employee, particularly when more than one key employee is present, is usually more difficult to determine than in the example above. The firm may have to consider various subjective factors to arrive at a proxy for the key employee's value. For example, the firm should consider replacement salaries and the training required for a replacement employee to become effective. A simple approach might be to take the key employee and pick some multiple of current salary as a proxy for his or her value.

Key Employee Life Insurance

A business can purchase life insurance on the life of the key employee to cover the risk of an income loss and/or increase in expenses resulting from the key employee's death. In most cases, some form of permanent insurance, usually ordinary life, is purchased, and the accumulating cash values are reflected as an asset on the business's books. If key person protection is needed for only a temporary period or if the primary concern is the key employee's dollar value to the business, term insurance is normally used. Decreasing term might be appropriate because the key employee exposure decreases as the insured approaches retirement and the business can expect to have his or her services for a fewer number of years.

Key employee insurance, however, is usually coupled with some other purpose such as providing a retirement benefit for the key employee. Permanent life insurance is typically purchased to meet this objective. The life insurance death benefit will be received by the business as indemnification for the income loss and/or increase in expenses resulting from the key employee's death. If the insured survives to retirement, the corporation can use the cash surrender value to fund a deferred-compensation retirement benefit. Another approach is for the business to transfer the policy to the employee at retirement.

The business should be the owner and beneficiary of key employee life insurance. This should pose no insurable interest problems since the business will suffer a financial loss at the death of the key employee. The premiums for key employee insurance will be nondeductible, while death benefits will be received income tax free. An additional benefit of key employee insurance is that no accumulated-earnings tax problems should result since the accumulation of earnings to insure the key employee death risk will meet the reasonable-business-needs test. For incorporated businesses key employee life insurance may, however, increase exposure to the alternative minimum corporate tax.

Funding Buy-Sell Agreements with Life Insurance

Business Continuation

An important form of business organization is the general partnership, which is subject to the rule of law that any change in the membership of the partnership causes its dissolution. In accordance with this rule, the death of a general partner dissolves the partnership, and the surviving partners become liquidating trustees, charged with the responsibility of paying over the deceased's fair share of the business's liquidated value to his or her estate. Liquidation of a business, however, almost invariably results in severe shrinkages of the business assets. Accounts receivable yield only a fraction of their book value, inventory is disposed of at sacrifice prices, furniture and fixtures are sold as secondhand merchandise, and goodwill is lost completely. Moreover, liquidation deprives the surviving partners of their means of livelihood.

In the absence of a prior agreement among the partners, any attempt to avoid liquidation is beset with legal and practical complications. Even if the surviving partners can raise the cash to purchase the deceased's interest—an unrealistic assumption in most cases—they have to prove, as liquidating trustees, that the price paid for the interest is fair. In some states, their fiduciary status prevents their purchasing the deceased's interest at any price because it is virtually tantamount to trustees purchasing trust property. Furthermore, it is seldom practical for the widow(er) or other heir to become a member of the reorganized partnership or to purchase the surviving partner's interests.

In order to avoid this impasse, it is common for the members of a partnership to enter into a buy-sell agreement. Such an agreement binds the surviving partners to purchase the partnership interest of the first partner to die at a price set forth in the agreement and obligates the deceased partner's estate to sell his or her interest to the surviving partners. The various interests are valued at the time the agreement is drawn up and revised from time to time thereafter. Each partner is insured for the amount of his or her interest, and either the partnership or the other partners own the insurance. Upon the first death among the partners, the life insurance proceeds are used by the partnership or the partners, as the case may be, to purchase the deceased's interest. Thus, the business continues in operation for the benefit of the surviving partners, and the deceased's heirs receive the going value of his or her business interest in cash.

All parties benefit by the arrangement. After the first death, the surviving partners can enter into a new buy-sell agreement, or they can continue under the original agreement with the necessary valuation and insurance adjustments. Life insurance is uniquely suited to financing such agreements since the very event that creates the need for cash also provides the cash.

The same sort of agreement is

Objectives of Buy-Sell Agreements

- Provide for transfer of deceased person's ownership interest.
- Establish an agreed-upon method of valuing the interest.
- Facilitate the continuation of the business despite the termination of the deceased person's participation and ownership.
- Establish the desired method of financing the ownership interest transfer(s).
- Provide an equitable method for terminating the interest of nonparticipating heirs.

desirable for the stockholders in a closely held corporation. Although the death of a stockholder does not legally dissolve the corporation, the same practical difficulties may be encountered in any attempt to continue the business. These difficulties arise because stockholders of a closely held corporation are also its officers, earnings are distributed primarily in the form of salaries, and no ready market exists for the stock.

Upon the death of a principal stockholder in a closely held corporation, the surviving stockholders are faced with three choices (apart from liquidation), all of which may prove undesirable: (1) to accept the widow(er) or other adult heir of the deceased into the active management of the corporation, (2) to pay dividends, approximately equivalent to the salary of the deceased stockholder, to the widow(er) or other heir without any participation in management on the heir's part, or (3) to admit outside interests to whom the deceased's stock may have been sold into active management of the company. The surviving spouse faces the possibility of having to dispose of the deceased's stock at a sacrifice price, either to the surviving stockholders or to outsiders, neither of whom would normally be inclined to offer a fair price, or of retaining the stock and receiving no dividends. These difficulties can be avoided through a binding buy-sell agreement financed by life insurance. Under such an agreement, the surviving stockholders will get the corporation's stock, and the widow(er) will receive cash for a speculative business interest.

Similar agreements can be arranged between a sole proprietor and one or more key employees. Life insurance can provide at least a portion of the purchase price, and the remainder can be financed by interest-bearing notes to be paid from the business's earnings after the proprietor's death.

Benefits of the Buy-Sell Agreement

Although contemplating death is not pleasant for anyone, proper estate planning employing a buy-sell agreement offers several advantages. The benefits of such an agreement can be summarized as follows:

- It guarantees a market for the business interest.
- It provides liquidity for the payment of death taxes and other estate settlement costs.
- It helps establish the estate tax value of the decedent's business interest, making the estate planning process more reliable for the owner.

- It provides that the business will continue in the hands of the surviving owners and/or employees.
- It makes the business a better credit risk as its probability of continuation is enhanced.

Basic Structure of a Buy-Sell Agreement

A properly designed buy-sell agreement has several provisions that will generally be included regardless of the type of agreement. The parties to a buy-sell agreement should be aware that the agreement is an important legal contract that carries out a critical purpose. The parties are advised to obtain competent legal counsel to assist in forming the agreement. Provisions of the typical buy-sell agreement include the following:

- *parties to the agreement.* All buy-sell agreements contain a provision that clearly identifies the various parties.
- *purpose of the agreement.* A buy-sell agreement should contain a statement indicating its purpose. One advantage of incorporating a statement of purpose is to document the intent of the agreement should a dispute arise later.
- *commitment of the parties.* The obligation of all parties to the agreement should be clearly stated. For example, it should be clear that the estate of the deceased business owner will sell the business interest to the parties who become purchasers under the terms of the agreement.
- *description of the business interest.* The agreement should clearly describe the business interest that is actually to be bought and sold.
- *lifetime transfer restrictions.* Most buy-sell agreements contain a first-offer provision preventing the parties to the agreement from disposing of the business interest to outsiders while the parties are living.
- *purchase price.* The buy-sell agreement should specify a purchase price or, in the alternative, a method for determining the purchase price at which the business interest will be bought and sold.
- *funding provisions.* The terms of the agreement should specify how the purchase price will be funded. For example, if the agreement is funded with life insurance, the agreement should indicate how such life insurance will be structured and funded.

- *details of the transfer.* The actual specifics of the transfer of the business should be described. For example, when and where settlement will occur are important terms of the agreement.
- *modification or termination of the agreement.* The agreement should provide for its modification or termination should all parties decide that the agreement in its current form no longer meets their goals.

Sole Proprietorship Continuation Agreements

The sole proprietorship is by far the most common form of business ownership. It is distinct from other forms of business ownership in many ways. Most important, there is no legal distinction between the business and personal assets of the owner. Only one individual can be the owner of a sole proprietorship. As such, when the sole proprietor dies or loses legal capacity to transact business, the sole proprietorship must terminate. Planning for this contingency is essential if the sole proprietor's family can expect to get full value for the business interest. The buy-sell agreement will bind the proprietor's estate to sell and the purchaser to buy the proprietorship assets.

Choosing a Purchaser—A critical step for a proprietorship buy-sell agreement is to find the appropriate purchaser. A natural successor to the sole proprietor may not exist. There are no co-owners of the sole proprietorship waiting to take over, and the sole proprietor may have no family successors who are capable and/or willing to step in at the sole proprietor's death. Choosing the appropriate buyer requires careful planning.

Often a key employee or group will be selected as purchaser. Such individuals, if available, are logical choices for two reasons:

- First, the key employee or employees of the sole proprietorship are familiar with the business interest. This is particularly important if the business requires unique skills to perform its function.
- Second, the key employees may be willing to enter into a buy-sell agreement to protect their own future employment. Without a buy-sell agreement, the sole proprietorship will often be liquidated or sold to outsiders at the death of the proprietor. This could leave the key employees unemployed and without a future in the proprietorship.

If there are no key employees or natural successors to the sole proprietor, a careful search will have to be made. It is often recommended that the sole proprietor hire and provide a training program for an employee who has the potential to take over the business. Or the sole proprietor could seek a buyer from competitors who may desire to take over the proprietor's business at some point in the future. This is particularly appropriate for a professional practitioner who has developed substantial goodwill and a large patient/client list. The death of the sole practitioner will result in the loss of that goodwill unless a purchaser can be found for a buy-sell agreement.

Life Insurance Funding—The life insurance arrangements for a sole proprietorship buy-sell agreement are relatively simple. The purchasing party is obligated to provide sale proceeds to the deceased proprietor's estate. Accordingly, the applicant, owner, and premium payer for such life insurance should be the purchasing party. The purchaser should obtain sufficient coverage on the life of the sole proprietorship to make the required payments to the estate. Insurable interest exists for such a policy because the purchaser has a financial obligation created by the buy-sell agreement. The insurance funding the agreement should be reviewed periodically, and the purchaser should obtain additional coverage necessitated by an increase in the value of the proprietorship.

Buy-Sell Agreements for Partnerships

A general partnership terminates by operation of law at the death of the partner unless the partnership agreement provides for continuation. Without lifetime planning a deceased partner's interest in the partnership will have to be liquidated by the surviving partner(s). The goal of the surviving partners is to continue the business of the partnership without interruption. Certainly, they would like to keep liquidation payments to a minimum. Therefore the surviving partners' goals are incongruent with those of the deceased partner's estate. Without a prearranged agreement, a dispute between the heirs and the surviving partners is nearly inevitable. The estate may be compelled to settle for far less than the fair market value of the business. If the surviving partners cannot make the required payments, the partnership may have to be sold or terminated—a result that generally benefits neither the heirs nor the surviving partners. The solution is a binding partnership buy-sell agreement.

Since there is more than one owner, the partnership buy-sell agreement must address the possibility that any of the partners will be the next to die. Therefore the partnership buy-sell agreement contains mutual promises between the partners that provide for different purchasers and sellers depending on the circumstances. Each partner will bind his or her estate to sell if he or she is the first to die. Each partner will also agree to purchase the partnership interest held by the deceased partner's estate if he or she is among the surviving partners.

Types of Partnership Buy-Sell Agreements

Entity Approach—Under the entity approach, the partnership is the purchaser in the buy-sell agreement. Technically, the partnership *liquidates* the interest held by the deceased partner's estate. Liquidation payments are divided into two components. The first component is a payment in exchange for the decedent's partnership interest. These payments are subject to capital-gain tax treatment. The remaining payments are ordinary income items that are taxable on the estate's income tax return, such as the deceased partner's share of partnership income and unrealized receivables. Under an entity buy-sell agreement both the partners and partnership are parties to the agreement providing for continuation of the partnership's business by the survivors.

Cross-Purchase Agreements—The cross-purchase agreement provides that the surviving partners are obligated to buy a prearranged share of a deceased partner's interest from his or her estate. The agreement is generally funded by life insurance policies owned by the individual partners. Each partner should purchase life insurance policies on the life of the other partners whose deaths will obligate the policyowner to purchase the decedent's partnership interest. Thus the individual partners become owners, beneficiaries, and premium payers for life insurance policies covering the lives of the other partners. At the death of a partner, the surviving partners receive the death proceeds from the policies, which will be transferred to the deceased partner's estate in exchange for the partnership interest. Each partner should secure a policy with a death benefit equal to his or her share of the purchase price of a deceased partner's interest.

Although the surviving partners purchase the interest from a deceased partner's estate, the tax treatment of the purchase and sale is similar, but not identical to, the entity approach. That is, some portion of the purchase price will be treated as the exchange of a capital asset—the partnership interest. The remaining portion of the purchase payments will be treated as distributions of income to the deceased partner's estate.

The choice between the entity or cross-purchase approach is a complex one. Details such as the number of partners, the differences in income tax treatment, the cost basis of the different partners, and the financial considerations of the partnership will dictate the appropriate choice. A partnership should not enter into a buy-sell agreement without careful consideration and planning with respect to the form of the agreement.

Generally the partnership should adopt the entity approach if it is in a better financial position to make the premium payments than the individual partners. This will be particularly true if some partners are younger and/or own smaller partnership interests. The partnership ownership of life insurance creates a pooling approach to fund the buy-sell agreement. The business might also adopt the entity approach if there are a large number of partners entering into the agreement. Fewer individual life insurance policies are usually required if the partnership has more than two partners.

Corporate Buy-Sell Agreements

A corporation is a separate legal entity apart from its shareholders. As such, it provides limited liability to its investors and is a separate taxpayer with entirely different tax rates and rules than those applicable to individual taxpayers. Although the corporation as a separate entity has, potentially, a perpetual life, the continuation problems that plague other forms of closely held enterprises often apply to closely held corporations as well. From a practical standpoint, a closely held business, regardless of its form, cannot continue without the services of at least one key individual. In a closely held corporation, the key individual or individuals usually include the shareholders. The death, retirement, or disability of these key individuals threatens the future of the corporation. For this reason, the closely held corporation and its shareholders should consider adopting a buy-sell agreement.

Types of Corporate Buy-Sell Agreements

Entity (Stock Redemption) Buy-Sell Agreement—Under a stock-redemption agreement the corporation is the "purchaser" of the stock at the death of a shareholder. Each shareholder subject to the agreement binds his or her estate to transfer the stock to the corporation in exchange for the required purchase price. The corporation redeems a deceased shareholder's stock in exchange for a redemption distribution, and either retires the stock or holds it as treasury stock. This reduces the number of shares of stock outstanding in the corporation. From the surviving shareholder's standpoint, the percentage ownership held by each surviving shareholder increases proportionately when a deceased shareholder's stock is redeemed.

The tax treatment of a stock redemption can be extremely complex. A stock redemption is treated as a distribution of cash or property from the corporation to a shareholder. Under some circumstances, the redemption distribution is treated as a taxable dividend to the redeemed shareholder. Under other circumstances, a redemption is treated as a sale or exchange subject to capital gains. It is essential to qualify the stock redemption as a sale or exchange to avoid disastrous tax consequences to the redeemed shareholder's estate. Generally speaking, a stock-redemption plan will not qualify for the desired sale-or-exchange treatment if family members of the decedent own stock in the corporation and plan to be the decedent's successors in the corporation.

Another tax problem associated with the stock-redemption agreement is the loss of income tax cost basis for the surviving shareholders. Since the corporation is the purchaser in the stock-redemption agreement, the surviving shareholders will not be treated as contributors to the purchase. Thus the surviving shareholders will not receive an increase in their income tax basis in their stock since the corporation, not the shareholders, provides the purchase price.

If life insurance is chosen as the agreement's funding mechanism, the corporation should be the applicant, owner, and beneficiary of the policies. Ownership of the policies is particularly important for a corporation that does not have an abundance of retained earnings. Under most state corporate laws, a corporation cannot make a distribution of any kind to a shareholder, including a stock redemption, unless the corporation has adequate surplus. The receipt of life insurance proceeds at a shareholder's death provides the necessary surplus to redeem the deceased shareholder's stock. Therefore the corporation should acquire life insurance on the life of each shareholder who becomes a party to the agreement. To ensure that the death proceeds will be adequate to meet the corporation's obligation, the stock-redemption agreement should be updated periodically to prevent the face amounts of life insurance coverage from becoming inadequate as the value of the corporation rises.

Corporate Cross-Purchase Buy-Sell Agreements—The corporate cross-purchase agreement is analogous to the partnership cross-purchase agreement discussed earlier. Each shareholder agrees to purchase a specified percentage of the shares of stock held by a deceased shareholder at the time of death, and also agrees to bind his or her estate to sell the stock owned at his or her death. The corporation is not a direct party to the buy-sell agreement. The corporation should, however, issue stock certificates endorsed with a statement that the stock is subject to the terms of the buy-sell agreement.

If few shareholders are involved, the cross-purchase agreement is advantageous from a tax standpoint in two respects. First, the sale of stock by a deceased shareholder's estate will always be treated as a sale or exchange. Thus the estate gets favorable capital gains tax treatment. This makes the cross-purchase agreement the preferable form of buy-sell agreement for a family corporation where a stock redemption would often result in taxable dividends to the estate. Second, the surviving shareholders are direct purchasers, and each receives an income tax cost basis in his or her stock equal to the amount of the purchase price paid.

If life insurance is the chosen funding mechanism for the agreement, each shareholder should purchase adequate life insurance on the life of the other shareholders. Each individual shareholder then becomes owner, beneficiary, premium payer, and beneficiary for the life insurance policies covering the lives of the other shareholders. At a shareholder's death the surviving shareholders will receive the death benefits from the policies and will transfer the death benefit proceeds to the deceased shareholder's estate in exchange for the appropriate amount of his or her stock. Since individual shareholders must be relied upon to maintain the funding for agreement, there is often the concern that some parties will not live up to the terms of the contract. To ensure that the cross-purchase agreement is carried out, a trustee is often used as an overseer to hold the policies and consummate the purchase and sale of stock at a shareholder's death.

Buy-Sell Agreements for S Corporations

For federal income tax reasons, many corporations make a special election to receive S corporation status. This election is particularly favorable for shareholders who desire a direct pass-through of tax items (taxable income, deductions, and so forth) directly to the individual shareholders. The S corporation generally pays no tax at the corporate level, and shareholders are taxed similarly, although certainly not identically, to partners of a partnership. The reader should be aware of the growing importance of S corporations and the special factors that need to be considered for continuation planning for such entities.

Preserving the S Election through Buy-Sell Agreements— Shareholders make the S corporation election for important tax reasons. It is imperative that they preserve this election to avoid adverse tax consequences. For this reason, continuation planning is particularly important for an S corporation. Actions that cause the S corporation to fail to meet the requirements for S status will cause termination of the S election. Unless the IRS deems the termination inadvertent, a future S election will be unavailable for 5 years.

Only certain corporations are eligible for S elections. A corporation is ineligible for S status if it has

- more than 75 shareholders
- shareholders who are corporations, partnerships, nonresident aliens, or ineligible trusts
- more than one class of stock
- ownership in a subsidiary corporation

A mandatory buy-sell agreement operative on the death of an S corporation shareholder can prevent the transfer of such stock to ineligible shareholders. Either the standard stock-redemption or cross-purchase agreement will cause the deceased S corporation shareholder's stock to be held by the entity or individuals who already qualify for the S election. Thus an effective buy-sell agreement for an S corporation prevents the termination of the S election by transfer to an ineligible shareholder. As with other buy-sell agreements, the provisions of the S corporation buy-sell agreement should be binding and enforceable on all parties.

Tax Treatment of the S Corporation Buy-Sell Agreement—Generally speaking, the cross-purchase arrangement will not change the tax implications of an S corporation buy-sell agreement. Since the entity is not involved in the agreement, the unusual tax characteristics of S corporations will not apply. Should a stock redemption agreement be adopted by the S corporation, the tax implications are distinctly different from those applicable to normal corporate stock-redemption agreements. The S corporation has its own unique tax accounting system for determining the reporting of tax items affecting the corporation. Generally, all income received by the S corporation will be reported proportionally by the shareholders of the S corporation on their individual income-tax returns. A stock-redemption agreement for the S corporation will normally be funded by policies owned by and payable to the corporation. Since such life insurance is an after-tax expense, the policies funding this stock redemption agreement will be paid for by dollars taxable to the individual shareholders. Thus, similar to a partnership entity buy-sell agreement, the S corporation shareholders pay for the funding of a stock redemption agreement in proportion to their ownership in the corporation. Finally, accounting rules that record the retained earnings of the S corporation are particularly complex. These accounting rules affect every aspect of the S corporation's participation in a stock-redemption plan.

Chapter Four Review

Key terms and concepts are explained in the glossary. Answers to the review questions and the self-test questions follow the Glossary.

Key Terms and Concepts

group term life insurance (Sec. 79)
executive bonus (Sec. 162)
group term carve out
split-dollar life insurance
endorsement method
collateral assignment method
equity split-dollar
economic benefit regime
loan regime
split-dollar rollout
Table 2001
rabbi trust
qualified terminal interest property (QTIP)

PS 58 Table
transfer-for-value
incidence-of-ownership
gift tax-future and present interest
ERISA
Sarbanes-Oxley Act
nonqualified deferred compensation
key person life insurance
buy-sell agreement
entity plan
cross-purchase plan
stock redemption plan
irrevocable life insurance trust

Review Questions

4-1. Identify the expenses commonly associated with a family breadwinner's death.

4-2. Identify the most common ongoing needs for funds to support surviving family members.

4-3. Explain why trusts are often used in providing for the support of surviving dependents.

4-4. Identify how life insurance can provide and protect retirement income.

4-5. Explain how life insurance can be used to make charitable donations or specific bequests.

4-6. Explain briefly the business uses for life insurance.

4-7. Briefly describe the tax and nondiscrimination rules for group term life insurance.

4-8.   Explain the executive bonus (Sec. 162) life insurance plan and its advantages.

4-9.   Explain the major components of split-dollar life insurance, how it is taxed, and how life insurance is used in these plans.

4-10. Explain how life insurance can be used in qualified retirement plans.

4-11. Explain the major features of deferred compensation plans and how life insurance is used in these plans.

4-12. Explain the need for key person life insurance and how this insurance plan works.

4-13. Explain the general needs for a buy-sell agreement, and the types of buy-sell plans that can be used for business continuation.

Self-Test Questions

Instructions: Read chapter 4 first, then answer the following questions to test your knowledge. There are 10 questions; circle the correct answer, then check your answers with the answer key in the back of the book.

4-1.   Which of the following statements concerning the surviving partners at the death of a partner is correct?

(A)   They must appoint trustees to liquidate the partnership assets.
(B)   They have a fiduciary responsibility to the deceased partner's estate and heirs.
(C)   They must continue to operate the partnership to maximize profits during estate administration.
(D)   They may enhance their own business careers because they can use the goodwill attached to the deceased partner's name.

4-2.   Which of the following statements concerning executive bonus (Sec. 162) life insurance plans is correct?

(A)   The plans must comply with the nondiscrimination rules of ERISA.
(B)   The participating employee is the owner of the policy covering his or her life.
(C)   The employer contributions to the plan are tax free to the participating employee.
(D)   The employer contributions are nondeductible because the death proceeds are received tax free.

4-3. Which of the following statements concerning key employee life insurance is correct?

(A) The key employee should name the beneficiary.
(B) The premiums paid by the employer are taxable income to the employee.
(C) The proceeds of the key employee policy are included in the estate of the key employee.
(D) The business should be the owner and beneficiary of the key employee life insurance.

4-4. Three partners have an equal 1/3 interest in a partnership valued at $1.2 million. If a cross-purchase type of buy-sell agreement is selected, how much coverage should each partner have on the life of the other partners?

(A) $200,000
(B) $300,000
(C) $400,000
(D) $600,000

4-5. The taxable amounts of coverage for group term life insurance are taxed according to

(A) PS 58 rates
(B) Table 2001 rates
(C) Table 1 rates
(D) Sec. 162 rates

4-6. Which of the following statements concerning dependent income needs is (are) true?

I. A child's dependency may continue beyond the death of both parents.
II. Trusts can be set up to protect children for their entire life.

(A) I only
(B) II only
(C) Both I and II
(D) Neither I nor II

4-7. Which of the following statements regarding life insurance death benefits is (are) correct?

   I. There may be delays in paying the death benefit if the policy is still contestable.
  II. Life insurance benefits payable directly to the beneficiary will not be subject to delays in settling the estate.

   (A) I only
   (B) II only
   (C) Both I and II
   (D) Neither I nor II

4-8. Which of the following statements is (are) true regarding the split-dollar collateral assignment method?

   I. The employee owns the policy and is primarily responsible to the insurance company for paying the entire premium.
  II. The employer makes what are in effect interest-free and non-taxable loans in the amount of the premium that the employer has agreed to pay under the split-dollar plan.

   (A) I only
   (B) II only
   (C) I and II
   (D) Neither I nor II

4-9. All of the following statements are correct concerning deferred compensation plans EXCEPT

   (A) Part of the employee's compensation over the employee's service-providing years is deferred until a later period.
   (B) Descrimination in favor of shareholder-employees and key executives is not permitted in nonqualified arrangements.
   (C) Deferred-compensation plans can be categorized as either *qualified* or *nonqualified*.
   (D) Qualified plans include pension plans, IRAs, profit-sharing plans, and Sec. 403(b) plans.

4-10. All of the following statements concerning qualified retirement plans are correct EXCEPT

(A)   A qualified plan must generally purchase life insurance in order to provide any substantial preretirement death benefit.

(B)   An insured preretirement death benefit can be provided in either a defined-benefit or defined-contribution plan.

(C)   An employer contribution may pay life insurance premiums if the amount qualifies under the tests for *incidental benefits*.

(D)   The IRS considers non-retirement benefits in a qualified plan incidental if the cost of these benefits is less than 50 percent of the cost of providing all the benefits under the plan.

5

Comparing Costs and Policy Illustrations

Overview and Learning Objectives

Chapter 5 investigates the meaning and methods of evaluating the costs of life insurance policies, especially on the basis of comparing one against another. The chapter then looks at policy illustrations, the most common technique for explaining an abstract and intangible financial product to a prospect. The chapter will examine illustrations in depth for the following important reasons:

- the importance and widespread use of illustrations by financial advisors in working with prospects
- the misrepresentations and other problems associated with the use of illustrations over the last few decades
- a need to understand the fine technical points in how they are constructed to eliminate these problems

By reading this chapter and answering the questions, you should be able to

5-1. List and explain the methods of comparing life insurance policies, and some strengths and weaknesses of each.

5-2 Describe the importance of interest adjustments in analyzing policy illustrations and determining the cost of a life insurance policy.

5-3. Explain the guidelines and regulations that effect the life insurance policy illustration.

5-4. Identify the issues that led to regulation of policy illustration content and organization.

5-5. Discuss the factors that affect the illustrated performance of a life insurance policy.

Chapter Outline

Methods of Comparing Life Insurance Policy Costs 3
     Net Cost Method 3
     Interest-adjusted Indexes 4
     Cash Accumulation Method of Comparison 11
     Equal Outlay Method 12
     Comparisons That Isolate Interest Rates 12
Policy Illustrations 17
     Types of Policy Illustrations 18
Guidelines and Regulations for Policy Illustrations 28
Chapter Five Review 41

Methods of Comparing Life Insurance Policy Costs

Net Cost Method

There are as many different methods of comparing life insurance policies as there are types of coverage. Historically the traditional *net cost method* has been widely used. Its procedure is quite simple, easy to calculate, understand and explain. The starting point is to specify the duration of coverage to be evaluated. Typically this is for either 10 years or 20 years, or until a specific age, such as 65. The actual mechanics of the evaluation involve taking all of the premiums paid under the policy and adding them together, then subtracting the cash surrender value for the term being considered and all dividends paid over that interval. One of the reasons this method is so easy to understand is that it does not take into account the *time value of money*. In other words, it ignores interest, which can be a significant factor in the cost of something over time. The time value of money concept focuses on when the money is paid or received and the role of interest in determining comparable financial cost and value. Without considering the time value of money, the results of this method can be misleading.

The final cost derived under net cost method can be considered the amount the insurance costs the client. The main criticism of this analysis is that after 20 years the net cost is usually negative. That is, the cash value amounts at the end of the interval, plus dividends paid over the interval, exceed the aggregate of premiums paid. The implication is that the policy owner has received insurance free of charge, and in fact made a profit on the premiums. The serious shortcoming of using this methodology is that it gives equal weight to payment amounts that may be separated by 10 or 20 years. Doing so totally ignores the opportunity costs of earnings forgone because the funds were not invested in an investment account. (See Table 5–5 at the end of this chapter).

The net cost method is not appropriate for comparing policies, whether they are the same type or different types. It is totally unacceptable under the state statutes and regulations for purposes of making replacement evaluations. In fact, under some state statutes insurance advisors are prohibited from using the net cost method. Policy illustrations and comparisons that do not take into account the effects of interest are by default making the assumption that the interest rate is zero and inflation is zero. Dollar amounts from different time periods are comparable only if money can be borrowed without cost (no interest charged) and if prices remain unchanged over time (no inflation occurred). This is obviously unrealistic and distorts the cost of a financial product that does not take interest and timing into account in its analysis of costs. This can result in a presentation that the life insurance is free or is even a good investment because the cash value eventually exceeds the total premiums paid, unless the premiums are adjusted for interest. Illustrations that include interest-adjusted figures are preferable because of their increased accuracy in the real world over unadjusted values.

Interest-adjusted Indexes

The logic of using *interest-adjusted indexes* is similar to that of the traditional net cost approach with the exception that interest-adjusted indexes explicitly take into account the time value of money. The *National Association of Insurance Commissioners (NAIC)* developed the interest-adjusted cost indexes and also derived model laws regarding their use. The NAIC is a voluntary association of state insurance regulatory officials that issues model insurance laws and regulations for state adoption to promote uniformity in the separate states.

The interest-adjusted index statutes were drafted and adopted during the 1970s prior to the high interest and inflation rates experienced in the late 1970s and early 1980s. Almost every one of the statutes mandates that the rate of interest to be used is 5 percent annually. The concern of these state statutes and regulations is not the accuracy of the interest rate in representing the actual future interest earned, but rather a need for the comparability of indexes for different policies and different companies. Indexes based on different interest rates are not directly or easily comparable. Thus, the prescribing of one interest rate results in comparison indexes that can be used without further adjustments.

The NAIC developed a Model Regulation to give consumers a way to compare the relative costs of different policies and to improve the quality of the cost information given to consumers. The *policy summary* on illustrations is required to contain two cost indexes of the issued policy. These indexes reflect the time value of money (interest) by recognizing that money is paid and received at different times and that costs can be better compared by using a specified interest assumption.

Premiums alone do not always reflect the true cost of a life insurance policy. This is especially true in permanent insurance. Naturally, the public perception is that the premium is the price of the contract, so the higher the premium, the higher the cost of the insurance within the policy. However this is also not always true.

The cost comparison methods described here apply to all life insurance policies. Where dividends are paid to the policy, usually in participating policies offered by mutual companies, there are provisions to properly account for their effect on the cost of the policy.

Actually, several factors (policy premiums, cash values, expenses and possibly dividends) determine the ultimate cost of the policy. We say "ultimate" here because until we know how long a policy will stay in force, we cannot know for certain what the final, true cost will be. The actual true cost cannot be determined until the policy ends, either through a death claim, lapse, or surrender, by looking at what actually occurred retrospectively. Although you cannot tell prospects the exact cost of the policy they bought today, there is a way of estimating fairly accurately what a policy will cost in different situations. This is done with special indexes of the annual cost per $1,000 of insurance if the insured died or surrendered the policy in a certain number of years, say, 10 or 20. That is the purpose of cost disclosure.

Surrender Cost Index

The *surrender cost index* represents the annual cost per $1,000 of life insurance if a policy is surrendered for its cash value. Unlike the net payment index, this index takes the cash value into consideration. It is most useful in comparing costs when cash accumulation is a primary concern.

Essentially, the surrender cost method takes all payments for premiums, when actually paid, and treats them as if they had been put into an interest-bearing account to accumulate interest until the end of

---

the interval for evaluation. In a like manner, all dividend payments are carried as if they are deposited in an interest-bearing account at a specific time (when they are projected to be paid), and that account balance is calculated for the end of the interval of evaluation. After all premium payments and all dividend payments have been adjusted to the end of the comparison interval, the policy cash value and accumulation dividends are subtracted from the accumulated value of all the premiums paid.

The next step is to take that future net cost and divide it by the future value of an *annuity due*, based on the specified interest rate and the period of time being evaluated. An annuity due is a series of payments of equal amounts made at the beginning of each of a number of consecutive periods. At 5-percent interest the annuity due factor to use for a 10-year evaluation period is 13.2068. Likewise, the annuity due factor to divide into the future value amount over a 20-year interval, again assuming a 5-percent interest rate, is 34.7193. The result represents the level annual cost for the policy. This will still be an aggregate amount that must be converted to a per-thousand amount, which is accomplished by dividing the level annual cost amount by the number of thousands of dollars in the policy death benefit. For example, the aggregate level annual cost for a $50,000 policy is 50 times greater than it would be for a $1,000 policy. We would therefore divide the level annual policy cost by 50 to determine the level annual cost per thousand dollars of coverage.

These future values appear on most sales presentation materials utilized by insurance advisors. For that reason there is usually no need to calculate them independently. The numbers presented will be based on the 5 percent mandated interest rate and the methods described in the statutes. The same procedures work for any other interest rate considered appropriate by the evaluating party. See Table 5-6, at the end of this chapter, for an example of a surrender cost index calculation..

Net Payment Index

The *net payment index,* sometimes called the payment cost index, represents the annual cost per $1,000 of insurance if the policy remains in force over a given period of time. It considers the amount of premiums paid, less dividends received, if any, but disregards the cash value. This index is useful in comparing costs when death benefit protection is emphasized. This is because if an insured with a permanent insurance policy died, the cash value would be included in the face amount.

Determining the net payment index is similar to calculating the surrender cost index except that there is no recognition of the end-of-period cash value. Under this calculation, dividends payable over the interval and terminable dividends at the end of period are the only items subtracted from the accumulated premium amounts. This gives a future value of net premiums that is then divided by the annuity due factor for the appropriate period and appropriate interest rate. Future values contained in advisors' sales materials are usually based on either a 10- or 20-year interval and a 5-percent annual interest rate. (See Table 5–7 for an example)

Sample Comparision—A simple example of a fictitious policy is presented in Table 5–8. In the example there is a premium of $15 per year over a 10-year interval and a dividend of $0.00 the first year and $1.00 the second year, increasing by $1.00 each year until it reaches $9.00 in the tenth policy year. The accumulation at 5 percent of all premiums paid is $198.10; the accumulation of all dividends is $54.14. Subtracting the accumulated value of dividends from the accumulated value of premiums yields a future value of net premiums equal to $143.96. Subtracting the cash value at the end of 10 years ($120) from that amount yields a future value of net cost equal to $23.96. This future net cost is then divided by the future value of an annuity due for 10 years, or 13.2068, which yields a surrender cost index of $1.814676. In the same table we can see that by ignoring the cash value, the payment cost index becomes $10.90.

Calculations under interest-adjusted indexes can be done by hand, but they are easier and quicker when done on a computer or financial calculator. Index values are sensitive to the interval being evaluated and the insured's age of issue for the policies being compared.

These cost indexes are an acceptable means of comparing similar policies. Usually the policy with the smaller numerical values for surrender cost and payment cost indexes is preferable to policies with higher index values. The method is not acceptable, however, for comparing dissimilar policies—for example, a term policy with a whole life policy. It is also not well suited for evaluating policy replacements.

Net Payment Index Computation

To compute the net payment index:

1. Accumulate the premiums at the desired interest rate (5 percent).
2. Accumulate the dividends (if applicable) at the desired interest rate (5 percent).
3. Subtract step 2 from step 1.
4. Divide step 3 by the amount to which one dollar paid each year will accumulate for the period selected (20 years) at the desired interest rate (5 percent). This amount is the future value of an annuity due factor for 20 years at 5 percent (the factor is 34.7193). The result represents the estimated level annual cost of the policy.
5. Reduce the result of step 4 to a cost per $1,000 of coverage by dividing it by the number of thousands of dollars in the policy's death benefit. The result is the estimated level annual cost per $1,000 of coverage.

Surrender Cost Index Computation

To compute the surrender cost index:

1. Accumulate the premiums at the desired interest rate (5 percent).
2. Accumulate the dividends (if applicable) at the desired interest rate (5 percent).
3. Subtract step 2 from step 1.
4. Subtract the cash value at the end of the period from step 3 and divide by the amount to which one dollar paid each year will accumulate for the period (20 years) selected at the desired interest rate (5 percent). This amount is the future value of an annuity due factor for 20 years at 5 percent (the factor is 34.7193). The result represents the estimated level annual cost of the policy.
5. Reduce the result of step 4 to a cost per $1,000 of coverage by dividing it by the number of thousands of dollars in the policy's death benefit. The result is the estimated level annual cost per $1,000 of coverage.

Notice that the steps are the same for the net payment and the surrender cost indexes, except that there is no subtraction of the 20th year cash value in the net payment cost index.

Calculation Example—In most cases, you can easily find a policy's interest-adjusted indexes on its policy summary or in commercial publications. However, the calculation procedure is illustrated here should you ever need to make the calculations yourself. You should also know how the cost indexes are calculated. By understanding this process, you can explain it to clients and help them understand what the indexes mean. Following are the calculations and, for this example, the assumptions used.

Example: Calculation Assumptions

Accumulated value of $1 per year for
20 years at 5 percent (future value of
an annuity due) $34.72

Per $1,000 Values

Annual premium...$21.00
20th year accumulation of cash value $370.00
20th year accumulation of dividends
at 5 percent $211.00

Calculation

1. Accumulation of premiums
   $21.00 x $34.72... ....$729.12

2. Accumulation of dividends*...............–$211.00
                                                              $518.12
   *Omit this step for policies that do not pay
   dividends

3. Net Payment Index:

$$\frac{\$518.12}{\$34.72} = \$14.92$$

4. Surrender Cost Index:

$$\frac{\$518.12 - \$370}{\$34.72} = \$4.27$$

Policies with net payment and surrender costs indexes lower than these would probably be better buys. Policies with higher index figures would probably be less favorable buys, all other things being equal.

A simple way to explain these indexes to your prospect or client is to treat the policy's premium as being split into three parts: the dividend, the cash value, and the company's share. Even though the premium remains level throughout the life of the policy, the size of these three parts varies through the years. In the early years, dividends and cash value accumulations are small and the company's share large, but as time passes, dividends and cash values increase and the company's share decreases.

Assume that the annual premium of $21 per thousand can be broken down into the average dividend of $6.08, the average cash value increment—coming directly from the premium, not from earned interest—of $10.65, and the average company share of $4.27. These averages take into consideration the time value of money.

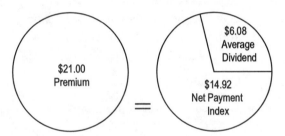

Subtracting the average dividend from the premium leaves the net payment index of $14.92. This is the policyholder's average yearly cost, assuming the policy is still in force 20 years from date of issue.

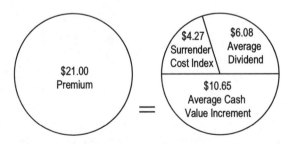

Subtracting the average dividend and the average cash value increment from the premium leaves the surrender cost index of $4.27.

This is the yearly cost—that portion of the premium the policy owner does not get back—assuming that the policy is surrendered for its cash value in the 20th year.

Equivalent Level Annual Dividend

A third index that might appear on the policy summary is the equivalent level annual dividend. This is a measure of the part that dividends play in the cost of a participating policy. This index—which is labeled the average dividend in the diagram we just illustrated—is an average of the total dividends with interest over the 20 years. It is found by dividing the 20th year accumulation of dividends by the appropriate accumulation of one dollar per year factor. Referring to our previous calculation example, this index would be $6.08, found by dividing $211 by $34.72.

Cash Accumulation Method of Comparison

The *cash accumulation comparison method* is much more complex than either the net cost method or the interest adjusted methods and requires a computer to make the calculations. A significant amount of data must be entered into the computer program in order to calculate the results accurately. One of the strengths of this method is that it can be used to compare permanent insurance policies with term policies. It can also be used for evaluation of replacement proposals.

The technique is simply to accumulate the premium differences between the policies being compared, while holding the death benefits of both policies constant and equal. For example, to compare a whole life contract with a term contract, set the death benefits equal at the beginning of the period, and use the yearly premium differences between the whole life policy and the term policy as the amount to deposit into a side fund to accumulate at interest. The calculation is essentially a buy-term-and-invest-the-difference approach to comparing the policies. At the end of the interval being evaluated, the side fund accumulation amount can be compared to the cash value in the whole life or other form of cash value insurance policy. All other things being equal, the policy with the greater accumulation at the end of the comparison interval is considered the preferable of the two contracts. As we will discuss in the next section on policy illustrations, caution must be taken with the validity and accuracy of any illustration, based on the assumption made that create the illustration. (See Tables 5–9 to 5–13.)

Equal Outlay Method

The *equal outlay method* is somewhat similar to the cash accumulation method. The same amount of premium dollars is expended, on the one hand for a cash value contract and on the other for a term policy. The amount by which the cash value contract premiums exceed the term premiums is deposited into a side fund, and the difference in premium amounts is accumulated at specified interest rates. Then the death benefit of the term insurance plus the accumulated side fund amounts are compared with the death benefit under the cash value contract in which dividends, if any, have been used to purchase paid-up benefit amounts, and the value of those paid-up additions. Under this type of comparison, the policy producing the greater death benefit is considered the preferable contract. (See Tables 5–14 to 5–18.)

Both this method and the cash accumulation method are very sensitive to the interest rate chosen for purposes of the side fund accumulation. Manipulating the interest rate can skew the comparison results. The higher the interest rate used, the more the equal outlay method will tend to favor the lower-premium term policy with the side fund combination.

Comparisons That Isolate Interest Rates

There are three other comparison methods that all utilize an assumed cost of coverage to isolate an interest rate for comparison purposes. One of the problems of comparing any life insurance policies is that there is variability in the many factors that influence the illustration. We cannot make a single-factor comparison without choosing assumptions for the other factors, and doing this in a way that holds those factors constant. In other words, if we want to calculate a policy's internal cost of insurance, we have to make some assumptions about interest rates; if we want to calculate interest rates, we have to make some assumptions about the cost of insurance. Further complicating the comparison is the fact that different companies create different policies, and the assumptions made can differ significantly. These assumptions are proprietary company information and often companies are reluctant to share them with competitors and the public.

Comparative Interest Rate Method

The *comparative interest rate method* is really a modification of the cash accumulation method, whereby we are calculating the interest rate that would make a term insurance policy side fund exactly equal to the cash value policy's surrender value at the end of the evaluation period. The comparative interest rate method looks for the interest rate that would make the buy-term-and-invest-the-difference comparison exactly equivalent in the death benefits provided. To make that calculation both the outlays for premiums and side funds and the death benefit levels must be held equal. This method is often referred to as the *Linton yield method,* named for actuary Albert Linton, who first published the approach in the early 1900s. (See Table 5–19). Its primary drawback is the complexity of the calculation, which requires not only a computer program to accurately calculate the interest rate desired but also a large amount of policy information that must be entered into the program before it can be calculated.

Another caution with using software for this type of comparison is that each comparison should use the same assumed term premium rates to derive the interest rate. Otherwise, there will have been manipulation (intentional or unintentional) of the interest rates derived by the calculations. The policy generating the highest comparative interest rate is assumed to be the preferable policy when making comparisons by this method.

Belth Yearly Rate-of-Return Method—Joseph Belth, a retired professor of insurance and publisher of the *Insurance Forum* newsletter, developed several cost comparison approaches. This chapter presents two of them. (See Table 5–20). He is quick to point out that there is no perfect comparison method because the wide range of objectives that insurance policies address requires different levels of priority to be placed on the death benefits and cash values in different situations. Each method puts its primary emphasis on the elements considered to be the highest priorities for that particular approach.

Under the *Belth yearly rate-of-return method,* only one year of the policy is considered in making an individual calculation. Such a calculation can be made for each year of coverage over the given interval. The objective is to identify the benefits provided by the policy during that year (the end-of-year cash value plus the dividends paid during the year and the net death benefit for the policy year) and the investments in the policy necessary to derive those benefits (a combination of the beginning-of-the-year cash value and the premium paid for that year of the policy). The yearly rate-of-return formula divides the sum of the benefits by the sum of the investments and then subtracts the number one from that amount. This process is repeated for each year over the comparison interval. The policy with the highest rates of yearly return in the largest number of years over the observation interval is considered the preferable policy. The calculation under the Belth yearly rate-of-return method depends on a realistic assumed term rate, not a manipulated rate that is (intentionally) so high or low that it skews the results. This method does not necessarily make it easy to identify a predominant policy. The highest yearly rate of return may change back and forth among the policies being compared.

Belth Yearly Price-of-Protection Method—Under the *Belth yearly price method* we must assume an investment or interest rate and thereby calculate the cost of protection. Again, the calculations are made one year at a time for each of the years in the comparison interval (usually 10 or 20 years as in most other comparison methods). Using this method, the beginning cash value plus the current premium are accumulated at the assumed rate of interest to derive a theoretical year-end surrender value. After computing the theoretical end-of-year value from the beginning cash value and the premium plus interest, we subtract the actual end-of-year cash value plus dividends paid during the year. This is the difference assumed to have been available to pay mortality charges.

$$\text{Cost per \$1,000} = \frac{(P + CVP) \times (1 + i) - (CSV + D)}{(F - CSV) \times (0.001)}$$

$$
\begin{aligned}
P &= \text{Premium} \\
CVP &= \text{Cash surrender value previous year} \\
i &= \text{Net after-tax interest rate} \\
CSV &= \text{Cash surrender value current year} \\
D &= \text{Dividend current year} \\
F &= \text{Face amount of coverage}
\end{aligned}
$$

The next step is to divide the difference between theoretical year-end values and actual year-end values plus dividends by the amount at risk per $1,000 of coverage. The actual formula looks quite formidable, but when its terms are defined, it is really quite simple and straightforward.

After making a yearly price-of-protection calculation for each policy being compared for each year in the comparison interval, it is then a matter of identifying the policy with the lowest cost of protection for the largest number of years over that interval. In most cases that policy would be the preferable one of those under consideration. The benchmark prices derived by Professor Belth (see table 5–1 below) are based on United States population data, rather than on insured lives data, and represent a relatively high cost of providing death benefits only; there is no allowance for company overhead or operations.

In most cases term rates for standard-issue policies to people in good health will be below these benchmark prices, which are only a crude yardstick and should not be used as the criterion for automatically rejecting a policy. These benchmark prices would have no validity at all for evaluating rates on policies issued or proposed to persons in poor health who are charged associated higher premiums. Such premiums might legitimately be multiples of the benchmark prices.

Both Belth methods of policy comparison are appropriately used for comparing similar and dissimilar policies. With some modification these methods are even appropriate for comparing replacement evaluations. Part of their attractiveness is their simplicity and their ability to be calculated without the need of a computer.

TABLE 5–1
Joseph Belth's Benchmark Prices of Insurance

Age	Price
Under Age 30	$ 1.50
30–34	2.00
35–39	3.00
40–44	4.00
45–49	6.50
50–54	10.00
55–54	15.00
60–64	25.00
65–69	35.00
70–74	50.00
75–79	80.00
80–84	125.000

Policy Illustrations

Life insurance sales usually rely on multiple-year and multiple page policy illustrations. Life insurance illustrations are typically used in the sales/planning process to show the prospective client how a life insurance policy works. They display the key policy values: the premium, guaranteed cash values, and guaranteed death benefits. Illustrations may also show hypothetical values based on certain performance assumptions such as interest rates, mortality charges, or dividend scales. This can be especially problematic when the cash value accumulation is based on variable interest rates or the value of underlying investments, or where alternative premium payment arrangements are being proposed.

Individuals do not always understand the differences between guaranteed and illustrative (hypothetical or current) values typically found in life insurance policy illustrations. If the differences are not clearly explained, a prospective client can easily be mislead into believing that the policy promises significantly greater values than those guaranteed in the contract. Allowing this misconception to exist, or actually fostering it, is a serious form of misrepresentation. In recent years more emphasis has been placed on proper formats of illustrations and a clear distinction of what is guaranteed in the contract and what is not by insurance regulators and insurers. As a result of the NAIC Life Insurance Illustrations Model Regulations (discussed later) insurers and state insurance departments require a full illustration, including all footnotes and explanation pages, of a product purchased by an individual to be signed by the prospect. The signature indicates that the prospect has read and understands the guaranteed and non-guaranteed elements in the illustration.

The full explanation of the illustration is especially important when focusing on the projected cash values, dividends or interest accumulations in the future. It is critical to show the client that the premium will still be required if the illustrated values are not achieved. Lower credited interest rates or dividends, and increases in administrative expense or mortality charges can all negatively affect the illustrated cash values.

The life insurance policy illustration is a tool designed to assist the advisor explain an intangible, abstract, and in many cases highly complex and sophisticated financial product. In the past few decades, with the advent of the personal computer and financial software, many advisors have turned to "illustration" selling. This involves selling the appealing numerical values on the printed illustration, rather than conducting a fundamental financial planning process, uncovering the client's needs based on sound fact-finding, and designing real solutions to real financial problems and concerns. The temptation to leave these preferred procedures behind and dwell on the columns of numbers must be avoided.

As will be discussed in detail later in this section, it is important to keep in mind that the policy illustration is based on a variety of assumptions, which may or may not occur in the future. It is an estimate of what may happen based on projections of past performance and interpretations of what may happen in the future. Although some of these projections may be accurate some of the time, the chance that all of these factors will interact consistently as proposed is almost impossible. In fact, the only real thing we can guarantee about a policy illustration is that what is projected will most likely not happen.

Types of Policy Illustrations

There are many, almost unlimited, types of policy illustrations. The simplest types merely show how much will have to be paid out-of-pocket to keep the policy in force. These illustrations will show premiums due, dividends projected, guaranteed cash value, and death-benefit values. Policy illustrations may show increasing death benefits based on the application of policy dividends to purchase paid-up, additional insurance. The use of dividends to purchase one-year term insurance, for example, is another type of illustration one might create to increase the policy death benefit without altering the policy. These simple illustrations can increase in sophistication to include complex combinations of term and permanent coverages, sometimes using policy cash values or dividends as funding.

Policy illustrations or ledger sheets usually cover at least 10 years of data and often cover 15 or 20 years. The years are usually presented in a single column of such an illustration, with the figures in this column referring to the number of years after the date of policy issue. Some illustrations present both the year column and an attained-age column in order to show the age of the insured at each displayed policy year. There are, however, some illustrations that present only the attained-age information and do not present the years of duration since policy issue. Presentation of only one of these columns is not a serious omission because the omitted column can be derived from the column that is included in the illustration. The one convention that is very frequently followed is to represent separate years on separate rows of the policy illustration. Each column generally represents a separate category of data such as age, premium, cash value, loan, death benefit, and so forth.

Policy illustrations can get very complex. The more complex illustrations can include techniques using policy loans, such as minimum-deposit, or withdrawing money from the policy for a variety of other purposes. Minimum deposit illustrations show how policy cash values can be used to pay policy premiums. Policy loans, dividend surrenders and cash value withdrawals (sometimes used for premium financing and funding of other financial objectives such educational, retirement or other needs) may be forecast. Additional premiums can be shown to serve a number of purposes, such as paying for additional benefits, potentially shortening the premium-paying period, or accumulating additional funds for future needs. These illustrations would typically include additional columns of numbers, showing loan amounts, loan interest, net cash values and death benefits.

Policy illustrations that have more than four columns of values often derive some of their data from information that is not provided in the illustration. The relationship between columns is sometimes defined in the footnotes to the policy illustration, but often the relationships between columns are only partially described, if at all.

Split dollar, executive bonus and other applications used for primarily business purposes incorporate the effects of marginal tax rates between the business and the business executives to show the after-tax cost of policies. Knowledge of the federal income tax system, as well as the concept behind the illustration, is necessary to interpret and present these illustrations, which can be quite complicated when they contain large amounts of numbers.

Policy comparisons, especially of term and whole life insurance, using the techniques discussed earlier in this chapter such as the cash accumulation method, compare a large amount of information regarding the costs of different policies. The cash accumulation method of illustration typically compares cash values and death benefits of whole life insurance with term insurance and a side fund investing the difference of premium at some assumed interest rate.

Lastly, some of the newer policies, such as universal and variable life and their variations, show performance under several different assumptions concerning mortality and expense charges, investment or interest earnings, and guaranteed and non-guaranteed values, which creates many columns and variations to consider.

In the last 10 years or so, many policy owners have been dissatisfied with policy performance and disappointed by policy illustrations that were vague, incomplete, and even misleading. As a result, state regulators and company compliance departments have instituted numerous requirements for illustrations that have expanded the policy illustration into a lengthy document. Explanations, caveats, definitions and page after page of numeric tables are now required on illustrations. The policy owner must also sign to indicate receipt of the illustration. These issues will be discussed later in the chapter.

Simple Illustrations—The Participating Policy

The following is an example of one of the simpler illustrations showing only policy year, gross annual premium, dividends, and net premium after dividends. This is an illustration of using dividends to reduce premiums. Policy Illustration 1 ($50,000 Graded Premium Paid-Up at Age 95 Policy) in Table 5-2 does not even present the cash values for the policy. Today these types of illustrations are known as supplemental illustrations, and must be shown with a complete illustration following state laws and company regulations.

There are some shortcomings with even this simple type of illustration. The summation of premium payments from the different years is improper unless the values are adjusted by an interest factor to make them comparable, as discussed earlier in this chapter. In fact, it is inappropriate to combine any dollar amounts from different time periods unless they are adjusted for interest.

It is appropriate to add or subtract values from the same time period. In the example, the dividends are deducted from the gross premium due in the same period to correctly determine the net premium due. These net-premium-due values can all be adjusted for interest to determine what beginning balance would be needed in an interest-bearing account to pay all of the net-premium-due amounts as they become payable. This adjusted amount is the present value of all 20 net-premium payments. When a 5-percent interest rate is used, the present value of the net premiums due is $2,273. In other words, an account with a present balance of $2,273, earning 5-percent interest, would be sufficient to pay all 20 premiums because the interest earnings of $1,484 plus the starting fund balance would cover the aggregate payments of $3,757.

Another way of adjusting payments from different time periods is to calculate the accumulated values, adjusting all payments to the end of the selected time period, as was done earlier in this chapter with the interest-adjusted indexes. The same result is obtained by depositing each net premium due into an interest-bearing account and letting the interest accumulate in the account. The balance in the account at the end of the period is the accumulated value for the specified interest rate, time period, and payments. This accumulated value for the example in policy illustration 1, based on 5 percent interest for the full 20 years, is $6,032. This value may be thought of as an opportunity cost of the premium payments. The policy owner is giving up the equivalent of the accumulated value that could have been invested had it not been allocated to life insurance premiums.

Obviously, the particular interest rate used has a strong influence on the adjusted present values and accumulated values. There is an inverse relationship between the interest rate and the resultant present values. That is, higher interest rates result in lower present values, and lower interest rates produce higher present-value amounts. To illustrate this point, reconsider the present value given above. The value was $2,273 when based on 5 percent interest. The calculated present value of the same premiums was $1,524 based on 10 percent interest. Similarly, the accumulated value of those 20 net premiums was $6,032 when based on 5 percent interest, but would have had an accumulated value of $10,252 if it had been based on 10 percent interest. This demonstrates the direct relationship between interest rates and accumulated values. Higher interest rates produce higher accumulated values and lower interest rates produce lower accumulated values.

The choice of the proper interest rate is both important and difficult. The difficulty arises from the fact that the rate chosen should represent actual after-tax investment rates of return for the particular policy owner over the selected future period. Any attempt to represent unknown future interest rates is necessarily an estimate or a guess. It is important to select an interest rate that is a relatively accurate representation of actual rates over the period because slight changes in the interest rate result in significant changes of the present values and accumulated values being calculated and compared.

TABLE 5-2
Policy Illustration 1

$50,000 Graded Premium Paid-Up at Age 95 Policy
Insured: Female, Aged 32   Initial Annual Premium: $170

Year	Gross Annual Premium	Dividend Used to Reduce Premiums	Premium Due
1	$ 170	$ 0	$ 170
2	170	50	120
3	175	52	123
4	180	53	127
5	185	53	132
	880	208	672
6	190	54	136
7	195	55	140
8	200	56	144
9	205	57	148
10	215	58	157
	1,885	488	1,397
11	230	59	171
12	245	60	185
13	260	61	199
14	275	65	210
15	295	70	225
	3,190	803	2,387
16	315	75	240
17	340	80	260
18	360	90	270
19	390	100	290
20	420	110	310
	$5,015	$1,258	$3,757

Dividends shown are not guarantees of future dividends. They are merely based on the current level of dividends, which may change in the future.

Combination Coverage

Policy illustration 2 in Table 5-3 is an example showing policy dividends used to purchase additional coverage. The basic policy is for $18,000 of whole life insurance, supplemented with additional term insurance and paid-up coverage purchased with dividends. The term insurance decreases each year as the paid-up insurance increases. The amount of term insurance equals the net amount at risk between the target face amount of $25,000 and the base whole life policy. Eventually the term insurance is totally replaced by paid-up additions. There are no figures in the illustration to indicate the level of the policy dividends, but there is a footnote indicating that the dividend levels assumed for the calculation are not guaranteed.

TABLE 5-3
Policy Illustration 2

Combination of Whole Life
and Additional Coverage Purchased with Policy Dividends

Whole Life	$18,000	
Additional Coverage	7,000	Insured: Female, Aged 40
Death Benefit	$25,000	Annual Premium: $320

Year	Gross Annual Premium	Total Paid-Up Value	Guaranteed Cash Value End of Year	Enhance-ment Reserve Fund	Total Cash Value End of Year	Total Cash Value Increase End of Year	CV Increase Less Net Payment
1	$ 320	$ 0	$ 0	$ 0	$ 0	$ 0	$ –320
2	320	285	101	0	101	101	–219
3	320	1,098	402	0	402	301	–19
4	320	1,863	704	0	704	302	–18
5	320	2,577	1,005	0	1,005	301	–19
6	320	3,291	1,324	0	1,324	319	–1
7	320	3,958	1,642	0	1,642	318	–2
8	320	4,583	1,960	0	1,960	318	–2
9	320	5,226	2,296	7	2,303	343	23
10	320	5,926	2,647	44	2,691	388	68
11	320	6,570	2,983	90	3,073	382	62
12	320	7,228	3,334	146	3,480	407	87
13	320	7,907	3,703	215	3,918	438	118
14	320	8,569	4,072	296	4,368	450	130
15	320	9,214	4,440	391	4,831	463	143
16	320	9,846	4,809	498	5,307	476	156
17	320	10,494	5,194	619	5,813	506	186
18	320	11,131	5,580	755	6,335	522	202
19	320	11,755	5,965	905	6,870	535	215
20	320	12,398	6,367	1,072	7,439	569	249
	$ 6,400					$ 7,439	$ 1,039

The current dividend scale is expected to continue, and it is now adequate to provide the needed $7,000 of benefits as term insurance for the first 8 policy years, then as whole life additions. The dividends are not guaranteed.

The first column lists the policy year. The second column shows the gross annual premium that is level for this policy. The third column of illustration 2 is labeled "total paid-up value." This label is ambiguous because it does not indicate whether the paid-up value is for the dividend additions only or for both coverages as a result of applying the cash values of both coverages. Study of the illustration reveals that a paid-up value occurs in the second policy year before there is any cash value associated with the coverage purchased with dividends. Thus, it can be deduced that the total paid-up value is the amount of fully paid-up coverage the policy owner is eligible for if the total cash value is applied to the purchase. This illustration is based on the assumption that the policy owner will not exercise any policy loans during the 20 years displayed.

The next column, titled "guaranteed cash value end of year," is relatively easy to interpret. The word "guaranteed" indicates that this is the scheduled cash value for the base whole life policy. Values for the supplemental coverage cannot be guaranteed because the dividends used to purchase the additional coverage are not guaranteed.

The "enhancement reserve fund" column shows the cash value for the paid-up supplemental policies purchased with policy dividends. The "total cash value end of year" column lists the sum of the guaranteed cash value and the enhancement reserve fund.

The last two columns in Illustration 2 show the relationship between the premium paid and the annual increase in the policy cash value. During the first through eighth policy years the policy premium exceeds the incremental increase in the cash value. The cash value increases exceed the policy premium in the ninth and all subsequent policy years.

The three column totals in Illustration 2 have the same flaw as those in the previous illustration: they are only appropriate if both interest rates and inflation rates are zero. The accumulated value of the $320 annual premium after 20 years is $11,110 based on 5-percent interest, or $20,161 if it is based on a 10-percent interest rate. The accumulated value of the last column in Illustration 2 is only $557 if based on a 5-percent interest rate. This is less than the column sum of $1,039 because of the negative quantities in the first 8 years, which accrued larger negative balances until they were counterbalanced in subsequent years with positive values. The accumulated value is $1,076 for a 10 percent interest rate.

The important concept to be discerned from this illustration is that the premium is sufficient to create an internal buildup of funds in the policy, which also earns investment income. These internal funds are essential for the level-policy mechanism to work.

Split-Dollar

Policy illustrations can become extremely advanced and require a good amount of expertise and experience to understand. For example, when illustrating split-dollar plans it is important to use a marginal tax rate in the policy illustration that is the same as the marginal tax rate for the prospective policy owner. Minor variations in the tax rate can result in significant changes in the after-tax costs to the policy owner and other involved participants. Illustrations based on tax rates that are significantly different from those of the prospect are misleading and could be considered *deceptive sales practices*. The size limitations of standard office stationery tend to limit the amount of information that can be displayed on a single sheet. Consequently, many related items are not included in policy illustrations, or are spread out over several pages. It is essential to show both the corporate information and the individual insured information for this type of illustration.

Universal Life

The final illustration presents an early version of a universal life policy. This particular policy provides a death benefit of $100,000 until the policy cash value exceeds $95,000. Thereafter a death benefit will be $5,000 higher than the policy cash value. Policy Illustration 3 in Table 5-4 shows the annual premium of $1,300 is paid for 25 years. The illustrations for universal life policies may include (as this one does) a column for partial withdrawals. These are policy owner withdrawals of funds from the policy cash value that are not policy loans and do not accrue interest, nor are they expected to be returned to the policy. Because universal life policies can have both policy loans and partial withdrawals, it is likely that some illustrations will have columns for both. If the total of all partial withdrawals ever exceeds the total premiums paid for the policy, the excess will be subject to federal income tax.

TABLE 5-4
Policy Illustration 3

Universal Life

Death Benefit: $100,000

Insured: Female, Aged 40, nonsmoker

Planned Annual Premium: $1,300

Policy Year	Annual Premium	Partial With-drawal	Premi-ums Less With-drawals	Guar. Cash Value	As-summed Cash Value*	Current Cash Value **	Current Death Benefit
				End of Year			
1	$ 1,300	$ 0	$1,300	$ 114	$ 153	166	$ 100,000
2	1,300	0	2,600	943	1,175	1,212	100,000
3	1,300	0	3,900	1,773	2,275	2,357	100,000
4	1,300	0	5,200	2,604	3,473	3,627	100,000
5	1,300	0	6,500	3,438	4,769	5,025	100,000
6	1,300	0	7,800	4,262	6,161	6,555	100,000
7	1,300	0	9,100	5,077	7,659	8,233	100,000
8	1,300	0	10,400	5,873	9,287	10,091	100,000
9	1,300	0	11,700	6,649	11,048	12,140	100,000
10	1,300	0	13,000	7,393	12,956	14,405	100,000
11	1,300	0	14,300	8,107	15,040	16,924	100,000
12	1,300	0	15,600	8,777	17,308	19,719	100,000
13	1,300	0	16,900	9,392	19,781	22,288	100,000
14	1,300	0	18,200	9,551	22,482	26,288	100,000
15	1,300	0	19,500	10,439	25,427	30,138	100,000
16	1,300	0	20,800	10,845	28,645	34,431	100,000
17	1,300	0	22,100	11,164	32,159	39,218	100,000
18	1,300	0	23,400	11,371	36,006	44,566	100,000
19	1,300	0	24,700	11,449	40,218	50,546	100,000
20	1,300	0	26,000	11,380	44,847	57,252	100,000
21	1,300	0	27,300	11,133	49,933	64,777	100,000
22	1,300	0	28,600	10,685	55,533	73,238	100,000
23	1,300	0	29,900	10,011	61,704	82,766	100,000
24	1,300	0	31,200	9,058	68,524	93,521	100,000
25	1,300	0	32,500	7,792	76,075	105,617	110,617
26	1,300	6,500	26,000	0	75,659	110,198	115,198
27	1,300	6,500	19,500	0	75,284	115,288	120,288
28	1,300	6,500	13,000	0	74,973	120,945	125,945
29	1,300	6,500	6,500	0	74,704	127,229	132,229
30	1,300	6,500	0	0	74,400	134,213	139,213

The guaranteed cash value is based on a 4% interest rate.

* Interest rate used for assumed cash value is 9%.

** Interest rate used for current cash value is 11%.

Essentials of Life Insurance Products

The premium less withdrawals column in Illustration 3 is a non-interest-adjusted column indicating the cumulative amount of past premiums paid after reductions for any partial withdrawals of funds. The present value of these premiums over 25 years and of withdrawals in the subsequent 5 years is $10,512 based on 5-percent interest. If the premiums had been deposited in a 5-percent interest-bearing account, that account would still have a balance of $45,432 after the five annual withdrawals of $6,500 each. Based on 10-percent interest, the same calculations indicate a present value of $10,478 and an accumulated value of $182,835. These adjusted figures negate the impression that the policy owner will have no investment in the policy at the end of the 30 years, as the unadjusted numbers might imply.

This illustration is quite different from a traditional policy illustration in that it has three separate cash value columns, each calculated for a different assumed rate of interest earnings for the cash value. The "guaranteed cash value" column is comparable to the traditional examples because it is based on the interest rate guaranteed in the policy. However, even the "guaranteed cash value" column has its own properties for universal life policies because the premium level is usually inadequate if the cash value interest earnings do not exceed the guaranteed rate. That is why the cash values peak at $11,449 in the 19th policy year and decline to zero by the 26th policy year.

The column showing the assumed cash value is calculated using the assumption that the cash value will earn 9 percent interest every year. At that level of investment earnings or higher, the $1,300 premium for 25 years is clearly adequate to keep the policy in force. This scenario would develop ever-increasing cash values for the policy. There are no guarantees or suggestions that the investment earnings will always equal or exceed 9 percent. This is merely an example of how the cash value would grow if the actual earnings turn out to be exactly 9 percent each policy year. Notice, though, that the cash value in the assumed rate is starting to fall slowly after reaching a peak in the 28th year ($74,973). If premiums do not continue, or additional withdrawals are taken from the policy, that cash value will decline precipitously as mortality charges increase rapidly at her attained ages over age 70.

The "current cash value" column is another example of how the cash value will increase at an even higher interest rate if that rate is earned every policy year. The interest rate used in Illustration 3 for the current cash value is 11 percent each year. These columns are just demonstrations of what compound interest can do at sustained high levels. During the 1981–82 high-interest-rate period, there were companies using rates as high as 14 percent in their illustrations. There were many arbitrary predictions during that time, one being that interest rates would never again drop below 12 percent. These predictions have already proven to be erroneous. It is unrealistic to expect interest rates to stay at historically high levels over any protracted period of time. There is a very low probability that the cash value of the policy in Illustration 3 will reach $134,000 in the 30th policy year. It is questionable whether even a 9-percent rate of return is achievable over such an extended period. The assumed cash value of $74,000 after 30 years may turn out to be overly optimistic.

As previously stated, this policy is of the earlier design and would not be offered with such a narrow final amount of at-risk death protection. The policies issued after the tax law change in October 1986 would provide a larger spread between the cash value and the death benefit. The cash value in the illustrated policy is too high for the $100,000 death benefit in the 24th policy year if the amounts in the "current cash value" column are actually attained. If the cash value of the policy attains the amounts in the "assumed cash value" column, there will be no problem of satisfying the test for life insurance in Sec. 101(f) of the Internal Revenue Code.

There are many other possibilities that could be illustrated for universal life policies and traditional policies. Universal life policies can be used in any type of situation in which whole life policies can be used. Whether they would be the preferred policy can only be determined after analysis and realistic estimation of future interest earnings in the policy.

Guidelines and Regulations for Policy Illustrations

The proliferation of illustrations in the early 1980's prompted calls for standards or guidelines. Computerized illustrations and software evolved rapidly, yet there were no regulations to monitor and control illustrations. Competitive pressures pushed companies to become more creative in having the best-illustrated policies. This led to companies creating assumptions for their illustrations that might be considered just short of fantasy. Projecting values for interest earnings, mortality improvements and expense reductions that might not be possible, let alone sustainable, became a part of the cat-and-mouse game of out-illustrating the competition.

Professional Practice Guidelines

To bring some sense to the "illustration game", the Society of Financial Service Professionals took the initiative and adopted the *Professional Practice Guideline*, which is a checklist of guidelines for sales material and presentations. Although these guidelines were not intended to be minimum standards, they did give explicit guidance on many issues concerning illustrations. This document was adopted by the membership of the Society of Financial Service Professionals at its 1988 annual meeting and is summarized in the following discussion. It was one of the first steps on the slow journey to establishing some standards for policy illustrations.

The principal items addressed in the checklist were interest rates, mortality expenses, dividends, benefit changes, surrender charges, waiver-of-premium benefit base, policy comparisons, and issues concerning replacement. This document can be used to ensure that all relevant questions have been explained to a prospect. Obviously, not every item will always be applicable. For example, dividends might not be involved in a proposal because of the type of coverage under consideration.

The *Professional Practice Guideline* is intended to serve as a checklist of information to be evaluated before a prospect or client is asked to make a buying decision. This checklist could be shared with prospects to see if they feel that all of their questions have been answered and that they understand all of the issues. An advisor could use separate guidelines for a nonparticipating policy, a participating policy, a universal life, each type of policy replacement, and any other anticipated situation. Making separate guidelines would eliminate any questions that are not appropriate for an individual situation.

It is critical for advisors to understand and be able to explain to their clients how changes in interest rates, investment gains, mortality, persistency, and expenses can affect the future performance of a life insurance policy. This understanding of where the figures come from and what they actually represent will enable advisors to better communicate the risks as well as the benefits of a life insurance contract to their clients. Agents can provide details on guaranteed and non-guaranteed elements inherent in the contract and help avoid disappointment in the future.

Most life insurance non-registered products sold today are adjustable, either as a traditional "participating" product or as one of the family of products referred to as "interest sensitive." While adjustable products incorporate guarantees, the sales illustrations and projections are usually designed to convey to the prospect what the benefits and/or costs may be under a set of assumptions more optimistic than the guarantees. Since the insurance company generally limits its responsibility to the guarantees, risks associated with the development of a higher benefit or lower cost than generated by the guarantees are borne by the policy owner.

The following guidelines for sales materials and presentations using policy illustrations are excerpted from the Society of Financial Services Professional's *Professional Practice Guide* (The Society Page, June 1988, a publication of the Society of Financial Service Professionals, Bryn Mawr, PA 19010). As you will see as you review these guidelines, there are many aspects and assumptions behind illustrations not normally revealed by the company (to advisors or their clients) that have a tremendous impact on the resulting policy illustrations. To properly understand the illustration being presented, an advisor and his or her client must understand which of the following factors may have an impact on the illustration being presented.

Exhibit 5-1
Excerpts from the Professional Practice Guideline

I. Mortality—The mortality expense used in an illustration may reflect
   1. the company's actual current or recent mortality experience
   2. actual current or recent mortality experience modified at an assumed rate of increase or decrease
   3. a combination of mortality and other expenses
   4. zero mortality

II. Interest Rate— The interest assumption used in an illustration may be based upon
   1. interest rates earned by the company on
      a. all investments now held
      b. new investments
      c. new investments over a certain number of past years
      d. other combinations of actual investments
   2. an independent index such as
      a. Treasury bills
      b. Moody's long-term bond index
      c. other indexes
   3. another basis not tied to company results or an index
   4. Interest rates may be the gross interest rate resulting from investments, indexes or other measures, or the gross interest rate reduced by

---

- investment expenses
- investment expenses and other expenses
- expenses and profit
- a fixed amount or percentage

How is interest portrayed in this illustration?

5. Interest assumptions may be constant or they may be assumed to change over future years. Which of the above is used in the illustration?

III. Basis of illustration

1. Is the policy of the traditional participating variety, or does it contain nonguaranteed pricing elements using a means other than dividends?

2. If the policy is not participating, describe the nonguaranteed elements involved (such as nonguaranteed interest crediting rates, mortality charges, loadings, and so on)

3. If the policy is participating, does the company state that the contribution principle** is being followed in the illustrative dividend scale? If it is not, how does it differ? (The contribution principle states that aggregate divisible surplus should be distributed in the same proportion as the policies are considered to have contributed to the divisible surplus.)

4. If the policy is not participating, what is the company's policy with respect to determination and redetermination of nonguaranteed pricing elements, with particular reference to (a) the degree of discretion reserved by the company and (b) whether any of the elements are guaranteed to follow an outside index?

5. Basis of dividends or nonguaranteed factors

- Are any of the underlying experience factors different from current experience? If so, describe how and for what factor(s).

- If the policy is participating, is there a substantial probability that the current illustrative dividend scale cannot be continued if current experience continues?

- If the policy is not participating, is there a substantial probability that current illustrations cannot be supported by currently anticipated experience?

IV. Special Considerations

A. Some contracts provide for future benefit increases. Are such increases subject to evidence of insurability?

B. Some Disability Premium Waiver provisions waive a term cost of insurance and some waive a level (permanent) cost. Specifically what is waived?

C. Are any surrender charges illustrated? Are surrender charges fixed or determined at company discretion?

D. Comparisons for replacement transactions:

1. Is the current experience of the product to be replaced being used and have all available amendments which might improve the performance of the product been taken into consideration?

2. Will suicide and incontestable provisions be extended by the replacement?

3. Are there any differences in assumptions of the old and new product that will affect the comparison?

4. Will the replacement produce a short-term loss? How long will it take any superior performance of the replacing product to offset any short-term loss?

5. Are any assumptions of either product contradicted by either carrier's past experience?

6. Is the replacement clearly to the advantage of the policy owner?

Reprinted with permission from Society Page, *June, 1988. Copyright by the Society of Financial Service Professionals, 270 S. Bryn Mawr Avenue, Bryn Mawr, PA 19010. Distribution prohibited without publisher's written permission.*

The advisor should frequently review the full checklist as a reminder of all the relevant issues. It is important to include a discussion of each applicable factor in presentations. Some additional items that fit each advisor's special needs might be added to the checklist.

Life Insurance Illustration Questionnaire

The Society took further initiative regarding policy illustrations in 1992 by adopting the *Life Insurance Illustration Questionnaire*. It was intended to stimulate advisors to question and more thoroughly understand the intricacies of illustrations, so they could better explain them to prospects. The questions were directed to the insurance company regarding the assumptions and methodology underlying the responding insurer's illustrations. Nearly all of the major life insurance companies responded to the questionnaire and provided their answers to their own advisors. The questionnaire has been since abandoned by the Society because of the labor-intensive nature of checking and compiling the reports coming from the life insurance companies. But the nature and types of questions asked in the questionnaire are still valid and useful to advisors.

Insurance companies are reluctant to provide their questionnaire responses to advisors from competing companies or to the consuming public. This is understandable because of both competitive concerns and the detailed nature of the information itself. It would take even the best of advisors a lot of time and effort to explain the intricate information provided in the questionnaire response of any one insurance company.

The Society of Financial Service Professionals had no power to impose a standard for illustrations, but its development of the Professional Practice Guidelines and the Life Insurance Illustration Questionnaire helped prod the National Association of Insurance Commissioners (NAIC) to adopt standards for life insurance policy illustrations in 1996.

It is generally acknowledged the policy illustrations work well to educate clients in the mechanics of how policies work. But policy illustrations are not an adequate tool for comparing costs of policies from different insurance companies. Illustrations do not create accurate projections of future performance because of differences in assumptions between insurance companies and the problems of estimating future performance of the company and the economy.

The Life Insurance Illustration Questionnaire is designed very much like the Professional Practice Guideline. It asks similar questions in similar formats, and has a similar purpose, which is to uncover the assumptions that make up the design of a life insurance policy illustration. The key factors examined by the Illustration Questionnaire are: general nature of the policy, mortality, interest or crediting rates, expenses and persistency. A summary of some of the questions from the Illustration Questionnaire (IQ) follows:

I. General
1. Is the policy participating or non-participating?
2. Describe the non-guaranteed elements. How may the company re-determine non-guaranteed pricing elements?
3. Do any experience factors underlying the dividend scale or other non-guaranteed elements used in the illustration differ from recent historical experience?
4. Is there a substantial probability that the current illustrative values will change if actual recent historical experience continues unchanged?
5. Is it company policy to treat new and existing policyholders of the same class the same or consistently with respect to the underlying factors in pricing?
6. With respect to joint and survivor policies, describe all the effects of the first death on the policy and riders.

II. Mortality
1. Do the mortality rates underlying the scale used in the illustration differ from actual recent historical experience?
2. Does the illustration assume mortality improvements in the future?
3. Do the mortality or cost of insurance charges used in the illustration include some expense charge?
4. Do the underlying mortality rates vary by product?
5. Indicate the approximation duration, if any, when all underlying mortality rates vary only by attained age (for example, when does select become ultimate?)

III. Interest or Crediting Rates
1. What is the interest rate used in the dividend scale or credited in the illustration? The portfolio rate, new money rate, gross rate, or net rate?
2. No interest rates reflect the earnings on all invested assets, a portion of assets, or just new investments?
3. Does the interest rate used in the illustration vary between new and existing policies?

4. Do the interest rates used in the illustration reflect actual recent historical earnings rates? At any point in the illustration do the interest rates used exceed the actual recent historical earnings?
5. Do the interest rates used in the illustration vary by policy duration, policy type, class or otherwise?
6. How does individual policy loan activity affect the illustrated interest rates?

IV. Expenses
1. Do the expense factors used in the illustration reflect actual recent historical company experience?
2. Are the expense charges used in the illustration adequate to cover the expenses in sales and administration? If not, how are remaining expenses covered?
3. How are investment expenses and all taxes assessed?
4. Are expense factors used in the illustration different for new and existing policies? Do they vary by product type, class, policy duration or otherwise?

V. Persistency
1. If the actual persistency was better than assumed, would that negatively affect illustrated values?
2. Does the illustration involve a persistency bonus (to policyholders who pay premiums for a specified number of years)? Is it guaranteed?
3. Is there any limitation or company discretion in deciding to pay the bonus?
4. What conditions must be met to pay the bonus?
5. What is the form of the bonus (cash, additional interest, refund of mortality and/ or loading charges)?
6. Does the company set aside any reserve or other liability earmarked for future bonuses?

NAIC Life Insurance Illustrations Model Regulation

In 1996 the National Association of Insurance Commissioners (NAIC) adopted a model regulation pertaining to life insurance illustrations. This was the NAIC's first attempt to set standards for policy illustrations. The stated purpose was to provide rules for life insurance policy illustrations that will protect consumers and foster consumer education. Its goals were to ensure that policy illustrations do not mislead purchasers of life insurance and to make illustrations more understandable. A key strategy in the regulation was to clearly define and distinguish for the consumer what is guaranteed in the contract and what was not.

There were some basic similarities among policy illustrations, such as a listing of the annual premium and the policy's cash value for each policy year, up to 20 years after policy issuance. However, despite the similarities, there were no uniform standards applicable to policy illustrations prior to 1997 with the introduction of this NAIC Model Regulation. The organization of illustrative information within a single report varied drastically from one insurance company to another, even if the same information was contained in the report. Rogue insurance companies could publish illustrations with any assumptions they wished without regulatory consequence.

The model regulation has had a tremendous impact on illustrations in all states because life insurance companies moved toward using the same illustration model in every state. Thus, they do not need different software systems for each state. Also, by making all their illustrations conform to the most stringent state's requirements, insurers could meet the regulatory requirements even in states that adopted the NAIC Model Regulations.

The life insurance illustrations model regulation does not apply to variable life, credit life, or life insurance with a face amount of less than $10,000. It does not apply to either individual or group annuity contracts. The regulation applies to all non-variable group and individual life insurance policies and certificates for more than $10,000 of death benefit.

The regulation requires the insurance company to declare to the state insurance department for each policy form whether or not it intends to use illustrations to market that form of coverage. A copy of each illustration the insurer intends to use must be forwarded to the state insurance department. The regulation contains significant minimum standards dealing with the format and content of any information provided in the illustration. Both the producer and the client must sign the initial illustration, with a copy provided to the insurance company and the client. If the issued policy differs in any way from the originally issued illustration, a revised Illustration must be submitted, following the same procedures as above.

Each illustration used in the sale of a life insurance policy covered by the regulation must be clearly labeled "life insurance illustration" and must include the following:

1. the name of the insurance company
2. the name and business address of the insurer's agent
3. the name, age, and sex of the proposed insured
4. the underwriting or rating classification upon which the illustration is based
5. the generic name of the policy (for example, whole life, universal life, and so on)
6. the initial death benefit amount
7. the dividend option election or application of nonguaranteed elements if applicable

The NAIC Model regulation prohibits insurers and their advisors from the following:

1. representing the policy as anything other than a life insurance policy
2. using or describing nonguaranteed elements in a manner that is misleading or has the capacity or tendency to mislead. The nonguaranteed elements must be labeled as nonguaranteed
3. stating or implying that the payment or amount of nonguaranteed elements is guaranteed. It must clearly be stated that these elementsare subject to change and that the actual results may be more or less favorable.
4. using an illustration that does not comply with the illustration regulation
5. using an illustration that is more favorable to the policy owner than the illustration based on the illustrated scale of the insurer
6. providing an applicant with an incomplete illustration
7. representing in any way that premium payments will not be required for each year of the policy in order to maintain the illustrated death benefits, unless that is the fact
8. using the term "vanish," "vanishing premium," or a similar term that implies the policy becomes paid up, to describe a plan for using nonguaranteed elements to pay a portion of future premiums
9. using an illustration that is not "self-supporting." The illustration must include actuarial assumptions of self-sustaining profitability.

The NAIC model illustration regulation specifies that all illustrations must be dated as of the date prepared. All pages must be marked to indicate both the individual page number and the total number of pages in the illustration (for example, "page 3 of 7"). The illustration must clearly indicate which elements are guaranteed and which are nonguaranteed. Any amount available upon surrender shall be the amount after deduction of surrender charges. Items presented in illustrations can be in the form of charts, graphs, or tabular values.

Each illustration must be accompanied by a narrative summary that describes the policy, premiums, and features, and defines column headings used in the illustration. The summary should also state that actual results might be more or less favorable than those shown in the illustration.

Universal Life Policies

The regulation states that illustrations for universal life policies must comply with the regulation requirements and additionally that the insurance company must issue annual reports to policy owners after the policy is issued. These annual reports must specify the beginning and ending dates for the reporting period.

The content of annual reports is specified in the NAIC model regulation to include:

- all transactions affecting the policy during the reporting period (debits and credits) and a description of each (for example, premiums paid, interest credited, loan interest debited, mortality charges, expenses debited, rider transactions, and so on)
- cash values at the beginning and end of the period
- death benefit at the end of the reporting period (for each life covered)
- the cash surrender value at the end of the period after deduction of surrender charge (if any)
- the amount of outstanding policy loans, if any, at the end of the report period
- a special Notice to Policy owners if the policy will not maintain insurance in force until the end of the next reporting period unless further premium payments are made

The regulation further stipulates that policy owners have the right to request an in-force illustration annually without charge. The insurer must provide information regarding where and how to direct such requests and must supply a current illustration within 30 days of the request. Such illustrations are to be based on the insurer's present illustrated scale.

Annual Certifications

Each insurer's board of directors must appoint at least one illustration actuary, who will certify that the illustrations are in compliance with the illustration regulation and are insurer-authorized. The regulation states the qualifications of an illustration actuary, including membership in good standing of the American Academy of Actuaries.

The illustration actuary must annually certify the method used to allocate overhead and expenses for all illustrations and file such certification with the insurance commissioner and with the insurer's board of directions. Further, the illustration actuary is required to report any mistakes found in previous certifications to both the commissioner and the board of directors. The insurance commissioner must also be notified of any change in the illustration actuary and the reasons for the change.

The model regulation sets forth limits on the methods used for calculating illustrations. These limits are intended to curb some of the overly optimistic projections that a few insurers were utilizing in past years in the absence of any standards or constraints. Most of the new constraints are contained in the definitions of currently payable scale, disciplined current scale, and illustrated scale:

- *currently payable scale*: a scale of nonguaranteed elements in effect for a policy form as of the preparation date of the illustration or declared to become effective within the next 95 days.
- *disciplined current scale*: a scale of nonguaranteed elements constituting a limit on illustrations currently being used by an insurer that is reasonably based on recent historical experience, as certified annually by an illustration actuary designated by the insurer. Further guidance in determining the disciplined current scale as contained in standards established by the Actuarial Standards Board may be relied upon if the standards

    (1) are consistent with all provisions of this regulation
    (2) limit a disciplined current scale to reflect only actions that have already been taken or events that have already occurred
    (3) do not permit a disciplined current scale to include any projected trends of improvements in experience or any

assumed improvements in experience beyond the illustration date, and

(4) do not permit assumed expenses to be less than minimum assumed expenses. *Illustrated scale*: a scale of nonguaranteed elements currently being illustrated that is not more favorable to the policy owner than the lesser of (1) the disciplined current scale, or (2) the currently payable scale.

Outlook

It is important to note that illustrations will never be an accurate prediction of future results or policy performance. Actual future situations will be influenced by the economy and by the investment performance of the specific insurance company's portfolio.

Illustrations are useful tools for showing how a policy works and its sensitivity to changes in factors such as interest, mortality, or expenses. However, illustrations are of limited value for comparing different policies, whether from the same insurer or from different insurers.

Policy illustrations are terrible tools for finding the "best" product, unless all the values are guaranteed, which is rarely the case, or unless all the assumptions that serve as the basis for the projections are provided. Policy illustrations do not show what a client *will get*, but rather what he or she *would get if* all the company's assumptions about the future came true, which is nearly impossible. How will mortality, interest and expense factors change over the next 20, 30, or 40 years? Obviously, none of these factors can be predicted with certainty.

Some companies make more conservative assumptions to minimize the chances that they will not meet expectations. Other companies are more aggressive to make their product look more attractive. The company with the "best" illustration may simply be the one that has the most optimistic assumptions about the future, not necessarily the one that will actually meet these expectations or deliver the most value to the client.

Therefore, do not fall into the illustration trap. Policy illustrations may be policy "illusions." Do your due diligence. Scrutinize the underlying assumptions of the policy and how it was created. Investigate the history of the company and their record of meeting policy projections in the past. What is the financial strength of the company? How well have they met their projections in the past?

The illustration regulation will no doubt eliminate some of the past abuses in illustrations where the assumptions were based on unfettered, pie-in-the-sky optimism. The regulations do *not* constrain illustrations to such an extent that we can compare apples to apples. It is still important to study all the questions about the underlying assumptions such as those set forth in the Professional Practice Guideline, the Life Insurance Illustration Questionnaire, and the NAIC Life Insurance Illustrations Model Regulation.

Chapter Five Review

Key terms and concepts are explained in the glossary. Answers to the review questions and the self-test questions follow the Glossary.

Key Terms and Concepts

net cost method
time value of money
interest-adjusted indexes
National Association of Insurance
Commissioners (NAIC)
policy summary
surrender cost index
annuity due
net payment index
cash accumulation comparison method

equal outlay method
comparative interest rate method
Linton yield method
Belth yearly rate of return method
Belth yearly price method
deceptive sales practices
Professional Practice Guideline
Life Insurance Illustration Questionnaire
NAIC Life Insurance Illustrations Model
  Regulation

Review Questions

5-1. Discuss the net cost method of comparing life insurance policy costs, how it is calculated, and its principle flaw.

5-2. Describe the interest-adjusted indexes, and explain how they differ from the traditional net cost method of comparing life insurance policy costs.

5-3. Describe the cash accumulation method of policy comparison, and explain its strengths and weaknesses.

5-4. Explain the equal-outlay method of policy comparison.

5-5. Explain the comparative interest rate method of policy comparison.

5-6. Describe the Belth yearly rate of return and yearly price approach methods of comparing life insurance policies

5-7. Describe the relationship between interest rates and accumulated values in policy illustrations.

5-8. What is the implicit assumption underlying policy illustrations that do not include interest adjustments?

5-9. Explain how the *Life Insurance Illustration Questionnaire* (IQ) from the Society of Financial Service Professionals differs from the *Professional Practice Guideline* from the same organization.

5-10. What type of information about mortality does the IQ elicit?

5-11. What type of information about interest or crediting rates does the IQ elicit?)

5-12. What type of information about expenses does the IQ elicit?

5-13. What type of information about persistency does the IQ elicit?

5-14. Describe the major elements of the NAIC Life Insurance Illustrations Model Regulation.

5-15. Describe the duties of an illustration actuary under the NAIC model regulation pertaining to illustrations.

Self-Test Questions

Instructions: Read the chapter first, then answer the following 10 questions to test your knowledge. Circle the correct answer, then check your answers in the answer key in the back of the book.

5-1. A serious shortcoming of the net cost method of comparing life insurance policies is that

(A) it gives equal weight to payment amounts that may be separated by 10 or 20 years
(B) it uses time value of money as the basis for its analysis of policy cost
(C) it looks for the interest rate that makes the buy-term-and-invest-the-difference comparison exactly equivalent
(D) it requires a computer in order to be efficient

5-2. The interest-adjusted indexes method of comparing policies is

(A) very well suited for evaluating policy replacements
(B) well suited for comparing dissimilar polices, such as term and whole life
(C) indicating that a policy with smaller numerical values (indexes) is preferable to a policy with higher indexes
(D) basically a buy-term-and-invest-the-difference approach

5-3. Which of the following policy comparison methods appear on most sales presentation materials used by insurance advisors?

(A) cash accumulation comparison method
(B) comparative interest rate method
(C) interest-adjusted indexes (surrender cost index and payment cost index)
(D) Linton yield method

5-4. Almost every state mandates that the interest rate to be used in comparing policies using the interest-adjusted cost indexes is:
(A) 3 percent
(B) 5 percent
(C) 6 percent
(D) a variable rate

5-5. It is generally held that policy illustrations are effective in serving which of the following purposes?

I. They work well to educate clients in the mechanics of how policies work.
II. They are an adequate tool for comparing costs of policies from different insurance companies.

(A) I only
(B) II only
(C) Both I and II
(D) Neither I nor II

5-6.   Which of the following statements concerning policy illustrations is (are) correct?

I.   They usually cover at least 10 years of data and often cover 15 or 20 years.
II.   The NAIC Life insurance Illustrations Model Regulation set standards applicable to policy illustrations.

(A)   I only
(B)   II only
(C)   Both I and II
(D)   Neither I nor II

5-7.   Which of the following statements concerning policy illustrations is (are) correct?

I.   The NAIC model regulation does not apply to variable life, credit life, or life polices with a face amount of less than $10,000.
II.   The NAIC Model Regulation applies to non-variable life and individual life policies for face amounts over $10,000

(A)   I only
(B)   II only
(C)   Both I and II
(D)   Neither I nor II

5-8.   All of the following statements concerning the interest-adjusted indexes are true EXCEPT

(A)   The NAIC developed these methods and model regulations requiring their use.
(B)   These methods treat premium payments as if they were put into an interest-bearing account to accumulate to the end of the interval.
(C)   The payment cost index is similar to the surrender cost index except it does not consider cash value at the end of the interval.
(D)   The surrender cost index is useful in comparing costs when death benefit protection is emphasized.

5-9. All of the following are questions asked on the Life Insurance Illustration Questionnaire (IQ) EXCEPT

(A) Are mortality rates equal to the most recent CSO Table?
(B) How are investment expenses and taxes assessed?
(C) What conditions must be met to pay or credit a bonus if an illustration includes a guaranteed bonus?
(D) Do the interest rates credited in the dividend scale or in the illustration vary by policy duration?

5-10. All of the following are statements concerning the Life Insurance Illustration Questionnaire (IQ) EXCEPT

(A) It is to be completed by insurance company's home office staff.
(B) Advisors can use it as a tool to educate themselves about policy illustrations.
(C) Its primary focus is to obtain detailed information about the guaranteed elements of policy illustrations.
(D) It was created by the Society of Financial Service Professionals.

TABLE 5-5 Traditional Net Cost

10-Year Traditional Net Cost		20-Year Traditional Net Cost	
Dividends	$ 2,178	Dividends	$10,487
Cash value	14,820	Cash value	35,900
Total	16,998	Total	46,387
Less		Less	
Premiums paid	21,870	Premiums paid	43,740
Cost	4,872	Cost	−2,647
Divide by $1,000's face	48.72	Per $1,000	−26.47
Divide by number of years	4.872	Per $1,000 per year	−1.3235

$100,000 Whole Life Policy Issue Age 48 Male Participating

Policy Year	Age	Premium	Cash Value	Dividend	Accum. Dividend	Accum. Premium
1	48	$2,187	$ 0	$ 0	$ 0	$ 2,296
2	49	2,187	1,456	76	76	4,708
3	50	2,187	2,963	120	200	7,239
4	51	2,187	4,516	170	380	9,898
5	52	2,187	6,119	185	584	12,689
6	53	2,187	7,775	217	830	15,620
7	54	2,187	9,470	280	1,151	18,697
8	55	2,187	11,210	325	1,534	21,928
9	56	2,187	12,992	390	2,001	25,321
10	57	2,187	14,820	415	2,516	28,883
11	58	2,187	16,698	455	3,097	32,624
12	59	2,187	18,625	550	3,801	36,551
13	60	2,187	20,605	615	4,606	40,675
14	61	2,187	22,638	707	5,544	45,005
15	62	2,187	24,720	775	6,596	49,552
16	63	2,187	26,857	845	7,771	54,326
17	64	2,187	29,042	952	9,111	59,339
18	65	2,187	31,276	1,020	10,587	64,602
19	66	2,187	33,559	1,140	12,256	70,128
20	67	2,187	35,900	1,250	14,119	75,931

TABLE 5-6 Interest-adjusted Net Surrender Cost Index

10-Year Surrender Cost Index		20-Year Surrender Cost Index	
Dividends	$2,515.779	Dividends	$14,119.04
Cash value	14,820	Cash value	35,900
Total	17,335.78	Total	50,019.04
Less		Less	
Premiums paid	28,883.24	Premiums paid	75,931.00
Cost	11,547.46	Cost	25,911.97
Divide by $1,000's face	115.4746	Per $1,000	259.1197
Divide by number of years	8.743575	Per $1,000 per year	7.463274
(13.2068)		(34.7193)	

$100,000 Whole Life Policy Issue Age 48 Male Participating

Policy Year	Age	Premium	Cash Value	Dividend	Accum. Dividend	Accum. Premium
1	48	$2,187	$ 0	$ 0	$ 0	$ 2,296
2	49	2,187	1,456	76	76	4,708
3	50	2,187	2,963	120	200	7,239
4	51	2,187	4,516	170	380	9,898
5	52	2,187	6,119	185	584	12,689
6	53	2,187	7,775	217	830	15,620
7	54	2,187	9,470	280	1,151	18,697
8	55	2,187	11,210	325	1,534	21,928
9	56	2,187	12,992	390	2,001	25,321
10	57	2,187	14,820	415	2,516	28,883
11	58	2,187	16,698	455	3,097	32,624
12	59	2,187	18,625	550	3,801	36,551
13	60	2,187	20,605	615	4,606	40,675
14	61	2,187	22,638	707	5,544	45,005
15	62	2,187	24,720	775	6,596	49,552
16	63	2,187	26,857	845	7,771	54,326
17	64	2,187	29,042	952	9,111	59,339
18	65	2,187	31,276	1,020	10,587	64,602
19	66	2,187	33,559	1,140	12,256	70,128
20	67	2,187	35,900	1,250	14,119	75,931

TABLE 5-7 Interest-adjusted Net Payment Cost Payment

10-Year Surrender Cost Index		20-Year Surrender Cost Index	
Accum. dividends	$2,515.779	Accum. dividends	$14,119.04
Accum. premiums	28,883.24	Accum. premiums	75,931.00
Future value of net premiums	26,367.46	Future value of net premiums	61,811.96
Convert to per $1,000	263.6746	Per $1,000	618.1196
Divide by factor 13.2068	19.96507	Per $1,000 per year (34.7193)	17.80334
Payment index	19.96507	Payment index	17.80334

$100,000 Whole Life Policy Issue Age 48 Male Participating

Policy Year	Age	Premium	Cash Value	Dividend	Accum. Dividend	Accum. Premium
1	48	$2,187	$ 0	$ 0	$ 0	$ 2,296
2	49	2,187	1,456	76	76	4,708
3	50	2,187	2,963	120	200	7,239
4	51	2,187	4,516	170	380	9,898
5	52	2,187	6,119	185	584	12,689
6	53	2,187	7,775	217	830	15,620
7	54	2,187	9,470	280	1,151	18,697
8	55	2,187	11,210	325	1,534	21,928
9	56	2,187	12,992	390	2,001	25,321
10	57	2,187	14,820	415	2,516	28,883
11	58	2,187	16,698	455	3,097	32,624
12	59	2,187	18,625	550	3,801	36,551
13	60	2,187	20,605	615	4,606	40,675
14	61	2,187	22,638	707	5,544	45,005
15	62	2,187	24,720	775	6,596	49,552
16	63	2,187	26,857	845	7,771	54,326
17	64	2,187	29,042	952	9,111	59,339
18	65	2,187	31,276	1,020	10,587	64,602
19	66	2,187	33,559	1,140	12,256	70,128
20	67	2,187	35,900	1,250	14,119	75,931

TABLE 5-8 Interest Adjusted Cost Method

	Premiums			Dividends		
Year	Per Year	Accum. @ 5%		Per Year	Accum. @ 5%	Cash Value
1	$ 15	$ 15.75		0	$ 0	$ 0
2	15	32.29		1	1.05	0
3	15	49.65		2	3.20	23
4	15	67.89		3	6.51	34
5	15	87.03		4	11.04	43
6	15	107.13		5	16.84	56
7	15	128.24		6	23.99	75
8	15	150.40		7	32.54	100
9	15	173.67		8	42.56	115
10	15	198.10		9	54.14	120
TOTALS	150	198.10		45	54.14	120

Surrender Cost Index

Future value of premiums	$198.1018
Minus FV of dividends	54.13574
FV of net premiums	$143.9661
Less net cash value	– 120
FV of net cost	$23.96606
Divide by annuity factor	13.2068
Surrender Cost Index	1.814676

Payment Cost Index

Accum. premiums	$198.1018
Less accum. dividends	–54.13574
FV of net premiums	$143.9661
Divide by annuity factor	13.2068
Payment Cost Indes	10.9009

TABLE 5-9
Cash Accumulation Comparison Method

Male Aged 48—$100,000 Whole Life
Dividends Buy Paid-up Additions
Annual Renewable Term (ART) Decreased to Equalize Death Benefits
Interest Rate 3% (on accumulations)

Policy Year	WL Premium	ART Premium	Prem Diff.	Accum. Diff. @ 3%	WL Cash Values	Term Plus Side Fund	WL + Paid-up Adds.	ART Face Amount
1	$2,187	$ 365	$1,822	$ 1,877	$ 0	$100,000	$100,000	$ 98,123
2	2,187	386	1,801	3,788	1,456	100,075	100,075	96,287
3	2,187	409	1,778	5,733	2,963	100,203	100,203	94,470
4	2,187	434	1,753	7,710	4,516	100,527	100,527	92,817
5	2,187	460	1,727	9,720	6,119	100,972	100,972	91,252
6	2,187	491	1,696	11,759	7,775	102,321	102,321	90,562
7	2,187	528	1,659	13,820	9,470	104,408	104,408	90,588
8	2,187	574	1,613	15,896	11,210	107,549	107,549	91,653
9	2,187	628	1,559	17,979	12,992	111,463	111,463	93,484
10	2,187	685	1,502	20,066	14,820	114,876	114,876	94,810
11	2,187	753	1,434	22,145	16,698	119,071	119,071	96,926
12	2,187	838	1,349	24,199	18,625	124,156	124,156	99,957
13	2,187	946	1,241	26,203	20,605	130,507	130,507	104,304
14	2,187	1,071	1,116	28,138	22,638	136,789	136,789	108,651
15	2,187	1,226	961	29,972	24,720	143,896	143,896	113,924
16	2,187	1,427	760	31,654	26,857	152,719	152,719	121,065
17	2,187	1,679	508	33,127	29,042	162,745	162,745	129,618
18	2,187	1,942	245	34,374	31,276	170,345	170,345	135,971
19	2,187	2,483	−296	35,100	33,559	183,682	183,682	148,582
20	2,187	3,127	−940	35,185	35,900	196,132	196,132	160,947

TABLE 5-10
Cash Accumulation Comparison Method

Male Aged 48—$100,000 Whole Life
Dividends Buy Paid-up Additions
Annual Renewable Term (ART) Decreased to Equalize Death Benefits
Interest Rate 5% (on accumulations)

Policy Year	WL Premium	ART Premium	Prem Diff.	Accum. Diff. @ 5%	WL Cash Values	Term Plus Side Fund	WL + Paid-up Adds.	ART Face Amount
1	$2,187	$ 365	$1,822	$ 1,913	$ 0	$100,000	$100,000	$ 98,087
2	2,187	386	1,801	3,900	1,456	100,075	100,075	96,175
3	2,187	408	1,779	5,963	2,963	100,203	100,203	94,240
4	2,187	433	1,754	8,104	4,516	100,527	100,527	92,423
5	2,187	457	1,730	10,325	6,119	100,972	100,972	90,647
6	2,187	486	1,701	12,628	7,775	102,321	102,321	89,693
7	2,187	521	1,666	15,008	9,470	104,408	104,408	89,400
8	2,187	564	1,623	17,463	11,210	107,549	107,549	90,086
9	2,187	615	1,572	19,987	12,992	111,463	111,463	91,476
10	2,187	666	1,521	22,583	14,820	114,876	114,876	92,293
11	2,187	729	1,458	25,243	16,698	119,071	119,071	93,828
12	2,187	806	1,381	27,955	18,625	124,156	124,156	96,201
13	2,187	905	1,282	30,698	20,605	130,507	130,507	99,809
14	2,187	1,019	1,168	33,460	22,638	136,789	136,789	103,329
15	2,187	1,159	1,028	36,212	24,720	143,896	143,896	107,684
16	2,187	1,342	845	38,910	26,857	152,719	152,719	113,809
17	2,187	1,570	617	41,504	29,042	162,745	162,745	121,241
18	2,187	1,804	383	43,981	31,276	170,345	170,345	126,364
19	2,187	2,300	−113	46,061	33,559	183,682	183,682	137,621
20	2,187	2,885	−698	47,631	35,900	196,132	196,132	148,501

TABLE 5-11
Cash Accumulation Comparison Method

Male Aged 48—$100,000 Whole Life
Dividends Buy Paid-up Additions
Annual Renewable Term (ART) Decreased to Equalize Death Benefits
Interest Rate 7% (on accumulations)

Policy Year	WL Premium	ART Premium	Prem Diff.	Accum. Diff. @ 7%	WL Cash Values	Term Plus Side Fund	WL + Paid-up Adds.	ART Face Amount
1	$2,187	$ 365	$1,822	$ 1,950	$ 0	$100,000	$100,000	$ 98,050
2	2,187	385	1,802	4,014	1,456	100,075	100,075	96,061
3	2,187	407	1,780	6,200	2,963	100,203	100,203	94,003
4	2,187	431	1,756	8,513	4,516	100,527	100,527	92,014
5	2,187	454	1,733	10,964	6,119	100,972	100,972	90,008
6	2,187	481	1,706	13,556	7,775	102,321	102,321	88,765
7	2,187	514	1,673	16,296	9,470	104,408	104,408	88,112
8	2,187	553	1,634	19,185	11,210	107,549	107,549	88,364
9	2,187	600	1,587	22,226	12,992	111,463	111,463	89,237
10	2,187	646	1,541	25,431	14,820	114,876	114,876	89,445
11	2,187	701	1,486	28,801	16,698	119,071	119,071	90,270
12	2,187	769	1,418	32,334	18,625	124,156	124,156	91,822
13	2,187	857	1,330	36,020	20,605	130,507	130,507	94,487
14	2,187	956	1,231	39,859	22,638	136,789	136,789	96,930
15	2,187	1,077	1,110	43,837	24,720	143,896	143,896	100,059
16	2,187	1,236	951	47,924	26,857	152,719	152,719	104,795
17	2,187	1,433	754	52,085	29,042	162,745	162,745	110,660
18	2,187	1,628	559	56,329	31,276	170,345	170,345	114,016
19	2,187	2,060	127	60,408	33,559	183,682	183,682	123,274
20	2,187	2,563	−376	64,235	35,900	196,132	196,132	131,897

TABLE 5-12
Cash Accumulation Comparison Method

Male Aged 48—$100,000 Whole Life
Dividends Buy Paid-up Additions
Annual Renewable Term (ART) Decreased to Equalize Death Benefits
Interest Rate 10% (on accumulations)

Policy Year	WL Premium	ART Premium	Prem. Diff.	Accum. Diff. @ 10%	WL Cash Values	Term Plus Side Fund	WL + Paid-up Adds.	ART Face Amount
1	$2,187	$ 365	$1,822	$ 2,005	$ 0	$100,000	$100,000	$ 97,995
2	2,187	385	1,802	4,188	1,456	100,075	100,075	95,887
3	2,187	405	1,782	6,566	2,963	100,203	100,203	93,637
4	2,187	428	1,759	9,158	4,516	100,527	100,527	91,369
5	2,187	448	1,739	11,987	6,119	100,972	100,972	88,985
6	2,187	473	1,714	15,071	7,775	102,321	102,321	87,250
7	2,187	501	1,686	18,432	9,470	104,408	104,408	85,976
8	2,187	535	1,652	22,093	11,210	107,549	107,549	85,456
9	2,187	574	1,613	26,076	12,992	111,463	111,463	85,387
10	2,187	610	1,577	30,149	14,820	114,876	114,876	84,457
11	2,187	652	1,535	35,149	16,698	119,071	119,071	83,922
12	2,187	703	1,484	40,297	18,625	124,156	124,156	83,859
13	2,187	767	1,420	45,888	20,605	130,507	130,507	84,619
14	2,187	836	1,351	51,963	22,638	136,789	136,789	84,826
15	2,187	918	1,269	58,554	24,720	143,896	143,896	85,342
16	2,187	1,026	1,161	65,687	26,857	152,719	152,719	87,032
17	2,187	1,157	1,030	73,388	29,042	162,745	162,745	89,357
18	2,187	1,265	922	81,741	31,276	170,345	170,345	88,604
19	2,187	1,555	632	90,610	33,559	183,682	183,682	93,072
20	2,187	1,867	320	100,023	35,900	196,132	196,132	96,109

TABLE 5-13
Cash Accumulation Comparison Method

Male Aged 48—$100,000 Whole Life
Dividends Buy Paid-up Additions
Annual Renewable Term (ART) Decreased to Equalize Death Benefits
Interest Rate 12% (on accumulations)

Policy Year	WL Premium	ART Premium	Prem Diff.	Accum. Diff. @ 12%	WL Cash Values	Term Plus Side Fund	WL + Paid-up Adds.	ART Face Amount
1	$ 2,187	$ 364	$ 1,823	$ 2,041	$ 0	$100,000	$100,000	$ 97,959
2	2,187	384	1,803	4,306	1,456	100,075	100,075	95,769
3	2,187	404	1,783	6,819	2,963	100,203	100,203	93,384
4	2,187	425	1,762	9,610	4,516	100,527	100,527	90,917
5	2,187	445	1,742	12,714	6,119	100,972	100,972	88,258
6	2,187	467	1,720	16,167	7,775	102,321	102,321	86,154
7	2,187	492	1,695	20,005	9,470	104,408	104,408	84,403
8	2,187	521	1,666	24,271	11,210	107,549	107,549	83,278
9	2,187	554	1,633	29,012	12,992	111,463	111,463	82,451
10	2,187	582	1,605	34,292	14,820	114,876	114,876	80,584
11	2,187	613	1,574	40,170	16,698	119,071	119,071	78,901
12	2,187	649	1,538	46,712	18,625	124,156	124,156	77,444
13	2,187	694	1,493	53,990	20,605	130,507	130,507	76,517
14	2,187	736	1,451	62,094	22,638	136,789	136,789	74,695
15	2,187	783	1,404	71,117	24,720	143,896	143,896	72,779
16	2,187	844	1,343	81,156	26,857	152,719	152,719	71,563
17	2,187	912	1,275	92,322	29,042	162,745	162,745	70,423
18	2,187	936	1,251	104,802	31,276	170,345	170,345	65,543
19	2,187	1,087	1,100	118,610	33,559	183,682	183,682	65,072
20	2,187	1,208	979	133,939	35,900	196,132	196,132	62,193

TABLE 5-14
Equal Outlay Comparison Method

Male Aged 48—$100,000 Whole Life
Dividends Purchase Paid-up Additions
Interest Rate 3%

Policy Year	WL Premium	ART Premium	Prem Diff.	Accum. Diff. @ 3%	WL Cash Values	Term Plus Side Fund	WL + Paid-up Adds.
1	$ 2,187	$ 372	$ 1,815	$ 1,869	$ 0	$101,869	$100,000
2	2,187	401	1,786	3,765	1,456	103,765	100,075
3	2,187	433	1,754	5,685	2,963	105,685	100,203
4	2,187	468	1,719	7,626	4,516	107,626	100,527
5	2,187	504	1,683	9,588	6,119	109,588	100,972
6	2,187	542	1,645	11,570	7,775	111,570	102,321
7	2,187	583	1,604	13,569	9,470	113,569	104,408
8	2,187	626	1,561	15,584	11,210	115,584	107,549
9	2,187	672	1,515	17,612	12,992	117,612	111,463
10	2,187	722	1,465	19,649	14,820	119,649	114,876
11	2,187	777	1,410	21,691	16,698	121,691	119,071
12	2,187	838	1,349	23,731	18,625	123,731	124,156
13	2,187	907	1,280	25,762	20,605	125,762	130,507
14	2,187	986	1,201	27,772	22,638	127,772	136,789
15	2,187	1,076	1,111	29,749	24,720	129,749	143,896
16	2,187	1,179	1,008	31,680	26,857	131,680	152,719
17	2,187	1,295	892	33,549	29,042	133,549	162,745
18	2,187	1,428	759	35,337	31,276	135,337	170,345
19	2,187	1,671	516	36,929	33,559	136,929	183,682
20	2,187	1,943	244	38,288	35,900	138,288	196,132

TABLE 5-15
Equal Outlay Comparison Method

Male Aged 48—$100,000 Whole Life
Dividends Purchase Paid-up Additions
Interest Rate 5%

Policy Year	WL Premium	ART Premium	Prem. Diff.	Accum. Diff. @ 5%	WL Cash Values	Term Plus Side Fund	WL + Paid-up Adds.
1	$ 2,187	$ 372	$ 1,815	$ 1,906	$ 0	$101,906	$100,000
2	2,187	401	1,786	3,876	1,456	103,876	100,075
3	2,187	433	1,754	5,912	2,963	105,912	100,203
4	2,187	468	1,719	8,012	4,516	108,012	100,527
5	2,187	504	1,683	10,180	6,119	110,180	100,972
6	2,187	542	1,645	12,416	7,775	112,416	102,321
7	2,187	583	1,604	14,721	9,470	114,721	104,408
8	2,187	626	1,561	17,097	11,210	117,097	107,549
9	2,187	672	1,515	19,542	12,992	119,542	111,463
10	2,187	722	1,465	22,058	14,820	122,058	114,876
11	2,187	777	1,410	24,641	16,698	124,641	119,071
12	2,187	838	1,349	27,289	18,625	127,289	124,156
13	2,187	907	1,280	29,998	20,605	129,998	130,507
14	2,187	986	1,201	32,759	22,638	132,759	136,789
15	2,187	1,076	1,111	35,563	24,720	135,563	143,896
16	2,187	1,179	1,008	38,400	26,857	138,400	152,719
17	2,187	1,295	892	41,256	29,042	141,256	162,745
18	2,187	1,428	759	44,116	31,276	144,116	170,345
19	2,187	1,671	516	46,864	33,559	146,864	183,682
20	2,187	1,943	244	49,463	35,900	149,463	196,132

TABLE 5-16
Equal Outlay Comparison Method

Male Aged 48—$100,000 Whole Life
Dividends Purchase Paid-up Additions
Interest Rate 7%

Policy Year	WL Premium	ART Premium	Prem Diff.	Accum. Diff. @ 7%	WL Cash Values	Term Plus Side Fund	WL + Paid-up Adds.
1	$ 2,187	$ 372	$ 1,815	$ 1,942	$ 0	$101,942	$100,000
2	2,187	401	1,786	3,989	1,456	103,989	100,075
3	2,187	433	1,754	6,145	2,963	106,145	100,203
4	2,187	468	1,719	8,415	4,516	108,415	100,527
5	2,187	504	1,683	10,804	6,119	110,804	100,972
6	2,187	542	1,645	13,321	7,775	113,321	102,321
7	2,187	583	1,604	15,970	9,470	115,970	104,408
8	2,187	626	1,561	18,758	11,210	118,758	107,549
9	2,187	672	1,515	21,692	12,992	121,692	111,463
10	2,187	722	1,465	24,778	14,820	124,778	114,876
11	2,187	777	1,410	28,021	16,698	128,021	119,071
12	2,187	838	1,349	31,426	18,625	131,426	124,156
13	2,187	907	1,280	34,995	20,605	134,995	130,507
14	2,187	986	1,201	38,730	22,638	138,730	136,789
15	2,187	1,076	1,111	42,630	24,720	142,630	143,896
16	2,187	1,179	1,008	46,692	26,857	146,692	152,719
17	2,187	1,295	892	50,915	29,042	150,915	162,745
18	2,187	1,428	759	55,291	31,276	155,291	170,345
19	2,187	1,671	516	59,714	33,559	159,714	183,682
20	2,187	1,943	244	64,155	35,900	164,155	196,132

TABLE 5-17
Equal Outlay Comparison Method

Male Aged 48—$100,000 Whole Life
Dividends Purchase Paid-up Additions
Interest Rate 10%

Policy Year	WL Premium	ART Premium	Prem Diff.	Accum. Diff. @ 10%	WL Cash Values	Term Plus Side Fund	WL + Paid-up Adds.
1	$ 2,187	$ 372	$ 1,815	$ 1,997	$ 0	$101,997	$100,000
2	2,187	401	1,786	4,161	1,456	104,161	100,075
3	2,187	433	1,754	6,506	2,963	106,506	100,203
4	2,187	468	1,719	9,048	4,516	109,048	100,527
5	2,187	504	1,683	11,804	6,119	111,804	100,972
6	2,187	542	1,645	14,794	7,775	114,794	102,321
7	2,187	583	1,604	18,037	9,470	118,037	104,408
8	2,187	626	1,561	21,558	11,210	121,558	107,549
9	2,187	672	1,515	25,381	12,992	125,381	111,463
10	2,187	722	1,465	29,530	14,820	129,530	114,876
11	2,187	777	1,410	34,034	16,698	134,034	119,071
12	2,187	838	1,349	38,922	18,625	138,922	124,156
13	2,187	907	1,280	44,222	20,605	144,222	130,507
14	2,187	986	1,201	49,965	22,638	149,965	136,789
15	2,187	1,076	1,111	56,184	24,720	156,184	143,896
16	2,187	1,179	1,008	62,911	26,857	162,911	152,719
17	2,187	1,295	892	70,183	29,042	170,183	162,745
18	2,187	1,428	759	78,036	31,276	178,036	170,345
19	2,187	1,671	516	86,407	33,559	186,407	183,682
20	2,187	1,943	244	95,317	35,900	195,317	196,132

TABLE 5–18
Equal Outlay Comparison Method

Male Aged 48—$100,000 Whole Life
Dividends Purchase Paid-up Additions
Interest Rate 12%

Policy Year	WL Premium	ART Premium	Prem. Diff.	Accum. Diff. @ 12%	WL Cash Values	Term Plus Side Fund	WL + Paid-up Adds.
1	$ 2,187	$ 372	$ 1,815	$ 2,033	$ 0	$102,033	$ 100,000
2	2,187	401	1,786	4,277	1,456	104,277	100,075
3	2,187	433	1,754	6,755	2,963	106,755	100,203
4	2,187	468	1,719	9,491	4,516	109,491	100,527
5	2,187	504	1,683	12,514	6,119	112,514	100,972
6	2,187	542	1,645	15,859	7,775	115,859	102,321
7	2,187	583	1,604	19,558	9,470	119,558	104,408
8	2,187	626	1,561	23,653	11,210	123,653	107,549
9	2,187	672	1,515	28,189	12,992	128,189	111,463
10	2,187	722	1,465	33,212	14,820	133,212	114,876
11	2,187	777	1,410	38,777	16,698	138,777	119,071
12	2,187	838	1,349	44,941	18,625	144,941	124,156
13	2,187	907	1,280	51,767	20,605	151,767	130,507
14	2,187	986	1,201	59,324	22,638	159,324	136,789
15	2,187	1,076	1,111	67,688	24,720	167,688	143,896
16	2,187	1,179	1,008	76,939	26,857	176,939	152,719
17	2,187	1,295	892	87,171	29,042	187,171	162,745
18	2,187	1,428	759	98,482	31,276	198,482	170,345
19	2,187	1,671	516	110,877	33,559	210,877	183,682
20	2,187	1,943	244	124,456	35,900	224,456	196,132

TABLE 5–19
Linton Yield Method—20 Year

Male Aged 48—$100,000 Whole Life
Dividends Purchase Paid-up Additions
Annual Renewable Term (ART) Decreased to Equalize Death Benefits
Interest Rate 3.132% (on accumulations)

Policy Year	WL Premium	ART Premium	Prem Diff.	Accum. Diff. @ 3.132%	WL Cash Values	Term Plus Side Fund	WL + Paid-up Adds.	ART Face Amount
1	$ 2,187	$ 365	$ 1,822	$ 1,879	$ 0	$100,000	$ 100.000	$98,121
2	2,187	386	1,801	3,795	1,456	100,075	100,075	96,280
3	2,187	409	1,778	5,748	2,963	100,203	100,203	94,455
4	2,187	434	1,753	7,735	4,516	100,527	100,527	92,792
5	2,187	460	1,727	9,759	6,119	100,972	100,972	91,213
6	2,187	491	1,696	11,814	7,775	102,321	102,321	90,507
7	2,187	528	1,659	13,896	9,470	104,408	104,408	90,512
8	2,187	573	1,614	15,995	11,210	107,549	107,549	91,554
9	2,187	627	1,560	18,105	12,992	111,463	111,463	93,358
10	2,187	683	1,504	20,222	14,820	114,876	114,876	94,654
11	2,187	752	1,435	22,336	16,698	119,071	119,071	96,735
12	2,187	836	1,351	24,429	18,625	124,156	124,156	99,727
13	2,187	944	1,243	26,477	20,605	130,507	130,507	104,030
14	2,187	1,068	1,119	28,460	22,638	136,789	136,789	108,329
15	2,187	1,222	965	30,347	24,720	143,896	143,896	113,549
16	2,187	1,422	765	32,086	26,857	152,719	152,719	120,633
17	2,187	1,672	515	33,622	29,042	162,745	162,745	129,123
18	2,187	1,934	253	34,936	31,276	170,345	170,345	135,409
19	2,187	2,472	-285	35,736	33,559	183,682	183,682	147,946
20	2,187	3,113	-926	35,900	35,900	196,132	196,132	160,232

TABLE 5-20
Belth Yearly Cost and Yearly Return Methods

Male Aged 48—$100,000 Whole Life
Dividends Buy Paid-up Additions
Annual Renewable Term (ART) Decreased to Equalize Death Benefits
Interest Rate 3.132% (on accumulations)

Policy Year	WL Premium	ART Rate	Dividends	WL Cash Values	Yearly Benefit	Yearly Investment	Yearly Return %	Yearly Cost
1	$ 2,187	3.72	$ 0	$ 0	$ 372	$ 2,187	−82.99	$ 22.96
2	2,187	4.01	76	1,456	1,927	2,187	−11.88	7.76
3	2,187	4.33	120	2,963	3,503	3,643	−3.84	7.65
4	2,187	4.68	170	4,516	5,133	5,150	−0.33	7.56
5	2,187	5.04	185	6,119	6,777	6,703	1.11	7.82
6	2,187	5.42	217	7,775	8,492	8,306	2.24	7.91
7	2,187	5.83	280	9,470	10,278	9,962	3.17	7.84
8	2,187	6.26	325	11,210	12,091	11,657	3.72	7.94
9	2,187	6.72	390	12,992	13,967	13,397	4.25	7.87
10	2,187	7.22	415	14,820	15,850	15,179	4.42	8.25
11	2,187	7.77	455	16,698	17,800	17,007	4.66	8.46
12	2,187	8.38	550	18,625	19,857	18,885	5.15	8.04
13	2,187	9.07	615	20,605	21,940	20,812	5.42	7.97
14	2,187	9.86	707	22,638	24,108	22,792	5.77	7.58
15	2,187	10.76	775	24,720	26,305	24,825	5.96	7.59
16	2,187	11.79	845	26,857	28,564	26,907	6.16	7.52
17	2,187	12.95	952	29,042	30,913	29,044	6.43	7.08
18	2,187	14.28	1,020	31,276	33,277	31,229	6.56	7.19
19	2,187	16.71	1,140	33,559	35,809	33,463	7.01	6.58
20	2,187	19.43	1,250	35,900	38,395	35,746	7.41	5.98

6

Selection and Classification of Risks

Overview and Learning Objectives

Chapter 6 examines the selection and classification of risks. The chapter conducts a thorough review of the underwriting process and all the detailed factors that enter into the selection and classification of life insurance applicants. The chapter concludes with a close look at the substandard risk and how it is treated in traditional underwriting processes.

By reading this chapter and answering the questions, you should be able to

6-1. Describe the fundamental guiding principles that govern the selection process.

6-2. Describe the various factors that affect proper risk selection.

6-3. Identify the sources of information regarding the applicant, and describe the role that each plays in the selection process.

6-4. Explain two methods of risk classification.

6-5. Describe the special considerations in the selection process when nonmedical insurance is available.

6-6. Describe the concerns regarding the issuance of life insurance at both extremes of age.

6-7. Explain the group concept applied to substandard risks.

6-8. Identify the broad substandard hazard groups for life insurance and give examples of each.

6-9. Identify and explain the methods life insurers use to deal with substandard risks and identify the types of risks for which each method is appropriate.

6-10. Explain the reasons for and against removing a substandard risk rating when the condition improves or another company finds the risk to be standard.

Chapter Outline

Selection of Risks 3
  Guiding Principles 5
  Factors Affecting Risk 6
  Sources of Underwriting Information 16
Classification of Risks 21
  Nonmedical Insurance 24
  Insurance at Extremes of Age 28
  Insurance of Substandard Risks 29
  Incidence of Extra Risk 30
  Treatment of Substandard Risks 31
  Removal of Substandard Rating 36
Chapter Six Review 39

Selection of Risks

The essence of the insurance principle is the sharing of losses by those exposed to a common hazard. This is made possible by contributions to a common fund by those exposed to loss from the common hazard. Each participant must pay into the fund a sum of money reasonably commensurate with the risk that the insured places on the fund. The function of the selection process is to determine whether an applicant's degree of risk for insurance corresponds with the premium established for people in the same classification being considered.

It is neither possible nor desirable to establish risk categories in which each component risk represents a loss potential that is identical to that of all the other risks in the category. For practical reasons, the categories must be broad enough to include risks with substantial differences in loss potential. In life insurance, the primary risk classification is the age of the applicant. Yet within each age group, the probability of death is greater for some than for others. These differences in risk stem from physical condition, occupation, sex, and other factors. The relative frequencies of mortality expectation represented in any randomly selected group of people who are the same age approximates the curve shown in Figure 6-1, with 100 percent representing average mortality for the group. The graph reveals a wide range of mortality expectations for a group of persons falling within a risk category (smoking) measured by age alone. Clearly, all should not be offered insurance on the same terms. Those persons subject to the lowest degree of mortality should pay a lower premium than those who represent an average risk; those with greatly impaired longevity expectations should be charged more than the standard premium or even declined altogether.

The insurance company must establish a range of *mortality classes* within which applicants will be regarded as average risks and hence entitled to insurance at standard rates or, conversely, the limits beyond which applicants will be considered either preferred or substandard and subject to a discount or surcharge. The insurance company should be guided by the principles set forth below.

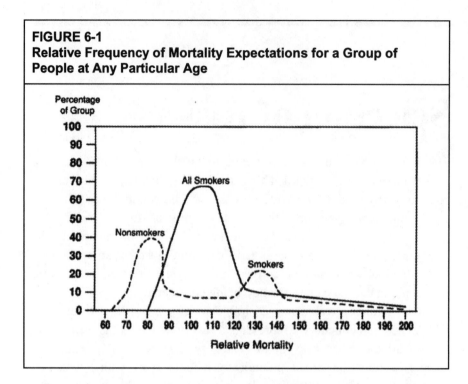

FIGURE 6-1
Relative Frequency of Mortality Expectations for a Group of People at Any Particular Age

After the limits for the various risk categories have been established, the company must adopt selection and classification procedures that will enable it to place applicants for insurance into the proper categories. This process is complicated by the fact that applicants for insurance may not fit the curve illustrated in figure 6-1. That curve depicts the mortality expectations of a randomly selected group, whereas applicants for insurance do not constitute such a group. Applications received by a life insurance company do not reflect randomness. They are biased by antiselection (or adverse selection). Many who seek insurance have knowledge or suspicion of a concealed impairment that might be expected to shorten their life span. A company's underwriting procedures must discover and either screen out such applicants or classify them into appropriate substandard groups.

Guiding Principles

There are certain fundamental principles that must govern the selection procedures of an insurance company if it is to operate on a sound basis. Some of these principles are mutually inconsistent, which means that a company must fashion its selection in such a manner as to balance these opposing principles.

Predominance of the Standard Group

The range of mortality expectations within which applicants will be regarded as average and hence entitled to insurance at standard rates should be broad enough to encompass the great percentage of applicants. That this principle is being observed in practice is evidenced by the fact that approximately 90 percent of the applicants for ordinary insurance in the United States are currently being accepted at standard rates. Only 3 percent are declined, the remaining 6 or 7 percent being insured at substandard rates. An excessive number of rejections undermines the morale of the agency force, increases the cost of doing business, and causes a loss of goodwill among the insurable public. The broader the base of standard risks, the more stable the mortality experience of the group is likely to be.

Balance within Each Risk or Rate Classification

A company must obtain and maintain a proper balance among the risks in each rate classification. If the overall mortality of the risks in each category is to approximate the theoretical average for the group—the goal of most companies—every risk that is worse than average must be offset by one that is better than average.

Irrespective of the underwriting procedures used by a company, if each risk classification is overbalanced with risks whose longevity prospects are less favorable than the assumed average for the classification, the company will end up with excessive mortality costs.

Equity among Policy Owners

The manner in which applicants are grouped for rating purposes should not unduly violate considerations of equity. The spread between the best and worst risks within a classification should not be so great as to produce injustice. If the spread is too great, the better risks may seek insurance with competing companies whose classification system is more equitable, leaving the first company with a disproportionate number of inferior risks.

Compatibility with Underlying Mortality Assumptions

The foregoing considerations tend to be relative matters, concerned primarily with equity and competition. There is another factor, however, that operates as an absolute regulator of a company's underwriting standards—the mortality assumptions entering into the company's premiums. All mortality tables used today reflect the experience of lives that were subject to some degree of underwriting selection. A company's underwriting standards must be at least as effective as those utilized by the companies that created the mortality table. Companies that might be tempted to lower their selection standards in a desire to capture a larger share of the life insurance market are virtually certain to experience higher mortality costs. The general improvement in mortality during recent decades cannot be expected to nullify the long-run consequences of lax underwriting standards.

Factors Affecting Risk

In order to place an applicant for insurance into the proper risk classification, an insurance company needs reliable information about every factor that might significantly affect an applicant's longevity. As a matter of practice, companies seek applicant information about the following:

- age
- build
- physical condition
- personal history
- family history
- occupation
- residence
- habits

- morals
- gender
- plan of insurance
- economic status
- aviation activities
- avocation
- military service

Age

The applicant's age is the most important single factor on individual mortality expectations. Except for the first few years of life, resistance to disease and injury weakens with the passage of time, and the probability of death increases with age. Each applicant is placed within the proper age classification and is then compared to the norm for that age to determine insurability.

Build

The applicant's build—the relationship between height, weight, and distribution of weight—is one of the basic determinants of mortality expectation because deviations are considered adverse factors for mortality. This was one of the first discoveries in the area of medical selection. The first comprehensive statistical study of the relationship between build and mortality was based on the experience of prominent life insurance companies and published in 1913. Today most companies use tables based on their own underwriting experience. These tables determine the minimum and maximum weight ranges, based on height, for each underwriting classification. These charts vary from company to company, so those seeking life insurance that may have a variation from average height and weight may be served well by investigating different companies for their guidelines on this matter.

Experience has shown that overweight increases the mortality at all ages. It can also magnify the significance of other physical ailments such as cardiac conditions. This is known as a co-morbid factor, because the weight condition tends to make another condition worse. Other examples of co-morbid factors would be smoking and high blood pressure.

Most companies uses tables showing average weights, and expected extra mortality is shown as a percentage of standard. Table 6.1 shows the mortality debits associated with each combination of height and weight in intervals of 25 points. As a group, people are expected to experience mortality 25-percent higher than normal (standard) if they fall within the first overweight column. Thus an applicant in that classification would be assigned a debit of 25 points for purposes of the numerical rating system described later in this chapter. There are also special juvenile build tables for people under age 15.

TABLE 6-1
Adult Build Table

Males and Females, aged 16 and over (feet and inches/pounds)

Ht.	Avg. Male Weight	Avg. Female Weight	+25	+50	+75	+100	+125	+150	+200	+250	+300
Ft. In.	Lbs.	Lbs.	Lbs.	Lbs.	Lbs.	Lbs.	Lbs.	Lbs.	Lbs.	Lbs.	Lbs.
4'8"	121	105	180	190	200	215	220	230	240	245	255
4'9"	124	108	185	195	205	215	225	235	245	255	260
4'10"	127	112	190	200	210	220	230	240	250	255	265
4'11"	130	116	195	205	215	225	235	245	255	260	270
5'0"	133	118	195	205	220	230	240	250	255	265	275
5'1"	136	122	205	210	225	235	245	250	260	270	280
5'2"	139	125	205	215	230	235	245	255	265	275	285
5'3"	143	129	210	220	230	245	255	265	275	280	290
5'4"	147	132	220	225	240	250	260	270	280	290	300
5'5"	151	135	225	235	245	255	265	275	285	295	305
5'6"	155	138	230	240	250	260	270	285	295	305	315
5'7"	159	143	235	245	255	270	280	290	300	310	320
5'8"	163	146	240	250	265	275	285	300	310	320	330
5'9"	167	151	250	260	270	285	295	305	320	330	340
5'10"	172	154	255	265	280	290	305	315	325	335	345
5'11"	176	158	260	275	285	300	310	325	335	345	355
6'0"	181	162	270	280	295	305	320	330	340	355	365
6'1"	185	166	275	290	300	315	325	340	350	360	370
6'2"	190	169	285	300	310	325	335	345	360	370	380
6'3"	195	173	290	305	320	330	345	355	365	380	390
6'4"	201	177	300	315	325	340	350	365	375	390	400
6'5"	207	180	305	320	335	345	360	370	385	400	410
6'6"	213	184	315	330	340	355	365	380	395	405	415
6'7"	219		320	335	350	365	375	390	405	415	425
6'8"	225		330	345	360	370	385	400	410	425	435
6'9"	231		335	350	365	380	395	410	425	435	450
6'10"	237		345	360	375	385	400	415	430	440	460
6'11"	243		355	370	385	390	410	420	435	450	465

Physical Condition

In the short run, an applicant's physical condition may outweigh all other factors in importance. In evaluating an application for insurance, the company wishes to know whether there are any impairments of body or mind that would tend to shorten the life expectancy of the applicant. Questions designed to elicit information on the applicant's physical status are included in the application. If a sizable amount of insurance is involved, the information is also confirmed and supplemented by a medical examination and laboratory testing. The primary purpose of the medical examination is to detect any malfunctioning of vital organs. The heart and other parts of the circulatory system are subjected to special scrutiny.

A combination of overweight and hypertension is always regarded seriously. Low blood pressure can usually be disregarded unless it is abnormally low or associated with some definite impairment, such as tuberculosis or congestive heart failure. High blood pressure that responds to treatment by returning to normal levels may receive favorable underwriting consideration,

> **Low Blood Pressure**
>
> - Low blood pressure by itself is not generally considered a high risk factor.
> - Low blood pressure associated with either congestive heart failure or tuberculosis is considered a high risk factor.

provided normal blood pressure levels are maintained for a reasonable period.

Blood Tests—Blood profile tests have provided insurers with useful information regarding applicants' renal and liver function, AIDS/HIV exposure, and blood lipids (fats, oils and waxes). The availability of this additional information has facilitated the proliferation of products offering preferred premium classifications.

Urinalysis—A standard feature of all medical examinations is the urinalysis. This important diagnostic procedure has a three-fold purpose: (1) to measure the functional capacity of the kidneys, (2) to detect infections or other abnormal conditions of the kidneys, and (3) to discover impairments of other vital organs of the body.

> **Urinalysis Can Detect**
>
> - kidney problems
> - infections
> - sugar in the urine (possible diabetes)
> - marijuana
> - cocaine
> - HIV antibodies
> - tobacco

The presence of an undue amount of sugar in the urine suggests the possibility of diabetes. The urinalysis is also used to screen for abnormalities of the bladder, prostrate, kidneys, urinary tract, and the use of illicit drugs such as cocaine and marijuana. Urine testing for the presence of antibodies to HIV is also available.

Personal History

The applicant's health record is usually the most important of the personal history factors. The person to be insured is asked to provide details about his or her health record, past habits, previous environments, and insurance status on the application for insurance. It is customary for the company to contact the attending physician or physicians for the medical details that normally would not be known to the applicant and might have a bearing upon insurability. It is not the practice to consider an application from any person who is scheduled for diagnostic testing or surgery, currently under treatment for any condition, or not fully recovered from any illness.

The company also wants to know whether the applicant has ever been addicted to the use of drugs or alcohol, because there is always a possibility that the "cure" will prove to be only temporary. The past abuse may have caused irrevocable damage to one or more body systems. The personal history may reveal that the applicant has only recently left a hazardous or unhealthful occupation, raising the possibility that he or she may retain ill effects from the job or might return to the job in the future. It may also disclose that the applicant has changed residence to improve his or her health or has had intimate association with a person who has a contagious disease such as tuberculosis.

Finally, the company wants to know whether the applicant has ever been refused insurance by any other company or offered insurance on rated terms. An affirmative answer would indicate a prior impairment that might still be present. Information as to existing insurance also enables the company to judge whether the amount of insurance, existing and proposed, bears a reasonable relationship to the applicant's needs and financial resources.

Family History

Family history is considered significant because certain characteristics are hereditary. Therefore, the applicant is asked to provide information about the ages and state of health of parents and siblings if they are living, or if deceased, their ages at death and causes of death.

It has been determined that if a group of applicants—all free of any known personal qualities that would adversely affect their longevity—is divided into classes on the basis of their family histories as revealed in their applications, the lowest mortality will be found in the class with the most favorable record, and the highest mortality will be found in the class with the poorest record. The best group shows a mortality of about 85 percent of the average for all classes, while the poorest group reflects a mortality of about 115 percent. Therefore companies usually give a credit of 15 points for a very good family history and a debit of 15 points for a very poor history.

Occupation

There are many occupations that are known to have an adverse effect on mortality. The higher mortality rate associated with these occupations may be attributable to a greater than normal accident hazard, unhealthful working conditions, or "socioeconomic" hazards.

Accident Hazards—All people working with machinery are exposed to some accident hazard. Construction workers, miners, electrical workers, and railroad workers are all subject to a high accident rate. Other groups subject to a higher than normal accident rate include fishermen, laborers, lumbermen, and farmers.

Socioeconomic Harzards—The socioeconomic hazard is associated with occupations that employ unskilled and semi-skilled labor and pay commensurately low wages. The extra mortality that occurs among such people is attributable primarily to their unsatisfactory living and working conditions and to inadequate medical care. The low economic status may reflect substandard physical or mental capacity. There are some occupations (bartenders, liquor salespeople, and cab drivers, for example) that are thought to have a socioeconomic hazard because of the environment in which the people work.

All insurance companies have occupational manuals in which they list occupations seen as having an adverse effect on mortality. An applicant employed in one of the listed occupations will pay an extra premium, even though all other factors may be favorable. If the applicant has a substandard rating and leaves that occupation, the rating may be removed. The company cannot, on the other hand, increase the premium if a policy owner changes from an unrated to a rated occupation after the policy has been issued.

Residence

The applicant's residence—present or prospective—is important, since mortality rates vary throughout different geographical regions of the United States and throughout the world. If the applicant is contemplating foreign travel or residence, the insurance company wants to know about it. It also wants to know whether the applicant has recently traveled or resided in a foreign country, particularly in the tropics. Differences among countries as to climate, living standards, sanitary conditions, medical care, political stability, and terrorist risk can be expected to have a decided effect on mortality.

Generally speaking, policies are not issued by United States companies to applicants whose permanent residence is in a foreign country, even though that country may have a climate and living conditions similar to those of the United States. Unless an insurance company has an organization and representatives in another country, it may not be able to get full information about applicants, and practical difficulties may arise in settling claims. Policies are freely issued to persons who plan to be abroad temporarily, provided they do not contemplate visiting crisis areas or making an extended stay in tropical countries.

Habits

The term habits, for underwriting purposes, refers to the use of alcohol and drugs. The company is concerned about an applicant's habitual use of alcohol because of the impairment of judgment and reactions during intoxication; it is concerned about the use of drugs because of the effect on the applicant's health and behavior. Of course, prolonged immoderate use of alcohol may also be harmful to a person's health.

All investigations of the effect of drinking on longevity indicate that there is substantial mortality increase among heavy drinkers. Successful completion of an in-house alcohol treatment program, combined with several years of total abstinence, will render prior abusers insurable on some basis with most life insurers.

A person who is known to be a drug addict cannot obtain insurance on any basis. Even after treatment, a former drug user may be considered uninsurable for as long a period as 5 years and, at best, will be rated heavily for a long period of years because of the possibility of resuming the habit.

Morals

It has been clearly established that departures from the commonly accepted standards of ethical and moral conduct involve extra mortality risks. Marital infidelity and other kinds of behavior that are considered immoral are regarded seriously, partly because they are frequently found in combination with other types of risky behavior, such as overindulgence in alcoholic beverages, gambling, and the use of drugs. The hazards to longevity are the impairment of health and the possibility of violence.

Unethical business conduct is another form of moral hazard. Companies do not care to insure persons who have a record of numerous bankruptcies, operate businesses that are just within the law, or have a general reputation for dishonesty. The companies fear the applicant's misrepresentation and concealment of material underwriting facts on the application. A person who is dishonest in general business dealings is not likely to make an exception for insurance companies, which have always been prime targets for unscrupulous schemes.

Gender

The superior longevity of women is the basis for offering women life insurance coverage at lower premiums. It is also the basis for higher annuity premiums and lower benefits under life-income options for women. Under the 2001 CSO mortality table, males face a higher probability of dying at earlier ages than do females.

Example: **Gender-based Life Expectancy**

Life expectancy at birth in

	2001	1977	1950	1900
Male	76.6 years	73.6	65.6	46.3
Female	80.8 years	79.4	1.1	48.3

Plan of Insurance

All other things being equal, the smaller the amount at risk, the more liberal the underwriting standards of the company. Thus, companies tend to be somewhat more liberal in underwriting single-premium and limited-payment policies, particularly when the extra mortality from a known impairment is not expected to be felt until middle or later life. This is because the higher initial premium discourages antiselection in connection with single premium and limited payment policies. The amount of antiselection is believed to be particularly great in connection with term insurance. The plan of insurance can be especially important in the consideration of substandard risks.

Economic Status

In the eyes of the law every person has an unlimited insurable interest in his or her own life. Thus, the burden of preventing overinsurance is placed on the insurance company. The company carefully investigates the applicant's financial status in order to make sure that family and business circumstances justify the amount of insurance applied for and carried in all companies. This investigation also reveals whether the amount of insurance applied for bears a reasonable relationship to the applicant's income. The company is interested not only in preventing too much insurance on the life of the applicant but also in keeping the insurance in force once issued.

Aviation Activities

Companies do not consider it necessary to impose any underwriting restrictions on passenger travel on any type of nonmilitary aircraft, whether it is a commercial airliner, a company plane, or a personal aircraft. Furthermore, no occupational rating or restriction is applied to crewmembers on regularly scheduled commercial aircraft.

The treatment of private pilots depends on the person's age, experience, training, and amount of flying. Most companies will treat as a standard risk a pilot between the ages of 27 and 60 who has at least 100 hours of pilot experience and does not fly more than 200 hours per year. A person who flies more than 200 hours per year will usually be charged a higher premium. Credits are commonly allowed for advanced training, such as attaining the Instrument Flight Rated (IFR) designation. The underwriting treatment of a crewmember of a military aircraft depends on the applicant's age and type of duty. Accidental death benefit riders often exclude aviation deaths if the insured was the pilot or crewmember of any type of aircraft.

When the applicant will be involved in any aeronautical activity that might present a special hazard, the applicant is usually required to complete a supplementary form that gives the company full details of past, present, and probable future aviation activities.

In the absence of a specific restriction, all basic policies cover the aviation hazard in full. In other words, there is no presumption that the hazard is not covered or is subject to a limitation of liability. It is only when the company discovers, usually through the applicant's own disclosure, that a hazard exists that the company must take special underwriting action.

Avocation

Certain avocations are sufficiently hazardous to justify an extra premium. Examples are racing automobiles, motorcycles, and speedboats; sky diving; skin diving (to depths below 50 feet); hang gliding and mountain climbing.

Military Service

At least since the Civil War, life insurance companies have taken special underwriting awareness of the extra mortality risk associated with applicants engaged in or facing military service during a period of armed conflict. The underwriting reaction has taken three principal forms: rejection of the applicant, limitation on the face amount of insurance issued, or the attachment of a so-called *war clause* that limits the insurer's obligation to return of premiums, less dividends, with interest, if the insured dies under circumstances as defined in the war clause.

The use of a war clause has been the most common method of dealing with the extra hazard of military service. Some companies have used a *"status" war clause*, which limits the insurer's obligation to return of premium if the insured should die while in military service outside the territorial boundaries of the United States, whether or not the cause of death can be attributed to military service. Other companies have used a *"results" war clause*, which limits the insurer's obligation only if the insured's death is the result of military service. While regarded as more liberal to the insured than the status clause, this provision limits liability even though the insured is no longer in a war zone at the time of death. Most companies have been willing to waive these clauses for an appropriate extra premium.

War clauses were widely used during both World Wars and the Korean Conflict in policies that were issued to persons of military age. After the cessation of hostilities, the clauses were generally revoked by the insurance companies without request from the insureds.

During the American involvement in Vietnam, there was no consensus among the companies as to the best approach to the problem, and a variety of practices were followed. One approach used by a number of companies was to refuse to write any coverage on military personnel at the lower ranks but to issue insurance in normal amounts to all other military persons, attaching a "results" type of war clause to policies written. Generally applications were not accepted on persons in combat units or on orders to combat zones.

Recent conflicts in the Middle East rekindled interest in the industry's risk classification practices. Some companies continued to issue unrestricted insurance; others sought to withdraw from the sale of insurance to military personnel in or under orders to report to areas of conflict. These companies cited their long-standing philosophies of not insuring *any* applicant (civilian or military) residing in or traveling to areas of political instability. Others simply defended their practice based on the extra risk of military duty in the Persian Gulf. However, faced with the threat by a number of state insurance department commissioners to label companies as unpatriotic in press conferences and to suspend their licenses for discriminatory practices (even for companies who maintained nondiscriminatory restrictions on military or civilian applicants in areas of political instability), companies generally provided such coverage with normal restrictions on insurance face amounts.

Sources of Underwriting Information

Having briefly examined the information required to classify insurance risks, we will now review how the insurance company acquires that information. Much of it comes from more than one source. This gives the company the means of verifying information that it considers critical to the underwriting decision and serves as a deterrent to conspiracy or fraud by any of the parties to the transaction.

The Agent

A company's field force is the foundation of the selection process. Most companies give their agents explicit instructions about the types of risks that will or will not be acceptable, and they instruct the agents to solicit only those risks they believe to be eligible under the company's underwriting rules.

The agent is usually asked to supply information in a statement that accompanies the application. The information typically includes the following: how long and how well the agent has known the applicant; an estimate of the applicant's net worth and

---

Information Often Asked of an Agent

- How long have you known the applicant?
- How well do you know the applicant?
- What do you estimate as the applicant's income/ net worth?
- What is the applicant's insurance in force?
- Are there other applications for coverage pending
- Does the applicant plan to terminate any existing coverage?
- Did the applicant initiate request for coverage?
- Was there another agent or broker involved in the origination of the application?

---

annual income; the applicant's existing and pending insurance, including any plans for the lapse or surrender of existing insurance; whether the applicant sought the insurance or whether the application was the result of solicitation by the agent; and whether the application came through another agent or broker.

The degree of selection exercised at the field level depends on the integrity and reliability of the agents and brokers. There is clearly some selection involved, since self-interest would cause the agent not to solicit insurance from persons who—because of obvious physical impairments, moral deficiencies, or unacceptable occupations—clearly could not meet the underwriting standards of the company. Beyond that, the amount of selection practiced by the agent is rather limited. Since the agent's compensation depends on the amount of insurance he or she sells, the motive exists to submit any application that stands a chance of being accepted. Hence the responsibility for applying the company's underwriting standards falls to the home office underwriters, who do not labor under the same motivation.

The agent is usually the only company representative to see an applicant face-to-face and make a visual assessment. If there is anything unusual about the applicant that requires an explanation, it is up to the agent to convey that information to the home office.

Experienced agents know what types of additional information the home office underwriters are likely to request when the application reveals specific health problems. These agents can expedite the process by asking for the supplemental reports at the same time the application is completed. Otherwise, the reports will not be generated until the home office staff has made a preliminary evaluation of the case and forwarded a request to the agent for the needed information.

Another advantage that some experienced agents have is a reputation with the home office underwriters for thoroughness, accuracy, and attention to detail in furnishing applications and supporting documents. This reputation can benefit applicants who are on the borderline between classifications and can be rated either way. They may get the benefit of the lower premium class because of their agent's reputation. Borderline cases from agents who send applications with less than complete information are more likely to be classified under the higher premium category when it is strictly a judgment call.

The Applicant

Much of the information a company needs to underwrite a case is supplied by the applicant. This information is contained in the application, which constitutes an important part of the offer and acceptance process and will become part of the contract if the policy is issued. Application blanks usually consist of two parts—the first containing identification and general questions and the second including questions to be asked by the medical examiner, or by the advisor subject to age and amount limitations under a "nonmedical" underwriting program, discussed later in this chapter.

Part one of the application is usually filled out by the agent on behalf of the applicant, who must sign it and certify the correctness of the information. The applicant's signature is generally witnessed by the agent.

Information Often Requested of an Applicant

- Identification
- Age
- Medical history
- Occupation and recent work history
- Amount and type of insurance applied for
- Existing insurance
- Intended policy owner
- Intended beneficiary
- Physicians consulted within last 5 years
- Use of alcohol and drugs
- Family health history

The answers to questions in the second part of the application normally must be recorded in the medical examiner's handwriting, and the applicant must sign the form to attest to the completeness and accuracy of its contents.

The Medical Examiner

In addition to recording the answers to part 2 of the application, the medical examiner is required to file a separate report or certificate, which accompanies the application but is not seen by the applicant. Some companies ask the examiner to review the applicant's driver's license or other form of identification to establish conclusive identification.

The basic purpose of the medical examiner's report is to transmit the findings of the physical examination. The medical examiner's report is considered to be the property of the insurance company and is carefully safeguarded at all times.

Attending Physicians

Attending physicians are a source of information on applicants who have undergone medical treatment prior to applying for insurance. When it appears that the information in the attending physician's files might influence the insurance company's underwriting decision, such information is sought as a matter of routine. The signed application gives the insurer the right to seek medical and personal information about the applicant.

Insurance companies have enjoyed a remarkable degree of cooperation from the medical profession regarding inquiries of this nature, with physicians normally providing all of the relevant information in their files. However, their response is not always prompt, and their delay suspends the policy issuance process. To expedite the physician's response, insurers usually send a check along with the letter of inquiry to cover the physician's expenses incurred to supply the information.

Inspection Report

Insurance companies attempt to verify all information from the previously mentioned sources, generally in one of two ways. The first method is through telephone interviews conducted by insurance company staff, which allows the insurer to structure the questions to best serve its purposes. The second alternative is to employ the services of an independent reporting agency. The unique advantage of these independent investigations is that they provide an evaluation of the applicant by a source having no interest in the outcome of the application.

The insurer's home office or its local agency may make the request for an *inspection report*. In either case, the report is filed directly with the insurance company's home office. Under provisions of the Fair Credit Reporting Act the applicant has the right to review the contents of the report at the offices of the agency that produced it.

The thoroughness of the inspection depends on the amount of insurance involved. When the amount of insurance is not large, the report is rather brief, commenting in a general way on the applicant's health, habits, finances, environment, and reputation. When a large amount has been applied for, the report tends to be comprehensive. It reflects the results of interviews with the applicant's neighbors, employer, banker, business associates, and others. The inspection focuses particularly on the applicant's business and personal ethics. The report calls attention to any bankruptcies and fire losses, and it comments on the applicant's use of alcohol, drugs, and other departures from "normal" social behavior. The inspection also occasionally uncovers physical impairments that were not revealed in the medical examiner's report.

The Medical Information Bureau

A final source of information is the *Medical Information Bureau (MIB)*. This organization is a clearinghouse for confidential medical data on applicants for life insurance. The information is reported and maintained in code symbols to help preserve its confidentiality.

Companies that are members of the Bureau are expected to report any impairments designated on the official list. The designated impairments are related primarily to the applicant's physical condition but also include hereditary characteristics and addiction to alcohol and narcotics. If they have a bearing on insurability, any suspicious tendencies revealed in an examination are reported in order to bring the matter to the notice of all companies using the Bureau's records. All impairments must be reported whether the company accepts, postpones, or declines the risk, or offers a modified plan of insurance. In no event does the company report its underwriting decision to the Bureau.

A company normally screens all of its applicants against the MIB file of reported impairments. If the company finds impairment and wants further details, it must submit its request through the MIB, but only after it first conducts its own complete investigation from all known sources. The company that reported the impairment is not obligated to supply further information, but if it agrees to do so, it provides the requested information through the MIB.

It should be emphasized that there is no basis for the widespread belief that a person who is recorded in the MIB files cannot obtain insurance at standard rates. The information contained therein is treated like underwriting data from any other source and, in the final analysis, may be outweighed by favorable factors. In many cases, it will enable a company to take favorable action, since favorable medical test results are reported as well as unfavorable ones. In any case, the rules of the MIB stipulate that a company cannot take unfavorable underwriting action *solely* on the basis of the information in the MIB files. In other words, the company must be in possession of other unfavorable underwriting facts or else determine through its own channels of investigation that the condition of impairment recorded in the MIB files is substantial enough to warrant an unfavorable decision.

Classification of Risks

After all available underwriting information about an insurance application has been assembled, the data must be evaluated and a decision reached as to whether the applicant is to be accepted at standard rates, placed in one of the various substandard classifications, or rejected entirely. This is clearly the focus of the vitally important selection process. Ideally the evaluation and classification system used by a company should (1) accurately measure the effect of each of the factors, favorable and unfavorable, that can be expected to influence an applicant's longevity; (2) assess the combined impact of multiple factors, including the situations in which the factors are conflicting; (3) produce consistently equitable results; and (4) be simple and relatively inexpensive to operate.

The Judgment Method of Rating

The earliest rating system used in the United States was the "judgment method." Routine cases were processed with minimum consideration by clerks trained to review applications, and doubtful or borderline cases were resolved by supervisors relying on their experience and general impressions.

The *judgment method* functions poorly when there are multiple unfavorable factors (offset perhaps by some favorable factors) or when the risk, if it does not qualify for standard insurance, must be fitted into the proper substandard classification. To overcome the weaknesses of the judgment method of rating, the numerical rating system, is used today by most insurers.

The Numerical Rating System

The *numerical rating system* is based on the principle that a large number of factors enter into the composition of a risk and that the impact of each of these factors on the longevity of the risk can be determined by a statistical study of lives possessing that factor. It assumes that the average risk accepted by a company has a value of 100 percent and that each of the factors that enter into the risk can be expressed as a percentage of the whole. Favorable factors are assigned negative values, called credits, while unfavorable factors are assigned positive values, called debits. The summation of the debits and credits, added to or deducted from the par value of 100, represents the numerical value of the risk. People with low mortality risks get lower scores. An older diabetic male military test pilot who smokes gets a higher score.

Assigning Weights to Risk Factors—Naturally, it would be impossible to assign weights to all the factors that might influence a risk. In practice, values are generally assigned to the following 10 factors:

1. build
2. physical condition
3. medical history
4. family history
5. occupation
6. aviation and avocation
7. residence
8. habits
9. morals
10. plan of insurance

The values assigned to the various factors are derived from mortality studies among groups of people possessing those characteristics or, in some cases, from estimates of what such mortality studies might be expected to show. For example, if the mortality experience of a group of insured lives with a particular medical history has been found to be 135 percent of that among all standard risks, a debit (addition) of 35 percentage points might be assigned to that medical history.

It should be noted that credits are generally not allowed when there are other ratable physical impairments or debits for blood pressure or other cardiovascular-renal impairments.

The ratings obtained by this method may go as low as 75 and as high as 500. The ratings that fall between 75 and 125 are usually classified as standard, although some companies, especially those that do not write substandard insurance, may include risks that produce a rating of 130 (or if the applicant is below age 30, even 140) in the standard category. Risks that produce ratings beyond the standard limit are either assigned to appropriate substandard classifications or declined. Many companies are willing to accept risks that indicate a mortality rate up to 500 percent of normal. Most companies feel that assessing mortality beyond 500 percent will yield results too erratic to price accurately.

Example: The applicant is a married man, aged 32, living in Philadelphia, Pennsylvania, with two children. He is 6-feet-one-inch tall and weighs 290 pounds. He is in good physical condition except that his expanded chest measurement is one inch less than the girth of his abdomen. His personal health record shows no operations or other ailments that would have an adverse effect on longevity. His family is long-lived, and the family history reveals no tuberculosis, insanity, cardiac conditions, malignancies, or diabetes. He has been employed for several years as a warehouseman in an industrial plant. His habits and morals are good. The plan of insurance is 20-payment whole life insurance.

The company might evaluate the facts as follows: The applicant is overweight, which calls for a debit of 50 points according to table 6-1. The unfavorable build (girth greater than chest expanded) is the basis for an additional debit of 20 points. The favorable family history receives a credit of 15 points, and the plan of insurance, 20-payment whole life, calls for an additional credit of 10 points. The residence is a neutral factor (only debits are assigned to residence, and debits are usually assessed only for a foreign or tropical residence). Regarding habits and morals, there is no credit for good behavior, only debits for bad behavior. The occupation is also a neutral factor with no debits or credits. Thus, the debits add up to 70 points and the credits add up to only 25. Hence, the numerical value of the risk is 145.

The analysis is summarized below:

Base = 100

Factor	Debit	Credit
Weight: overweight	50	–
Physical condition: favorable	–	–
Build: unfavorable	20	–
Family history: superior	–	15
Occupation: favorable	–	–
Residence: normal	–	–
Habits and morals: favorable	–	–
Plan of insurance: 20-payment whole life	–	10
	70	25

Rating = 145

Nonmedical Insurance

A substantial portion of all new insurance is written without a medical examination. Neither group nor industrial life insurance ordinarily requires a medical examination and large amounts of term and ordinary life insurance are being sold without a medical examination. While any type of insurance sold without a medical examination might logically be called *nonmedical insurance*, the expression usually refers to ordinary insurance sold in that manner.

Because nonmedical insurance is subject to higher than normal mortality, at least for the first several policy years, insurance companies have set a limit on the amount that will be made available to any one applicant.

Companies also impose a limit on the ages at which nonmedical insurance will be issued. Studies have shown that the extra mortality resulting from waiving the medical examination increases with age and after a point will exceed any savings in selection expense. The point at which the extra mortality costs will exceed the expense savings is obviously a function of the underwriting age limit, but most companies place it around age 50. There is usually no lower age limit; most companies offer nonmedical insurance down to age zero.

A third safeguard is the general limitation of nonmedical insurance to standard risks. As a broad class, substandard risks must submit to medical examinations. Exceptions are commonly made, however, for risks that are substandard because of an occupational, aviation, or avocational hazard.

A final safeguard is the increased attention given to underwriting information from sources other than the medical examiner. A urine specimen and blood profile may be required for home office analysis. If the applicant has recently been under the care of a physician, a statement may be necessary from the attending physician (at the expense of the company). If any adverse medical information is revealed by the applicant's statement, the inspection report, or other source, the company may demand a complete medical examination.

A particularly heavy responsibility is placed on the agent, with great reliance on the agent's judgment and integrity. Agents may submit nonmedical applications only from applicants who appear to meet the company's underwriting requirements from a physical, medical, occupational, and moral standpoint. The agent must elicit from the applicant and accurately document most of the information that a medical examiner would seek. A detailed agent's certificate that records the agent's underwriting impressions of the applicant is also required. It is understandable that the privilege of submitting nonmedical business is not bestowed indiscriminately on the field force.

Inspection reports are sometimes ordered to supplement the larger nonmedical insurance applications, even though such information would not be requested for medically underwritten cases for the same or larger amounts of coverage.

Economics of Nonmedical Insurance

Several advantages are associated with nonmedical insurance. It lessens the demands on the time and talents of the medical profession, it eliminates the delays and inconvenience connected with medical examinations, and it removes one of the greatest psychological barriers to the sale of insurance. Important as these advantages are, insurers could not enjoy them if nonmedical insurance did not rest on a solid economic foundation. It must justify itself on a dollars-and-cents basis.

Nonmedical insurance is subject to a higher rate of mortality than medically examined business. This extra mortality is believed to stem from (1) impairments known to the applicant but deliberately concealed and (2) impairments not known to the applicant that could have been discovered by a medical examination. This extra mortality can be measured and expressed as a dollar amount per $1,000 of insurance.

The procedure customarily used to measure the extra mortality is to compare the mortality experience on nonmedical business with the mortality at the same ages, years of issue, and durations on business that was subject to a medical examination. This does not give a perfect answer since the two groups may not be comparable in all respects. For example, they might differ as to ratio of males to females, income level, and size of policies.

Studies reveal that most of the extra mortality occurs during the first 10 years after issue, although some extra mortality is observable up to 15 years after the policy is issued. The disparity between nonmedical and medical mortality increases with age of issue, both in absolute amount and as a percentage of the base mortality rate. This seems to indicate that up to a point at least, the importance and effectiveness of the medical examination grows greater with age. Extra death claims are offset by the savings in medical examiners' fees and incidental home office expenses, less the increase in expenditures for inspection reports and attending physicians' statements. Note: This net saving is realized on every application that does not involve a medical examination, while the extra mortality is experienced only on those policies that remain in force until they become claims—a much smaller number because of lapses and surrenders. The savings in selection expenses are expressed as an amount per policy and range from $30 to $100.

Example: ***Trade-off between extra mortality costs and savings in underwriting expense***

When the extra mortality per $1,000 and the expense savings per policy are known, it is a matter of simple arithmetic to determine the proper limits for nonmedical insurance. If, at ages below 30, the extra mortality cost per $1,000 is $0.75 and the expense savings per policy is assumed to be $100, the company could safely offer about $133,000 of nonmedical insurance to applicants under 30 ($100 ÷ 0.75 = $133 rounded to nearest whole number). With the same expense savings and an extra mortality cost of $1.50 per $1,000 at ages 30 to 34, the proper limit for persons in that age group would be $67,000 ($100 ÷ 1.50 = $67 rounded). By the same logic, the limit for applicants aged 35 to 39 might be about $30,000.

> Thus, the need for age limits and the equity of variable limits are apparent.

In practice, companies are inclined to offer larger amounts of nonmedical insurance than the above figures suggest. While the amount made available to any one applicant might seem excessive, all applicants do not request the maximum. Because the company's objective is to break even on its nonmedical business in the aggregate, it may safely set its limits higher than the precise relationship between the expected extra mortality and expense savings would support.

Furthermore, at ages under 30, the absolute rate of mortality is so low and the probability of finding impairments on examination so small that the nonmedical rules can be greatly relaxed. The increased use of blood and urine screening tests also allows for increased nonmedical limits.

Paramedical Examination

Somewhere between the medical examination and nonmedical evidence is another alternative—the paramedical examination. This examination is conducted by nurses or other medical technicians and consists of securing basic examination from measurements: height, weight, blood pressure, pulse rate and waist measurement. Blood and urine specimens may also be taken.

The chief advantages of *paramedical examinations* are their reduced cost compared to a physician's fees and their convenience for the client: most services offer traveling examiners. The paramedical examinations, however, do not include the more-sophisticated tests or detailed reports typically provided by an insurance medical examiner.

Example: The convenience of paramedical examiners coming to the home or workplace of the applicant eliminate potential delays in the process that scheduling a medical examination might impose. These traveling examiners have expedited the evaluation process and reduced some of the costs.

Insurance at Extremes of Age

Applications for insurance at both extremes of age must be carefully underwritten. In both cases, the basic obstacle is limited insurable interest—which, if not recognized, may lead to speculation and excessive mortality.

In some families, there is a demand for juvenile insurance, and most companies will write insurance on the lives of very young children, even down to 15 days old. These insurers attempt to cope with the lack of insurable interest in three ways: (1) by limiting the coverage to amounts much smaller than those available to adults, particularly at the early ages, (2) by seeing that the insurance on the child bears a reasonable relationship to the amounts in force on the other members of the family, especially the breadwinner, and (3) by seeking a large volume of juvenile insurance applications to minimize adverse selection.

From the standpoint of the basic mortality risk, juvenile risks are very attractive. With the exception of the first few weeks after birth, the death rate is very low and does not begin to climb until around age 10. The death rate is high immediately after birth because of the hazards of childbirth to the child, congenital defects, and the naturally delicate physique of a newborn infant. This period of heavy mortality can be avoided by limiting coverage to children who have attained the age of one, 3, or perhaps 6 months. Family economic circumstances seem to have greater influence on mortality at the younger ages than later in life, which makes it necessary to inquire about family finances. In general, juvenile insurance is sold without a medical examination.

At extreme older ages, the volume of insurance issued is not yet large enough to yield predictable mortality results. The restricted demand for insurance at those ages reflects the high cost of the insurance, the general inability to satisfy the medical requirements, and the limited need for new insurance. In the second place, a high degree of adverse selection is associated with applications received at those ages. Low volume in itself is suggestive of adverse selection, but when it is accompanied by burdensome premium payments, the environment is even more conducive to adverse selection. This antiselection may be exercised by the insureds themselves, aware of a serious impairment, or by a third party, perhaps a relative, who seeks insurance on the life of an elderly person for speculative reasons. A third factor, related to the others, is the relative ineffectiveness of the medical examination for elderly people. A routine medical examination does not reveal many conditions of a degenerative nature that can materially shorten the life of the elderly applicant.

Estate tax law changes have led to a dramatic expansion of the marketing of life insurance, particularly joint-life and survivorship products, to applicants of advanced age. This has resulted in the extension of insurable ages to 80 or 85 by some insurers.

Insurance of Substandard Risks

Using the numerical rating system or some other method of rating, an insurance company classifies certain risks as *substandard risks*. A group or classification of risks rated substandard is expected to produce a higher mortality rate than a group of normal lives. The group concept must be emphasized, because—as with insuring standard risks—there is no certainty about any one individual's longevity expectations. All calculations, therefore, are based on the anticipated average experience of a large number of individuals, and the experience of any one individual is merged into that of the group.

This is an elementary concept, but it needs to be repeated in any consideration of substandard insurance, involving, as it does, extra cost to or restricted benefits for the policy owner or beneficiary. It is commonly supposed that if an individual is placed in a substandard classification and subsequently lives to a ripe old age, the company erred in its treatment of the case. However, if 1,000 persons, each of whom is suffering from a particular physical impairment, are granted insurance, it is certain that the death rate among them will be greater than the death rate among a group of people the same age who are free from of any discernible impairments. To allow for the higher death rates that will certainly occur within the substandard group, the company must collect an extra premium from—or impose special terms on—all who are subject to the extra risk since it is not known which of the members of the group will be responsible for the extra mortality. It is not expected that every member of the group will survive for a shorter period than the normal life expectancy. In fact, it is a certainty that this will not be the case; it is known merely that a larger proportion of people in a normal group will attain normal life expectancy.

The fact that certain members of the impaired group reach old age is, therefore, no indication that an error was made in their cases. If they had paid no extra premium, a still higher premium would have been required from the others. Generally speaking, nothing could—or should—be refunded to members of a substandard group who live beyond the normal life expectancy, provided that the extra premiums charged (or other special terms imposed) were a true measure of the degree of extra hazard represented by the group.

Incidence of Extra Risk

If a group of substandard risks is to be fairly treated, the degree of extra mortality represented by the group and the approximate period in life when the extra mortality is likely to occur must both be known within reasonable limits. It makes a great deal of difference financially whether the extra claims are expected to occur primarily in early life, at middle age, old age, or at a level rate throughout the individuals' lifetimes. If the extra mortality occurs during the early years of the policies when the amount at risk is relatively large, the burden on the company will be greater than if it occurs later when the amount at risk is relatively small. Hence, between two substandard groups representing the same aggregate amount of extra mortality, the group whose extra mortality is concentrated later in life should pay a smaller extra premium than the group whose extra mortality occurs earlier.

There are innumerable variations in the distribution of the extra risk among different classes of substandard risks. It is impractical, however, for companies to recognize all the many patterns of risk distribution. The majority of companies therefore proceed on the assumption that each substandard risk falls into one of three broad groups. In the first group, the additional hazard increases with age; in the second group, it remains approximately constant at all ages; in the third, it decreases with age.

Examples of each type of hazard are easy to find. High blood pressure presents an increasing hazard. Occupational hazards represent a constant hazard, as do certain types of physical defects. Even though most constant hazards tend to increase somewhat with age, they are treated as if they remain constant. Impairments attributable to past illnesses and surgical operations are hazards that decrease with time, although not all illnesses and operations fall into this category.

Treatment of Substandard Risks

Several methods have been devised to provide insurance protection to people with impaired health. With the exception of the lien, most American life insurance companies utilize all the available methods. In general, companies make an effort to adapt the method to the type of hazard represented by the impaired risk, but departures from theoretically correct risk treatment are frequently made for practical reasons.

Increase in Age

One method of treatment, widely used in the past and still favored by many companies for joint-and-survivor products, is to "rate up" the age of the applicant. Under this method, called the *increase-in-age method*, the applicant is assumed to be a number of years older than his or her real age, and the policy is written accordingly. The number of years older is usually determined by adding the amount estimated as necessary to provide for the extra mortality to the net premium for the applicant's actual age, and then finding the premium in the standard table that most closely matches that total, and deriving the rate-up from the standard age in the table. For example, assume the net level premium for an ordinary life contract issued at age 25 is $12.55 per $1,000. If a male applicant for such a contract, aged 25, should be placed in a substandard classification that is expected to produce an extra mortality equivalent to $3.67, the correct net premium for the applicant would be $16.22 per $1,000. The net level premium in the standard table closest to this amount is $16.43, which is the premium for age 33. Therefore, the applicant is rated up 8 years and is thereafter treated in all respects as if he were 33 years of age. His policy would contain the same surrender and loan values and would be entitled to the same dividends, if any, as any other ordinary life contract issued at age 33.

Example: **Increase-in-Age Method**

In some substandard cases, the estimated extra mortality charge will be added to the net premium for the applicant's actual age to determine the appropriate net premium level. Then the insurer will offer a policy for the age associated with the higher net premium.

The policy will have higher premiums and build

---

cash values (if any) faster than a policy based on actual age. For example, an extra mortality charge of $10 per $1000 of coverage for someone aged 30 might be the equivalent of a net premium for a 35-year-old for a specific insurer. The insurer would propose a policy and premiums based on age 35 instead of age 30.

This method of dealing with substandard risks is suitable only when the extra risk is a decidedly increasing one and will continue to increase indefinitely at a greater rate. Although few impairments give rise to such a consistent and rapid increase in the rate of mortality as provided in the rated-up age method, the method is considered to be appropriate for all types of substandard risks where the extra mortality, in general, increases with age.

The chief appeal of the method for the insurance company is its simplicity. Policies can be dealt with for all purposes as standard policies issued at the assumed age. No separate set of records is required; no special calculations of premium rates, cash and other surrender values, reserves, and dividends are involved. For the applicant, the method is attractive because the higher premium is accompanied by correspondingly higher surrender values and dividends (if participating). Thus, a portion of each extra premium is refunded as a dividend, and another portion is applied to the accumulation of larger surrender values than would be available under a policy issued at the applicant's true age. If the policy is surrendered for cash, the additional cash value is equivalent to a refund of a portion of the extra premium paid. To protect themselves against the use of the surrender privilege for this purpose, some companies add a slight loading to the original extra premium.

Extra Percentage Tables

The most common method of dealing with risks that present an increasing hazard is to classify them into groups based on the expected percentage of standard mortality and to charge premiums that reflect the appropriate increase in mortality (*extra percentage method*). The number of substandard classifications may vary from three to 12, depending to some extent on the degree of extra mortality the company is willing to underwrite. Some companies are unwilling to underwrite substandard groups whose average mortality is expected to exceed 200 percent of standard, and they usually establish three substandard classifications with expected average mortalities of 150, 175, and 200 percent, respectively.

Table 6-2 shows a scale of substandard classifications widely used by companies offering coverage up to 500 percent of standard mortality.

TABLE 6-2 Scale of Substandard Classifications			
Class	Mortality (Percent)	Class	Mortality (Percent)
1	125	6	250
2	150	7	275
3	175	8	300
4	200	10	350
5	225	12	400
		16	500

In effect, a special mortality table reflecting the appropriate degree of extra mortality is prepared for each substandard classification, and a complete set of gross premium rates is computed for each classification. The gross premium rates at specified ages quoted by one company for an ordinary life contract under substandard tables A, B, C, and D, are set forth in Table 6-3. For purposes of comparison the rate for a standard risk at each 5-year age period is also given.

Perhaps the most notable feature of these premiums is that they do not increase in proportion to the degree of extra mortality involved. The rates under substandard table D, for example, are not double the rates at which insurance is made available to standard risks. Neither are the rates under table B one-and-one-half times the standard rates. There is a twofold explanation of this apparent inconsistency. In the first place, the rates illustrated in Table 6-3 are gross premium rates, and the amount of loading does not increase from one rate classification to the other, except for commissions and premium taxes but remains constant (with minor exceptions). In the second place, the percentage of extra mortality is computed on the basis of actual—rather than tabular—mortality. Additions to standard premiums to arrive at the substandard rates reflect only the excess mortality for the substandard classifications over the actual standard mortality. Therefore, the rates for the substandard classifications are not proportionally greater than the premiums for the standard risks.

For example, using Table 6-3, the standard rate for a 50-year-old is $41.31. Although substandard class A represents a 25-percent increase in mortality, the class A premium of $45.69 represents only a 10-percent increase in premium.

TABLE 6-3
Illustrative Gross Annual Premium Rates at Selected Ages for Ordinary Life Contract under Substandard Tables A, B, C, and D

| Age | Rate for Standard Risks | Substandard Tables | | | |
		A 125 Percent	B 150 Percent	C 65 Percent	D 200 Percent
15	$14.46	$15.74	$16.67	$17.53	$18.37
20	16.15	17.62	18.67	19.68	20.63
25	18.21	19.90	21.15	22.33	23.45
30	20.81	22.82	24.33	25.75	27.12
35	24.14	26.56	28.41	30.19	31.88
40	28.45	31.38	33.70	35.93	38.07
45	34.01	37.59	40.50	43.32	46.04
50	41.31	45.69	49.40	52.99	56.48
55	50.99	56.41	61.11	65.71	70.22
60	64.03	70.74	76.73	82.67	88.54
65	81.82	90.08	97.69	105.34	112.97

The extra mortality under the extra-percentage method is relatively small at the early ages, unless the percentage of extra mortality is high, since the normal (or base rate) mortality at such ages is small. As the base death rate increases, however, the margin for extra mortality increases very greatly. This explains why the method is appropriate for substandard risks whose impairments are expected to produce an increasing rate of extra mortality. Like the increase-in-age method, extra-percentage substandard tables should, in theory, be used only when the hazard is expected to increase at a greater rate. In practice, however, they are used for all types of impairments that are expected to worsen as the years go by.

The reserves under policies issued in accordance with extra percentage tables must be calculated on the basis of the mortality assumptions underlying the premiums, which require separate classification records and tabulations. Depending on company practice and state law, surrender values may be based on the special mortality table or may be the same as surrender values under policies issued to standard risks. Many companies do not make the extended-term insurance nonforfeiture option available under extra-percentage-table policies, especially at the higher percentages, and those that do compute the period on the basis of the higher mortality rate even when only the normal surrender value is allowed.

Extra percentage tables are sometimes used as a basis for determining the extra premiums needed under other methods of underwriting substandard risks. Thus, the risk may first be assigned to an extra percentage table, after which the rating is translated into the equivalent age markup. This is a convenient way to determine the necessary step-up in age when statistics on the additional mortality expected from a particular impairment are available.

| *Example:* | A substandard health condition that is expected to result in an increasing rate of extra mortality with aging is an appropriate situation for either the increase-in-age approach or the extra-percentage method. |

Flat Extra Premium

A third method of underwriting substandard risks is by assessing a flat extra premium. Under this method, the standard premium for the policy in question is increased by a specified number of dollars per $1,000 of insurance. Assessed as a measure of the extra mortality involved, the flat extra premium does not vary with the age of the applicant. It may be paid throughout the premium-paying period of the policy, or it may be terminated after a period of years when the extra hazard has presumably disappeared.

The *flat extra premium* method is normally used when the hazard is thought to be constant (deafness or partial blindness, for example) or decreasing (as with a family history of tuberculosis or the aftermath of a serious illness or surgical operation, in which case the flat extra is usually temporary in duration). The flat extra premium is widely used to cover the extra risk associated with certain occupations and avocations. When used for this purpose, the extra premium usually ranges from $2.50 to $10 per $1,000 of insurance. Unless a permanent impairment is involved, the extra premium is generally removed if the insured leaves the hazardous occupation or avocation.

At first glance, a flat extra premium for an extra hazard that adds an approximately constant amount to the rate of mortality at each age appears to be a fair arrangement. In practice, however, it works out equitably only if an allowance is made for the fact that the amount at risk is not a level sum under most policies. Except for term policies, the net amount at risk decreases with each year that elapses. Thus a flat extra premium becomes an increasing percentage of the amount at risk and, in effect, provides for an increasing extra risk.

When the extra risk is constant, the extra premium for a cash value contract should diminish each year in the proportion that the amount at risk decreases. To avoid the labor and expense that would be involved in such an annual adjustment, and in recognition of the fact that the flat extra premium is an approximation, most companies compute the flat extra addition on the basis of the average amount at risk. Some companies vary the extra premium with the plan of insurance, charging less for high-cash-value policies than for policies with lower reserve elements.

The flat extra premium is not reflected in policy values and dividends. It is assumed that the entire amount of the extra premium is needed each year to pay additional claims and expenses. The dividends and guaranteed values are identical to those of a comparable policy without the flat extra premium. Thus, the policy owner must regard the flat extra premium as an irrecoverable outlay.

Removal of Substandard Rating

Frequently, a person who is classified as a substandard risk and insured on that basis by one company subsequently applies for insurance with another company—or even the same company—and is found to be a standard risk in all respects. Under these circumstances, the person's natural reaction is to request the removal of the substandard rating.

Theoretically, the rating should not be removed unless the impairment on which it was based was known to be temporary or was due to occupation or residence. At the time the policy was originally issued, the insured was placed in a special classification of risks whose members were presumably impaired to approximately the same degree. It was known by the company that some of the members of the group would die within a short period, while others would survive far beyond their normal expectancy. It was likewise known that the health of some of the members would deteriorate with the passage of time, while some members would grow more robust. By the time the insured under consideration is in normal health, the health of many others in the original group has undoubtedly worsened. Many of them cannot now get insurance on any terms, while others are insurable only at a greater extra premium than that charged. If the company reduces the premiums for those whose health has improved, it should be permitted to increase the premiums of those whose health has deteriorated. Because the premiums of those in the latter category cannot be adjusted upward, the premiums of those in the former category should not be reduced.

As a practical matter, however, the company is virtually forced to remove the substandard rating of a person who can demonstrate current insurability at standard rates. If it does not do so, the policy owner will almost surely surrender the extra-rate insurance and replace it with insurance at standard rates in another company. Knowing this, most companies calculate their initial substandard premiums on the assumption that the extra premium will have to be removed for people who subsequently qualify for standard insurance. Thus, the common practice is to remove the extra premium upon proof that the insured is no longer substandard.

Where an extra premium has been imposed because of occupation, residence, or a temporary risk, it is proper to discontinue the extra premium upon termination of the condition that created the extra hazard and adjust the premium to standard. It is necessary to exercise care in these cases, however, particularly when the source of the rating was occupation or residence. There is always a possibility that the insured may subsequently return to the hazardous

> **Removal of a Substandard Rating Often**
>
> - Waiting period of one or 2 years
> - Medical examination(s)

occupation or residence, or that his or her health has already been affected adversely. Hence, it is customary in such cases to require that a specified period of time, such as one or 2 years, must elapse after cessation of the extra hazard before the rating will be removed. Occasionally, a medical examination is also required. At the end of the period, the adjustment is usually made retroactively to the change of occupation or residence.

Chapter Six Review

Key terms and concepts are explained in the glossary. Answers to the review questions and the self-test questions follow the Glossary.

Key Terms and Concepts

mortality classes
"status" war clause
"results" war clause
inspection report
medical information bureau (M.I.B.)
judgment method of rating
numerical rating system

nonmedical insurance
paramedical exam
substandard risks
increase-in-age method
extra-percentage tables
flat extra premium

Review Questions

6-1. What is the function of the selection process?

6-2. Jimmy and Johnny were both born on the same date. Does this mean that they will always pay the identical premium if they both purchase the same type of life insurance policy on the same day? Explain.

6-3. What is the potential result if each risk classification used in the selection process is overloaded with risks whose longevity prospects are less favorable than the assumed average for the classification?

6-4. Why should a company's underwriting standards be at least as effective as those utilized by the companies that supplied the data for the mortality table used in risk classification?

6-5. Why are the following considered an important factor in classifying applicants for life insurance?

    a. age
    b. build
    c. physical condition

6-6. What is the purpose of blood tests and urinalysis diagnostic procedures?

6-7. What information can be acquired by completing the applicant's personal history questionnaire?

6-8. Why is family history significant in the selection process?

6-9. How do the following factors associated with various occupations have an adverse effect on mortality and therefore effect the selection and/or premium charge for applicants engaged in such occupations?

    a. accident hazards
    b. socioeconomic hazards

6-10. What relevance does an applicant's residence or morals have in the life insurance selection process?

6-11. How can aviation activities affect the risk classification of an applicant for life insurance?

6-12. a. What three principal forms of underwriting action have historically been associated with applicants engaged in or facing military service during a period of armed conflict?
    b. How does the "status" clause differ from the "results" cause?

6-13. What are the roles of the following in the selection process?

    a. the advisor
    b. the applicant
    c. the medical examiner
    d. the Medical Information Bureau (MIB)

6-14. What characteristics should a company include in its evaluation and classification system?

6-15. Under what circumstances will the judgment rating method function effectively?

6-16. What is the basic assumption on which the numerical rating system is based? What criticisms have been leveled against the numerical rating system?

6-17. What factors are assigned weights when the numerical rating system is used to evaluate and classify risks and how are the values assigned to these factors?

6-18. How does each of the following work as an underwriting safeguard in the issuance of nonmedical insurance?

a. limiting the amount of insurance
b. limiting the age of issue
c. limiting insurance to standard risks
d. relying on other sources of information

6-19. What factors might contribute to a higher rate of mortality for nonmedical insurance than for medically examined applicants?

6-20. What are the problems associated with writing life insurance for elderly and very young applicants?

6-21. When an individual who was placed in a substandard classification lives to old age, it is often argued that the company made an error in its treatment of that case. Explain why this is not necessarily an indication that an error in classification was made.

6-22. List the three broad additional hazard groups that most companies assume substandard risks fall into, and give examples of additional hazards that would cause life insurance applicants to fall into each of these three categories.

6-23. Using the increase-in-age method of dealing with substandard risks, explain the following:
a. how this method provides for the extra mortality of a substandard risk
b. types of risks for which it is considered appropriate to use this method
c. why this method is appealing to an insurance company and an applicant

6-24. Using the extra-percentage-tables method of dealing with substandard risks, explain the following:
a. how this method provides for the extra mortality of a substandard risk
b. types of risks for which it is considered appropriate to use this method
c. why the gross premiums derived under this method do not increase in proportion to the degree of extra mortality involved
d. what implications this method has for the determination of policy reserves and cash surrender values, and the availability and/or determination of the coverage period for the extended-term nonforfeiture option

6-25. Using the flat-extra-premium method of dealing with substandard risks, explain the following:

a. how this method provides for the extra mortality of a substandard risk

b. types of risks for which it is considered appropriate to use this method
c. how companies adjust for the use of a flat extra premium to handle constant extra risk for policies with increasing cash values in order to approximate equitable treatment of the policy owners
d. the effect that this method has on policy values and dividends

6-26. Explain the reasons (both theoretical and practical) for and against removing a substandard rating when a person classified as a substandard risk subsequently applies for insurance with another company (or even with the same company) and is found to be a standard risk in all respects.

Self-Test Questions

Instructions: Read the chapter first, then answer the following 10 questions to test your knowledge. Circle the correct answer, then check your answers in the answer key in the back of the book.

6-1. The method most commonly used by life insurance companies for dealing with substandard risks that present an increasing hazard is to

(A) create a lien against the policy for a number of years
(B) assess a flat extra premium
(C) charge a premium based on a mortality table that reflects the degree of extra mortality for the substandard class into which a risk is classified
(D) make no extra charge but place the members of the group in a special class for dividend purposes, adjusting the dividends in accordance with actual experience

6-2. Which of the following statements concerning factors used in the selection and classification process of applicants for life insurance is correct?

(A) Applicants must submit documented proof of age as part of the application
(B) Any past health record of the applicant is of little relevance in the selection process
(C) The determination of an applicant's mortality expectation involves an examination of he relationship between height, weight, and girth
(D) The influence of heredity may be more significant when evaluating a young person's relationship between height, weight, and girth

6-3. Which of the following statements concerning the underwriting of life insurance is (are) correct?

   I. Urinalysis detection of excess sugar could lead to a higher premium or refusal to issue coverage.
   II. Detection of low blood sugar usually results in refusal to issue coverage.

   (A) I only
   (B) I only
   (C) Both I and II
   (D) Neither I nor II

6-4. Which of the following statements concerning substandard risk underwriting of life insurance is (are) correct?

   I. The gross premium for a 200-percent extra percentage case will be two times the gross premium for a standard case.
   II. Deafness is an example of a constant hazard appropriately handled with a flat extra premium.

   (A) I only
   (B) II only
   (C) Both I and II
   (D) Neither I nor II

6-5. Which of the following statements concerning the higher mortality associated with the issuance of nonmedical insurance is (are) correct?

   I. The extra mortality normally does not manifest itself until 20 to 25 years after the policy is issued.
   II. The extra mortality is believed to stem from impairments known to the applicant but deliberately concealed.

   (A) I only
   (B) II only
   (C) Both I and II
   (D) Neither I nor II

6-6. Which of the following statements concerning methods used by life insurance companies to handle substandard risks is (are) correct?

    I. If a male applicant aged 40 is rated up to age 45 under the increase-in-age method, the premium will be that for a policy issued to a male aged 45, but the surrender values will be the same as those for a policy issued to a male age 40.

    II. When the flat extra premium method is issued, cash surrender values and dividends are increased to reflect the additional premium paid.

    (A) I only
    (B) II only
    (C) Both I and II
    (D) Neither I nor II

6-7. Which of the following statements concerning the application for life insurance is (are) correct?

    I. It is used to obtain important information directly from the applicant.
    II. It must be completely filled out by the applicant.

    (A) I only
    (B) II only
    (C) Both I and II
    (D) Neither I nor II

6-8. All the following statements concerning methods used by life insurance companies to handle substandard risks are correct EXCEPT

    (A) The chief appeal of the increase-in-age method to the insurance company is its simplicity.
    (B) The increase-in-age method is appealing to the applicant because the higher premium is accompanied by correspondingly higher surrender values and dividends if a policy is participating.
    (C) When the degree of extra mortality is small, members of the group may be placed in a special class for dividend purposes rather than being assessed an extra premium charge.
    (D) The flat extra premium method is normally used when the hazard is thought to be increasing, as opposed to decreasing or constant.

6-9. All the following are guiding principles that must govern the risk-selection procedures of an insurance company if it is to operate on a sound basis EXCEPT

(A) predominance of the standard group
(B) avoidance of inferior risks
(C) equity among policy owners
(D) compatibility with underlying mortality assumptions

6-10. All the following are correct statements concerning the numerical rating system used in the classification of risks EXCEPT

(A) The summation of the debits and credits, added to or deducted from the par value of 100, represents the numerical value of the risk.
(B) Favorable underwriting factors are assigned positive values and are called credits. Unfavorable factors are negative and called debits.
(C) The average risk accepted by the company has a value of 100 percent.
(D) The system is based on the principle that only a small number of factors enter into the composition of risk.

7

Policy Provisions

Overview and Learning Objectives

Chapter 7 reviews life insurance policy provisions. This important discussion features those provisions that constitute the insurance contract and dictate how the policy will be carried out when it is put into effect. An insightful and accurate understanding of these provisions is essential for the financial advisor to effectively perform his or her professional duties of advising and providing service to clients.

By reading this chapter and answering the questions, you should be able to

7-1.   Explain the standard policy provisions in a life insurance contract.

7-2.   Identify the provisions that are required by law in life insurance policies.

7-3.   Identify and explain the types of provisions from which insurers are prohibited in life insurance policies.

7-4.   Explain the concepts of waiver and estoppel.

7-5.   Briefly describe the provisions: accidental death, guaranteed purchase option, automatic premium loan, and waiver of premium.

7-6.   List and describe the required surrender options in a cash value policy.

7-7.   Explain how a policy loan affects surrender options, especially extended term insurance.

Chapter Outline

Policy Provisions 3
  Contract of Adhesion 3
  Policy Face Page 4
  Standard Policy Provisions 5
  Required Provisions 6
  Prohibited Provisions 23
  Optional Provisions 26
  Waiver and Estoppel 28
  Additional Common Provisions 30
  Policy Filing and Approval 40
Chapter Seven Review 41

Policy Provisions

Contract of Adhesion

A *contract of adhesion* is one that is not negotiated. It is drafted entirely by one party. The other party to the contract is not permitted to alter the terms of the contract but may only accept or reject the contract. Because the drafting party has the freedom to choose the words of the contract, the law requires that party to abide by the words it has chosen. This means any ambiguities are interpreted in favor of the other party.

A life insurance contract is a contract of adhesion. This means that the policy owner and the insurer do not negotiate the terms of the contract. The prospective policy owner performs only these two functions in the creation of a life insurance contract:

- He or she applies for the policy (the contract) by filling out the application and supplying any medical information required by the insurer. This is not a negotiation. The applicant is merely specifying what type of contract he or she would like to be offered. Based on this information, the insurer will make an offer by issuing a policy.
- The applicant is then asked to accept or reject the contract as offered by the insurer.

The applicant accepts the offer by paying the initial premium. The applicant rejects the offered contract by refusing delivery of the policy. Even after the applicant accepts the insurer's offer of coverage and a contract is binding on the insurer, the policy owner may reject the contract and get a full refund based on the 10-day free look provision.

Because the prospective policy owner can only accept or reject the contract offered by the insurer, the contract of adhesion rules provide that all ambiguities in the contract of insurance will be resolved in favor of the policy owner and against the insurer.

State law generally requires that the contract avoid complex legal terminology. The goal is to make the contracts easier for the consumer to read and understand.

A number of required, prohibited, and optional provisions are controlled by state law. Before a policy may be sold in a particular jurisdiction, its provisions must be filed with that state's insurance department for approval.

Policy Face Page

Although the placement of the provisions may vary from company to company, the face pages of most life insurance contracts are quite similar. The face page of the contract usually contains the following information:

- the name of the insurance company
- some specific details for that policy—for example, the name of the insured and the name of the policy owner, the face amount of the policy, the policy number, and the policy date or issue date (some include both dates)
- a general description of the type of insurance provided by that policy contract. For example, the face page of a traditional participating whole life policy might read as follows:

> Whole Life—Level Face Amount Plan. Insurance payable upon death. Premiums payable for life. Policy participates in dividends. Dividends, dividend credits, and policy loans may be used to help pay premiums.

- a statement about the policy's *free look provision*. This is a provision that gives the policy owner a period of time, usually 10 days, to return the policy after acceptance. The following is an example of such a provision:

> Not later than 10 days after you get this contract, you may return it to us. All you have to do is take it or mail it to one of our offices or to the agent who sold it to

you. The contract will be canceled from the start, and a full premium refund will be made promptly.

- the insurer's promise to pay. This is the heart of the insurance contract and is called the insuring clause.
- the signatures of the officers (usually the president and the secretary) of the company, which binds the company to the terms of the contract

The remainder of the required and optional provisions is not usually included on the face page.

Examples: **Typical Promise-To-Pay Statements**

– We will pay the beneficiary the sum insured under this contract promptly if we receive due proof that the insured died while this policy was in force. We make this promise subject to all the provisions of this contract.

– We will pay the benefits of this policy in accordance with its provisions.

– We agree to pay the death benefits of this policy to the beneficiary upon receiving proof of the insured's death; and to provide you with the other rights and benefits of this policy.

Standard Policy Provisions

The state insurance codes generally impose a requirement that unless specifically exempted from the law, all life insurance policies delivered or issued for delivery in the state must contain language substantially the same as certain specified provisions. Insurers are also generally given the option to insert different provisions than those specified in the statute if the language in the insurer's provisions is more favorable to policy owners. The insurance department determines whether an alternative provision is more favorable to consumers.

Required Provisions

Grace Period

The *grace period clause* grants the policy owner an additional period of time to pay any premium after it has become due. Because of the provision, a policy that would have lapsed for nonpayment of premiums continues in force during the grace period. The premium remains due, however, and if the insured dies during the grace period, the insurer may deduct one month's premium from the death benefit.

Note that although insurers could charge interest on the unpaid premium for the late period, they do not normally do so. If the insured survives the grace period but the premium remains unpaid, the policy lapses (except for any nonforfeiture options).

As with all renewal premiums, the policy owner has no obligation to pay the premium for the insurance coverage provided under the grace period provision.

The standard length of the grace period is 31 days. If the last day of the grace period falls on a nonbusiness day, the period is normally extended to the next business day.

Example: **A Typical Grace-Period Provision**

We allow 31 days from the due date for payment of a premium. Your insurance coverage continues during this grace period. *Note:* If the insured dies during the grace period, the past due premium will be deducted from the death benefit.

Late Remittance Offers—It is important to make a distinction between the grace period rules and a late remittance offer; they are not the same. There is usually no provision in the contract concerning late remittance offers. Such offers are made solely at the insurer's option. The late remittance offer is not a right of the policy owner or an obligation of the insurer that is included in the insurance contract under the requirements of the law.

Some insurers will make a *late remittance offer* to a policy owner whose coverage has lapsed after the grace period has expired. This is not an extension of the grace period and coverage is not continued as a result of the offer. Late remittance offers are intended to encourage the policy owner to reinstate the policy; they do *not* extend coverage. The inducement from the insurer is that coverage can be reinstated without having to provide evidence of insurability. The policy owner accepts the late remittance offer by paying the premiums that are due and meeting any other conditions imposed by the insurer.

Policy Loans

The law requires that the insurance contract permit policy loans if the policy generates a cash value. To understand this requirement it is necessary to make a distinction between loans, policy loans, and advancements.

> *Loan*—a transfer of money (or other property) with an obligation to repay the money plus interest (or to return the asset transferred) at a certain time

> *Policy loan*—an advance of money available to the policy owner from a policy's cash values. Interest is accrued on the amount borrowed from the policy. Although there is no fixed time for repayment of the money to the insurer, the amount of the loan plus any unpaid interest will be deducted from any policy values payable under the policy.

> *Advancement*—money or other property transferred to someone prior to the anticipated time of payment or delivery

The term *policy loan* is a misnomer. A policy loan is actually an advance against the policy's cash surrender value or death benefit. It is not technically a loan because the policy owner assumes no obligation to repay the money taken from the policy. Thus, it is not technically correct to say that the policy owner borrows from the insurer and the loan is secured by the policy cash values. It is more accurate to say that the policy owner makes an advance withdrawal of cash values otherwise available when the policy is surrendered or when the insured dies.

Example:	Ms. Policyowner obtains a policy loan of $8,000; it is subject to an 8 percent interest rate. Her repayment options are to:

- repay none of it
- repay interest only
- repay some of balance due
- repay all $8,000 plus interest due

(*Note:* the timing and amount of any repayments are totally at the discretion of Ms. Policyowner unless either the insured dies or the policy is terminated.)

After 2 years at an 8-percent interest rate, the loan balance will be $9,331.20 if no repayments have been made.

$$\$8,000 + \$640 + \$691.20 = \$9,331.20$$

If Ms. Policyowner pays the $640 interest charge each year, the loan balance will remain level at $8,000. Death benefits will be reduced by the loan balance, plus any unpaid interest, such as the $9,331.20.

One might ask, if it is not a loan, why is the insurer permitted to assess an interest rate against the amount borrowed? The policy owner is expected to pay interest on the "loan" because he or she has withdrawn assets from the insurer that were intended to support the level premium concept. If the policy owner withdraws those assets, it is fair to expect him or her to pay an interest rate that would approximate what the insurer would earn if the money were left with the insurer to invest.

Automatic premium loans are another type of policy loan. These loans are advances the insurer makes from policy cash values to pay any unpaid premiums. They will be discussed later in this chapter with optional provisions.

Incontestable Clause

This is a provision that makes the life insurance policy incontestable by the insurer after it has been in force for a certain time period. This means the insurance company can refuse payment of a claim, usually due to a misrepresentation or fraud on an insured's application. The laws of the states differ as to the form of the clause prescribed, but no state permits a clause that would make the policy contestable for more than 2 years.

Example: **A Typical Incontestable Clause**

Except for nonpayment of premium, we will not contest this contract after it has been in force during the lifetime of the insured for 2 years from the date of issue.

After a policy has been in effect for the period of time prescribed by the incontestable clause, the insurance company cannot have the policy declared invalid. The courts have generally recognized three exceptions to this rule: (1) If there was no insurable interest at the inception of the policy, (2) if the policy had been purchased with the intent to murder the insured, or (3) if there had been a fraudulent impersonation of the insured by another person (for example, for purposes of taking the medical exam), then the incontestable clause is deemed not to apply because the contract, which includes the incontestable clause, was void from its inception.

Example: Abigail and Diane were identical twins, but they had different states of health. Diane had a heart murmur for the decade prior to her death. Four years prior to her death, she purchased a life insurance policy by concealing her heart problem and having healthy Abigail take the physical examination the insurance company requested.

The insurance company discovered the impersonation when they investigated for the death claim, but the policy had been in force for 4 years.

Will the insurer be liable for the death claim?

No. The contract was void from the inception because of the fraudulent impersonation at the physical examination. But if there had not been any

---

> fraudulent impersonation and merely concealment, then the policy would have been voidable until the end of the contestable period. After 4 years, the policy would be incontestable in the absence of fraudulent impersonating.

Divisible Surplus

The *divisible surplus provision* applies only to participating policies. It requires the insurer to determine and apportion any divisible surplus among the insurer's participating policies, typically at annual intervals.

A typical divisible surplus provision from an insurance contract reads as follows:

> While this policy is in force, except as extended term insurance, it will be entitled to the share, if any, of the divisible surplus that we shall annually determine and apportion to it. This share is payable as a dividend on the policy anniversary.

In addition, some contracts provide that payment of a dividend is conditioned upon payment of all premiums then due. The provision in most contracts notes that a dividend is not likely to be paid before the second anniversary of the policy.

Entire Contract

Ordinarily we expect that a contract of any type to include all the provisions that are binding on the parties. However, this is not always the case. Sometimes one contract will include the terms of another document without actually including that second document in the contract. This is accomplished by referring to the other document and incorporating it into the contract by that reference. This is known as incorporation by reference. Entire contract statutes grew out of an attempt to prohibit insurers' use of incorporation by reference and to make life insurance contracts more understandable by consumers.

Some states require a provision disclosing that the contract and the application constitute the *entire contract*; other states simply provide that the contract and the application are the contract regardless of what the policy may say.

Example: **A Sample Provision**

> This policy and any attached copy of an application form the entire contract. We assume that all statements in an application are made to the best of the knowledge and belief of the persons who make them; in the absence of fraud, they are deemed to be representations and not warranties. We rely on those statements when we issue the contract. We will not use any statement, unless made in an application, to try to void the contract, to contest a change, or to deny a claim.

Reinstatement

Reinstatement provisions allow a policy owner to reacquire coverage under a policy that has lapsed. This right is valuable to both the policy owner and the insurer. The various state laws and the insurance contracts impose certain requirements that the policy owner must meet to reinstate the policy. New York law requires that life insurance policies contain a provision granting the policy owner the right to reinstate the policy ". . . at any time within three years from the date of default, unless the cash surrender value has been exhausted or the period of extended term insurance has expired, if the policyholder makes application, provides evidence of insurability, including good health, satisfactory to the insurer, pays all overdue premiums with interest at a rate not exceeding six per centum per annum compounded annually, and pays or reinstates any other policy indebtedness with interest at a rate not exceeding the applicable policy loan rate or rates determined in accordance with the policy's provisions. This provision shall be required only if the policy provides for termination or lapse in the event of a default in making a regularly scheduled premium payment."(N.Y. Insurance Law, Section 3203(a)(10), McKinney 1985.)

Normally, insurers do not permit reinstatement of a policy that has been surrendered for its cash value, and this prohibition is often included in the contractual definition of the requirements for reinstatement.

Example:	**A Sample Reinstatement Provision**
	This policy may be reinstated within 3 years after the due date of the first unpaid premium, unless the policy has been surrendered for its cash value. The conditions for reinstatement are that (1) you must provide evidence of insurability satisfactory to us, (2) you must pay all overdue premiums plus interest at 6 percent per year, and (3) you must repay or reinstate any policy loan outstanding when the policy lapsed, plus interest.

Misstatement of Age or Gender

The age and gender of the insured are fundamentally important factors in the evaluation of the risk assumed by a life insurance company. Inaccurate statements about the insured's age or gender are material misrepresentations. Rather than voiding the contract based on such misrepresentations, the practice after discovering the inaccuracy is to adjust the policy's premium or benefits to reflect the truth. Adjustments in the policy's premiums or benefits based on misstatements of age or gender are not precluded by the incon-testability clause. This is because incontestability clauses preclude contests of the *validity* of the policy. If a misstatement of age or gender clause appears in the contract, an adjustment based on that clause would be an attempt to enforce the terms of the contract, not invalidate it.

A sample provision might say: If the age or gender of the insured has been misstated, we will adjust all benefits payable under this policy to that which the premium paid would have purchased at the correct age or gender.

Example:	Janet understated her age when she purchased a life insurance policy. The premium she paid was $900 annually but would have been $1000 annually for her correct age. The policy face amount will be adjusted down to the amount of coverage she could have purchased with a $900 annual premium based on her true age.

Note that if the insured is still alive when it is discovered that the insured's age or sex has been misrepresented, it may be that the parties will elect to adjust the premium to the correct amount rather than to adjust the benefits.

The New York insurance code requires insurance contracts to contain a provision stipulating that if the age of the insured has been misstated, any amount payable or benefit accruing under the policy will be what the premium would have purchased at the correct age (N.Y. Ins. Law Sec. 3203(a)(5). A majority of states have a similar provision.

Nonforfeiture Provisions

When insurers developed the concept of level premium insurance policies, the goal was to make life insurance more affordable to older policy owners. This was accomplished by charging a lifetime level premium. In the earlier years of the policy this level premium was higher than necessary to cover the mortality costs. The excess portion of the premium in the policy's early years (and the interest it earned) built up a cash reserve that was used to pay the mortality costs at older ages, which then exceeded the level premium being charged. A question soon arose concerning who was entitled to those reserves when a policy lapsed. Initially, these reserves were forfeited by the policy owner and kept by the insurer. This was clearly inequitable, and the practice was soon modified. Today, the states require that insurers assure policy owners who voluntarily terminate their contracts a fair return of the value built up inside some policies. These laws are known as the nonforfeiture laws.

The Standard Nonforfeiture Law require that surrender values are at least as large as those that would be produced by the method the law prescribes. In addition, each policy must contain a statement of the method used to find the surrender values and benefits provided under the policy at durations not specifically shown.

These laws require that after a cash value policy has been in effect for a minimum number of years—usually 3—the insurer must use part of the reserved excess premium to create a guaranteed minimum cash value. In addition, the insurer must make that value available to the policy owner in cash as a surrender value and must give the policy owner a choice of two other nonforfeiture options: (1) extended term insurance for the net face amount of the policy or (2) paid-up insurance at a reduced death benefit amount. If the policy owner has not elected between them, the policy must provide that one of these two options will be effective automatically if the policy lapses. This is typically extended term, for then, assuming the lapse is unintentional and the premium may be paid or the policy may be reinstated, the beneficiary will be protected for the full face amount.

Surrender (Nonforfeiture) Options

The surrender values provided under the Standard Nonforfeiture Law can be taken by the policy owner in one of three forms:

- cash
- paid-up cash value life insurance
- extended or (paid-up) term insurance

Example: **Standard Nonforfeiture Law**

Marshall Artiste purchased a $100,000 whole life policy.

$10,000 = cash value
$ 6,000 = outstanding policy loan

This policy has been in effect the minimum number of years and the Company has given Marshall his choice of

- Cash surrender value—$4,000 of cash surrender value would be paid, after subtracting the $6,000 outstanding policy loan from the $10,000 cash value.

- Extended term insurance—$94,000 of coverage would be extended for as long as the $4,000 net cash value will purchase that as a single premium.

- Paid-up insurance—a paid-up whole life policy will be provided for whatever face amount can be purchased with the $4,000 net cash value (based on the age of the insured). The face amount will be significantly less than $94,000.

These forms are properly referred to as *surrender benefits,* but because the policy owner has the option or privilege of choosing the form under which the surrender value is to be paid, the benefits are usually referred to as *surrender options.*

The Standard Nonforfeiture Law requires that a surrender benefit be granted whenever a value appears under the formula. This may be as early as the end of the first year under some policies and later than 3 years under other policies. Under most plans and at most ages of issue, a surrender value will appear in the second policy year. Formerly, no cash or other surrender benefits were required in the case of term insurance policies of 20 years or less. Under the current law a level-premium term policy for more than 15 or 20 years—or one that expires after age 65, regardless of its duration—must provide surrender benefits if the mandated formula indicates that one exists.

The nature and significance of the various standard forms of surrender benefits are discussed in the following sections.

Cash—The simplest form in which the surrender value may be taken is cash. After the policy has been in force long enough to have no surrender charges, there is an exact equivalence between the surrender value of a policy and the cash that can be obtained upon its surrender, leading many persons to refer to the surrender value generically as the *cash surrender value.* The new law requires that the surrender value of a policy be made available in the form of cash, but it does not compel a company to grant cash values until the end of 3 years in the case of ordinary insurance. This limitation on cash values was provided in order to relieve the companies of the expense of drawing checks for the relatively small values that might have developed during the first and second policy years. It does not, however, relieve the company of the obligation to make available in some non-cash form of benefit any surrender value that might accumulate during the first 2 years. Most companies waive this statutory provision and provide a cash value as soon as any value develops under the policy.

The law permits a company to postpone payment of the cash surrender value for a period of 6 months after demand thereof and surrender of the policy. This *delay clause* was given statutory sanction in order to protect companies against any losses that might otherwise arise from excessive demands for cash during an extreme financial emergency. The law has made the inclusion of a delay clause mandatory and has made the delay period of 6 months uniform. It is contemplated that the clause would be invoked only under the most unusual circumstances.

As might be expected, provision is made for deduction of any policy indebtedness (policy loans plus accrued interest) from the cash value that would otherwise be available.

Impact of Electing Surrender Benefits—The impact of the election of each surrender benefit on the structure of the underlying insurance contract is illustrated in Figures 7-1 through 7-4. In each case the underlying contract will be assumed to be a whole life policy, but the principle involved is applicable to any type of contract, with some modification.

Figure 7-1 shows the change produced in cash value life insurance contracts by the exercise of the cash surrender option. The figure indicates that up to the point of surrender, the contract is a combination of protection and cash value. By surrendering the policy for cash, however, the policy owner takes the cash value element of the contract and, in so doing, terminates the protection element as well. Subject only to any reinstatement privilege that might exist, the company has no further obligations under the contract. Generally, the reinstatement rights are available only to policies that have terminated for reasons other than a cash surrender.

Reduced Paid-Up Insurance—This form of surrender benefit is referred to as *reduced paid-up insurance,* in recognition of the fact that under this option, the withdrawing policy owner receives a reduced amount of paid-up cash value insurance, payable upon the same conditions as the original policy. If the original policy was either an ordinary life or a limited-payment life policy, the insurance under this option will be paid-up whole life insurance. If the original policy was an endowment contract, this option will provide an endowment with the same maturity date but in a reduced amount. Some companies make this option available under a term policy, in which case an appropriately reduced amount of term insurance is paid up to the expiry date of the original term policy.

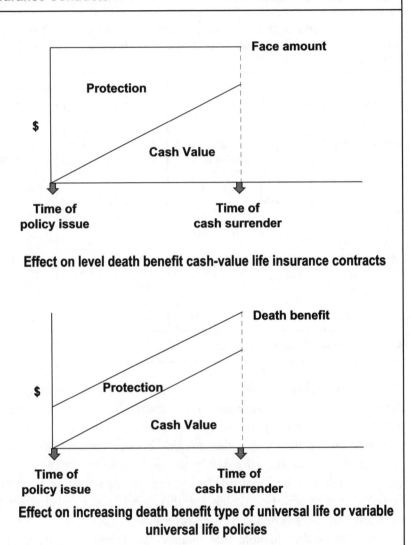

FIGURE 7-1
Effect of Cash Surrender on Structure of Several Types of Life Insurance Contracts

Face amount

Protection

$

Cash Value

Time of
policy issue

Time of
cash surrender

Effect on level death benefit cash-value life insurance contracts

Death benefit

$ Protection

Cash Value

Time of
policy issue

Time of
cash surrender

Effect on increasing death benefit type of universal life or variable universal life policies

The amount of paid-up insurance provided under this option is the sum that can be purchased at the insured's attained age by the net surrender value (cash value, less any policy indebtedness, plus the cash value of any dividend additions or deposits) applied as a *net single premium* computed on the mortality and interest bases specified in the policy for the calculation of the surrender value. The amount of paid-up insurance available at various durations under an ordinary life and under a 20-payment life policy, issued at age 35, is shown in Table 7-1.

TABLE 7-1
Example of Surrender Benefits at Selected Durations for Ordinary Life and 20-Payment Life (Issue Age 35, Male 1980 CSO Mortality, 4.5 Percent Interest)

	Ordinary Life				20-Payment Whole Life			
Policy Year	Cash Value	Reduced Paid-up Insurance	Extended Term Insurance		Cash Value	Reduced Paid-up Insurance	Extended Term Insurance	
			Yrs.	Days			Yrs.	Days
3	6	28	1	297	7	29	2	42
5	28	122	6	261	40	157	9	216
10	92	331	13	211	142	468	20	318
15	168	498	16	15	266	743	25	145
20	250	630	16	170	420	1,000	7	242
25	336	721	15	186	487	1,000	22	175
30	429	794	14	9	558	1,000	18	88
35	523	850	12	119	629	1,000	14	300

All values are per $1,000 of insurance.

Paid-up insurance is provided under this option at net premium rates, despite the fact that maintenance and surrender or settlement expenses will be incurred on the policies. The law made no specific allowance for expenses on the theory that the margins in the mortality and interest assumptions underlying the net rates are sufficient to absorb any expenses that will be involved. In the case of participating insurance, however, any margins available for this purpose are reduced by the payment of dividends on the paid-up insurance.

It is interesting to note that there is a surrender privilege under reduced paid-up whole life and endowment policies. The law states that such policies can be surrendered for cash within 30 days after any policy anniversary, provided. the original policy was in force long enough to grant a cash value. In other words, the cash surrender privilege of the paid-up policy cannot be used to subvert the provision in the law that cash values need not be granted until the end of 3 years.

The effect of the reduced paid-up insurance option on the structure of the whole life policy is illustrated in Figure 7-2. It is readily apparent that the most important impact is on the protection element of the contract. In the example, the cash value before surrender had accumulated to a sum half the face of the policy, which at age 60, for instance, would purchase a paid-up whole life policy in an amount approximately 75 percent of the original face. The entire shrinkage comes out of the protection element, however, since the investment element continues to increase until it equals the reduced face at the end of the mortality table. The same phenomenon occurs with a surrender at any duration. As was pointed out, this cash value element of a reduced paid-up policy can be converted into cash by surrendering the policy pursuant to its terms.

Universal life insurance and variable universal life policies provide a nonguaranteed form of reduced paid-up option. The policy owner can reduce the death benefit so that the existing cash value is sufficient to cover all future charges, helped by the future earnings credited to the cash value. The nonguaranteed element is the fact that the variable universal policy owner bears the investment risk, and if the earnings on the cash value drop below the level anticipated when the policy benefit was reduced, further adjustment(s) may be needed.

The policy owner has to explicitly request a death benefit reduction to create the equivalent of a reduced paid-up surrender option for a universal or variable universal life policy.

Extended Term Insurance—The extended term insurance option provides paid-up term insurance in an amount equal to the original face of the policy, increased by any dividend additions or deposits and decreased by any policy indebtedness. The length of the term is that which can be purchased at the insured's attained age by the application of the net surrender value as a net single premium. This gives effect to the statutory requirement that the present value at the time of surrender of any paid-up surrender benefit must be at least the equivalent of the surrender value. The period for which term insurance is provided for various durations under an ordinary life policy, and under a 20-payment life policy, issued at age 35, is shown in Table 7-1.

Universal and variable universal life insurance policies do not have a *guaranteed* extended term surrender option. However, they are automatically configured to work similarly to extended term insurance. These policies have no fixed or required premiums, and the viability of the contract depends on the account balance of the policy's cash value.

The policy will remain in force as long as the cash value is sufficient to cover the next 60 days of charges for mortality (term charges) and administration, and until these charges consume the cash value.

It is readily apparent that the policy loan should be deducted from the surrender value to determine the net single premium, since it is only the *net* value that is available for the purchase of extended insurance, but many persons do not understand why it is also necessary to deduct the policy loan from the face of the policy. The requirement is founded on underwriting considerations. If the policy indebtedness is not deducted from the face of the extended policy, the companies will be exposed to a dangerous form of antiselection.

Consider the case of a person suffering from an incurable illness who has a $200,000 life insurance policy with a $100,000 cash value. If, to meet the cost of medical treatment or for any other reason, he or she borrows the maximum amount against the cash value, say $95,000, and then dies shortly thereafter, the company will be obligated to pay only $105,000, since the policy loan is an encumbrance against both the cash value and the death proceeds. The total return will thus equal the face of the policy, or $200,000. If, on the other hand, he or she borrows $90,000, surrenders the policy, and applies the remaining equity, $10,000, to the purchase at net rates of $200,000 of extended term insurance, death within the next few years will result in a total payment of $290,000 (the face plus the loan). Under present practice as required by law, the ill policy owner can extend only $110,000, thus limiting the total obligation of the company to $200,000, as was the original intent.

> **Extended Term Insurance Surrender Option**
>
> - Amount of coverage is reduced by the amount of policy loans
> - Surrender value available to purchase extended coverage is reduced by policy loans

The deduction of policy loans is based on the theory that the cancellation of an unliquidated policy loan constitutes a prepayment of a portion of the face amount. To ignore policy indebtedness in determining the face amount of extended insurance would be to make available, without medical or other evidence of insurability, additional term insurance equivalent to the policy indebtedness. This strategy would violate all the tenets of sound underwriting.

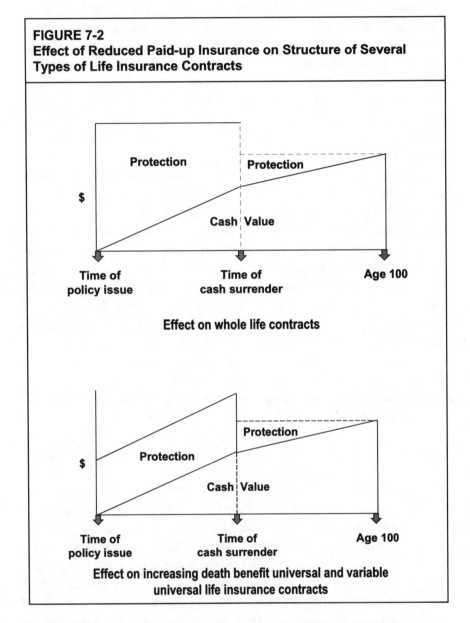

FIGURE 7-2
Effect of Reduced Paid-up Insurance on Structure of Several Types of Life Insurance Contracts

Effect on whole life contracts

Effect on increasing death benefit universal and variable universal life insurance contracts

   The effect of deducting the policy loan from *both* the surrender value and the amount of extended insurance is to produce a shorter period of term insurance than would be available if no loan existed. This is a natural consequence of the fact that the deduction is a much greater proportion of the cash value than it is of the face amount of the policy. Theoretically the amount of term insurance should not be the face amount less the loan, as required by law, but should be the face amount less the portion thereof having a cash value equal to the loan; in other words, a proportionate part of the *policy* would be *surrendered* to pay the loan, and only the remainder would be continued as term insurance. If this method were used, a lower amount of coverage would be extended and the *period* of term insurance would not be affected by policy indebtedness. The rule laid down by law in effect *increases* the total insurance extended and thus reduces the term, since the net cash value remains the same.

Thus, if a policy of $1,000 has a cash value of $500 and policy indebtedness of $200, the net cash value of $300 (*one-half* of the death benefit it will support) will support a $600 benefit. Seen from the loan perspective, a $400 reduction in coverage will be required to offset $200 of loan forgiveness. The proper amount of extended insurance is $600, instead of $800, as presently provided. In other words, the *amount* of the term insurance is reduced by 20 percent, whereas the *cash value* available to purchase it is reduced by 40 percent. The *period* of insurance, therefore, must be less than it would be if no indebtedness existed.

From the standpoint of the companies, paid-up (extended) term insurance is a more attractive surrender benefit than paid-up whole life or endowment insurance. Companies consider the favorable features of extended term insurance to be

1. the relatively large amount of insurance involved, with the correspondingly low expense *rate*
2. the definite date of expiry, which limits the maintenance expenses and minimizes the problem of tracing policy owners
3. the uninterrupted continuation of the original amount of coverage, as modified by dividend additions and policy loans, for those persons who contemplate eventual reinstatement
4. its adaptability to liberal reinstatement requirements, which stems from the fact that the amount at risk is normally decreased by reinstatement, in contrast to the increase in the amount at risk that occurs on the reinstatement of reduced paid-up insurance

The only real disadvantage of extended term insurance from the insurer's standpoint is the adverse mortality selection encountered, and this can be hedged through the use of the higher mortality assumptions authorized by law or minimized through making the extended-term option the *automatic* paid-up benefit. All things considered, the extended-term option is so attractive that most companies designate it as the option to go into effect automatically if the insured does not elect another available option within 60 days after the due date of the premium in default.

FIGURE 7-3
Effect of Extended Term Insurance Option on Structure of Several Types of Life Insurance Contracts

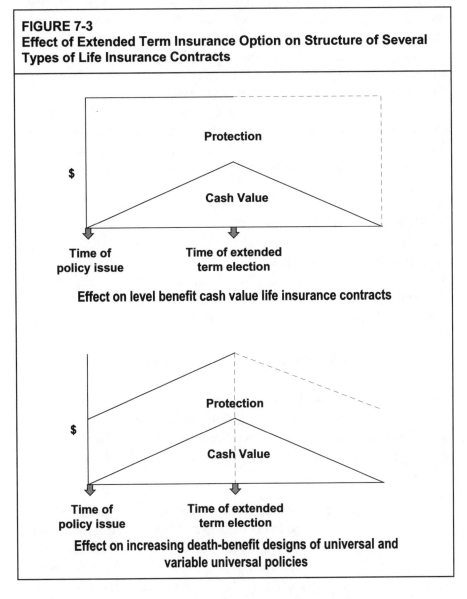

Effect on level benefit cash value life insurance contracts

Effect on increasing death-benefit designs of universal and variable universal policies

The change produced in the structure of a whole life insurance policy by its surrender for extended term insurance is plotted in Figure 7-3. This diagram reveals that, in direct contrast to the situation under reduced paid-up insurance, the protection element grows progressively larger, and the investment element progressively smaller, until the policy finally expires. The investment element is at a peak at the time of surrender but is gradually used up in the payment of term insurance premiums, being completely exhausted at the point of expiry. Because of the complementary nature of the protection and investment elements in any insurance contract, the protection element becomes constantly larger, eventually equaling the face of the extended insurance. This explains why the amount at risk is *reduced* through the reinstatement of a policy that has been running under the extended term option.

The investment element of a paid-up term insurance policy can be obtained by surrendering the insurance for cash, subject to the same conditions governing the surrender of reduced paid-up insurance. Extended term insurance is normally nonparticipating with respect to dividends.

Settlement Options

State laws require that a life insurance policy must include certain settlement options tables if the settlement options include installment payments or annuities. These tables must show the amounts of the applicable installment or annuity payments. This topic will be discussed in the next chapter.

Prohibited Provisions

Although the state laws are not uniform, most states prohibit insurers from including certain provisions in their policies. For various reasons, courts or state legislatures have determined that these prohibited contract provisions violate public policy. There are five generally prohibited provisions:

- The insurance producer, who is the agent of the insurance company, cannot be made the agent of the insured for purposes of filling out the application for insurance. If the producer could be made the insured's agent rather than the company's agent, then the insurance company could not be charged with knowing facts presented to the agent but not communicated to the insurance company by the agent.

- Nonpayment of a loan cannot cause a forfeiture. The state laws generally provide that so long as the cash value of the policy exceeds the total indebtedness on the policy, the policy owner's failure to repay the loan or to pay interest on the loan cannot cause a forfeiture of the policy.
- *Less-value statutes* preclude an insurer from promising something on the face of the policy and taking it away in the fine print. These laws are called less-value statutes because the insurer is prohibited from providing a settlement option of less value than the death benefit of the policy.
- There are limitations on the time for filing lawsuits against the insurer. All states have *statutes of limitation* that control how long a person may wait before bringing a lawsuit of any type against another party. These statutes are designed to force people to sue in a timely fashion rather than waiting in the hope that evidence favorable to the other side will be lost. After the time period specified in the statute has expired, the courts will not hear the lawsuit.

   The statutes of limitation have different lengths for different types of lawsuits. Ordinarily, the time period during which a lawsuit based on a contract must be brought is quite long; 10 years is not an unusual length. Sometimes the parties to a contract will agree to a shorter time period for initiating a lawsuit (based on a breach of that contract) than the period prescribed by the state law. The insurance codes of several states prohibit insurers from issuing policies that greatly reduce the length of the statute of limitations on contract actions. These statutes permit insurers to shorten the period to a reasonable length but not to eliminate it entirely. The permissibly shorter periods range from one to 6 years. Some states do not permit insurers to reduce the statute of limitations period at all.

   These laws protect the interests of the insurers and the public. Insurers are protected because the laws allow them to impose shorter limitation periods than otherwise permitted in the state. This benefits insurers because it requires plaintiffs to sue while information relevant to the insurance policy is still easy to obtain. The public is protected because the statutes do not allow insurers to shorten the limitation period so much that the public does not have sufficient time to determine whether or not a lawsuit is worthwhile.

- No lengthy backdating to save age is allowed. *Backdating* a policy means issuing the policy as if it had been purchased when the insured was younger. This practice has an advantage and a disadvantage. The advantage is that the insured will pay lower annual premiums for each increment of the policy because the premium will be based on the younger age. The disadvantage is that the insured must pay the premium applicable to the length of the backdating. This means that the insured will have paid for insurance protection during a period of time before the policy was issued when no coverage was provided. The statutes generally limit backdating to no more than 6 months.

Optional Provisions

In addition to the required provisions and the prohibited provisions, there are numerous other provisions that are neither required nor prohibited:

- **Suicide provision**—An insurer may elect to include suicide as a covered risk from the day the policy is issued. However, this is not normally the case, and as a general rule most insurance contracts do not provide coverage for a death by suicide within the first one or 2 years after the policy is issued. If the policy does not contain a suicide exclusion provision, then a death by suicide is covered by the policy and the death benefit is payable to the beneficiary regardless of when the suicide occurs.

Example: **A Typical Suicide Provision**

Suicide of the insured, while sane or insane, within 2 years of the issue date, is not covered by this policy. In that event, we will pay only the premiums paid to us less any unpaid policy loans.

- **Ownership provision**—Ordinarily the insured is the applicant and owner of the policy. The ownership provision in the life insurance contract describes some of the rights of the owner. The typical ownership provision stipulates that the owner of the policy is the insured unless the application states otherwise. The provision also usually states that the policy owner may change the beneficiary, assign the policy to another party, and exercise other ownership rights. If these powers are described, the provision will also define how such powers are to be exercised in order to be recognized by the insurance company.

- **Assignment provision**—As with most contracts and most interests in property, the policy owner has, as a matter of law, the right to transfer some or all of his or her rights to another person. In contract law this is generally known as the *right to assign*. The act of transferring a property right is an assignment. The right to assign an ownership interest in an insurance policy exists even without an assignment provision in the contract. However, most contracts include an assignment clause because it sets out clearly the conditions upon which an assignment can be made. If the policy contains a provision prohibiting an assignment, any attempted assignment by the policy owner will not be binding on the insurer. If the policy sets conditions for an assignment, the policy owner must comply with these restrictions.

Example: **Assignment Clause**

You may assign this policy if we agree. We will not be bound by an assignment unless it has been received by us in writing at our home office. Your rights and the rights of any other person referred to in this policy will be subject to the assignment. We assume no responsibility for the validity of an assignment. An absolute assignment will be the same as a change of ownership to the assignee.

- **Plan change**—This provision gives the policy owner an important power to change the plan of insurance and provides that the parties may agree to make other changes in the terms of the contract.

Example:	**Contract Change Provision**
	Subject to our rules at the time of a change, you may change this policy for another plan of insurance, you may add riders to this policy, or you may make other changes if we agree.

- **Accelerated benefits**—As a result of the AIDS epidemic and public concern about other terminal illnesses, some insurers have added a provision that permits the insured to withdraw policy death benefits under certain circumstances. These accelerated benefits or living benefits provisions state that if the insured develops a medical condition that drastically reduces an insured's life expectancy (to two years or less), then he or she may withdraw a portion of the policy's death benefit.

Waiver and Estoppel

The concepts of waiver and estoppel are quite similar and easy to confuse. Some courts treat waiver and estoppel as two parts of the same theory.

> **Waiver**—the voluntary and intentional surrender of a known right. By a waiver, a party relinquishes a right. For example, if an insurer issues a policy even though the medical questionnaire has not been completed and was not signed by the applicant, the insurer will have waived the right to have that information.

Nevertheless, the law is clear that some waivers are forbidden. No party to an insurance contract may waive a right that also partly benefits the general public. For example, the insurable interest requirement benefits the public as well as the insurer; thus an insurer may not waive its right to demand that the applicant have an insurable interest in the life of the insured at the time the policy is applied for. Similarly, a policy owner may not waive his or her rights to nonforfeiture values or premium notices.

Granting a waiver is not necessarily permanent. An insurer may elect to waive a particular right for one time and one purpose only. If so, the waiver will have no effect on future actions between the parties. If a party has repeatedly waived a contractual right in the past, it can reclaim that right simply by notifying the other party that it intends to reassert that right in the future.

Estoppel—the loss of the ability to assert a defense because the party has acted in a manner inconsistent with that defense. For example, if an insurer has repeatedly accepted payment of late premiums after the end of the grace period without requiring the insured to comply with the reinstatement process, the insurer may be prohibited (estopped) from requiring a reinstatement for future late premiums. This may be the result even if the prior late premiums were accepted by mistake and without recognizing that they were late.

There is a fine distinction between the example above and the rule that the concept of estoppel may not be used to create coverage or to extend coverage beyond that assumed by the insurer in the contract.

Example:	A classic case is *Pierce v. Homesteaders Life Association.* The policy in that case provided that the death benefit was payable only if the insured died before age 60. The policy owner paid and the insurer accepted premium payment through the end of September of the year in which the insured turned 60. The insured's 60th birthday was on March 3, and she died on March 11. The insured's beneficiary filed a claim for the death benefit asserting that because the insurer had accepted a premium payment for a period beyond the insured's 60th birthday, the insurance company had waived that contractual limitation and should, therefore, be estopped from denying coverage. The court held for the insurer and asserted that coverage cannot be created by waiver.

The essence of the distinction between the example and the case is narrow but clear. In the case, no coverage was to be provided after the insured reached age 60. Estoppel could not be invoked to create something that never existed. In the example, coverage existed for the insured subject to the condition that premiums must be paid on time. The insurance company's actions were inconsistent with the existence of that timely premium payment condition; thus, the insurance company was estopped from asserting it.

Additional Common Provisions

Other common policy provisions are those concerning accidental death benefits, and the waiver of premium in the event of the insured's disability, the guaranteed purchase option (also known as the guaranteed insurability option), and the automatic premium loan provision.

Accidental Death Benefits

This provision is added to some insurance contracts in the form of a rider, or amendment, to the policy. It is also known as the double indemnity provision because it normally doubles the standard death benefit if the insured dies accidentally.

Because this benefit is payable only in the event of the insured's *accidental* death, that term requires definition. In the absence of a specific definition in the rider, the word *accident* means an unintentional event that is sudden and unexpected. An *accidental death* is one that is caused by an accident. This statement seems quite clear, but it is not always easy to apply. There have been cases where an insured has been mortally injured in an accident, but the actual cause of death is a disease. In this case, is the accidental death benefit payable? The answer is yes only if the accident was the cause of death. If the insured is in an automobile accident but dies from a heart attack, the accidental death benefit will be payable only if the accident can be proven to have triggered the heart attack.

Example: The insured died when driving an automobile. The car was severely damaged in an accident associated with the death. The cause of death was determined to be a heart attack.

The policy had a face amount of $50,000 and

> included an accidental death benefit rider.
>
> The insurance company claims the heart attack occurred first and caused both the death and the accident.
>
> The beneficiary spouse with minor children thinks the auto accident occurred first and was the cause of the heart attack. The burden of proving this in order to collect the accidental death benefit is almost impossible to satisfy.
>
> The most likely outcome is that the insurer will only pay a $50,000 death benefit. Money spent by the beneficiary trying to collect the accidental death benefit usually results in squandering part of the basic benefit on legal costs.

The problems caused by cases in which there is potentially more than one cause of death are eased somewhat by the standard practice of putting a time limit in the accidental death benefit provision. In the most common type the death must occur within 90 days of the accident that is said to have caused the injury.

These basic definitions preclude coverage for any death that is the natural and probable result of a voluntary act. It is an unchallenged principle of law that people are presumed to expect and intend the probable or foreseeable consequences of their actions. This concept is sometimes described by the term *assumption of the risk*. If one plays Russian roulette, jumps off buildings, or runs with the bulls in Pamplona, Spain, his or her death as a result of those activities cannot be described as accidental.

There are two types of accidental death clauses: (1) the *accidental result* type and (2) the *accidental means* type.

Example 1:   **Accidental Result Death Benefit Provision**

We will pay this benefit to the beneficiary when we have proof that the insured's death was the result, directly and apart from any other cause, of accidental bodily injury, and that death occurred within one year after that injury and while this rider was in effect.

Example 2:   **Accidental Means Death Benefit Provision**

We will pay this benefit to the beneficiary when we have proof that the Insured's death was caused directly, and apart from any other cause, by accidental means, and that death occurred within one year after that injury and while this rider was in effect.

The most common type of provision that insurers use is the accidental result type. This is because the accidental result clause is more favorable to the consumer. It is also because most courts have recognized that the difference between the two clauses is too difficult for many consumers to understand and have therefore ceased to recognize a distinction between the two types of clauses.

The distinction can be explained as follows: under an accidental means clause both the cause (means) of the death and the result must be unintentional. Under an accidental result clause, only the result must be unintentional. For example, assume that an insured is participating in an obstacle course race at a family reunion, and the race requires the racers to dive over a barrel, do a somersault, and run to the next event. The insured breaks her neck and is killed doing the somersault. Because she was doing exactly what she intended to do, the means was not accidental although the result was certainly an accident. The accidental means clause would not require the payment of the benefit, but the accidental result clause would.

There is another factor that has made accidental means clauses less attractive to insureds and thus less frequently used by insurers. This is the provision requiring that, in addition to being accidental, the means (cause) of death must also be violent and caused by an external agency. Courts have been liberal in their interpretation of these limitations in favor of the public.

Most accidental death benefit clauses do not provide coverage in the event of the insured's death by suicide. If suicide of the insured (whether sane or insane) is excluded, then an examination of the insured's mental state at the time of the suicide is avoided. If the insured is sane at the time of the suicide, then it is an intentional act that would not qualify as an accident. If the insured is insane, the suicide might be classified as unintentional because the insured may be presumed not to have been able to intend the consequences of his or her act.

Waiver of Premium

A waiver-of-premium provision in the event of the insured's disability is another extremely valuable coverage.

According to a typical waiver-of-premium provision, if the insured becomes totally disabled as defined in the life insurance contract, the insurance company will waive payment of premiums on the policy during the continuance of the insured's disability.

The disability waiver of premium has some limitations. For example, the waiver will not be granted if the insured's disability begins after a specified age, typically age 60 or 65. In addition, the provision (as in the sample below) will typically not waive premiums if the disability is self-inflicted or the result of an act of war. As with all contracts, it is important to pay close attention to the language used. Seemingly small differences in the language of the provision can make large differences in the obligations the insurer incurs.

Example: **Disability Waiver-of-Premium Rider**

Waiver of premiums. We will start to waive the premiums for this policy when proof is furnished that the Insured's total disability, as defined in this rider, has gone on for at least 6 months in a row.

If a total disability starts on or prior to the anniversary on which the Insured is age 60, we will waive all premiums that fall due during that total disability. If it goes on until the anniversary on which the Insured is age 65, we will make the policy fully paid-up as of that date, with no more premiums due.

If a total disability starts after the anniversary on which the Insured reaches age 60, we will waive only those premiums that fall due during that total disability and prior to the anniversary on which the insured is age 65.

Premiums are waived at the interval of payment in effect when the total disability started. While we waive premiums, all insurance goes on as if they had been paid. We will not deduct a waived premium from the policy proceeds.

Definition of Total Disability—"Total Disability" means that, because of disease or bodily injury, the Insured cannot do any of the essential acts and duties of his or her job, or of any other job for which he or she is suited based on schooling, training, or experience. If the Insured can do some but not all of these acts and duties, disability is not total and premiums will not be waived. If the Insured is a minor and is required by law to go to school, "Total Disability" means that, because of disease or bodily injury, he or she is not able to go school.

"Total Disability" also means the Insured's total loss, starting while this rider is in effect, of the sight of both eyes or the use of both hands, both feet, or one hand and one foot.

Total Disabilities for Which Premiums are Not Waived—We will not waive premiums in connection with any of these total disabilities.

1. Those that start prior to the fifth birthday of the insured, or start at a time when this rider is not effect.
2. Those that are caused by an injury that is self-inflicted on purpose.
3. Those that are caused by any kind of war, declared or not, or by any act incident to a war or to an armed forces of one or more countries while the insured is a member of those armed forces.

Proof of Total Disability—Written notice and proof of this condition must be given to us, while the insured is living and totally disabled, or as soon as it can reasonably be done. As long as we waive premiums, we may require proof from time to time. After we have waived premiums for 2 years in a row, we will not need to have this proof more than once each year. As part of the proof, we may have the insured examined by doctors we approve.

Payment of Premiums—Premiums must be paid when due, until we approve a claim under this rider. If a total disability starts during a grace period, the overdue premium must be paid before we will approve any claim.

Refunds of Premiums—If a total disability starts after a premium has been paid, and if it goes on for at least 6 months in a row, we will refund the part of that premium paid for the period after the policy month when the disability started. Any other premium paid and then waived will be refunded in full.

Values—This rider does not have cash or loan values.

Contract—This rider, when paid for, is made a part of the policy, based on the application for the rider.

Incontestability of Rider—We have no right to contest this rider after it has been in force during the lifetime of the insured for 2 years from its date of issue, unless the insured is totally disabled at some time within 2 years of the date of issue.

Dates and Amounts—When this rider is issued at the same time as the policy, we show the rider premium amount on the front page of the policy. The rider and the policy have the same date of issue.

When this rider is added to a policy that is already in force, we also put in an add-on-rider. The add-on-rider shows the date of issue. The rider premium amount is shown in a new Premium Schedule for the policy.

When Rider Ends—You can cancel this rider as of the due date of a premium. To do this, you must send the policy and your signed notice to us within 31 days of that date. If this rider is still in effect on the anniversary on which the insured is age 65, it will end on that date.

This rider ends if the policy ends or is surrendered. It will not be in effect if the policy lapses or is in force as extended or paid-up insurance.

Guaranteed Insurability Option

Another popular policy provision is the *guaranteed insurability option*, which is also called the *guaranteed purchase option*. This provision helps to protect policy owners against the possibility that they might become uninsurable. Under the typical provision, the policy owner receives the right to acquire additional insurance in specified amounts at specified times or ages. Typically, this provision allows additional purchases every 3 years and after the birth of a child, provided the events occur before the insured reaches a specified maximum age (often 45). The right to purchase additional insurance can be very valuable because the insured does not have to provide *evidence of insurability* to exercise the option. Another benefit of this option is that the new coverage is normally not subject to a new suicide provision or a new incontestability clause.

The additional insurance need not be on the same plan as the basic policy to which the option is attached; the option is exercisable in favor of any standard whole life or other cash value insurance policies offered by the company. Premiums for the new insurance are payable at standard rates on the basis of the insured's attained age on the option date. If the original policy contains a waiver-of-premium provision and accidental death benefits, the new policies will, at the insured's option, contain the same features. If premiums are being waived on the original policy at the time an option for additional insurance is exercised, premiums on the new policy will be waived from the beginning and will continue to be waived if the insured is totally disabled, until the insured recovers.

Example: Larry purchased a policy with a guaranteed purchase option when he was age 7. He exercised his right to purchase more coverage every 3 years until his 39th birthday. Because his children had entered college and the costs of tuition were squeezing his budget severely, he did not purchase more coverage when he was 42. Unfortunately, he was found to have cancer at age 44. Consequently, he wants to exercise his guaranteed purchase option at age 45.

    The insurance company informed Larry that the option lapsed when he did not use it at age 42.

The options vary as to details, but typically the policy owner is permitted, with the knowledge and consent of the insured, to purchase up to $10,000 of additional insurance at 3-year intervals beginning with the policy anniversary nearest the insured's 25th birthday and terminating with the anniversary nearest the insured's 40th birthday. Under current policies, the amount of insurance that can be obtained on each specified policy anniversary is usually limited to some percentage of the original face amount up to a specified maximum dollar amount, such as $60,000. Some policies also specify an aggregate limit (for example, two times the original face amount) on the amount of coverage that can be purchased under this option without evidence of insurability. Option amounts vary from company to company but may be as high as $100,000 per exercise option with some insurers. When the insured passes an age or event that triggers the right to purchase additional insurance but he or she does not exercise that option, the option lapses.

Some contracts also permit the purchase of additional insurance upon the insured's marriage or following the birth of the insured's first child or subsequent children. Some contracts even provide coverage automatically for 60 to 90 days after each option date.

The option is available only for an extra premium that varies, not in proportion to the number of option dates remaining, as might be supposed, but with the age of issue. The schedule of annual premiums charged for the option by one company begins at $0.50 per $1,000 at age 0 and increases to approximately $2.00 per $1,000 at age 37. These premiums reflect the company's estimate of the average amount of extra mortality that it will experience on policies issued without evidence of insurability and, from the standpoint of the insured, may be regarded as the cost of ensuring his or her insurability. Premiums for the option are payable to the last anniversary at which it can be exercised—usually age 40—or to the end of the premium-paying period of the basic policy, whichever is earlier.

Some insurers also offer guaranteed insurance under cost-of-living adjustments that increase policy amounts based on rises in economic inflation indicators, such as the Consumer Price Index. The insured typically can accept or refuse this offer, but if the insured refuses, the provisions may terminate. Guaranteed insurance under cost-of-living adjustments is typically offered at 3-year intervals from the issue date of the policy.

Automatic Premium Loans

A policy provision found in some—but not all—policies that bears a resemblance to the paid-up term insurance option but is technically not a surrender option (because the policy is not surrendered) is the automatic premium loan feature. It grew out of the conventional premium loan clause, which states that at the request of the policy owner any premium may be paid by means of a loan against the surrender value, provided that a surrender value is then available and large enough to cover the loan. Such a loan usually bears interest at the rate applicable to all policy loans.

The *automatic premium loan provision* provides that any defaulted premium will be automatically paid and charged against the cash value without request from the policy owner unless he or she elects to surrender the policy for cash or one of the paid-up insurance options. This automatic option must result from an explicit request previously by the policy owner.

The effect of the premium loan clause is to extend the original plan of insurance for the original face amount decreased by the amount of premiums loaned with interest. Such extension will continue as long as the cash value at each premium due date is sufficient to cover another premium. It should be noted that each premium loan increases the cash value, lengthening the period during which the process can be continued. At the same time, however, the indebtedness against the cash value is growing, not only by the granting of additional premium loans but also by the accrual of interest. Eventually a premium due date will be reached when the unencumbered cash value is no longer large enough to cover another full premium.

The principal advantage to the policy owner of an automatic premium loan provision is that in the event of inadvertent nonpayment of the premium or temporary inability to pay the premium, the policy is kept in full force. Several collateral advantages flow from this basic fact. First, premium payments can be resumed at any time (as long as the equity in the policy remains sufficient to pay premiums as they become due) without furnishing evidence of insurability. This is in contrast to the reinstatement of policies surrendered for paid-up insurance, in which case evidence of insurability is almost invariably required. Second, special benefits—such as waiver of premium, disability income, and accidental death or double indemnity—remain in full force, contrary to the situation under the paid-up insurance options. Finally, if the policy is participating, the policy owner continues to receive dividends, which is usually not true of paid-up term insurance and might not be true under reduced paid-up insurance.

On the other hand, unless the provision is used only as a temporary convenience, as intended, it may prove disadvantageous to the policy owner. If premium payments are not resumed, not only will the *period* during which the policy is kept in force usually be less than under extended insurance, but the *amount* payable in the event of death will be less, and the disparity will become greater with each passing year.

In the event of the insured's death during the period covered, the insurer is better off financially under the automatic premium loan arrangement than under extended term insurance because the former receives additional premiums by way of deduction from the policy proceeds. However, offsetting this advantage to some extent are the additional outlays for commissions, premium taxes, and dividends (if participating).

The effect of the automatic premium loan feature on the structure of a whole life policy is shown in Figure 7-4. Upon default of the first premium the effective amount of protection is reduced by the amount of the *gross* premium. Each year thereafter that the feature is permitted to operate, the amount of protection is reduced by the gross premium due that year, plus interest on that premium and all unpaid premiums of previous years. Hence, the protection element will decline at a constantly increasing rate. The surrender value will be exhausted, however, before the protection element is reduced to zero.

The effective or unencumbered investment element also turns downward, but not immediately, and it never declines at the same rate as the protection element, so the solid and broken lines are not parallel. The nominal investment element (cash value) increases with the payment of each gross premium (regardless of the source of the funds) by the amount of the net premium, plus interest at the contractual rate and benefit of survivorship, less the cost of insurance.

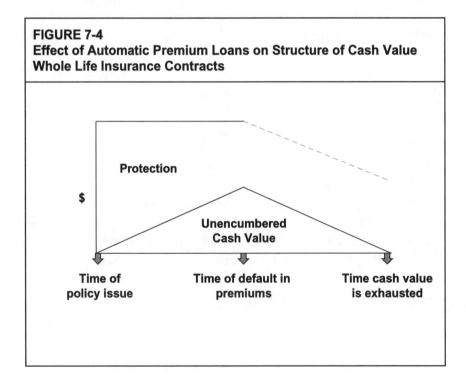

FIGURE 7-4
Effect of Automatic Premium Loans on Structure of Cash Value Whole Life Insurance Contracts

Protection

$

Unencumbered Cash Value

Time of policy issue

Time of default in premiums

Time cash value is exhausted

Policy Filing and Approval

If a policy is sold in a state but does not include a required provision or has not been filed with the state for approval, the courts will treat the policy as if it did include all the required provisions under the law of that jurisdiction. The policy owner or beneficiary will be permitted to enforce the policy against the insurer as if it complied in all respects with the applicable state law. The state insurance commissioners are charged with the responsibility to see that the insurance companies doing business in their state are complying with that state's law regarding the permitted and prohibited policy provisions. To enable the insurance department to do its job, a policy may not be issued or delivered in a state until it has been approved by the department. In some states, the insurer may assume that the policy has been approved if it has not been advised otherwise within a fixed period of time, such as 30 days, after it has been submitted to the state insurance department. In other states, the insurer may not issue the policy until it has received notice of approval from the department.

If an insurer issues a policy that has not been approved by the insurance department, the policy owner may seek a refund of premiums paid or seek to enforce the policy. If suit is brought, the courts will enforce the unapproved contract against the insurer on behalf of the beneficiary. If the unapproved policy does not include a provision that would have been required for approval, the policy will be treated by the courts as if it does contain such a provision. Furthermore, if a required provision is more favorable to the policy owner than one actually included in the contract, the courts will treat the contract as if it included the more favorable provision. The insurer that violates the laws requiring filing of the policy and approval of its provisions by the state will also be subject to fines or other penalties (such as revocation of the insurer's right to do business in that state).

Chapter Seven Review

Key terms and concepts are explained in the glossary. Answers to the review questions and the self-test questions follow the Glossary.

Key Terms and Concepts

contract of adhesion

free look provision

grace period clause

late remittance offer

policy loan

incontestable clause

divisible surplus provision

entire contract provision

reinstatement provision

misstatement of age or gender

nonforfeiture (surrender) options

cash surrender value

delay clause

reduced paid up insurance

net single premium

extended term insurance

automatic premium loan provision

prohibited provisions

backdating

optional provision

suicide provision

ownership provision

assignment provision

accelerated benefits

waiver

estoppel

accidental death benefits

guaranteed insurability (purchase)

option

waiver of premium

surrender options

automatic premium loan

Review Questions

7-1. Describe the two functions the prospective policy owner plays in the creation of a life insurance contract.

7-2. Explain how ambiguities in a life insurance contract are generally resolved by the courts.

7-3. List the types of information generally found on the face page of a life insurance policy.

7-4. Explain why standard policy provisions might be more accurately called required provisions.

7-5. What benefit does the grace period provide for the policy owner?

7-6. How do the rules applicable to late remittance offers differ from the grace period rules?

7-7. Though a policy owner is not obligated to pay back a policy loan, why is the insurer allowed to assess an interest charge against the amount borrowed?

7-8. List the goals of entire contract statutes.

7-9. List the typical requirements that must be met for a policy owner to reinstate a life insurance policy.

7-10. When Jim purchased $100,000 of life insurance, he told the company he was 35 years old and was charged $1,500 per year. When Jim died 20 years later, it was discovered that he had understated his age and was 38 at the time he purchased the policy. The premium for a 38-year old would have been $1,667 per year. Explain how the insurer would handle this situation.

7-11. List the key requirements of the Standard Nonforfeiture Law.

7-12. A policy owner intends to surrender her policy with a reported $60,000 cash value. Two years ago she took out a $10,000 policy loan with an 8-percent fixed policy loan rate. None of the loan has been repaid, and there are no applicable surrender charges. How much will she receive as a result of surrendering the policy?

7-13. Explain the reinstatement rights normally available to a policy owner after surrendering a policy for cash.

7-14. When the reduced paid-up insurance nonforfeiture option is elected, what type and amount of coverage is provided?

7-15. How does the reduced paid-up insurance nonforfeiture provision in a whole life policy differ from a similar reduction under a variable life or a universal life policy?

7-16. Describe the extended term insurance nonforfeiture option.

7-17. A policy owner elects the extended term insurance option for a policy having $30,000 cash value, a $100,000 face amount, and indebtedness of $10,000.

    a. How much extended term insurance will be provided?

    b. How much will be available to purchase the extended term coverage?

7-18. Why do life insurers prefer the extended term insurance nonforfeiture option to other surrender options?

7-19. Explain how the automatic premium feature works on fixed-premium policies.

7-20. Explain why certain policy provisions are prohibited.

7-21. List the five generally prohibited policy provisions.

7-22. Explain how statutes that prohibit insurers from contractually reducing the period for filing a lawsuit against them to a period shorter than that specified in the statute protect the interests of both insurers and the public.

7-23. Explain how the backdating of a life insurance policy provides both an advantage and disadvantage for the policy owner.

7-24. Sally purchased a $250,000 life insurance policy containing a one-year suicide provision. How much would the insurer have to pay if Sally committed suicide

    a. during the first year of coverage?

    b. during the fifth year of coverage?

7-25. What limitations are typically found in accidental death benefit coverage?

7-26. Explain the difference between the two types of accidental death clauses. Why does the accidental death provision most commonly use the accidental result type terminology?

7-27. Explain how the guaranteed insurability option helps policy owners protect themselves against the possibility that they, as insureds, may become uninsurable.

7-28. Describe the possible consequences if an insurer issues a policy that has not been filed and approved by the insurance department as required by state law.

Self-Test Questions

Instructions: Read the chapter first, then answer the following 10 questions to test your knowledge. Circle the correct answer, then check your answers in the answer key in the back of the book.

7-1. When the premium for Irene's life insurance policy was still unpaid at the end of the grace period, what action would the insurance company have taken on her 10-year-old whole life plan with $8,000 cash value and the APL (automatic premium loan) option?

    (A) cancelled the policy
    (B) surrendered it for the $8,000 cash value
    (C) advanced the premium payment automatically as a loan from the $8,000 cash value
    (D) moved the policy to an extended term plan under the settlement options

7-2. A contract of adhesion is one where

(A) both parties contribute to the terms and conditions
(B) the values exchanged are not equal
(C) both parties make a legally enforceable promise
(D) one party has the option of affirming or rejecting

7-3. If an insured dies during the grace period, the insurance company can

(A) consider the death claim invalid
(B) deduct overdue premium plus interest from the settlement
(C) require new evidence of insurability to reinstate the policy
(D) activate the automatic premium loan provision, if selected

7-4. If the insured is found to be younger at death than was stated in the application for an insurance policy, the company will

(A) do nothing
(B) refund all premiums
(C) increase the amount to what the premiums would have purchased
(D) decrease the amount to what the premiums would have purchased

7-5. The nonforfeiture provisions of a policy would be used in which of the following situations?

(A) at the death of the insured
(B) at the termination of the policy
(C) to guarantee dividends
(D) in either a term or permanent policy

7-6. Which of the following statements concerning surrender options under universal life and variable life policies is (are) correct?

I. These policies provide a nonguaranteed form of reduced paid-up option.
II. These policies do not have a guaranteed extended term option.

(A) I only
(B) II only
(C) Both I and II
(D) Neither I nor II

7-7. Which of the following statements concerning reduced paid-up insurance is (are) correct?

    I. There is no surrender privilege under reduced paid-up life and endowment policies.

    II. A reduced paid-up policy is payable on the same conditions as the original policy.

    (A) I only
    (B) II only
    (C) Both I and II
    (D) Neither I nor II

7-8. All of the following statements concerning the automatic premium loan provision are correct EXCEPT

    (A) If the policy is participating, the policy owner continues to receive dividends.
    (B) Special benefits such as waiver of premium and accidental death benefit remain in force.
    (C) The policy owner must furnish evidence of insurability to resume premium payments.
    (D) An automatic premium loan usually bears interest at the rate applicable to all policy loans.

7-9. All of the following are typically requirements for reinstating a lapsed policy EXCEPT

    (A) The company may require that any outstanding policy loan be paid.
    (B) Proper evidence of insurability has been submitted and accepted by the company.
    (C) Back and current premiums must be paid, with interest.
    (D) The policy must first be surrendered for cash.

7-10. All of the following statements concerning the waiver of premium ride are correct EXCEPT

    (A) The waiver will not be granted if the insured's disability begins after a specified age.
    (B) The waiver will not be granted if the insured's disability is self-inflicted or the result of war.
    (C) The typical rider requires that the disability last at least 2 or 3 weeks before premiums will be waived.
    (D) The definition of disability used in the rider determines whether premiums will be waived.

8

Settlement Agreements and Ethical Issues of Classifying Risks

---

Overview and Learning Objectives

Chapter 8 examines life insurance contract settlement options, including the concepts and rules that govern them, the options available, and the rights and privileges available to policyowners and beneficiaries. The chapter then discusses the ethical issues involved in classifying risks, and the responsibilities the advisor, client and company have to each other in the insuring process.

By reading this chapter and answering the question, you should be able to

8-1. Understand the underlying concepts and rules of settlement options.

8-2. Describe the basic settlement option choices available to policyowners and policy beneficiaries.

8-3. Explain the settlement agreement provisions concerning contract and current rates, rights of withdrawal and commutation, and minimum-amount requirements.

8-4. Describe the structure, characteristics, and functions of the four fundamental settlement options.

8-5. Understand the use of settlement options to meet family needs such as estate liquidity, mortgages, emergencies, education, and income.

8-6. Discuss the ethical issues of classifying risks.

8-7. Outline the responsibilities the advisor has to the client and the insurance company.

Chapter Outline

Settlement Agreements 3
   General Concepts and Rules 3
   Characteristics and Types of Settlement Options 9
   Use of Settlement Options 24
Ethical Issues of Classifying Risk 30
Chapter Eight Review 47

Settlement Agreements

Most life insurance policies provide that upon maturity the proceeds shall be payable to the designated beneficiary in one sum, generally referred to as a *lump sum*. Many life insurers now make the lump-sum death benefit payable through an interest-bearing account against which the beneficiary can draw checks. The way these accounts work is similar to the way a money market fund works. The beneficiary can withdraw the total proceeds in one transaction or make partial withdrawals as funds are needed, merely by writing checks. The balance in the account continues to earn interest until withdrawn. Even though the beneficiary can leave the benefits in the account and earn more investment income, over 90 percent of beneficiaries still choose a single lump-sum withdrawal and take possession of all the proceeds.

As an alternative to a lump sum payment, life insurance companies have a wide range of periodic income options available to beneficiaries and policyowners. Collectively, these contractual choices are known as *settlement options*. They constitute an important feature of a life insurance contract and can play a vital role in the protection of the insured's dependents.

General Concepts and Rules

When the proceeds of a life insurance policy are payable in a lump sum, the company's liability under the policy is fully discharged with the payment of such sum. If, however, the company retains the proceeds under one of the optional methods of settlement, its liability continues beyond the maturity of the policy and must be evidenced by some sort of legal document. That document is the *settlement agreement*.

The typical settlement agreement is one entered into between the insurance company and the insured, or policyowner, to control the distribution of the policy proceeds to third-party beneficiaries after the insured's death. Depending on company practice, the agreement may be a basic part of the insurance policy, or it may be separate and distinct from the policy. It can be drawn up at the time the policy goes into effect or at any time prior to the insured's death. Although the insured (policyowner) can revoke the agreement at any time and substitute a new agreement, he or she can revoke the beneficiary designation only if such right has been specifically reserved. The policyowner may or may not give the primary beneficiary the right to set aside the prior agreement after the insured dies. Upon the insured's death, the insurance company's obligation under the original contract terminates, and it assumes a new obligation, which is defined by the terms of the settlement agreement.

The insured may also enter into a settlement agreement with the insurer to provide payments to himself or herself from a surrendered policy's cash value. If the agreement relates to the proceeds of an endowment policy, it can be entered into at the policy's inception or at any time prior to the policy's maturity.

If the insured did not elect a deferred settlement or did elect one but gave the primary beneficiary the right to set it aside, under the rules of most companies the beneficiary may elect a settlement option and enter into an agreement with the company to govern the distribution of the proceeds. The beneficiary is usually given 6 months after the insured's death in which to elect a settlement option, provided the check offered by the insurer in full settlement of the death claim has not been cashed. Insurers pay interest on the portion of proceeds still held by the insurer after the insured dies. The interest starts accruing from the date of death (even if the election of the specific option is made long after the insured dies) and continues accruing until the underlying proceeds are distributed to the beneficiary.

Parties to Settlement Agreements

- Insurance company
- Policyowner
- Beneficiary may have the option of becoming a contracting party after the insured dies (if so provided by the policyowner)

When a beneficiary elects the settlement option or when the policyowner elects a deferred settlement for his or her own benefit, a spendthrift clause cannot be included in the settlement agreement (if it is included, it will not be enforceable). A *spendthrift clause* states that the proceeds will be free from attachment or seizure by the beneficiary's creditors. This clause may properly be embodied in a life insurance policy or settlement agreement procured by one person for the benefit of another, but it cannot be incorporated into an agreement at the request of the party for whose benefit the agreement is being drawn up. This offers an argument for having the policyowner elect the settlement option on behalf of the beneficiary, especially if the beneficiary has credit problems (or may be expected to have them in the future).

Under the rules of many companies, a settlement agreement entered into between the company and the beneficiary must provide that any proceeds unpaid at the time of the beneficiary's death will be paid either to his or her estate in a lump sum or in a single sum or installments to irrevocably designated contingent beneficiaries. In other words, the beneficiary cannot designate *revocable contingent beneficiaries*.

Companies that impose this limitation fear that designating revocable contingent beneficiaries to receive proceeds that are already in existence at the time the designation is made might be construed as a disposition of property to take effect at the primary beneficiary's death. If the beneficiary's action should be so construed, the settlement agreement would be ineffectual as to the residual proceeds unless the agreement had been executed with all the formalities of a will—which, of course, is not the practice. Some insurance companies, however, feel that such a construction of the settlement agreement is a remote contingency and they, therefore, permit the beneficiary to designate contingent beneficiaries with the right of revocation.

Contract Rates versus Current Rates

The liability of the insurer at the maturity of a life insurance policy is generally stated in terms of a single-sum payment. In making other modes of settlement available, the company promises a set of installment benefits, based on various patterns of distribution, that have a present value precisely equal to the lump-sum payment. The policy contains tables that show the amount of periodic income that will be payable under the different options for each $1,000 of proceeds left with the company. Under each option a specified rate of income per $1,000 of proceeds is guaranteed in the policy; these are referred to as *contract rates*. It is important to note that insurers can and often do credit investment earnings in excess of the guaranteed rate to the funds supporting settlement options.

From time to time, a company will modify the actuarial assumptions underlying the benefits provided under the optional modes of settlement, which means that the amount of periodic income per $1,000 of proceeds will change. Historically, because of declining interest yields and growing longevity, these modifications have produced lower benefits per $1,000 of principal. Such benefit modifications are, of course, reflected only in those policies and settlement agreements issued after the change.

The benefits under existing agreements cannot be modified without the specific consent of the policyowner. Consequently, insurers rarely take steps to modify existing settlement agreements. In order to distinguish the rates of income available under existing policies and settlement agreements from rates that are applicable to contracts currently being issued, the latter are referred to as *current rates*. For policies and agreements issued since the latest rate changes there is, obviously, no difference between the contract and current rates. For all others, however, the distinction can be significant.

Contract rates are always available to the policyowner, except for options that can be "negotiated"—that is, options not contained in the original policy. If a policyowner wants the proceeds to be distributed in a manner not provided for in the original policy and his or her request is granted, the benefits will almost invariably be based on the rates in effect at the time the option was requested. Thus, if a policy does not contain all the options that the applicant thinks he or she might want to utilize, the applicant should try to have them added to the policy by endorsement at the time the policy is issued or as soon thereafter as possible.

Interest Rates in Settlement Options

- Contract interest rates (such as 3.5 percent) are guaranteed as a lower limit on current rates when interest rates in the economy drop below the guaranteed rate.
- Contract interest rates remain fixed for the entire contract duration.
- Current rates (such as 5.8 percent) are rates actually being paid under the settlement agreements.
- Current rates usually exceed contract rates.
- Current rates fluctuate along with economic conditions

Under most companies' rules, a beneficiary who is entitled to a lump-sum payment can choose to leave the proceeds with the company under the interest option or elect one of the liquidating options at contract rates. Contract rates are usually available to the beneficiary if a liquidating option (any option other than the interest option) is elected within a specified period after the insured's death—usually somewhere in the range of 6 months to 2 years. If within the 6-month period, the beneficiary elects the interest option, he or she can switch to a liquidating option at contract rates up to 2 years after the insured's death. Moreover, if—during the prescribed period of 6 months to 2 years—the beneficiary elects to have a liquidating option go into effect at some specified date beyond the 2-year period, contract rates will apply. On the other hand, if the beneficiary requests a change of option after the permissible period, the requested benefits will be made available only at current rates, if at all.

It is important to grasp the rationale of the restrictions on contract rates. They are *not* designed primarily to prevent an indefinite projection

---

of contract rates into an uncertain future. Rather, they are intended to protect the insurance company from adverse mortality and financial selection. For example, if a beneficiary could elect a life-income option at any time, his or her attitude toward that right would be influenced by the condition of his or her health. If, after the insured's death, the beneficiary's health deteriorated, he or she would not consider a life-income option appropriate, unless it were the cash-refund type. On the other hand, if the beneficiary's health over the years were excellent, he or she might elect a life-income option. Because beneficiaries as a group could be expected to react in this manner, without a time limit or option selection the company would find itself with an undue proportion of healthy annuitants.

Likewise, if a beneficiary has the choice of withdrawing the proceeds and placing them in some other type of investment or leaving them with the company to be liquidated under one of the installment options, he or she would probably place the investment burden on the insurer if it provided a higher return than could be obtained in the open market. The reverse would be true if the market yield were higher than that provided by the insurer. While the behavior of one or a few beneficiaries has little impact on the insurance company, the adverse action of tens of thousands could be financially devastating to the insurer.

Right of Withdrawal

The beneficiary may be given the right to withdraw all or a portion of the proceeds held by the insurer under a deferred-settlement arrangement. If the beneficiary can withdraw all of the proceeds at any one time, subject only to a delay clause, he or she is said to have an *unlimited right of withdrawal*. However, if the privilege is subject to restrictions, it is generally identified as a *limited right of withdrawal*.

The right of withdrawal may be limited as to the following:

- the frequency with which it can be invoked
- the minimum amount that can be withdrawn at any one time
- the maximum amount that can be withdrawn at any one time
- the maximum amount that can be withdrawn in any one year
- the maximum amount that can be withdrawn in the aggregate

The first two types of limitations are imposed by the insurers to control the cost of administration, while the last three are imposed by the policyowner (often a parent of the beneficiary) to prevent dissipation or too rapid exhaustion of the proceeds by the beneficiary. The right of withdrawal can usually be invoked only on dates when regular interest or liquidation payments are due. Most companies permit withdrawals on any such dates, but some restrict the privilege to a stated number of withdrawals per year, such as three, four, or six. Although some insurers have no minimum requirement, the minimum amount that can usually be withdrawn at any one time ranges from $10 to $1,000.

Most policies reserve the right to delay cash withdrawals under settlement options for a period of up to 6 months. This is a counterpart to the delay clause required by law in connection with loan and surrender requests.

The policyowner may provide that the *right of withdrawal* will be *cumulative*. This means that any withdrawable amounts that are not withdrawn during a particular year can be withdrawn in any subsequent year, in addition to any other sums that can be withdrawn pursuant to the terms of agreement. Thus if the settlement agreement permits the beneficiary to withdraw up to $1,000 per year in addition to the periodic contractual payments and provides that the right will be cumulative, the beneficiary's failure to withdraw any funds during the first year would automatically give him or her the right to withdraw $2,000 during the second year. No withdrawals during the first or second years would bestow the right to withdraw $3,000 during the third year, and so on. A *noncumulative right of withdrawal*, whether exercised or not, expires at the end of the period to which it pertains. Most limited rights of withdrawal are noncumulative.

A right of withdrawal is included in a settlement agreement in order to provide flexibility. It can be invoked to obtain funds for unexpected emergencies or to meet the problem of a rising price level. It is especially desirable during the period when the beneficiary is caring for dependent children. In most cases, however, the right should be hedged with reasonable restrictions in order to prevent premature exhaustion of the proceeds.

Right of Commutation

The right of *commutation* is related to the right of withdrawal. To commute, in this sense, is to withdraw the present value of remaining installment payments in a lump sum. The term is properly applied only to a right attaching to proceeds distributed under a liquidating option. Hence it does not apply to proceeds held under the interest option. For all practical purposes, however, the right of commutation is identical to an unlimited right of withdrawal.

The right of commutation is not implicit in an installment arrangement; in order to be available, it must be specifically authorized in the settlement agreement. Commutation is specifically and intentionally denied the beneficiary in the spendthrift clause that is sometimes made part of the settlement agreement.

Minimum-amount Requirements

To hold down the cost of administering proceeds under deferred-settlement arrangements, life insurance companies will not hold small amounts (such as $10,000) under a settlement option. These minimum amounts are subject to change and rarely stated in the policy. Most companies will not make monthly payments of less than $5 per $1,000 under this option. This special rule is designed to assure liquidation of all proceeds and interest within a reasonable period of time.

Characteristics and Types of Settlement Options

Life insurance settlement options, as a group, embody three basic concepts:

- retention of proceeds without liquidation of principal
- systematic liquidation of the proceeds without reference to life contingencies
- systematic liquidation of the proceeds with reference to one or more life contingencies

A number of options have evolved from this conceptual foundation, but they can be reduced to these four fundamental options:

- the interest option
- the fixed-period option
- the fixed-amount option
- the life income option

These four options will be discussed in the following section under the conceptual classifications mentioned above.

Retention of Proceeds Without Liquidation of Principal—*The Interest Option* The simplest and most flexible of all settlement options is the *interest option*. The company pays interest to the beneficiary but the proceeds are held until the expiration of a specified period or until the occurrence of some specific event. Thus it postpones the ultimate disposition of the proceeds and must be followed by a liquidating option or a lump-sum distribution.

The company guarantees a minimum rate of interest on the proceeds, which is payable at periodic intervals, usually monthly. If the policy was participating, the proceeds will be credited with the actual rate of interest earned by the company or, more likely, a rate approximately equal to the interest factor in the dividend formula. Excess interest is usually paid once a year on one of the normal interest-payment dates.

To determine how much principal must be left with the company to provide an interest income of a desired amount, see Tables 8-1 and Table 8-2. These tables are based on the assumption that the proceeds will yield even percentages between 3-percent and 8-percent annual interest.

The primary beneficiary can be given varying degrees of control over proceeds held by the company under the interest option. If the policyowner wants the proceeds to go intact to the contingent beneficiaries eventually, he or she will give the primary beneficiary no rights in the proceeds other than the right to receive the interest for a lifetime or for some other specified period. If the policyowner wants to provide flexibility to meet unforeseen needs, he or she may grant the primary beneficiary a limited right of withdrawal.

Interest-Only Option

- The interest-only option is frequently used for the primary beneficiary (keeping the proceeds intact for liquidation on behalf of a contingent beneficiary).
- Most often the interest-only option is payable to a surviving spouse. Frequently, the contingent beneficiaries are the children.

Further flexibility and control may be provided by giving the primary beneficiary the right to elect a liquidating option within a specified period or at any time. The settlement agreement itself may stipulate that after a specified period of time, or upon the occurrence of a stipulated contingency, the proceeds will be applied under a liquidating option for the benefit of either the primary beneficiary or the contingent beneficiaries, or both.

The beneficiary may be given complete control over the proceeds by receiving an unlimited right of withdrawal during his or her lifetime, as well as the right to dispose of the proceeds after his or her own death.

The only forms of disposition by the beneficiary that many insurance companies will permit are payment to the beneficiary's estate or payment to irrevocably designated contingent beneficiaries. If the primary beneficiary is given an unlimited right of withdrawal, the guaranteed rate of interest may be lower than would otherwise be the case. If the beneficiary is entitled to a lump-sum settlement but chooses to leave the proceeds with the insurer under the interest option, she or he can retain any privileges the insurance company is willing to grant.

Most companies are willing to retain proceeds under the interest option throughout the remaining lifetime of the primary beneficiary or for 30 years, whichever is longer. Thus, the interest option may be available to contingent beneficiaries. A few companies will hold the proceeds throughout the lifetime of the primary beneficiary and the first contingent beneficiary. From the company's standpoint, some limit is necessary to control the cost of administration and to avoid an indefinite projection of contract rates. (If the insured or the beneficiary elects a liquidating option for the contingent beneficiaries to commence upon termination of the interest option, contract rates will be applicable.)

As a general rule, a company will not accumulate the interest credited to proceeds retained under the interest option. In other words, it insists upon paying out the interest at least annually. This is to avoid any conflict with the laws in several states that forbid the accumulation of trust income except that payable to a minor beneficiary.

Systematic Liquidation Without Reference to Life Contingencies

Proceeds left with a life insurance company to be liquidated at a uniform rate without reference to a life contingency must be paid out either over a specified period of time, with the amount of each payment being the variable, or at a specified rate, with the period of time over which the liquidation is to take place being the variable. The *fixed-period option* provides payments over a stipulated period of time, while the *fixed-amount option* provides payments of a stipulated amount. The two options are based on the same mathematical principles and differ only as to whether emphasis is attached to the duration of the payments or to the amount of the payments. If the insured or the beneficiary wants the assurance of some income, however small, over a specified period, he or she should select the fixed-period option. If, however, the need is for temporary adequacy of income, irrespective of its duration, the insured or the beneficiary should choose the fixed-amount option.

The Fixed Period Option—The essence of the fixed-period option is the certainty of the period over which the proceeds will be distributed. Hence, any developments that increase or decrease the amount of proceeds available are reflected by variation in the size of the monthly payments and not in the duration of the payments. Additional proceeds payable by reason of the insured's accidental death increase the amount of the monthly payments. Dividend accumulations and paid-up additions have the same effect. If prepaid or discounted premiums are considered part of the proceeds, they can be applied under a settlement option and, in the case of the fixed-period option, raise the level of payments. (Under the provisions of some policies, however, such premium deposits are treated as belonging to the insured's estate and do not become part of the proceeds payable to third-party beneficiaries.) Policy loans, if still outstanding at the policy's maturity reduce the proceeds available and, hence, the size of the monthly benefits. Some companies permit the beneficiary to repay a policy loan after the insured's death in order to have the full amount of proceeds payable under a settlement option. Excess interest, if any, may be paid in one sum at the end of each year or added in pro rata proportions to each of the regular benefit payments during the following year.

The fixed-period option is a very inflexible arrangement. The only flexibilities are to permit the beneficiary to choose the date on which the option becomes operative, rather than having it go into effect automatically at the policy's maturity, and to grant the beneficiary the right of commutation. If the option is designed not to go into operation automatically upon maturity of the policy, the proceeds are held under the interest option until such time as the beneficiary indicates that liquidation should commence. Limited withdrawals are not permitted, presumably because of the administrative expense involved in recomputing the benefits and recasting the agreement after each withdrawal. Insurers are willing, however, to permit the settlement agreement to be terminated by the beneficiary's withdrawal of all proceeds remaining with the company.

The Fixed-period Option—
Calculating the Benefit

If a given principal sum is to be liquidated at a uniform rate over a specified period of years, the amount of each annual payment can be derived from a financial calculator or from compound discount tables. For example, if $1,000 is to be liquidated in annual installments over a 20-year period and the undistributed proceeds are assumed to earn interest at the rate of 3.5 percent, the amount of each payment *due at the beginning of the year* will be $1,000 ÷ $14.71 = $67.98. In other words, the present value of a series of annual payments of $1, at 3.5 percent interest, *due at the beginning of the year,* for a period of 20 years, is $14.71. If $14.71 will provide $1 per year for 20 years, then $1,000 will provide an annual payment equal to 67.98 times $1 since it takes $14.71 to support each series of $1 payments, and $1,000 will support 67.98. The monthly payment for 20 years at 3.5 percent interest from $1,000 is $5.78. The amount of annual, semiannual, quarterly, or monthly payment for each $1,000 of proceeds for any period of years can be computed using a financial calculator. Table 8-1 shows the guaranteed installments for each $1,000 of proceeds at 3.5 percent interest. Obviously, the numbers in the table would change if a different interest rate were used.

The Fixed-amount Option—is based on the simple proposition of distributing a specified sum each month, or at some other periodic time interval, until the proceeds are exhausted. Mathematically, it is based on the same compound discount function that underlies the fixed-period option. The application is different, however.

TABLE 8-1
Guaranteed Installments per $1,000 of Proceeds (3.5 Percent Interest, Beginning-of-period Payments)

Number of Years Payable	Annually	Semiannually	Quarterly	Monthly
1	$1,000.00	$504.34	$253.30	$84.67
2	508.60	256.54	128.84	43.08
3	344.86	173.98	87.41	29.22
4	263.04	132.72	66.69	22.29
5	213.99	107.99	54.27	18.14
6	181.32	91.51	45.99	15.37
7	158.01	79.76	40.09	13.40
8	140.56	70.96	35.67	11.92
9	127.00	64.12	32.24	10.78
10	116.18	58.66	29.50	9.86
11	107.34	54.21	27.26	9.11
12	99.98	50.50	25.40	8.49
13	93.78	47.37	23.83	7.96
14	88.47	44.70	22.49	7.52
15	83.89	42.39	21.33	7.13
16	79.89	40.37	20.32	6.79
17	76.37	38.60	19.43	6.49
18	73.25	37.03	18.64	6.23
19	70.47	35.63	17.94	5.99
20	67.98	34.37	17.31	5.78
21	65.74	33.24	16.74	5.59
22	63.70	32.26	16.23	5.42
23	61.85	31.28	15.76	5.26
24	60.17	30.43	15.33	5.12
25	58.62	29.65	14.94	4.99
26	57.20	28.94	14.58	4.87
27	55.90	28.28	14.25	4.76
28	54.69	27.67	13.95	4.66
29	53.57	27.11	13.67	4.56
30	52.53	26.59	13.40	4.48

The principle can be explained in terms of $1,000 to be distributed in equal annual payments of $100, the first payment being due immediately. It is obvious that the liquidation will extend over a minimum period of 9 years because the principal alone will provide payments for that period of time. The problem is to determine how much longer the payments can be continued because of crediting compound interest to the unliquidated portion of the principal.

Because the amount of each payment is fixed under this option, any augmentation in the volume of proceeds or interest lengthens the period over which payments will be made; any diminution in the amount of proceeds shortens the period. Thus, dividend accumulations, paid-up additions, accidental death benefits, and excess interest extend the period of liquidation, whereas loans outstanding at the insured's death and withdrawals of principal by the beneficiary shorten the period. This is true even though the payments are to terminate at a specified date or at the occurrence of some specified event, with the balance of the proceeds being distributed in some manner.

The fixed-amount option offers a great deal of flexibility. As with the fixed-period option, the beneficiary can be given the right to indicate when the liquidation payments are to begin. In the meantime, the proceeds will be held at interest, with the interest payments going to the primary beneficiary. Unlike the fixed-period option, the beneficiary can be given either a limited or an unlimited right of withdrawal. Under this option, withdrawals will merely shorten the period of installment payments and will not necessitate recomputing benefit payments.

The beneficiary can also be given the right to accelerate or retard the rate of liquidation. That is, he or she can be given the privilege of varying the amount of the monthly payments, subject to any limitations the policyowner might wish to impose. For example, the policyowner might direct the company to liquidate the proceeds at the rate of $3,000 per month, while giving the beneficiary the option of stepping up the payments to $5,000 per month or reducing them to any level acceptable to the company. Under such circumstances, the insured is not likely to prescribe any minimum rate of liquidation.

Furthermore, the beneficiary can be given the privilege of discontinuing payments during particular months of the year or from time to time. For example, when the proceeds of an educational endowment policy are being paid out to a beneficiary who is enrolled in a college or university, payments can be discontinued during the summer vacation months. Similarly, larger-than-usual payments can be provided for months in which tuition and other fees are payable. Such flexibility stems from the fact that the fixed-amount option basically creates a savings account from which withdrawals can be made to suit the beneficiary's convenience.

Finally, this option can include a provision for transferring the remaining proceeds to another liquidating option. If the transfer is to take place at a specified date or age, contract rates will be available. If the beneficiary has the right to transfer the proceeds at any time, the conversion will be subject to current rates.

Systematic Liquidation with Reference to Life Contingencies

The proceeds of a life insurance policy may be liquidated at a uniform rate over the lifetime of one or more beneficiaries. This type of arrangement, unique to life insurance companies, is of very great value. It protects a beneficiary against the economic hazard of excessive longevity—that is, it protects the beneficiary against the possibility of outliving his or her income.

Life Income Options—Any settlement option based on a life contingency is called a *life income option.* The principle underlying a life income option is identical to that underlying an annuity. In fact, a life income option is simply the annuity principle applied to the liquidation of insurance proceeds (each payment is composed partly of principal and partly of income on the unliquidated principal). Hence, there are as many variations of the life income option as there are types of immediate annuities. Among the single-life annuities, there are the

- pure or straight life annuity
- life annuity with guaranteed installments
- installment-refund annuity
- cash-refund annuity

There are other types of annuities based on two or more lives, and combinations of the above types.

While there is a counterpart among the life income options for every type of *immediate annuity*, it is not customary for a company to include the whole range of annuity forms in its life insurance policies. The typical policy provides for a life income with payments guaranteed for 10, 15, and 20 years and the installment-refund option. Some companies include the joint-and-last-survivor annuity, and a few show the straight life annuity. Virtually all will make additional options available upon request.

Mathematically, the *straight life income* option is equivalent to a pure immediate annuity. To be precisely accurate, it is the same as a life annuity due because the first payment is due immediately upon maturity of the policy or upon election of the option, whichever is later. The monthly income provided per $1,000 of proceeds depends on the age and gender of the beneficiary and the insurer's assumptions of mortality and interest. Although the schedules of income guaranteed under various insurers' policies are similar, there is currently little uniformity among companies as to the combination of mortality and interest assumptions used to calculate the income payments. Benefits are provided at *net* rates, and there is no charge for the use of the life income settlement.

The *life income option with a specified period of guaranteed payments* is mathematically a combination of a fixed-period installment option of appropriate duration and a pure *deferred life annuity*. For example, a life income option that promises to provide payments of a specified amount to a beneficiary aged 45 throughout his or her remaining lifetime, and in any event for 20 years, is a combination of a fixed-period installment option running for 20 years and a pure life annuity deferred to the beneficiary's age 65. If the beneficiary does not survive to age 65, the portion of the proceeds allocated to the deferred life annuity is retained by the insurance company without further obligation.

Because the life income settlement options are essentially annuity contracts available without any applicable sales commissions or other expense loadings, they often provide more benefits for the same contribution than do separate annuity contracts. The only way to be certain that the settlement option is less costly is to make price and benefit comparisons with the annuity contracts available from other insurers. If an annuity contract is found to be more advantageous than the settlement option, that life insurer should be carefully scrutinized to determine its long-term financial strength.

The *installment refund option* is a combination of a pure immediate life annuity and decreasing term insurance in an amount sufficient to continue payments until the proceeds, without interest, have been paid out in full. This option promises to continue the monthly payments beyond the annuitant's death until the purchase price of the annuity or, in this case, the proceeds of the life insurance policy have been returned. At the inception, the term insurance is in an amount equal to the proceeds, less the first payment due immediately, but it decreases with each periodic payment and expires altogether when the cumulative benefit payments equal or exceed the life insurance proceeds committed to the installment-refund option.

The *cash-refund option* is likewise a combination of a pure immediate life annuity and decreasing term insurance. Since the refund is payable in cash rather than payable in installments, however, a slightly larger amount of term insurance is required.

To use a life income option in planning a client's estate, the advisor needs two types of tables. The first type enables the advisor to compute the amount of insurance required to meet the life income needs of the beneficiary or beneficiaries. It shows the amount of principal needed to provide $10 a month under the various life income options for a wide range of male and female ages. The values for such a table, based on one set of actuarial assumptions, are presented in tables 8-2 and 8-3.

These tables (8-2 through 8-5) are based on the individual 1983 annuity tables. Though there are newer annuity tables that reflect improving mortality, the 1983 tables are still used for tort settlements, worker's compensation, and long-term disability claims. The newest individual table is the Annuity 2000 Mortality Table, which can be used for rate making to create tables such as those displayed here. State insurance offices, which use these tables for statutory annuity valuation reserves, vary in their reserving requirements regarding which tables are permitted for use. The 1983 tables are used here for illustrative and educational purposes, and as such are not intended to reflect current annuity rates.

The second type of table shows the amount of monthly income that will be provided for each $1,000 of proceeds under the life income options and ranges of ages. After the advisor determines how much insurance in multiples of $1,000 is needed, he or she can demonstrate to the client, through the second type of table, exactly how much income can be provided with the actual and contemplated insurance. The values for this type of table, calculated on the same basis as the values for Tables 8-2 and 8-3, are shown in Tables 8-4 and 8-5.

Because the life income option contemplates the complete liquidation of the proceeds during the beneficiary's lifetime, it follows that any circumstances that enlarge the volume of proceeds will increase the amount of each periodic payment, while shrinkages in the proceeds will decrease the size of the payments. It is interesting to note that excess interest is usually payable only under the annuity form calling for a guaranteed number of payments and, even then, only during the period of guaranteed installments. In other words, excess interest is payable on the portion of the proceeds applied under the fixed-period installment option but is not payable on that portion of the proceeds allocated to the deferred life annuity. Some companies guarantee a lower rate of interest on the fixed-period option portion of the arrangement than under the deferred life annuity.

TABLE 8-2
Principal Amount Needed to Provide Life Income of $10 per Month at Selected Male Ages

Age	Life Annuity	10-Year Certain + Life	20-Year Certain + Life
50	$2,074.72	$2,092.4386	$2,151.0323
51	2,043.45	2,062.7682	2,126.4265
52	2,011.56	2,032.5134	2,101.7083
53	1,979.00	2,001.6522	2,076.9307
54	1,945.73	1,970.1663	2,052.1523
55	1,911.70	1,938.0465	2,027.4383
56	1,876.88	1,905.2949	2,002.8620
57	1,841.21	1,871.9240	1,978.5044
58	1,804.65	1,837.9573	1,954.4541
59	1,767.18	1,803.4327	1,930.8080
60	1,728.77	1,768.4122	1,907.6737
61	1,689.46	1,732.9815	1,885.1662
62	1,649.31	1,697.2468	1,863.4048
63	1,608.41	1,661.3293	1,842.5077
64	1,566.86	1,625.3595	1,822.5883
65	1,524.77	1,589.4676	1,803.7493
66	1,482.26	1,553.7817	1,786.0778
67	1,439.45	1,518.4284	1,769.6418
68	1,396.43	1,483.5328	1,754.4876
69	1,353.31	1,449.2195	1,740.6381
70	1,310.18	1,415.6112	1,728.0929
71	1,267.12	1,382.8293	1,716.8311
72	1,224.21	1,350.9933	1,706.8147
73	1,181.51	1,320.2200	1,697.9912
74	1,139.07	1,290.6243	1,690.2966
75	1,096.96	1,262.3231	1,683.6587
76	1,055.28	1,235.4283	1,677.9980
77	1,014.12	1,210.0381	1,673.2300
78	973.61	1,186.2301	1,669.2662
79	933.85	1,164.0560	1,666.0169
80	894.98	1,143.5380	1,663.3935
81	857.11	1,124.6717	1,661.3114
82	820.36	1,107.4297	1,659.6907
83	784.85	1,091.7671	1,658.4572
84	750.68	1,077.6228	1,657.5428
85	717.92	1,064.9197	1,656.8857

Male 1983 Individual Annuity Table (4 percent interest net rates)

TABLE 8-3
Principal Amount Needed to Provide Life Income
of $10 per Month at Selected Female Ages

Age	Life Annuity	10-Year Certain + Life	20-Year Certain + Life
50	$2,237.91	$2,244.7293	$2,272.6161
51	2,208.92	2,216.6597	2,247.8142
52	2,179.14	2,187.8547	2,222.5817
53	2,148.53	2,158.3038	2,196.9426
54	2,117.07	2,127.9981	2,170.9289
55	2,084.73	2,096.9326	2,144.5825
56	2,051.51	2,065.1151	2,117.9610
57	2,017.38	2032.5550	2,091.1317
58	1,982.33	1,999.2603	2,064.1720
59	1,946.35	1,965.2489	2,037.1739
60	1,909.45	1,930.5356	2,010.2380
61	1,871.65	1,895.1533	1,983.4812
62	1,832.98	1,859.1360	1,957.0284
63	1,793.45	1,822.5286	1,931.0152
64	1,753.15	1,785.3961	1,905.5879
65	1,712.08	1,747.7927	1,880.8914
66	1,670.28	1,709.7883	1,857.0756
67	1,627.71	1,671.4403	1,834.2843
68	1,584.36	1,632.8252	1,812.6609
69	1,540.18	1,594.0268	1,792.3413
70	1,495.16	1,555.1662	1,773.4541
71	1,449.38	1,516.4019	1,756.1091
72	1,402.92	1,477.9123	1,740.3840
73	1,355.91	1,439.8962	1,726.3185
74	1,308.52	1,402.5704	1,713.9114
75	1,260.89	1,366.1510	1,703.1193
76	1,213.21	1,330.8508	1,693.8614
77	1,165.59	1,296.8726	1,686.0267
78	1,118.20	1,264.4172	1,679.4831
79	1,071.14	1,233.6701	1,674.0847
80	1,024.57	1,204.8069	1,669.6856
81	978.63	1,177.9807	1,666.1476
82	933.48	1,153.3068	1,663.3430
83	889.29	1,130.8537	1,661.1568
84	846.23	1,110.6411	1,659.4863
85	804.47	1,092.6360	1,658.2403

Female 1983 Individual Annuity Table (4 percent interest net rates)

Essentials of Life Insurance Products

TABLE 8-4
Monthly Lifetime Benefit for Male per $1,000 Annuity Purchase (Net Rates)

	Life Annuity	10-Year Certain + Life	20-Year Certain + Life
50	$ 4.82	$ 4.78	$ 4.65
51	4.89	4.85	4.70
52	4.97	4.92	4.76
53	5.05	5.00	4.81
54	5.14	5.08	4.87
55	5.23	5.16	4.93
56	5.33	5.25	4.99
57	5.43	5.34	5.05
58	5.54	5.44	5.12
59	5.66	5.54	5.18
60	5.78	5.65	5.24
61	5.92	5.77	5.30
62	6.06	5.89	5.37
63	6.22	6.02	5.43
64	6.38	6.15	5.49
65	6.56	6.29	5.54
66	6.75	6.44	5.60
67	6.95	6.59	5.65
68	7.16	6.74	5.70
69	7.39	6.90	5.75
70	7.63	7.06	5.79
71	7.89	7.23	5.82
72	8.17	7.40	5.86
73	8.46	7.57	5.89
74	8.78	7.75	5.92
75	9.12	7.92	5.94
76	9.48	8.09	5.96
77	9.86	8.26	5.98
78	10.27	8.43	5.99
79	10.71	8.59	6.00
80	11.17	8.74	6.01
81	11.67	8.89	6.02
82	12.19	9.03	6.03
83	12.74	9.16	6.03
84	13.32	9.28	6.03
85	13.93	9.39	6.04

Male 1983 Individual Annuity Table (4 percent interest net rates)

TABLE 8-5 Monthly Lifetime Benefit for Female per $1,000 Annuity Purchase (Net Rates)			
Age	Life Annuity	10-Year Certain + Life	20-Year Certain + Life
50	$ 4.47	$4.45	$4.40
51	4.53	4.51	4.45
52	4.59	4.57	4.50
53	4.65	4.63	4.55
54	4.72	4.70	4.61
55	4.80	4.77	4.66
56	4.87	4.84	4.72
57	4.96	4.92	4.78
58	5.04	5.00	4.84
59	5.14	5.09	4.91
60	5.24	5.18	4.97
61	5.34	5.28	5.04
62	5.46	5.38	5.11
63	5.58	5.49	5.18
64	5.70	5.60	5.25
65	5.84	5.72	5.32
66	5.99	5.85	5.38
67	6.14	5.98	5.45
68	6.31	6.12	5.52
69	6.49	6.27	5.58
70	6.69	6.43	5.64
71	6.90	6.59	5.69
72	7.13	6.77	5.75
73	7.38	6.94	5.79
74	7.64	7.13	5.83
75	7.93	7.32	5.87
76	8.24	7.51	5.90
77	8.58	7.71	5.93
78	8.39	7.91	5.95
79	9.34	8.11	5.97
80	9.76	8.30	5.99
81	10.22	8.49	6.00
82	10.71	8.67	6.01
83	11.24	8.84	6.02
84	11.82	9.00	6.03
85	12.43	9.15	6.03
Female 1983 Individual Annuity Table (4-percent interest net rates)			

The life income option is extremely inflexible. Benefits are calculated on the basis of the age and sex of the primary beneficiary, and once the payments have begun, no other person can be substituted for the designated beneficiary, even with an adjustment in the benefits. No right of withdrawal is available and no commutation privilege exists for benefits payable under a deferred life annuity. Otherwise, persons in poor health would be inclined to withdraw the proceeds. When the benefits are guaranteed for a specified period of time, however, a few companies will permit the proceeds payable under the fixed-period installment option to be commuted. If the commutation privilege is exercised, the beneficiary is usually given a deferred life annuity certificate. This certificate provides for life income payments to the beneficiary if he or she survives the period during which the guaranteed payments were to have been made.

Use of Settlement Options

Adaptation of Settlement Options to Basic Family Needs

Earlier chapters of this book described the basic family needs that life insurance can meet. The manner in which settlement options can be adapted to a family's various needs is outlined below.

Lump-Sum Cash Needs of the Family—*Cleanup or Estate Clearance Fund.* The first need in point of time is a fund to meet the expenses that arise from the insured's death and to liquidate the current outstanding obligations. These are claims against the insured's probate estate and must be satisfied before any property can be distributed to the heirs. The size of the fund varies, but for estates of less than $1,000,000, it averages 15 percent of the probate estate. For larger estates the percentage is higher because of the progressive nature of death tax rates.

The conventional method of handling proceeds intended for estate clearance is to have them paid to the insured's estate in a lump sum. This recognizes that payment of the claims against the estate is an obligation of the executor or administrator, and fulfilling this obligation requires cash within a relatively short time after the insured's death. For estates of more than the federal estate tax exemption amount (unified credit), estate taxes can be avoided by having the policy owned by the spouse or a life insurance trust. By making the life insurance proceeds payable to the spouse or the trust, funds can be made available to the insured's estate either by purchasing noncash assets from the estate or by loaning money to the estate.

Under the interest-only option, the beneficiary may leave the proceeds with the insurer to earn interest until they are needed by the beneficiary or the executor. If the insurance is more than adequate for the needs of the estate, the excess can go to the insured's dependents without having to pass through the probate estate and incurring any accompanying delay and expense. These advantages are especially important when the potential estate liabilities are large but unpredictable and a substantial amount of insurance is involved. While some insurers do not permit executors or trustees to elect life-income settlement options, most are willing to make the interest option available to a trustee or an executor during the period of estate administration.

If the probate estate is modest and the insured's spouse is the sole or major beneficiary of the estate, it may be advantageous to have the insurance intended for estate clearance payable to the widow(er) under the interest option with the unlimited right of withdrawal. He or she can use whatever portion of the proceeds is needed to pay the debts of the insured's estate and apply the remainder to his or her own needs, perhaps in the form of a deferred settlement. This procedure will reduce the cost of estate administration, particularly the executor's fee. It will also take advantage of the special inheritance tax exemption available in most states when insurance proceeds are payable to third-party beneficiaries, especially the insured's widow(er) and child(ren). This advantage is offset to the extent that payment of the insured's debts out of the insurance proceeds enlarges the taxable distribution from the estate unless funds were made available through loans to, or asset purchases from, the estate. By using the interest option and a spendthrift clause, the insured can protect the proceeds from the beneficiary's creditors.

The obvious disadvantage of this arrangement is that the beneficiary, through poor judgment, may pay claims that were not valid or, through stupidity or greed, refuse to use the insurance proceeds for the purposes for which they were intended. This behavior is, of course, more likely when the beneficiary is not the sole heir of the estate, and it may result in forced liquidation at great sacrifice of valuable estate assets. Another risk in this arrangement, unless properly safeguarded, is that the widow(er) might die before clearing the insured's estate, with the proceeds going to his or her estate or to minor contingent beneficiaries. Both situations would then make it impossible for the proceeds to be used to pay the insured's debts. To guard against such an unpleasant development, it is possible to make the insured's estate the contingent beneficiary if the widow(er) should predecease the insured or die within 6 months after the insured's death. If the primary beneficiary survives the insured by 6 months, the child(ren) can become the contingent beneficiaries of any unused proceeds.

If the estate liabilities are large and a life insurance trust is going to be used for other purposes, the estate clearance fund can be made payable to the trustee in a lump sum or under the interest option (if permissible). A provision in the trust agreement authorizes the trustee to lend money to the estate or to purchase estate assets. Thus, the trust may come to hold assets formerly held by the estate.

Mortgage Cancellation Fund. If there is a mortgage on the insured's home, the insured usually attempts to provide enough insurance to liquidate the mortgage upon his or her death so that the family can continue to occupy the home. In some cases, the insurance is provided through a special mortgage redemption policy, embodying the decreasing term insurance principle.

If the mortgage can be prepaid, there is usually a provision for a lump-sum payment either to the insured's surviving spouse or to his or her estate. This is predicated on the assumption that it takes less insurance to liquidate the mortgage with a single-sum payment than to provide a monthly income equal to the regular monthly payments. If the mortgage has no prepayment privilege or can be prepaid only with a heavy penalty, an income settlement can be arranged to provide funds in the required amount and frequency for the mortgage

Mortgage Cancellation
• Lump sum payment to fully repay is common
• Continuation of mortgage payments is an option if
– there is an onerous prepayment penalty
– the mortgage interest rate is very low relative to available investment yields

payments. Either the fixed-period option or the fixed-amount option is satisfactory, although the fixed-period option would be difficult to use if elected before the insured's death.

Emergency Fund. If a life insurance trust is not created, perhaps the most satisfactory arrangement for emergency funds is by electing the interest option with a limited or an unlimited right of withdrawal. The widow(er) is normally the beneficiary. Another method of making emergency funds available is through the fixed-amount option with appropriate withdrawal privileges. Under this arrangement, a somewhat larger fund can be set aside than that needed for the regular installments.

Educational Fund. The fixed-amount option is ideally suited to liquidating proceeds intended to finance a college education or professional training. However, the interest option, with appropriate withdrawal privileges, can also be used to cope with inflation. The payments can be made directly to the student, to the educational institution on his or her behalf, or to an adult relative or friend.

Income Needs of the Family—*Readjustment Income.* The readjustment period is the interval of time—usually one to 3 years in duration— immediately following the insured's death, during which income is usually provided at or near the level enjoyed by the family during the insured's lifetime. In the dependency period thereafter, the income drops to a more realistic and sustainable level.

Theoretically, the income for the readjustment period can be provided through the fixed-period option, the fixed-amount option, or the interest option with the right of withdrawal. If a step-down within the period is contemplated, which may be advisable if the dependency period income represents a drastic reduction, the fixed-amount option can be used because it allows adjustments to the amount. Some estate planners provide the same contractual income in the readjustment period as in the dependency period, with the thought that the widow(er) can use the withdrawal privilege to cushion the financial shock during the readjustment period.

Dependency Period Income. Broadly speaking, the dependency period extends from the date of the insured's death until the youngest child is self-sufficient or perhaps in college. In planning terminology, however, the dependency period is the interval between the end of the readjustment period and the youngest child's self-sufficiency, usually assumed to occur at age 18, unless a child is mentally or physically handicapped.

In practice, a combination of Social Security survivorship benefits and the interest on life insurance proceeds being held for other purposes frequently meets a substantial portion of the family's income needs during this period. If not, additional income can be provided through the fixed-period or fixed-amount options. If, for example, at the time the program is being set up, the youngest child is 6 years old and additional income of $600 per month is desired until the child is 18, it does not seem to matter whether proceeds in the amount of $68,530 are set aside under a fixed-period option providing $600 per month for 12 years or whether the same sum is set aside under a fixed-amount option providing $600 per month as long as the proceeds hold out, which would be exactly

12 years if there were no withdrawals from the fund and no excess interest over the assumed 4-percent rate were credited to it. Under most circumstances, however, the fixed-amount option will prove to be more satisfactory.

Perhaps most significant is that the right of withdrawal can be granted in connection with the fixed-amount option but not with the fixed-period option. In some cases, it may be unwise to give the beneficiary this privilege, but in general, it injects an element of flexibility into the settlement plan that may be urgently needed, particularly with the prospect of continued inflationary pressures. Moreover, moderate withdrawals will not necessarily shorten the period of income payments because the withdrawals may be offset in whole or in part by dividend accumulations and excess interest credits. Another argument in favor of the fixed-amount option is that provision can be made for increasing the size of the monthly payments to offset the loss of income from Social Security as each child reaches age 18.

Life Income for Surviving Spouse. In life insurance planning, it is necessary to break the widow(er)'s basic need for life income into two periods. One period runs from the youngest child's 18th birthday to the widow(er)'s 62d, and the other starts when the widow(er) reaches age 62. This breakdown is necessary because the widow(er)'s income from Social Security terminates when the youngest child reaches age 18 (unless a child is totally disabled) and does not resume until the widow(er) reaches age 62. A permanently reduced benefit is available at age 60. The period in between is usually called the Social Security gap or the *blackout period.*

Income during the blackout period can be provided by making the life income option operative upon the insured's death or upon termination of the Social Security survivorship benefits. Alternatively, the interest-only option can be left in place until the surviving spouse needs more income and then converted to a life income option.

In most cases, after the blackout period, income to the surviving spouse will be provided by Social Security benefits and payments under a life income option, the only practical way of ensuring a definite income for the remainder of the widow(er)'s life. If a large sum of insurance is available and the beneficiary is both financially able and desires to preserve the principal for the benefit of contingent beneficiaries (such as children), the interest option can be used until the primary beneficiary's death.

The primary beneficiary's age and health should be considered before making a life income settlement option election. If the beneficiary is unlikely to survive very long because of poor health or very old age, choosing a life income option could result in a significant forfeiture. Selecting a period-certain guarantee would at least limit such forfeiture. The beneficiary is less likely to be concerned about a possible forfeiture if there are no children or grandchildren to receive such residual funds.

Ethical Issues of Classifying Risk

Ethics is a social system of rules created to allow people to resolve disputes rationally without resorting to physical force, so that the relationships affected by the dispute can endure and even flourish. Because most disputes are generated over the question of who is entitled to certain goods, the pursuit of goods and the avoidance of harm are at the core of any moral system.

Ethics deals primarily with enhancing the quality of life on the one hand, and the issues of fairness and justice on the other. The basic ethical rule can be summarized: pursue your interests fairly and unselfishly. Fair treatment means "the same should be treated the same." Consequently, a difference in treatment is justified only when there are relevant differences. Selfish behavior is behavior in which the pursuit of self-interest is without regard for the interests of, or at the expense of, others. This notion of fairness and rational thinking underlies the principle of the Golden Rule: "Do unto others as you would have others do unto you." This principle reinforces the notion that others are the same as you in most relevant respects.

Reflecting on the principle of fairness helps us see the unethical nature of selfishness. By "selfishness" we do not mean just the pursuit of self-interest. The pursuit of self-interest is a perfectly natural and acceptable activity. Selfishness is the pursuit of self-interest *at the expense of another* when one is not entitled to the good pursued. When a person is being selfish, he or she puts his or her own interest first in a situation where pursuing that interest will hurt another. For example, if there is one piece of cake allotted to each person at a party, and I take two pieces, I have deprived someone of their share of the cake. In such a case whoever pursues his or her own interest will do so at the expense of the other. It is for situations like this that society has created rules of fair distribution. If two people have a desire or need for the good, why should it go to one and not to the other? We need rules to decide. These are the ethical rules of society.

The demands for justice and enhanced quality of life require a set of ethical rules for appropriate behavior that govern any existing society. How are such rules established? It is easy to see how ethical rules rest on the more general prohibitions against selfishness and unfairness. For example, stealing is wrong because it is fundamentally unfair or selfish. If a person has acquired property through a process the society deems fair, only to have it taken by another who has no right to it, such stealing violates fairness and involves selfishness.

One of the processes for distribution of goods is the process of free markets. The free exchange of goods in a market requires the informed consent of both parties. For example, if we view a life insurance sale as a market transaction, we can see that certain types of fraud that misrepresent the product or withhold significant information do not allow informed consent, so they constitute misappropriation of the buyer's goods. Such a sale involves a type of stealing that is unfair and unjust.

To be fair or just requires society to work out procedures for the distribution of the benefits and burdens of the world. Some relationships exist simply because we share the same world. Other relationships exist because we have entered into a type of relationship with another that involves a commitment to them. In societies there are various relationships, some natural and some conventional (literally based on agreements), that help in the smooth functioning of those societies. Many of those conventional relationships are based on promises made— implicit or explicit contracts to which people are committed. For example, if I become a parent, I have implicitly committed—and my society expects me—to meet certain obligations to care for and educate my child.

In this section we will apply the ethics of relationships to the insurance industry, and specify the rights and responsibilities of the various individuals and constituencies in the world of insurance. We will look at some particular practices that are ethically suspect and try to show why they are inappropriate and, if they are problematic, show the reasons both for and against them.

Insurance is first of all a cooperative social system created to minimize the risk of financial loss from specific unforeseen future events. It minimizes the risk of financial loss both to oneself and to dependants. To enter into a private insurance contract is, in effect, to enter into a group of one's own free will in order to collectively help one another minimize the risks involved. (This applies to private insurance; public insurance is a compulsory group.) The collective nature of insurance immediately raises ethical questions about the fairness or unfairness of discriminating for some and against others who wish to join a group.

For example, if a group of healthy people joins together to insure their lives, the cost of insurance would be much cheaper if they could exclude people with unhealthy characteristics, histories, and/or lifestyles. One could ask if it is "fair" for such a group to be exclusionary. If someone significantly less healthy than the others wants to pay, what is the fair price for entrance? There is a dispute about whether someone *should* be allowed to join a group. The joining would be at the expense of the others. Under what conditions would causing that harm to others be justified by the benefit of including the unhealthy person? What reasons can be given in answer to such questions? The reasons that can be given constitute the fundamental ethical concepts.

When we consider life insurance in particular, as opposed to property and casualty insurance, a relevant difference arises. Life insurance is primarily designed to provide support for dependents. Property and casualty insurance is meant to minimize the risk to oneself rather than benefit survivors.

Life insurance was originally designed to respond to an ethical belief that people have a moral responsibility for the support and maintenance of their children during the children's dependent years. Given that fact, life insurance is an exceptional financial instrument in that the benefit goes to a person other than the one who makes the investment and the sacrifice. Before the use of life insurance as an investment or a viatical tool, or a source of long-term care, it required the setting aside of one's self-interest for the sake of others. That is the very essence of unselfish behavior, and selfishness is characteristic of unethical behavior. Consequently, a life insurance advisor becomes a promoter of this type of altruistic behavior.

While the original concept of insurance is remarkably simple—a group of people joining to pool their resources to protect themselves from risk—the products and their distribution have become quite complex over the years. All-important ethical issues, questions of what is fair and right and beneficial to whom, have gotten similarly complex. We will now take a look at some of the ethical issues and responsibilities that face the various actors in the drama of the life insurance industry.

There has been intense interest in the ethics of market behavior, focused on the misrepresentation of the values of certain products, or on the unnecessary replacement of policies to further the interests of the advisor, thereby helping the advisor meet quotas to further the profits of the company. But this is only one type of ethical difficulty present in the field of life insurance. Other problems involve the ethics of underwriting or conflicts between the demands of the company and the demands of the client. Some of the issues are merely matters of selfishness or greed on the part of the advisor, while others involve conflicts of obligations where the advisor is in a no-win situation.

There are at least three groups of people (four if we distinguish between the insured and the insured's beneficiaries) involved in the ethics of insurance: the insurer (the company), the insured (the client or beneficiary), and the advisor. Each of these has a relationship to the other and carries ethical responsibilities. The remainder of the chapter will investigate those relationships and the moral responsibilities that arise from them. The three relationships we will examine are: 1) the advisor/client relationship, 2) the advisor/insurer relationship, and 3) the insured/insurer relationship.

The Advisor/Client Relationship

The Advisor's Responsibility to the Client—As stated in the "Special Notes to Advisors" in the front pages of this text, this series uses the term "financial advisor" or "advisor" as a generic reference to professional practitioners that sell, service, or advise clients regarding life insurance and other financial products. That usage will be carried through in the following discussion, except when the use of the term "agent" specifically refers to "one who acts for another." Agency is defined as the relationship that results from the consent by one person or entity (the principal) that another party (the agent) will act on the principal's behalf. The agent is subject to the principal's control, and there must be consent to the agency by the agent.

When you commit to be an insurance advisor, you commit to meet certain responsibilities toward your clients and company. Focusing on these responsibilities is to adopt an approach to ethics that has been called *role morality*. Role morality means that one's situation in life, which results from commitments to others, brings with it specific duties.

Analyzing the ethical aspects of the advisor/client relationship without reference to the insurer is somewhat problematic because, in insurance, there is really a three-part relationship in which the advisor is a mediator between the company and the client. However for purposes of discussion we will focus on the various two-part relationships that exist and recognize the added dimensions when necessary.

In the advisor/client relationship it is important to note that the responsibilities change toward the client during the course of the relationship. For example, the client is technically only a prospective client before the policy goes into effect. In the early stages of contact between advisor and client, the client is a customer and the advisor is a salesperson. In that context, the ethics of marketing hold. In a marketing situation the advisor is obliged to adhere to the requirements of honest marketing, such as necessary disclosure and the avoidance of undue pressure which could limit the client's freedom to buy or not to buy. After the insurance goes into effect the customer is then an "insured" and a client, and new obligations emerge. The advisor's responsibilities now include servicing, helping with claims, and updating policies.

The differences can be prevented by the adoption of a general principle to cover all phases of the relationship. Most people would agree that the advisor should follow the Golden Rule and treat clients as the advisor would like to be treated. The professional pledge to which all CLU and ChFC designees commit specifically applies that Golden Rule when it states: "I shall, in light of all conditions surrounding those I serve, which I shall make every conscientious effort to ascertain and understand, render that service which, in the same circumstances, I would apply to myself." This rule exists and needs to be followed because insurance advisors, like everyone else, are subject to the conflict between self-interest and the interests of others.

Advisors should make recommendations based on their client's needs, but obviously they need to sell policies to make a living and their company needs to sell policies to stay in business. Consequently, from time to time, there can be pressure based on the advisor's personal financial situation or from the advisor's company and manager to sell the client what he or she does not need. According to *The Market Conduct Handbook for Agents*, "The insurer may say it wants the field force to provide a careful needs analysis but, in fact, the reward system for the advisor is based on sales—not service. If an advisor discovers that less service and needs analysis can result in quicker sales, then the advisor faces the ethical conflict of whether to make more sales and more money at the expense of the clients' needs." Of course, for the advisor to act for reasons of self-interest at the expense of another is the very core of selfishness; it is an attitude universally condemned.

Other than the avoidance of selfishness, and the refusal to sell what does not need to be sold, what other responsibilities does an advisor have to a client by virtue of his or her role as an advisor? That advisor certainly has an obligation to ascertain a client's needs for life insurance. The attempt to sell a client an unnecessary insurance policy would tend to involve lying and/or deception, practices universally considered unethical.

There might be times when such a sale does not involve deception but is the result of the advisor's ignorance about the product. The advisor might not have known what the client needed and subsequently recommended an unsuitable product. If the advisor does not know but could reasonably be expected to know, that advisor has an obligation to divulge the ignorance and to learn more. If the advisor thinks he knows but does not, we might hold the advisor responsible for his ignorance. Whatever the resolution of these issues, we can see that the obligation to analyze needs puts the further requirement of product knowledge on the shoulders of the advisor.

In addition to adherence to the Golden Rule in selling and looking out for the client's best interests, other obligations are inherent in the advisor/client relationship.

Confidentiality. In the course of writing a policy and performing a needs analysis, the advisor acquires a great deal of private information about the client. It is an obligation of the advisor to keep such information confidential, which means it should only be shared with those who have a legitimate right to such information after the client has authorized a release.

Obligations Associated with Delivering the Policy. The advisor is responsible for delivering the insurance policy to the insured and often also collects any premium that may be due at the time of policy delivery. Since some coverages do not take effect until the policy is delivered, timely delivery is crucial. Obviously, the advisor should take the time to explain all the policy provisions, including riders and exclusions, to see one more time if the policy meets the needs of the client, and to explain how the agency handles ongoing service. Finally, the advisor needs to explain any changes that have been made to the policy that were not in the original application.

Claims Handling. When the situation arises for the owner or beneficiary to make a claim, the advisor has a responsibility to help in various ways: explaining what the beneficiary is obliged to do in order to collect on a claim, helping the beneficiary expedite the claim settlement, mediating between the beneficiary and the insurer, and explaining the final settlement if the settlement is not what the owner or beneficiary expected.

Other Servicing. The advisor should review the client's policies to see if they are up to date with reference to beneficiaries and, more importantly, to see if they provide the coverages currently needed.

Ethics of Market Conduct. Thus far we have looked at what the advisor should do. All the above aside, most attention to ethics in the insurance industry is paid to market misconduct and the most notorious examples of unethical behavior on the part of advisors comes under the heading of unfair trade.

One unfair trade practice is misrepresentation, including misrepresenting the benefits or terms of a policy; misrepresenting dividends as guaranteed when they are not; misrepresenting the financial condition of the insurer; misrepresenting a life insurance policy as some other instrument; or, finally, misrepresenting oneself by perhaps claiming to be a financial planner when one is not.

Coercion that restricts free choice of products is also unethical. For example, for a bank to coerce one of its clients into buying the mortgage insurance it is selling rather than a competitor's insurance as a condition of granting a loan is clearly unethical. This obviously violates the conditions of a free market exchange and informed consent as discussed.

Other well-known types of unethical behavior are *twisting* and *churning*. Twisting occurs when a policyowner is induced to discontinue and replace a policy through advisor or insurer distortion or misrepresentation of the facts. When a policy is replaced unnecessarily it is known as churning. These practices are obviously unethical to the extent they exemplify the advisor pursuing self-interest at the expense of the client. If the replacement were really beneficial to the client, it would be the ethically correct thing to do.

There is also the practice of *rebating*, which is usually considered unethical, although there is some argument. Rebating is defined as any inducement in the sale of insurance that is not specified in the insurance contract. An offer to share a commission with an applicant is an example of such an inducement, and is illegal in most states except California and Florida. Rebating is generally considered wrong because it gives one advisor an unfair advantage over other advisors, or is seen as unfair to those clients who are not given a rebate. Defenders of rebating argue that it is not unfair, but rather should be viewed simply as a competitive market ploy.

It is also generally unethical, as well as illegal, for an advisor to charge fees in addition to a policy premium for services that are not 'truly' extra. Currently there is a good deal of argument concerning the proper way to compensate advisors. Because of recent abuses in the replacement of policies in order to take advantage of front-end-loaded commissions, the question is raised about the appropriateness of front-end-loaded commission-based selling as opposed to level commissions or fee-based selling.

It goes without saying that the advisor owes the client the truth. Knowing that, we see that it is unethical to do what is called *company bashing.* It is clearly unethical to tell lies or to misrepresent the strengths and weaknesses of the competition whether it is another advisor or another company. Yet there are numerous examples of advisors who suggest that another advisor or company is disreputable. Certainly if a product is not meeting a client's needs, or if clients are being misguided by another advisor, the first advisor has an obligation to disclose that fact, but it should be based on facts, not the needs and desires of the advisor to replace the company business of another advisor.

Discrimination against clients for reasons other than sound actuarial principles is unethical. Discrimination—which used to be a neutral term to describe the process of choosing to include or exclude people on the basis of some relevant characteristic(s)—has become an offensive term. Unethical discrimination is exclusion committed on the basis of some unjustified bias or hatred toward a person or group. Hence, discrimination committed on the basis of such considerations as race, gender, religion, nationality, or ethnic group is unethical when those considerations are irrelevant and when they are done from motivations such as sexism, racism, or antireligious bias.

There are, of course, insurance companies that are tied to a particular religious or national group. Their exclusion of nonmembers is not unethical. But if a company is not an exclusive company from its inception, then such exclusionary policies are unethical. There are, however, legitimate reasons in underwriting for exclusion. A famous case of whether the discrimination was permissible concerned granting of premiums to young women drivers that were lower than the premiums applied to men. Actuarially, as a group, young women had safer driving records than their male counterparts. Was this sexist? Because it was not based on denigrating women, and in fact favored them, it was not deemed discriminatory in the ethical sense.

It is unethical for the advisor to discriminate against a client based on considerations such as race, for this violates one of the first principles of a market economy: in any exchange only relevant economic factors should apply. Questions that should be asked include "Is the person worth the risk?" and "Does the person have the ability to pay?"

These, in brief, are the ethical responsibilities an advisor has toward his or her client. We now need to consider the responsibilities the client has toward his advisor or the company.

Client Responsibilities. The advisor/client relationship is not a one-way street. Thus far we have talked mainly of the advisor's responsibilities to the client. The client has ethical responsibilities to the advisor as well. Again the principle is simple: the client should do nothing that is deceitful, unfair, or harmful to the advisor or the company. The insured owes the company the truth. The chief examples of a client's unethical behavior include fraudulent claims, lying to the advisor and withholding information on an application.

There is a widespread practice involving fraudulent claims, particularly in the disability income area where back injuries are faked in order to collect compensation. The fact that such practices exist does not make them ethically acceptable. They are fraudulent and unfair because their cost is borne by those who pay premiums and/or by those who receive less return on their investments. Another type of unethical practice is lying or withholding information on an application. There are a number of stories told in which a client, while smoking a cigarette, has told the advisor he is a nonsmoker. What should an advisor do? There are advisors who write the policy the way the applicant wants. The honest advisor will not do this, but the client puts that advisor in an uncomfortable situation by asking him to violate his obligation to the company. In this case we are focusing on the ethics of the client. It is unethical to put an advisor into that kind of situation and it is unethical to lie. Once again, as in the fraudulent claims case, the fact that many people lie on their applications does not make it right.

The following example shows the subtle kind of unethical behavior engaged in by the client when he puts the advisor into a conflict-of-interest situation.

Example: Your brother-in-law, Sam, an attorney, is undergoing treatment for an inoperable malignant brain tumor. Because of the aggressive nature of the treatment, he may live for up to 3 years. On the other hand, he may not make it 3 months.

Sam feels he is woefully underinsured. He is concerned for his family's financial welfare after his death. So are you.

Sam has always been a bit of a spendthrift. He has lived the good life, spending everything he has earned over the course of the years—and then some. You know that you will probably have to help support his family if he dies without adequate life insurance.

Sam comes to you, an experienced, professional life insurance advisor and asks for your help and understanding. Sam wants to apply for life insurance—not a big policy, but $100,000 of annual renewable term, which he feels is just enough to guarantee his children's college education. He plans to deny his medical history when he is examined for the policy. He will claim that he has no attending physician.

Sam is prepared to take his chances that he will live beyond the policy's contestable period. As an attorney, he believes that he fully understands the implications of what he is about to do, at least as far as those implications may affect his beneficiaries.

He does not however seem to have given much thought to how they may affect you and your career.

What are your ethical obligations to Sam, to Sam's family, to your company (if you give it the business), and to yourself?

The example is interesting because selfishness on the advisor's part is not involved, rather there is a conflict of loyalty. Sam, as a member of the advisor's family, puts a claim on the advisor in the name of family loyalty and, in this situation, the family's interest conflicts with the company's interest.

There are other cases in which the self-interest of an advisor is involved. For example, when an advisor knows the applicant is a smoker, or has cancer, and also knows that if he does not write the policy, someone else will. So the advisor is losing a client and the commission that goes with it. What is the ethical thing to do in that case? What does the advisor owe the company? Because honesty in filling out the application will cost the advisor the commission, there is great temptation to submit false data on the application. There is also a conflict between the advisor's, client's, and company's interest (the interests of the shareholders and other policyowners of the company). Clearly misrepresenting the fact of smoking on an application is unfair as well as dishonest because it lets the current applicant play on an uneven field.

What these examples show is that clients have at least three obligations: 1) to tell the truth on an application, 2) to file honest claims, and 3) to not put the advisor into an unnecessary conflict-of-interest situation. Acquiescence by the advisor is essentially collusion against the insurer and the other policyowners.

The Advisor/Insurer Relationship

The Advisor's Responsibilities to the Company—An advisor (and, in some cases, a broker) serves as an agent of the company in accord with agency law. That means the agent is empowered to act on behalf of the company (the principal) and acts performed by the agent bind the company. Thus, in certain situations and under certain conditions, when the agent signs an application or binds an insurance contract, he or she binds the company to that contract. However, because an agent is expected to act in the best interest of the company, there are times the agent's interests are expected to be subordinated to those of the company. There is a stipulation here, however. An agent is never required to do anything illegal or unethical for the sake of the company. It is an interesting phenomenon that a vital ethical issue among office assistants is whether they are required to lie on behalf of their bosses. Something as seemingly innocuous as telling a caller with relevant business that the boss is not in—when he or she is—takes on moral import.

If the agent is bound to look out for the best interest of the principal, part of defining the responsibilities of the agent to the company will require a look at the interests of the company. In insurance there are three types of companies: mutual, publicly owned for profit, and state run. The mutual company is theoretically a group of individual insureds with a mutual interest who pool their resources in order to protect themselves from undue risk. The publicly owned for-profit company is a business set up with a pool of resources that allows one to purchase protection from risk at a price. State funded insurance programs may or may not be considered insurance companies depending on one's definition of risk management. Nevertheless, the purpose of the state-run program is to provide public services for private individuals who, in some cases, do not enter the program voluntarily but are required to belong. The focus here will be on the mutual and for-profit companies.

It has been said (by such as Milton Friedman) that the primary and only responsibility of for-profit businesses is to maximize profit for the shareholders. Hence, as an agent for the company, the agent must act on behalf of the company, and act in ways that will make money for the company, not cost the company money.

There is a popular hypothetical case in which a husband cancels a life insurance policy covering himself. His wife had encouraged him to purchase the policy, and he had reluctantly agreed. The cancellation took place late on a Friday. The agent did the paper work and gave the client a cancellation slip, but did not send the requisite paperwork to the company because the mail had already been collected for the weekend. The husband was killed in a hunting accident on Saturday and his wife called the agent on Sunday because she was unable to find the policy, all she had found was the cancellation memorandum. This scenario raises many questions. What should the agent do? What obligations does the agent have to the company? What obligations does the agent have to the wife?

If we concentrate on the obligation to the company we can state that though sympathy favors ripping up the return receipt and the paperwork, that is not fair to the company. The agent's first loyalty is to the company. As harsh as it sounds, it is nonetheless true that giving the money to the wife is tantamount to giving stockholder's money to her. Of course, considerations of good public relations and a compassionate image might persuade the company to pay the benefit if they knew the truth. But that raises the question of what obligations companies have to clients or former clients.

Some people would argue that the agent should withhold the information from the company while others would argue that as an agent, committed to looking out for the best interests of the company, he would be obliged to inform the company of the cancellation. The law clearly maintains the latter position. The courts hold that a company is aware of all information known by any of its agents. When polled on this issue, agents are likely to be split in their response as to which course of action is ethical.

Not all situations are as difficult to resolve as the one above. In most situations the obligations are clear. The agent's contract or agency agreement spells out many of the agent's (or broker's) responsibilities to the company.

The Company's Responsibilities to the Agent—*Agent Support and Training.* Companies have two obligations with respect to training their agents. First, they owe it to their agents to insure that they have the competence to do adequate analyses of the various needs of their clients. Secondly, they owe it to their agents to teach them what behavior is ethically acceptable and what is not. One might expect young recruits to be able to distinguish between the acceptable and the unacceptable, but a young, inexperienced person might be more easily swayed into thinking that a somewhat shady practice is standard operating procedure. For example, one company (not an insurance company) taught its young salespeople to slip a contract and a pen into the hands of a prospective client on the premise that only 5 percent of people would have enough fortitude to hand back a contract without signing it if the sales presentation were handled correctly. That is a real hard-sell technique. What is valued by such a hard-sell artist is not whether the client's needs have been met but whether the sale is made. The sales manager who trains his recruits that such behavior is intolerable meets his ethical obligation; the hard-sell artist does not.

Provide Clear Sales Materials. In addition to offering the agent training, the company should provide the agent with good tools—sales material that is clear and non-deceptive.

Fair Commission Structures. One cannot pick up literature about how to influence ethical behavior without sooner or later encountering the question of the effects of commission structures on ethical behavior. The move to level commissions and/or fee for services is a direct result of the attempt to dissuade purely commission-driven sales. We can see why when we look at the next obligation, the obligation to reward ethical behavior.

Reward Ethical Behavior. Abraham Lincoln once threw a man out of his office, angrily refusing a substantial bribe. "Every man has his price," Lincoln explained, "and he was getting close to mine." Human beings are self-interested and subject to temptations. Consequently they can be motivated by the rewards their companies choose to put in place. If the only behavior rewarded is productivity, not honesty, the company is not meeting its responsibility to encourage ethical behavior. Richard O. Lundquist of the Equitable Life Assurance Society once said, "Most companies give numerous awards for achievement and accomplishment for sales, for growth, for longevity and loyalty; but there are no medals in the business world for honesty, compassion, or truthfulness." Numerous studies have shown the significant correlation between behavior and rewards. Common sense tells us that what the boss rewards is what the boss expects. To the extent that a company needs to promote ethical behavior, it has a responsibility to set up systems that reward that behavior. Many of the unethical practices of the past can be traced to undue pressure from the home office to do business without regard for how that business was done.

The Insured/Insurer Relationship

Company's Responsibilities to the Insured—Many of the following considerations concerning the relationship of the agent to the insured have been discussed in the previous sections. As the company's agent, the agent is responsible for acting on behalf of the company. His responsibilities therefore are inherent in the fact that he is an agent. Now we will focus on the company's responsibilities.

The company's responsibilities are based on the various functions it fulfills. The company develops and markets the product. After the product is applied for, the company must underwrite the product. This underwriting makes the company the custodian of a great deal of sensitive private information about the insured. Finally, the company promises to meet the insured's legitimate claims. Each of these relationships carries ethical responsibility.

Product Creation. As with all products, insurance policies should be quality products that are dependable and not harmful. More than most products, the insurance policy is an ethical instrument because it is a promise to pay compensation given the occurrence of a specific harmful event. This places a moral burden on the company to be fiscally sound so it is able to meet its payment obligations. The product should not be excessively risky and should be fairly priced. The product is generally too complicated for the average untrained person to adequately determine its value, hence, the company is responsible for giving fair value to the client.

Marketing. It should be clear that there are many ethical constraints on the marketing of the insurance product. The utilization of the principle of *caveat emptor* (buyer beware) should no longer guide corporate philosophy. Products today—from pharmaceuticals, to electronics, to automobiles, to food, to insurance policies—are far too complicated for the average buyer to know their quality, safety factors, or fair market value. Liability laws indicate that society has moved from favoring *caveat emptor* to favoring *caveat vendor* (seller beware). The burden to be open and honest in marketing has shifted to the producer.

An insurance company owes the client what any company owes a prospective customer: truth in advertising. As we have seen, the basis of the market is ideal exchange, and ideal exchange requires full information and autonomous individuals making the choice to exchange freely. In medical ethics the operative ideal is known as *informed consent.* For a client to give informed consent requires there be no misleading, coercive or manipulative advertising. Such advertising takes the decision out of the hands of the client. An ad that says "guaranteed renewable" when in reality it is not, is deceptive and unethical.

Underwriting. Knowledge of health risks is relevant for underwriting purposes. One of the classic ethical puzzles is whether a company should underwrite a client who is a known health risk, such as in the case of a prospective client who has AIDS. Should insurance companies insure those with AIDS? Obviously they are not a good health risk. But most risks can be insured. So the question is not so much should companies insure people with AIDS, but rather into what insurance pool should they be placed? More humanitarian, egalitarian groups might insist on putting the AIDS group into the general pool. Of course those in that pool might call it unfair for they would, in a sense, be subsidizing the AIDS policyowner. On the other hand, if we were to create a pool only for those who have AIDS, the cost of the premiums would be prohibitive. Some people might argue that this is an area where the insurance needs to be social insurance and, therefore, be funded through taxes.

A different problem for insurance companies is whether—and to what extent—to engage in genetic testing and/or genetic screening. This results in an actuarial paradox because the more we can predict about the future health and time of death of a person, the greater the role the risk factor plays in the decision of who gets covered and for how much. If I knew a client would cost X number of dollars to care for by a certain date, then should I not in all fairness to the other policyholders and the owners of the company, underwrite a policy in such a way that there is no loss of revenue? Companies make promises to deliver money upon certain contingencies. They have a responsibility therefore to stay in sound fiscal shape so they can deliver on those promises. The inclusion of people with known and highly predictable health risks into an insurance group at premiums that cannot be soundly underwritten is a violation of the company's trust to others who depend on its soundness. What looks hard-hearted may be the ethical path.

It could be said that the company has the right—possibly even the duty—to be discriminatory, but not unfairly discriminatory, and this involves fair underwriting. A company is obliged to treat its constituency fairly, with requirements set forth in the canons of fairness that govern marketplace transactions.

One practice that is prohibited by the NAIC's Unfair Trade Practices Act is the practice of redlining. At one time realtors drew red lines around a geographic area on a map to keep certain people out of that area. Redlining is a form of unfair discrimination and is more common in auto insurance than in life insurance. There are companies that do not want to insure in certain geographic areas. This is not to say there are not genuine underwriting issues involved, but one must look carefully at the exclusion of anyone to see that it occurs on legitimate grounds and not on the basis of racist or sexist biases. Of course, there can be lively debate as to what counts as legitimate grounds.

As a result of the underwriting process, and given the amount of information required on insurance applications, insurance companies receive an extraordinary amount of private information about people, particularly in life insurance contracts where physical examination may be required. Thus the company is obliged to practice due care that this private information—the disclosure of which could be harmful to the client—does not become available to anyone without a reason to possess it. It is a very important responsibility for a company to keep confidentialities, including the maintenance of privacy and the protection of confidential health records.

What constitutes the proper use of health records? Clearly, only those with legitimate claims to such knowledge should have access to it. Does a pharmaceutical company have a right to access the list of a Health Maintenance Organization's client records so it can push its prescription drugs? No matter what the case, to have information on someone is to hold that information in trust and it is unethical to divulge it except to those who are legitimately entitled to it—those the client has authorized to receive the information.

Claims Settlement Practices. The insured has a right to prompt, fair, and equitable settlement. Prompt settlement is the efficient processing and payment of a claim within a reasonable time. Fair settlement means paying what a claim is worth. If a company attempts to settle a claim for less than what a reasonable person could expect, the company is acting unethically. The company also has an obligation to give reasons for any compromise claims settlement and the company has the responsibility to make known when and where appeals procedures are available.

Fair Cancellations and Nonrenewals. Suppose a company that sells guaranteed renewable disability insurance finds that such a policy is not profitable and discontinues the line. On the policy there is an automatic reinstatement period following the expiration of the contractual thirty-one day grace period, so if a policyowner missed the end of the grace period, he could get identical coverage automatically reinstated. Suppose as a result of poor financial conditions, the company changes its procedure and requires policyowners to apply and qualify for reinstatement. That reinstatement however, when granted, is on a modified basis. Beneficial riders are dropped in some cases and some promises of return of premiums are discontinued.

In this case it would appear that the company is adopting a policy that harms policyholders in order to minimize loss. What is the responsibility of a company that finds itself with commitments that are far more costly than they seemed originally? To what extent can the pursuit of profit override obligations to the insured? What should happen when circumstances change so that the terms of a contract now benefit one party and injure another far more than was foreseen? If the purpose is to make contracts as a hedge against those times, shouldn't they be honored? Should the insurer's main concern be profit or the benefit of the client? On the other hand, if a company needs to make adjustments to long-standing agreements in order to stay in business, aren't those adjustments ethically defensible? In our system one cannot benefit the client without remaining competitive in the marketplace.

Due Diligence in Hiring, Firing, and Retaining Agents. Another responsibility of the company is to practice due diligence in the hiring and firing of agents. It has been said that one of the problems with retention is recruitment. If you do not recruit well, you will not retain your agents. We could add that if you do not recruit well, you may acquire unethical agents. Along with the responsibility of diligence in the hiring of agents, the company also has an obligation to provide for the training of its agents.

On another issue, should a company keep a top producer if it becomes clear that top producer writes business by cutting ethical corners? Recently a CEO of a major insurance company that had recently ceased commission payments on internal replacements contemplated offering no commissions for external replacements. The reason was simple—such a move would disincentivize replacements. Clearly, this was an insurance executive who took the company's responsibility to its clients very seriously. But is such a plan fair to the agents who also had to work hard on replacements? Would it be fair to the shareholders of the company if it forced productive agents to look for another company? This example shows that responsibilities are not simply one-sided but involve a multitude of responsibilities, some of which may be in conflict.

These relationships and obligations that arise among the agent, client, and insurer are multidimensional and involve a wide range of stakeholders. When there is a multitude of stakeholders, inevitably and occasionally conflicts of obligation with respect to two or more of those stakeholders will occur. The CEO mentioned above has duties to many stakeholders: his stockholders (or policyowners in the case of a mutual company), his agents, his clients, his family, and himself. What should be done when these duties conflict? The ethical course of action would be to try to resolve the difficulty without hurting someone in the process, and to try to be fair and true to oneself.

Chapter Eight Review

Key terms and concepts are explained in the glossary. Answers to the review questions and the self-test questions follow the Glossary.

Key Terms and Concepts

lump sum
settlement options
settlement agreement
spendthrift clause
revocable contingent beneficiaries
contract rates
current rates
unlimited right of withdrawal
limited right of withdrawal
cumulative right of withdrawal
noncumulative right of withdrawal
commutation
rebating
caveat emptor
dependency period income
churning
twisting
blackout period

caveat vendor
interest option
fixed-period option
fixed-amount option
life income option
immediate annuity
straight life annuity
life annuity with guaranteed installments
installment refund annuity
cash refund annuity
deferred life annuity
estate clearance fund
mortgage cancellation fund
emergency fund
educational fund
readjustment income

Review Questions

8-1. Compare insurance company liability when policy proceeds are paid in a lump sum and when an optional method of settlement is selected.

8-2. Explain when a spendthrift clause in a settlement agreement is enforceable.

8-3. An applicant for life insurance discovers that the policy does not contain a settlement option he thinks he will want to use. Why should he request to have the desired settlement option added to the policy by endorsement at the time the policy is issued?

8-4. Describe the ways a beneficiary's right of withdrawal of proceeds held by the insurer under a deferred-settlement arrangement may be limited.

8-5. Describe how a cumulative right of withdrawal differs from a noncumulative right of withdrawal.

8-6. Cathy is the beneficiary of her father's life insurance policy. Under a settlement option, the policy provides that Cathy has a cumulative right to withdraw $4,000 per year in addition to periodic contractual payments. During the next 5 years, Cathy exercises the right of withdrawal according to the following pattern: year one, a $1,500 withdrawal; year 2, no withdrawal; year 3, a $2,000 withdrawal; year 4, no withdrawal; year 5, a $2,500 withdrawal. Ignoring other sums that can be withdrawn pursuant to the terms of agreement, what is the maximum amount Cathy can withdraw under the cumulative right of withdrawal in year 6?

8-7. Describe the three basic concepts of life insurance settlement options.

8-8. Describe the four fundamental settlement options that have evolved from settlement option concepts.

8-9. Explain why the interest option is simple and flexible.

8-10. Define the fixed-period option and the fixed-amount option.

8-11. What factors must be taken into account to determine the amount of each payment when the liquidation period is a fixed period of time or if the amount of each payment is fixed in advance?

8-12. Describe developments that may increase or decrease the amount of proceeds available under the fixed-period option.

8-13. Describe the flexibility features available with the fixed-amount option.

8-14. Explain the underlying principle of a life income option.

8-15. Describe the following life income options:

   a. straight life income option

   b. life income with guarantee (period certain)

   c. installment-refund option

   d. cash-refund option

8-16. Explain why life income options are considered to be inflexible.

8-17. Discuss the advantages of having a life insurance trust own the policy when the insured's estate is substantial.

8-18. Describe how an election of the fixed-period option and the fixed-amount option can be used to provide a mortgage cancellation fund for the mortgage on the insured's home.

8-19. Greta and Hal are 33 and 35 years old, respectively, and have been married for 8 years. They have two children, Jimmy, age 6, and Joanie, age 2. Currently Hal is the only income provider. Although all family members enjoy excellent health, Hal wants his family to be provided for in the event that he dies while his children are young. Discuss what Greta and Hal should consider in selecting a settlement option that will provide income during the dependency period for Greta and their children.

8-20. Discuss the differences between selfish behavior and self interest with regard to ethical behavior.

8-21. Discuss the responsibilities the agent has toward the client.

8-22. Briefly list examples of unethical market conduct that the advisor should avoid.

Self-Test Questions

Instructions: Read the chapter first, then answer the following 10 questions to test your knowledge. Circle the correct answer, then check your answers in the answer key in the back of the book.

8-1. The spendthrift clause is intended to protect life insurance proceeds from attachment or seizure by

   (A) the insured's creditors
   (B) the surviving spouse's creditors
   (C) the beneficiary's creditors
   (D)   both the insured's and the beneficiary's creditors

8-2. Which of the following settlement options will pay both principal and interest for a specific time period?

   (A) life income
   (B) fixed-period income
   (C) specified amount
   (D) interest income

8-3. A 65-year-old policyowner who has cash value of $15,000 asks to be paid $1,200 annually under a settlement option. The policyowner has selected the

(A)   life income option
(B)   fixed-period option
(C)   specified-amount option
(D)   guaranteed-interest option

8-4. Inducing a policyowner to discontinue or replace a policy through agent distortion or misrepresentation of the facts is known as

(A)   churning
(B)   rebating
(C)   company bashing
(D)   twisting

8-5. The life income option with a specified period of guaranteed payments is mathematically a combination of

(A   a fixed-period installment option and a pure deferred life annuity
(B)   an installment refund annuity and an interest only option
(C)   a fixed-amount option and a fixed-period option
(D)   a pure deferred annuity and a principal-only option

8-6. Which of the following statements regarding ethics is (are) correct?

I.   Ethics deals primarily with enhancing, not diminishing, the quality of life.
II. The basic ethical rule can be summarized: Pursue your interests fairly and unselfishly.

(A)   I only
(B)   II only
(C)   Both I and II
(D)   Neither I nor II

8-7. Which of the following statements concerning life settlement options is (are) correct?

I. A life-income option and an annuity are based on the same principle.
II. The life income option is flexible, and after payments have begun, changes can be made to the income amount and who receives them.

(A) I only
(B) II only
(C) Both I and II
(D) Neither I nor II

8-8. Which of the following statements regarding ethics is (are) correct?

I. Selfish behavior is behavior in which self-interest is pursued without regard for, or at the expense of, others.
II. By "selfishness" we mean just the pursuit of self-interest, which is ethically unacceptable.

(A) I only
(B) II only
(C) Both I and II
(D) Neither I nor II

8-9. All of the following are types of life-income settlement options EXCEPT

(A) pure or straight life annuity
(B) life annuity with guaranteed installments
(C) cash-refund annuity
(D) interest-only annuity

8-10. Life insurance settlement options accomplish one of the following EXCEPT

(A) retention of proceeds and interest
(B) retention of proceeds, without liquidation of principal
(C) systematic liquidation of the proceeds without reference to life contingencies
(D) systematic liquidation of the proceeds with reference to life contingencies

Glossary

accelerated benefits—a provision in a life insurance policy that allows death benefits to be paid to the policyowner prior to the insured's death when the insured is terminally ill and has a limited life expectancy

accidental death—an unexpected death caused directly, unintentionally, and apart from any other cause and that occurred within a specified period after the event

accidental death benefit—a life insurance rider that increases the death benefit, usually doubling it, when the insured dies accidentally

adjustable life policy—life insurance that can be configured anywhere from short-duration term insurance through single premium whole life and that gives the policyowner the right to request and obtain a reconfiguration of the policy at specified intervals

adverse selection—occurs when premiums increase as a member ages, prompting healthy members to withdraw from the plan due to the premium increase, thus producing an abnormal increase in mortality rates for those less healthy members still in the plan

amount at risk—the difference between the face amount of an insurance policy and its reserve

annuity—a stream of periodic (monthly, quarterly, annual) payments whose function is to liquidate a principal sum in a scientific manner regardless of how that sum was created

annuity certain—an agreement under which periodic payments are made for a definite period of time without being linked to the duration of a specified human life, such as a mortgage or bank loan or as period-certain guarantee for an annuity pay out

annuity due—an annuity with payments at the beginning of the period

assignment provision—a life insurance policy provision that specifies the conditions under which a policyowner can transfer some or all of his or her rights in the policy to another

attained age—the number of years a person has already lived

attained-age method of conversion—an insurance policy conversion method that uses the insured's date of exchange as the effective age for future premiums

automatic premium loan provision—an insurance contract provision that stipulates that any defaulted premium will be automatically paid and charged against the cash value without request from the policyowner unless he or she elects to surrender the policy for cash or one of the paid-up insurance options

back-end withdrawal penalties—surrender charges that apply during the early years of life insurance and annuity contracts as well as federal income taxes applicable to annuity contracts up to age 59-1/2

Belth yearly price method—a price-of-protection method for life insurance cost comparisons. It assumes an interest rate or investment rate and, thereby, calculates the cost of protection to be compared with costs calculated in the same way for other policies being evaluated. It requires premium, dividend, face amount, beginning and ending cash values for the year, and assumed interest rate information.

Belth yearly rate-of-return method—a method of comparing life insurance costs that considers only one year of the policy when making an individual calculation. The yearly rate of return formula divides the sum of the benefits by the sum of the investments and then subtracts the number one from that amount. This process is repeated for each year over the comparison interval.

blackout period—the time between when the benefit to children of a surviving spouse ceases and when that spouse can start to collect Social Security retirement benefits

broker—a full-time insurance producer who works independently and has no primary relationship or minimum production requirements with any company

buy-sell agreement —a contract binding the owner of a business interest to sell the business interest for a specified or determinable price at his or her death or disability and a designated purchaser to buy at that time

capital needs analysis—a method of computing a desired income level that can continue indefinitely

capitalized value—the monetary value of the future earnings and total economic values of a human life to others that can be created to replace the economic value of that life to that person's dependents.

cash accumulation comparison method—a method of comparing life insurance costs. The technique is to accumulate the premium differences between the policies being compared while holding the death benefits of both policies constant and equal. The calculation is basically a buy-term-and-invest-the-difference approach. At the end of the interval being evaluated, the side fund accumulation amount can be compared to the cash value in the whole life or other form of cash value insurance policy. The policy with the greater accumulation at the end of the comparison interval is considered the preferable of the two contracts.

cash needs—the lump-sum needs at death for money to pay for expenses that a person would like to have taken care of for his or her survivors. These may include funds for final expenses, debts, mortgage cancellation or a rent fund, estate administration and taxes, if applicable, an emergency fund, and any prefunding of future anticipated needs, such as children's education.

cash refund annuity—a type of refund annuity that promises that upon the death of the annuitant it will pay to the annuitant's estate or a contingent beneficiary a lump sum that is the difference, if any, between the purchase price of the annuity and the sum of the monthly payments already distributed

cash value—the amount of equity in a policy against which a loan can be made. It is a savings element that results when premiums during the early years of a whole life policy exceed what is necessary to pay death claims. This excess is set aside and accumulates for the benefit of the insured.

cash surrender value—the cash values provided under nonforfeiture law, based on the level premium concept that creates a prefunding of death benefits and cash value.

cash value accumulation test—a procedure by which the cash value of a policy is generally limited to the net single premium that would be needed to fund the policy's death benefit

caveat emptor—buyer beware

caveat vendor—seller beware

churning—the process of generating brokerage commissions through unnecessary securities transactions; advising a client to make unnecessary transactions is also considered churning.

cleanup fund—a source of money to meet final expenses resulting from an insured's death and to liquidate all current outstanding obligations; also known as a probate fund or estate clearance fund

collateral assignment method—the technique used with split-dollar life insurance whereby the employee owns the policy and has the responsibility for paying the premium. The employers' share of the policy proceeds is secured by an assignment.

Commissioners Standard Ordinary (CSO) Morality Tables— Developed by the NAIC to serve as the standard (statutory) mortality tables for calculating minimum policy reserves, surrender values, and company assets and liabilities. Company solvency is the primary concern. The 1980 tables were the first to establish separate male/female and smoker/non-smoker rates. The 2001 tables are currently being introduced and approved for use throughout the various states and will gradually take effect over the next few years.

commutation—properly applied only to a right attaching to proceeds distributed under a liquidating option, it is to withdraw the present value of remaining installment payments in a lump sum. This does not apply to proceeds held under the interest option, but for all practical purposes, this right is identical to an unlimited right of withdrawal; it is not implicit in an installment agreement and must be specifically authorized in the settlement agreement.

company bashing—an unethical practice in which lies are told or facts are purposely misrepresented concerning the strengths or weaknesses of the competition whether it is another agent or another company

comparative-interest method—a modification of the cash-accumulation method of comparing life insurance costs whereby it is necessary to calculate the interest rate that would make a term insurance policy side fund exactly equal to the difference between the available cash value policy death benefit and the term insurance death benefit; often referred to as the Linton yield method

compound interest—interest earnings that are not distributed but are added to the original principal and reinvested at the same interest rate or a different rate of interest; it is interest on interest

contestability—an insurance company's right to refuse payment of a claim, often due to fraud or misrepresentations on an insured's application

contract of adhesion—a contract that is not negotiated. It is drafted entirely by one party (insurance company). The other party can only accept or reject the contract. Ambiguities will be interpreted in favor of the now-drafting party.

contract rates—a specified rate of income per $1,000 of proceeds guaranteed in a policy

convertibility—a feature in term life insurance that allows the insured to replace the term coverage with permanent individual life insurance without having to show evidence of insurability. In group insurance, the right is available only at certain times, including termination of the insured from the group or from an eligible class within the group.

cost of insurance—the amount a policyowner must pay for protection; the sum that each policyowner must contribute as their pro rata share of death claims in any particular year

cross-purchase agreement—a contract that provides that the surviving partners are obligated to buy a prearranged share of a deceased partner's interest from his or her estate

cumulative right of withdrawal—a right of withdrawal, whether exercised or not, that does not expire at the end of the period to which it pertains; any withdrawal amounts that are not taken out during a particular year can be withdrawn in any subsequent year, in addition to any other sums that can be withdrawn pursuant to the terms of agreement

current assumption whole life—a variation of traditional whole life insurance that lies somewhere between adjustable life and universal life with a redetermination feature that essentially recasts the premium amount, and in some instances, the death benefit in reaction to the most recent interval of experience. It is differentiated from universal life insurance by the absence of total premium flexibility in the renewal years.

current rates—rates that are applicable to contracts currently being issued, or the rate that is being paid on an existing policy.

death-benefit-only (DBO) plans—nonqualified plans designed to provide death benefits to a participant's heirs

decreasing term insurance—term insurance that provides systematic decreases in the amount of insurance from year to year

deferred (life) annuity—an agreement under which a period longer than one payment interval must elapse after purchase before the first benefit payment is due. This contract is usually, but not always, purchased with periodic premiums payable over a number of years, up to the date income benefits commence; a contract that provides an income for life to begin at some future date or time and continue for life.

delay clause—a legally sanctioned postponement of payment of the cash surrender value for a period of 6 months after demand thereof and surrender of a life insurance policy. The inclusion of a delay clause is mandatory and has made the delay period of 6 months uniform.

dependency period income—the expanse of time that extends from the date of the insured's death until the youngest child is self-sufficient or perhaps completes the desired level of education

direct recognition—an attempt to increase the equity (fairness) of dividend distributions reflects the "contribution" principle; that is, that policy choices made by a policyowner are reflected in the dividend. This is commonly found where a policy with a loan may receive a lower dividend.

discounting—a process by which today's value (present value) is calculated (at a specific rate of interest) from a given sum due at a designated time in the future

dividend (policyowner)—a refund to the policyowner of a portion of a life insurance premium after the company meets such obligations as claims, expenses, and reserves (not to be confused with a dividend to stock owners of stock insurance companies)

divisible surplus—that portion of insurance company surplus that is available for distribution to participating policyowners as policyowner dividends

economic benefit regime—Under the *economic benefit regime* the owner of the life insurance contract is treated as providing economic benefits to the non-owner of the contract. The value of the life insurance coverage or other benefit provided to an employee under a split-dollar plan is valued and taxed to the employee as additional taxable income.

economic value of a producer—the future earning capacity (dollar value) of an individual producer represented by native ability and acquired skills

educational fund—an amount set aside to provide for educational/training needs

emergency fund—an amount set aside to cover unexpected financial needs

endorsement method—the technique used with split-dollar life insurance whereby the employer owns the policy and has the primary responsibility for paying the premium. The beneficiary designation provides for the employer to receive a portion of the death benefit equal to its premium outlay (or some alternative share), with the remainder of the death proceeds going to the employee's designated beneficiary.

endowment life insurance—a variation of whole life insurance that provides level death benefits and cash values that increase with duration so a policy's cash value equals its death benefit at maturity, and allows the purchaser to specify the policy's maturity date

entire contract provision—in life and health insurance, a provision that specifies that the policy and the attached application constitute the entire agreement between the parties

entity plan—a business buy-sell agreement in which the business itself is the designated purchaser of the deceased's business interest. The business buys life insurance on the owners and in the event of an owner's death, purchases that owner's share of the business from his or her heirs.

equal outlay method—a method of comparing life insurance costs. Basically, a buy-term-and-invest-the-difference approach. The amount by which the cash value contract premiums exceed the term premiums is deposited into an interest-bearing side fund. The term insurance plus the side fund is compared to the cash value policy, including any paid-up additions. Under this type of comparison, the policy producing the greater death benefit is considered the preferable contract.

equity split dollar—An arrangement in which the employer's interest is limited to the actual premiums the employer paid and the excess cash surrender value vests in the employee. Current life insurance protection as well as any other benefit received by the employee during the year, presumably including any increase in the employee's vested interest in the policy's cash value, constitute taxable compensation income under the new (2003) regulations.

estate clearance fund—a source of money to meet final expenses resulting from an insured's death and to liquidate all current outstanding obligations; also known as a probate fund

estoppel—the loss of the ability to assert a defense because the party has acted in a manner inconsistent with that defense. For example, repeated acceptance of late payment may preclude the insurer from enforcing timely payment of premiums in the future.

exclusion—a provision that limits insurance policy coverage of certain risks; items listed in a policy that are not covered

executive bonus—shareholder-employees and executives apply for, own, and name the beneficiary on permanent life insurance policies covering their lives. The corporation provides the premiums through a bonus payment. Premiums are treated as income to the employee, subject to the employee's normal individual income tax rate.

extended term insurance—an option that provides paid-up term insurance in an amount equal to the original face of a policy, increased by any dividend additions or deposits and decreased by any policy indebtedness; the length of the term is such that it can be purchased at the insured's attained age by the application of the net surrender value as a net single premium

extra percentage tables—a special mortality table that reflects the appropriate degree of extra mortality for each substandard classification

financial needs analysis—a method of determining budgetary needs with an expected termination date

fixed-amount option—provides that proceeds of a life insurance policy may be liquidated in payments of a stipulated amount; also known as an installment amount option

fixed-period option—provides that proceeds of a life insurance policy may be liquidated in payments over a stipulated period of time; also known as an installment time option

flat extra premium—a method of underwriting substandard risks in which the standard premium for the policy in question is increased by a specified number of dollars per $1,000 of insurance; assessed as a measure of the extra mortality involved, the flat extra premium does not vary with the age of the applicant

free-look provision—gives a policyowner a period of time, usually 10 days, to return the policy after acceptance

future interest—the postponed right of use or enjoyment of gifted property

future value—the amount to which any given principal sum will accumulate at a later date

gift tax—a tax imposed on transfers of property by gift during a donor's lifetime

grace period—a period of 30 or 31 days after the premium due date that the insurance company will accept late payments without requiring reinstatement to continue coverage. Coverage will extend for this period as well, but the past-due premium will be deducted from the death benefit.

gross premium—the premium actually paid by the policyowner; it is the net premium increased by an allowance for the insurer's expenses and contingencies

group term insurance—insurance protection provided to a specific group for a limited period of time, for example, employer-provided group health insurance

group term life insurance (IRC Sec. 79)—insurance protection provided to a specific group for a limited period of time, for example, by an employer. Section 79 allows a tax deduction for employer-paid group term premiums and provides up to $50,000 of coverage tax-free to participants

group term carve-out—the practice of excluding certain classes of employees from a benefit plan and providing benefits to them under an alternative arrangement. Carve-outs are generally used to contain employee costs or provide broader or tax-favored benefits to key employees and executives.

guaranteed issue—underwriting that does not go beyond a group screening. If the group is acceptable, the insurance company dispenses with individual underwriting and agrees in advance to accept all applications for insurance up to a formula-determined limit.

guaranteed insurability (purchase) option—an option to acquire additional increments of coverage at future dates and events without further evidence of good health or insurability

habits—for underwriting purposes refers to the use of alcohol and/or drugs

human life value—the present value of that portion of a person's estimated future earnings that will be used to support dependents

human life value approach—a way of determining how much life insurance a person should carry based on the proposition that a person should carry life insurance in an amount equal to the capitalized value of his or her net earnings until retirement

illustrated scale—a scale of nonguaranteed elements currently being illustrated that is not more favorable to the policyowner than the lesser of (1) the disciplined current scale or (2) the currently payable scale

immediate annuity—an agreement under which the first payment is due one payment interval after the date of purchase

immediate annuity with guaranteed payments—an annuity contract that starts paying out benefits the next payment interval after it is purchased (for example, one month after purchase if paid out monthly) that guarantees to pay some specified amount even if the annuitant does not live long enough to collect that amount during his or her lifetime. Benefit payments will cease at the later of the annuitant's death or the end of the guaranteed payments.

incident-of-ownership—any right to the economic benefits of a piece of property, such as a life insurance policy

income needs—the ongoing income needs of the surviving dependent family members that continues until those members become self-supporting. These include readjustment period income, dependency period income, and income for the surviving spouse.

incontestable clause—a provision in the life insurance contract that gives the insurance company up to 2 years to void the contract on the basis of material misrepresentation, concealment, or fraud in applying for coverage. After that 2-year period, the insurer will not be able to void the coverage on those grounds unless the insured died during that period.

increase-in-age method—this method of providing life insurance for substandard risks involves "rating up" the age of the applicant. The applicant is assumed to be a number of years older than his or her real age to provide for the extra mortality that he or she poses to the insurer.

increasing term insurance—term insurance that provides systematic increases in the amount of insurance from year to year

indeterminate premium whole life—a policy under which there is a periodic recasting of the premium amount based on recognition of the most recent interval of experience

inspection report—insurance companies verify information collected in the application process, and collect additional information, by using telephone interviews with the applicant by company employees or outside independent reporting services

installment refund annuity—a type of refund annuity that promises that if the annuitant dies before receiving monthly payments equal to the purchase price of the annuity, the payments will continue to a contingent beneficiary or beneficiaries until the full cost has been recovered

interest—represents the difference between the principal—the value of the original capital invested—and the amount that must be repaid by the borrower after a specified term. To an insurer it is the income from invested capital; to a borrower it is the price paid for the use of money.

interest option—a life insurance settlement option under which the death proceeds are retained by the insurer temporarily, with only the interest earnings thereon distributed to the beneficiary

interest-adjusted indexes—a method that takes all payments for both premiums and dividends and treats them as if they had been put into interest-bearing accounts to accumulate interest until the end of the interval for evaluation. Essentially, this is the net-cost method refined to recognize interest earnings.

interest-sensitive whole life insurance—a contract in which mortality and expense charges are guaranteed because excess interest (credited interest minus guaranteed interest) credited to the cash value becomes the only non-guaranteed element in the contract

joint annuity—a contract that covers two or more lives and that provides that the income will cease upon the first death among the lives involved

joint and survivor annuity—a contract that covers two or more lives and that provides that the income will continue for as long as either of the covered persons live

joint-life annuity—a contract that provides an income of a specified amount as long as the two or more persons named in the contract live. The income ceases at the first death among the covered lives.

joint-life policy—an insurance contract written on the lives of two or more persons and payable upon the death of the first person to die; also known as a first-to-die-joint-life policy

judgment method of rating—routine cases are processed with a minimum of consideration by underwriters or clerks trained in the review of applications. Doubtful or borderline cases are resolved by supervisors who rely on their experience and general impressions.

key persons—those individuals whose unique talents and experiences are crucial to the success of a business entity

key person life insurance—insurance designed to protect a business firm against the loss of income that results from the death or disability of a key employee

lapse—refers to termination of a life insurance policy through nonpayment of premiums before surrender values are available

late remittance offer—an offer made by an insurer to the owner of a lapsed life insurance policy that invites him or her to pay the premium and reinstate the coverage without having to provide evidence of insurability

law of large numbers—asserts that in a series of trials, the ratio of the number of occurrences of an event to the number of trials approaches the actual underlying probability of the event as the number of trials increases; it is more formally known as *Bernoulli's Law*

legal reserves—a fund maintained by a life insurance company for future claims; subject to state regulation

level premium insurance—a plan of insurance under which premiums do not increase from year to year but, instead, remain constant throughout the premium-paying period

life annuity—an agreement under which payments are made for the duration of a designated life; also known as a single-life annuity or whole life annuity

life annuity certain—a type of refund annuity that provides a certain number of annuity payments whether the annuitant lives or dies, and payments will continue for the whole of the annuitant's life if he or she lives beyond the guaranteed period

life annuity due—a contract under which the first payment is due at issue or contract date and continue as long as the annuitant lives

life annuity immediate—a contract under which the first payment is due at the end of one payment interval and continue as long as the annuitant lives

life expectancy—the average number of years a person is expected to live; it is an average future lifetime for a representative group of persons at the same age

life income option—any settlement option based on a life contingency. Payments cease when the specified person(s) die(s)

Life Insurance Illustration Questionnaire—developed by the Society of Financial Service Professionals in 1992, this was intended to stimulate agents to question and more thoroughly understand the intricacies of illustrations so they could better explain them to purchasers and prospects. Questions were directed to the insurance company regarding the assumptions methodology underlying the responding insurer's illustrations. *See* policy illustration.

Life Insurance Illustrations Model Regulation—standards for policy illustrations set by the National Association of Insurance Commissioners (NAIC) in 1996. This regulation applies to all non-variable group and individual life insurance policies and certificates for more than $10,000 of death benefit.

limited right of withdrawal—the right of a beneficiary under a deferred-settlement agreement to withdraw all of the proceeds at any one time, subject to restrictions

limited-payment life insurance—a type of whole life insurance for which premiums are limited by contract to a specified number of years; thereafter, the policy is fully paid up

Linton yield method—the comparative interest rate method seeks to determine the interest rate that would make a term insurance policy side fund exactly equal to the surrender value of a cash value policy providing the same death benefits

loading—the amount added to the net premium to cover expenses of operation, to provide for contingencies, and to allow any profit

loan—a transfer of money (or other property) with an obligation to repay the money plus interest (or to return the asset transferred) at a certain time

loan regime—Under the *loan regime,* the non-owner of the life insurance contract is treated as loaning premium payments to the owner. The loan regime is the default treatment for split-dollar plans that don't meet the specified requirements for the economic benefit regime. Thus, loan treatment will apply to plans of the type that have been referred to as "collateral assignment plans" where the employee or the employee's trust or beneficiary is the owner of the contract.

lump sum—receiving the cash value in one payment or depositing a premium in a large amount at one time.

market conduct—how an insurer and its advisors operate in relation to the insurance-consuming public as to products sold and prices charged, particularly in light of compliance to insurance regulations and ethical codes of behavior.

Medical Information Bureau (M.I.B.)—an organization sponsored by its member life insurance companies to gather and maintain principally medical information disclosed by applicants for life insurance

misstatement of age provision—a life insurance policy provision that specifies that, if the insured's age or sex has been misstated, the benefits payable under the policy will be adjusted to what the premium paid would have purchased at the correct age or sex

model regulation—various insurance regulations promulgated by the National Association of Insurance Commissioners intended for adoption by each state insurance department. They promote uniform regulation of insurance in all states.

modified endowment contract (MEC)—a life insurance contract defined in the federal tax law to be treated as an investment rather than most life insurance policies. Single premium life insurance policies and other policies that become fully paid up in 7 years or less fail the so-called "7-pay test" and become classified as an MEC. Withdrawals from an MEC are considered to be ordinary income until all internal gain has been taxed.

modified premium—a premium that has been changed from the regular premium for a similar policy (reduced in early years and increased to a stepped-up amount in later years)

mortality expectations—The insurance company must establish a range of *mortality expectations* within which applicants will be regarded as average risks and hence entitled to insurance at standard rates or, conversely, the limits beyond which applicants will be considered either preferred or substandard and subject to a discount or surcharge. After the limits for the various risk categories have been established, the company must adopt selection and classification procedures that will enable it to place applicants for insurance into the proper categories.

mortality rate—a ratio of deaths within a total population. This ratio can be refined by such factors as age, cause, or gender.

mortality table—a list of mortality experience used to estimate longevity and the probability of living or dying at each age; it is used to figure the risk factors toward determining a gross premium rate

mortgage cancellation fund—money provided to liquidate the mortgage upon an insurer's death so the family can continue to occupy the home. This can be provided through a special mortgage redemption policy, which embodies the decreasing term insurance principle.

National Association of Insurance Commissioners (NAIC)—a membership organization for state insurance commissioners formed in 1871 that promotes uniformity in state laws, regulations and work product, and recommends model legislation

needs analysis approach—a way of determining how much life insurance a person should carry by analyzing the various needs a family or other dependents would experience if the income producer died

net-cost method—a way of comparing life insurance policies in which all net premiums paid under the policy are added together, then the cash surrender value for the interim under consideration and all dividends paid over that period are subtracted from the total. This method does not consider the time value of money (interest).

net payment cost comparison index—an index that helps to compare costs at some future point in time if premiums continue to be paid and cash values are not withdrawn; it is especially useful when the main concern is that benefits are to be paid at death

net premium—life insurance premium based on mortality and interest only that ignores the costs of company operations. It is used for reserve calculating.

net single premium—the sum of the present values of all the expected benefits of an insurance contract based on mortality and interest only (ignores operational expenses). It is the amount needed today for all insureds in a classification, together with future investment earnings, to pay all claims within that class of insureds

noncumulative right of withdrawal—a right of withdrawal, whether exercised or not, that expires at the end of the period to which it pertains; most limited rights are noncumulative

nonforfeiture laws—statutes that define the minimum amount that must be returned upon surrender of a policy to prevent forfeiting equity accumulated in level premium policies

nonforfeiture options—a set of choices available regarding how a life insurance policyowner can use the policy's cash value; alternative forms that the policyowner can select are the cash surrender value, reduced paid-up insurance, and extended term insurance

nonlevel term insurance—refers to insurance policies in which the amount of insurance may increase or decrease throughout the term

nonmedical insurance—refers to ordinary life insurance sold without a medical examination

nonparticipating policy—an insurance contract under which a policyowner does not share in the profits experienced by the insurer; also called a guaranteed cost policy

nonqualified deferred compensation—Qualified plans must meet an overabundance of federal nondiscrimination and administrative compliance standards. Nonqualified plans allow a deferral of the employer's tax deduction until such benefits are paid. Because closely held corporations often want to maximize the benefits for shareholder-employees, the goal of their retirement plans is to discriminate in favor of shareholder-employees and key executives to the fullest extent of the nondiscrimination rules. Since discrimination is permitted in nonqualified arrangements, these plans are often more favorable to the closely held corporation.

nonrefund annuity—a contract that provides a fixed life income with payments ceasing at an annuitant's death

numerican rating system—is based on the principle that a large number of factors enter into the composition of a risk and that the impact of each of these factors on the longevity of the risk can be determined by a statistical study of lives possessing that factor. It assumes that the average risk accepted by a company has a value of 100 percent and that each of the factors that enter into the risk can be expressed as a percentage of the whole. Favorable factors are assigned negative values, called credits, while unfavorable factors are assigned positive values, called debits. The summation of the debits and credits, added to or deducted from the par value of 100, represents the numerical value of the risk. People with low mortality risks get lower scores. An older, diabetic male military test pilot who smokes gets a higher score.

OASDI—Old-Age, Survivors and Disability Income (commonly called Social Security)

optional provisions—In addition to the required provisions and the prohibited provisions, there are numerous other provisions that are neither required nor prohibited. These include suicide, ownership, assignment, plan change, and accelerated benefits.

ordinary annuity—an annuity with payments at the end of each period

ordinary life insurance—a type of whole life insurance for which level premiums are based on the assumption that they will be paid until the insured's death; also known as continuous premium whole life insurance

original age—the age of the insured when the policy was originally taken. When a conversion is effective as of the original policy date at the original age, the premium rate for the permanent insurance is that which would have been paid had the new contract been taken out originally, and the contract is that which would have been issued originally

ownership provision—in life insurance, a provision that specifies that the insured is the owner of the policy, unless the application states otherwise, and that the owner can exercise ownership rights, such as changing the beneficiary (unless irrevocable), assign the policy, take a policy loan, and so on.

PS 58 cost—the pension service term insurance rates used to value the economic benefit of life insurance offered as an employee benefit, used in traditional split-dollar plans. These rates were replaced by the 2001 Table.

paid-up insurance—a policy that has been paid in full but has not yet matured

paid-up term—a type of insurance policy surrender option that provides paid-up term insurance in an amount equal to the original face amount of the policy, increased by any dividend additions or deposits and decreased by any policy indebtedness. The length of the term is that which can be purchased at the insured's attained age with the net cash value applied as a net single premium.

paramedical exam—used as a source of underwriting information, this exam is conducted by nurses or other medical technicians and consists of obtaining medical information from a questionnaire and measurements such as height, weight blood pressure, and waste measurement. It may also include blood and urine specimens.

permanent insurance—refers to whole life, universal life, and other cash value types of insurance, as distinguished from the temporary protection afforded by term insurance; also called *permanent plan insurance*

policy illustration—a numerical spreadsheet projecting what could happen under a policy if actual experience mirrored all the assumed factors used to calculate the illustration. The NAIC model regulation strictly defines what and what cannot be shown in an illustration.

policy loan—an advance of money available to a policyowner from a policy's cash values

policy summary—most states require that a policy summary be delivered with a life insurance policy. This form, normally produced by the home office with the policy, gives the main features of the issued policy, such as premiums, cash values and guarantees and non-guaranteed elements

preferred risk—an individual whose health, occupation, and life style indicate an above-average life expectancy, who should experience a lower rate of mortality than that among insured lives generally because of more rigorous underwriting requirements

present interest—one in which the donee's (recipient of a gift) use, possession or enjoyment begins at the time the gift is made. A gift must be of present interest to qualify for the annual gift tax exclusion.

present value—what something is worth today; the value today that is equivalent to a given sum due at a designated time in the future

present value of $1 per annum—the current value of a series of an annuity (or annuity due) if the payments are discounted at an appropriate interest rate

Professional Practice Guideline—a checklist of guidelines for sales material and presentations. Developed by the Society of Financial Services Professionals, it was designed to provide guidance on issues concerning policy illustrations, particularly the assumptions made in developing the policy values shown in the illustration.

prohibited provisions—most states prohibit insurers from including certain provisions in their policies. For various reasons, courts or state legislatures have determined that these prohibited contract provisions violate public policy.

prospectus—thorough and accurate information provided to prospective variable insurance and annuity contract purchasers that provides information about the company as well as a full disclosure of all of the provisions of the contract, including expenses, investment options, benefit provisions, and policyowner rights under that contract. It must be provided to the investment prospect before any discussions of a variable product to be purchased.

pure annuity—an agreement that provides periodic (usually monthly) income payments that continue as long as the annuitant lives but terminate at the person's death; also referred to as a *straight life annuity*

pure endowment—a contract that pays only if the insured survives the specified period of years

qualified terminal interest property trust (QTIP)—a trust in which a lifetime income is paid to the surviving spouse, and the trust corpus is then distributed to children (or others) after the spouse dies

rabbi trust—a trust, usually irrevocable, established by a corporate employer to finance payment of deferred-compensation benefits for an employee

rate—a number that equates to the value of benefits under an insurance contract

rate making—the process by which the promises of an insurance contract are valued

readjustment income—an amount closely equivalent to the family's share of the producer's earnings at the time of his or her death. The length of the financial readjustment period depends largely on the magnitude of the change(s) the family will have to make in living standards.

readjustment period—the time following the death of a wage earner during which a person or family needs to become acclimated to the changes in their finances

rebating—a reduction of an insurance premium or gift of some other valuable consideration not specified in a policy to the buyer as an inducement to purchase insurance

redetermination—a process in which an insurance company reviews the actual experience for a block of policies compared to the previous review and decides what adjustments, if any, are necessary based on the assumption that past experiences are indicative of what to expect in the period before the next review. The level of premiums influences the frequency of redetermination.

reduced amount of paid-up whole life—a type of insurance policy surrender option that allows the insured to take a reduced amount of coverage payable upon the same conditions as the original policy. The protection continues in the reduced amount until the insured's death unless the reduced policy is surrendered for cash, and no further premiums are called for under this plan.

re-entry term insurance—a term insurance policy intended to charge higher premiums to those in poorer health when they renew their term insurance

refund annuity—any type of annuity that promises to return (in one manner or another) a portion or all of the purchase price of the annuity

reinstatement—a procedure a life insurer follows to put back in force a policy that had lapsed because of nonpayment of renewal premiums

reinsurance—a device by which one insurance company or insurer transfers all or a portion of its risk under an insurance policy or a group of policies to another company or insurer

reinsurer—the insurance company to which an insured risk is transferred; also called the assuming company

renewability—a feature commonly found in individual term life insurance that allows the policyowner to renew (extend) the policy for another period of protection, up to a stated point in time, without having to show evidence of insurability

replacement—a transaction in which a new life insurance or annuity contract is to be purchased and it is known, or should be known, by the proposing agent or company that, because of such transaction, an existing life insurance or annuity has been or will be terminated, converted, or otherwise reduced in value

reserve—the present value of future benefit payments (surrender and death) minus the present value of future incoming premiums. It is an amount that must be maintained by the insurer in order to meet definite future obligations

"results" war clause—limits an insurer's obligation only if the insured's death is the result of military service

retention limit—the maximum amount of insurance a company will retain on any one life

retirement needs—fund that will be sufficient to take care of the post-retirement needs of the insured and the spouse, if applicable

retroactive conversion—an insurance policy conversion method that uses the insured's age on the original date of the term policy as the effective age for future premiums

revocable contingent beneficiaries—alternate beneficiaries named by the policyowner to cover the possibility the primary beneficiary predeceases the insured; the beneficiary can be changed by the policyowner without the beneficiary's permission

risk pooling—group sharing of losses on an equal basis by persons exposed to similar loss

Sarbanes-Oxley Act—As part of the wave of corporate governance regulation arising out of the Enron collapse and similar events in 2001 and 2002, Congress enacted this law containing a range of corporate accountability provisions. Included was a provision banning publicly traded corporations from making personal loans to any director or executive officer, which may impact eligibility for split-dollar plans.

savings—the amount remaining from more efficient and economical operations than were assumed when a policy premium was set

Sec. 7702 of the Internal Revenue Code (extended the corridor test)—a test for flexible-premium life insurance developed by Congress—to all life insurance policies, including fixed-premium endowments, entered into after October 22, 1986

select and ultimate term insurance—a term insurance policy intended to charge higher premiums to those in poorer health when they renew their term insurance, thereby reducing the degree of adverse selection. The product is commonly called *re-entry term insurance*.

select mortality table—a presentation of data that shows the rate of mortality not only by age but also by duration of insurance; it recognizes the experience of recently selected lives evaluated to be in good health. It reflects the effects of selection.

separate account assets—assets segregated from those of the general account for the purpose of funding variable life insurance, variable universal life insurance, variable annuities, pensions, and other benefits

separate account liabilities—these consist of reserves established for the variable life insurance, variable annuities, pensions and other benefits funded through separate accounts

separate accounts—funds managed and invested separately for use in variable life and annuity products. These funds are separate from the other company assets.

settlement agreement—a document provided when the insurance company retains the proceeds under one of the optional methods of settlement because its liability has continued beyond the maturity of the policy. This agreement contains the designation of the various classes of beneficiaries and a detailed description of the manner in which the proceeds are to be distributed.

settlement options—periodic income choices available to beneficiaries and policyowners for payout of death benefits, including the interest option, fixed-amount option, fixed-period option, and life income option

seven-pay test—one of two tests applied to a life insurance policy to determine if it is a modified endowment contract (MEC). If the premium paid at any time during the first 15 years of the policy exceeds the level premium necessary to fully pay up the policy in 7 years with level payments, the policy will be an MEC. Tax law discourages single premium and other highly funded variations of life insurance.

single life insurance—a life insurance policy on a single life, as opposed to insurance on two or more persons found in joint life

special needs of surviving spouse and family—certain needs not found in every family situation, such as care and therapy for disabled family members, specially equipped vehicles, medication, and so on

spendthrift clause—a statement in a settlement agreement that says the proceeds of the policy will be free from attachment or seizure by the beneficiary's creditors

split-dollar life insurance—a plan that splits a life insurance policy's premium obligations and policy benefits between two individuals or entities, normally between an employer and an employee. This arrangement has gone through significant tax-law changes in 2001 and 2002.

split-dollar rollout—a solution that transfers the insurance and other benefits in split-dollar plan to the employee through a termination of the agreement. The employer is repaid for its contributions through policy loans, withdrawals, or some other financing arrangements.

Standard Nonforfeiture Law—a law requiring life insurance surrender values to be at least as large as those that would be produced by the method the law prescribes. Each policy must contain a statement of the method used to fund the surrender values and benefits provided under the policy at durations not specifically shown. This law does not require specific surrender values.

standard provisions—certain specified items that states require in their life insurance contracts, either as set forth in the statute or whose effect is the same in substance to those in the statute

"status" war clause—limits an insurer's obligation to return of premium if the insured should die while in military service outside the territorial boundaries of the United States, whether or not the cause of death can be attributed to military service

statutory financial statement—a financial statement mandated by NAIC and filed with each state in which the company is licensed to do business

statutory table—a mortality table specified by law that must be used for calculating reserves and minimum cash values

stock redemption agreement—a buy-sell agreement that binds the corporation to purchase a shareholder's interest at the occurrence of certain events, such as death or retirement

straight life annuity—an agreement that provides periodic (usually monthly) income payments that continue as long as the annuitant lives but terminates at the person's death; also referred to as a *straight life annuity*

substandard risks—a rate based on the anticipated average experience of a large number of individuals expected to produce a higher mortality than a group of normal lives; those whose personal characteristics suggest worse-than-average mortality

suicide provision—a life insurance policy provision that specifies that if an insured, whether sane or insane, commits suicide during the first 1 or 2 years of the policy, the insurer will be liable only for a return of the premium

surplus—an amount that results when insurance company assets are greater than its liabilities

surrender—refers to termination of a life insurance policy through nonpayment of premiums after surrender values are available

surrender charge—an amount deducted from the surrender value if the policyowner terminates the policy during its early years

surrender cost comparison index—an index that compares the costs of surrendering an insurance policy and withdrawing the cash value at some future point in time. It is especially useful when the main concern is the level of the cash values.

surrender options—a set of insurance contract provisions increasingly used to adapt policy coverages to changing circumstances and needs, also known as nonforfeiture options. Most policies stipulate that the surrender value may be taken in one of three forms: cash, a reduced amount of paid-up life insurance, or paid-up term insurance.

Survivorship life insurance (second-to-die)—a type of life insurance policy that covers two or more persons in which the proceeds are payable on the death of the last person to die

Table 2001—A new transitional table adopted in IRS Notices 2001-10 and 2002-8 for split-dollar arrangements. Table 2001 replaces the PS 58 table for valuing economic benefit. The Table 2001 rates are much lower than the PS 58 rates.

target premium—a suggested premium to be paid on a level basis throughout the universal life contract's duration or for a shorter period of time if a limited-pay approach was originally intended to fund a policy. It is merely a suggestion and carries no liability if it is inadequate to maintain the contract to any duration, much less to the end of life.

term insurance—a contract that pays death benefits only if the insured does not survive the specified period

time value of money—the concept that a specific amount of money received (paid) in a specific time period has a different value than the same amount received (paid) in a different time period. This concept is expressed as an interest rate that represents or creates these different values.

three-factor contribution plan—a distribution plan that recognizes only three major sources of surplus: mortality savings, excess interest, and loading savings

transfer-for-value—a rule that specifies that, subject to certain exceptions, if a life insurance policy is transferred from one owner to another for valuable consideration, the death proceeds will be subject to federal income taxation

twisting—occurs when a policyowner is induced to discontinue and replace a policy through an agent's distortion or misrepresentation of the facts

ultimate mortality table—a presentation of data that excludes the effects of selection and reflects only the rates of mortality that can be expected after the influence of selection has worn off

universal life insurance—a variation of whole life insurance that offers truly flexible premiums and includes provisions similar to those contained in the adjustable life contract. The policyowner has the right to withdraw part of the cash value without having the withdrawal treated as a policy loan; the policyowner also has the choice of either a level-death benefit or an increasing-death benefit design.

unlimited right of withdrawal—the right of a beneficiary under a deferred-settlement agreement to withdraw some or possibly all of the proceeds at any one time, subject to restrictions

variable adjustable life insurance—a policy that can be negotiated to change the death benefit level up or down, or to increase or decrease premium amounts to a new fixed level, which can shorten or lengthen the premium-paying period. The policyowner has the ability to choose the investment portfolio, within limits.

variable annuity—a type of contract that attempts to protect the purchasing power of annuity benefits by providing benefits that vary with changes in the insurer's investment performance; the annuity owner chooses the asset allocation from among available fund options

variable life insurance—a market-driven life insurance policy that provides a guaranteed minimum death benefit, but the actual death benefit or cash value is dependent upon investment fluctuations of the funds selected by the policyowner

variable universal life insurance—a variation of whole life insurance, this policy incorporates all of the premium flexibility and policy adjustment features of the universal life policy with the policyowner-directed investment aspects of variable life insurance. This policy eliminates the direct connection between investment performance above or below some stated target level and the corresponding formula-directed adjustment in death benefits. Then it adopts the death benefit designs applicable to universal life policies: either a level death benefit or an increasing death benefit design where a constant amount at risk is paid in addition to the cash accumulation account.

waiver—the voluntary and intentional surrender of a known right, such as waiving premiums if the insured is disabled

waiver-of-premium provision—if the insured becomes totally disabled as defined in the life insurance contract, the insurance company will waive payment of premiums on the policy during the continuance of the insured's disability

yearly renewable term insurance—insurance provided for a period of one year only that permits the policyowner to renew the policy for successive periods of one year each without the necessity of furnishing evidence of insurability

Answers to Questions

Chapter 1

Answers to Review Questions

1-1. In risk pooling or group sharing of losses, persons exposed to loss from a particular source combine their risks and agree to share losses on some equitable basis. The risks may be combined under an arrangement whereby the participants mutually insure each other, called "mutual insurance," or they may be transferred to an insurer that, for a consideration called the "premium," is willing to assume the risks and pay the resulting losses. Risk pooling is a basic principle that makes insurance possible.

1-2. *Yearly Renewable Term (YRT) insurance* is the simplest form of insurance offered by regular life insurance companies. It provides insurance for a period of one year only but permits the policyowner to renew the policy for successive periods of one year, each without the necessity of furnishing evidence of insurability. The policyowner can renew the policy without submitting to a medical examination or providing other evidence of good health, simply by paying the renewal premium. The premium for yearly renewable term insurance is determined by the death rate for the attained age of the individual involved. To calculate the premium, the company takes the mortality rate for age/gender group, determines the number of deaths from the group, and multiplies by the face amount of the policy (measured by number of thousands).

1-3. If the surviving members of the insured group renew their insurance year after year, the steadily increasing premiums would cause many to question continuing the insurance. There would be a tendency for the healthy individuals to give up their protection or find a less-costly plan, while those in poor health would continue to renew their policies, regardless of cost. This is *adverse selection* against the insurance company. The withdrawal of the healthy members would accelerate the increase in the death rate among the continuing members and could produce death claims in excess of premium income. In this event, the loss would be borne by the company, because the rates at which the policy can be renewed are guaranteed for the entire period of renewability.

1-4. *Level premium insurance* has premiums that remain constant throughout the premium-paying period. Premiums that would otherwise increase with each passing year are leveled out; the premiums paid in the early years of the contract will be more than sufficient to meet current death claims, while those paid in the later years will be less than adequate to meet incurred claims. The redundant premiums in the early years of the contract create an accumulation that is held by the insurance company for the benefit and to the credit of the policyowners. This accumulation is called a *reserve* and is sufficient to pay all claims as they come due.

1-5. Life insurance is concerned with the *economic* value of a human life, which is derived from its earning capacity and the financial dependence of other lives on that earning capacity. The *human life value approach* is based on the proposition that a person should carry life insurance in an amount equal to the capitalized value of his or her net future earnings.

1-6. 1) Estimate the individual's average annual earnings from personal efforts over the remaining years of his or her income-producing lifetime. 2) Deduct federal and state income taxes, life insurance premiums, and the cost of self-maintenance. 3) Determine the number of years between the individual's present age and the contemplated age of retirement. 4) Select a reasonable rate of interest at which future earnings will be discounted. 5) Multiply (1) minus (2) by the present value of $1 per annum for the period determined in (3), discounted at the rate of interest selected in (4).

1-7. The types of needs covered in a needs analysis include the following:

1) Cleanup fund—a fund to meet the expenses resulting from the insured's death and to liquidate all current outstanding obligations: the costs of daily living for survivors; final expenses such as funeral costs, cemetery plot and burial; repairs and replacements associated with events surrounding the family member's death, state and federal estate taxes, and the cost of estate administration (including executor's or administrator's fee, appraisers' fees, legal fees, and probate court expenses)
2) Readjustment income—the need for income approximately equivalent to the family's share of income from the producer prior to death that will continue for a period of readjustment
3) Income during dependency period—income may need to be provided to support children until they are self-sufficient and able to support themselves.
4) Life income for surviving dependent spouse—income that will allow the surviving spouse to maintain a desired standard of living
5) Special needs—needs that may not be found in every situation but require attention according to specific family goals and lifestyle demands.
   - Mortgage redemption needs—A common desire is to have the surviving family have a rent- or mortgage-free home that will give peace of mind, adequate and comfortable living, and reduce monthly income requirements.
   - Educational needs—If college or other educational goals are desired, additional funds or income will be needed.

- Emergency needs—A liquid fund should be set up from which additional income can be provided if and when it is needed.
6) Retirement needs—This need can provide funds in the event of death during retirement. In the event of a long life, a cash-value policy can provide funds to supplement retirement income.

1-8. Post-death financial needs are separated into two main categories: cash (lump sum) needs at death and ongoing income needs. First, project future cash flow income needs, then find the present value of all those needs. Then identify and deduct all of the existing sources of income (Social Security, investments, employee benefits, and so on) to determine the income deficit. This amount equals the unfunded amount that can be made up with life insurance. Future income payments can be comprised solely of investment earnings on a capital sum, or they can be a combination of investment earnings and liquidation of part of the capital sum. Within the life insurance industry the liquidating approach is often referred to as the *financial needs analysis*, and a non-liquidating approach is often referred to as the *capital needs analysis*.

Answers to Self-Test Questions

1-1. B
1-2. D
1-3. B
1-4. C
1-5. A
1-6. C
1-7. C
1-8. B
1-9. B
1-10. D

Chapter 2

Answers to Review Questions

2-1. Term insurance provides life insurance protection for a limited period only. The face amount of the policy is payable if the insured dies during the specified period, and nothing is paid if the insured survives. The period may be as short as one year, or it may run to age 65 or above. Such policies may insure for the agreed term only, or they may give the insured the option of renewing the protection for successive terms without evidence of insurability. Term insurance may be regarded as temporary insurance. The premium for term insurance is initially relatively low, despite the fact that it contains a relatively high expense loading and an allowance for adverse selection. The reason premiums can be low is that most term contracts do not cover the period of old age when death is most likely to occur and when the cost of insurance is high.

2-2. Variations of term insurance include

- Renewable term—contains an option to renew for a limited number of additional periods of term insurance, usually of the same length, without evidence of insurability
- Convertible term—contains a provision that permits the policyowner to exchange the term contract for a contract on a permanent plan without evidence of insurability
- Re-entry term—a term insurance policy intended to charge a higher premium to those in poorer health when they renew their term insurance, thereby reducing the degree of adverse selection
- Long-term contracts—term contracts designed to provide insurance over a long period, such as term to age 65
- Non-level term—the amount of insurance may either increase or decrease throughout the term of the policy

2-3. Renewable term insurance contracts contain an option to renew for a limited number of periods of term insurance, usually of the same length. The key to the renewable feature is the right to renew the contract without providing evidence of insurability. Where the term policy contains no renewal privilege, or where evidence of insurability is required, the insured may find it difficult or impossible to continue a contract, or obtain any other form of life insurance, due to poor health, dangerous occupation or hobby, or some other reason. Renewability prevents this. Its chief function is to protect the insurability of the insured.

2-4. If a term policy is converted as of the current date, conversion is referred to as an *attained-age method*, because the current age determines the premium. A conversion using the original date of the term policy is referred to as the *original-age method* or a *retroactive conversion*. Advantages of original-age conversions include (1) the lower premium and (2) the possibility that the contract being issued at the original date contains actuarial assumptions or other features more favorable than those being offered in current policies. A major disadvantage is the financial adjustment involving a payment by the insured to the company, which may be quite substantial if the term policy has been in effect for a number of years. The payment is calculated as the larger of (1) the differences in the reserves (or cash values) under the policies being exchanged or (2) the differences in the premiums paid on the term policy and those that would have been paid on the permanent plan, with interest on the difference at a stipulated rate.

2-5. The purpose of a time limit on term conversions is to minimize adverse selection. As the time limit on conversion approaches, those insureds in poor health are more likely to convert and pay the premium than those who believe they are in good health. Typically a policy will require conversion within 10 years of the policy date, or before age 60 or 65.

2-6.   Select and ultimate term (re-entry) insurance is a policy subject to two different premium schedules. The lower premium rate is based on select rates given to those who have recent, favorable evidence of insurability. Select rates are available at renewal if the insured submits satisfactory evidence of insurability. The higher-premium rate schedule is based on ultimate rates, which are those rates applicable after 10-20 years of previously providing evidence of insurability. The insured who cannot or wishes not to show good health to the insurer when required will pay considerably higher rates to renew their coverage.

2-7.   Term-to-65 policies (1) are designed to provide long-term protection, (2) often give prospective policyowners the option to purchase waiver of premium and accidental death benefits, and (3) customarily provide for cash and other surrender values.

2-8.   Term insurance is useful and suitable when either the need for protection is temporary or the insured cannot afford the premiums for permanent insurance. Temporary needs can and should be solved through term insurance. Examples of a suitable use of term insurance include younger adults with limited income, families with dependent children, covering a loan, mortgage redemption, to protect a speculative investment or business venture, or key person insurance on a person instrumental to the success of a business or similar venture.

2-9.   Most arguments against permanent (whole life) insurance focus on two allegations: (1) whole life overcharges for the premium, and (2) the accumulation and protection element should be separated. The first argument is only true if a person dies within a short time of purchasing the policy. We do not know when we will die. Permanent insurance protects the insured against living too long as well as dying too soon. In a long life term, premiums can exceed the policy death benefit payable. By paying a level premium, the policyowner shifts the financial risk of death to the insurance company, preventing the need to pay prohibitive premiums in old age for term insurance. The argument that the cash value (reserve) is paid out with the face amount as a death benefit, and not in addition to it, is because the reducing risk amount is part of the assumption made initially in calculating the premium. The second argument that the accumulation and protection elements should be separated is based on the proposition of "buying term and investing the difference" of the two premiums. This argument assumes that the individual can invest more wisely and with a greater return than the insurance company. When looking at the investment objectives of safety, yield and liquidity, the insurance industry is difficult to outperform. Yield and safety are inverse, and as one increases the other decreases. Whole life also offers a number of tax advantages and loan privileges that enhance its value.

2-10.   The general features of whole life include

- permanent protection—provides for the payment of the face amount upon the death of the insured, regardless of when death occurs
- reserve and cash value—increases over the duration of the policy and eventually equals the face amount at the end of the policy period (usually age 100)
- policy loans—give the policyowner access to the cash value that accumulates inside the policy without having to terminate the policy. Policy loans do involve interest charged on the borrowed funds. The policyowner has the option of paying the policy loan interest in cash or having the unpaid interest charge added to the balance of the outstanding loan(s) so that additional interest charges will be applied to the unpaid interest amount. If the policy loan and accrued interest are not paid in cash, the life insurer can recover the outstanding balance of the loans and accrued interest in the following ways: (1) from the death benefits if the insured dies or (2) from the cash surrender value if the policy is terminated. In fact, the policy will automatically terminate if the policy loan balance plus unpaid interest ever exceeds the policy cash value.
- automatic premium loan—when this option is selected, a delinquent premium will be paid automatically by a new policy loan. This will keep the policy in force as long as there is adequate cash value to cover each delinquent premium. However, the policy will terminate if the cash value is exhausted.
- nonforfeiture or surrender options—the surrender value may be taken in cash, a reduced amount of paid-up insurance, or paid-up term insurance
- annuity or retirement income—the surrender value can be used to purchase an annuity or retirement income
- participating versus nonparticipating—can be purchased on a participating (pay policyowner dividends) or nonparticipating (do not provide for policyowner dividends) basis

2-11.   Unlike ordinary life policies where premiums are paid until the insured's death, limited-payment life insurance is a type of whole life insurance for which premiums are limited by contract to a specified number of years. The limitation may be expressed as a number of annual premiums (for example, 20-pay life) or of the age beyond which premiums are not required (for example, life paid up at 65).

2-12.   A joint-life policy is one written on the lives of two or more persons. There are two types of joint-life policies, depending on when the death benefits are paid. First, a joint life –policy pays the death benefit upon the death of the first insured to die. These policies might fund business buy-sell agreements, or be used by married homeowners as mortgage insurance. The second type, called *survivorship life* or a *second-to-die policy*, pays the death benefit upon the death of the last of two or more lives insured under a single policy. These policies have become popular to provide funds to pay estate taxes and settlement costs for wealthy couples that wish to maximize deferral of estate taxes at the first death.

2-13. A policy loan reduces the death benefit that a beneficiary would receive on the death of the insured by the amount of the loan and accrued interest. It reduces the cash surrender value by the amount of the loan and accrued interest for the policyowner, if the policy is surrendered or terminated. The outstanding loan would also reduce the extended-term insurance or reduced paid-up insurance benefits available upon lapse.

2-14. The key functions of whole life are to provide protection against long-range or permanent needs, and to accumulate a savings fund that can be used for general purposes or to meet specific needs or objectives.

Answers to Self-Test Questions

2-1. B
2-2. C
2-3. A
2-4. B
2-5. A
2-6. D
2-7. C
2-8. B
2-9. B
2-10. C

Chapter 3

Answers to Review Questions

3-1 While a whole life insurance contract provides a survivorship benefit at age 100 that is equal to the death benefit that would have been payable prior to the insured's age 100, endowment contracts make the same full-survivorship benefit payable at younger ages. Among the wide variety of endowments that have been sold are 10-, 15-, 20-, 25-, 30-, 35-, and 40-year endowments (or longer), or the maturity date can be a specific age of the insured, such as 55, 65, 70, or older. Endowment policies have nearly disappeared from new policy sales, because changes in the federal income tax laws in the mid-1980s took away the tax preference for newly sold endowments. Interest earned on the cash value of a newly sold endowment would now be taxed annually rather than tax deferred as with other life insurance policies.

3-2. A variable life insurance policy provides no guarantees of either interest rate or minimum cash value. As the SEC pointed out, in order for policyowners to gain the additional benefit of better-than-expected investment returns, they also have to assume all of the downside investment risk. Consequently, the SEC required variable life policies to be registered with the SEC and all sales to be subject to the following requirements applied to other registered securities:

- Policy sales can be made only after the prospective purchaser has a chance to read the policy prospectus.
- An insurance company issuing a variable life insurance policy must be registered as an investment company and all sales agents must be registered with the SEC for the specific purpose of variable life insurance policy sales.
- Agents who sell variable life insurance policies must be licensed as both life insurance agents and securities agents.

3-3. Because the primary reason for life insurance is to provide death benefits, it makes sense to link superior investment performance with increases in the death benefit level. A variable life insurance policy has a minimum death benefit equal to the initial face amount when the policy was first purchased. However, if the policy's actual investment performance exceeds a target level of investment performance, the excess investment return is used to purchase additional life insurance under either the level additions method or the constant ratio method. Under both methods, the amount of additional coverage in excess of the initial face amount will fluctuate depending on actual investment performance. If investment earnings are negative (the actual earnings are lower than the target rate), then the adjustments will have to be downward from any previously attained levels above the policy's initial face value. If investment earnings are positive (the actual earnings are above the target rate), the adjustments will be upward.

3-4. Life insurance companies are now offering many more investment fund options than they made available in the early stages of the variable life product's development. Some insurance companies have more than a dozen funds from which to choose in their current product offering. There are usually a variety of stock funds, including growth stock funds, income stock funds, balanced stock funds, and international stock funds. Bond fund offerings are likewise more robust and include different durations and different types of issuers (large corporations, small corporations, state governments, and the federal government) as well as Government National Mortgage Association funds (GNMAs) and collateralized mortgage obligations (CMOs). Many insurance companies offer a managed fund as one of the portfolio choices, and have formed alliances with large mutual fund groups that make their entire range of mutual funds available.

3-5. Unlike a whole life policy, where the cash value increases over time due to the crediting of at least the guaranteed interest rate, the cash value of a variable life policy fluctuates daily depending on the net asset value of the separate account funds that make up the policy portfolio.

3-6. The prospectus is a full disclosure of all of the provisions of the contract, including expenses, investment options, benefit provisions, and policyowner rights under the contract. The prospectus has very thorough information about all of the expense charges levied by the insurance company against variable life insurance contracts. This includes commissions paid to soliciting agents, state premium taxes, administrative charges, collection charges, and fees for specific future transactions. The prospectus explains how charges are made against the asset account to cover the cost of insurance under the contract. It also explains the manner in which charges are levied against the separate account itself— the fees associated with managing the various mutual fund type of accounts from which the policyowner can choose. Part of that charge is always some specified percentage (usually less than one full percent) of the assets in the separate accounts themselves. The prospectus explains the surrender charge applicable to policy surrenders. This information is often set forth in a table, giving the policy year and the applicable percentage for the surrender charge in that year. Surrender charges are commonly levied during the first 10 to 15 years of the contract. The prospectus sets forth the investment objectives of each of the available investment funds and a record of their historical performance. Any investment restrictions applicable to these portfolios are fully disclosed. There are also projections of future performance under the contract if portfolio funds generate a fixed level of investment earnings over the projected interval. Under SEC regulations, the permissible rates of return that can be projected are the gross annual rates after tax charges but before any other deductions at 0, 4, 8, 10, or 12 percent. The insurance company can decide the permissible rates it chooses to project.

3-7. With a variable life insurance policy, the policyowner assumes the investment risk and, therefore, can participate in favorable investment returns. The fixed-premium provision does not allow the policyowner to increase or decrease the death benefit as an option; favorable results automatically translate into increased death benefit amounts. The policy does guarantee a minimum death benefit level equal to the original face amount of the contract, regardless of how negative the investment performance. If all of the required premiums are paid, the insurance company guarantees that the death benefit equal to the original face amount of the policy will be paid even if the investment funds are otherwise inadequate to support the policy. Therefore, the variable feature of this contract can provide additional coverage if warranted by investment experience, but the policyowner will never be required to pay more or permitted to pay less than the guaranteed premium.

3-8. Both the variable adjustable life policy and the adjustable life policy permit the policyowner to make changes in the death benefit level up or down, or to change the premium (increase or decrease) amount to a new, fixed level, which can shorten or lengthen the premium-paying period. However, with the variable adjustable life policy, the policyowner also has the ability to choose the investment options.

3-9.   Universal life insurance was introduced in 1979 as a revolutionary new product. It was the first variation of whole life insurance to offer truly flexible premiums. The policy death benefit can be adjusted upward (sometimes requiring proof of insurability) or downward to meet the policyowner's needs. Two other features also were initiated with universal life policies: (1) the policyowner's ability to withdraw part of the cash value without having the withdrawal treated as a policy loan and (2) the choice of either a level death benefit design or an increasing death benefit design.

3-10. The true innovation of universal life insurance was the introduction of completely flexible premiums after the first policy year, the only time a minimum level of premium payments for a universal life policy is rigidly required. The first year's premium can be arranged on a monthly, quarterly, semiannual, or annual basis. The insurance company requires only that a minimum specified level of first-year premium payments be equaled or exceeded. After the first policy year, it is completely up to the policyowner the amount of premium to pay (limited only by the maximums contained in the income tax definition of life insurance) and even whether or not to pay the premiums. Of course, premiums can be skipped altogether only if the policy cash value is at least adequate to cover the next 60 days of expense and mortality charges. Otherwise, the policy would lapse if no additional premium was paid by the end of the grace period.

3-11. A universal life policy permits the policyowner to make partial withdrawals from the policy's cash value without incurring any indebtedness. In other words, money can be taken out of the policy cash value, but no interest is charged on the amount withdrawn, as there would be with a policy loan. Withdrawals do affect the policy's future earnings because the fund still intact to earn interest for future crediting periods is reduced by the amount of the withdrawal. Its effect on the death benefit depends on the type of death benefit in force. Partial withdrawals do not reduce the death benefit amount under the level death benefit design. They do, however, decrease the amount of the policy's cash value and correspondingly increase the amount at risk. Partial withdrawals under the increasing death benefit design will, in fact, reduce the death benefit payable because the withdrawal decreases the cash value that constitutes part of the death benefit amount.

3-12. Nearly every universal life policy is issued with a target premium amount. The target amount is the suggested premium to be paid on a level basis throughout the contract's duration or for a shorter period of time if a limited-pay approach was originally intended to fund the policy. The target premium amount is merely a suggestion and carries no liability if it is inadequate to maintain the contract to any duration, much less to the end of life. Some insurance companies have introduced a secondary guarantee associated with their target premium. These companies have pledged contractually to keep the policy in force for, say, 15 or 20 years and to pay the full death benefit as long as the premium has been paid in an amount equal to or greater than the target premium amount at each suggested premium-payment interval.

3-13.	Universal life insurance gives policyowners a choice between level death benefits and increasing death benefits. The level death benefit design is much like the traditional whole life design. When the death benefit stays constant and the cash value increases over the duration of the contract, the amount at risk or the protection element decreases. The one new aspect of a level death benefit design under universal life policies results from a tax law definition of life insurance that was added to the Code shortly after the introduction of universal life insurance policies. Thisrequired that a specified proportion of the death benefit be derived from the amount at risk. Whenever the cash value in the contract gets high enough that this proportion is no longer satisfied, the universal life policy starts increasing the death benefit even though the contract is called a level death benefit contract. This is known as the corridor test. The increasing death benefit design is a modification that was introduced with universal life policies. Under this approach, there is always a constant amount at risk that is superimposed over the policy's cash value. As the cash value increases, so does the total death benefit payable under the contract. A reduction in the cash value will reduce the death benefit. This design pays both the policy's stated face amount and its cash value as benefits at the insured's death. There is nothing magical about this larger death benefit amount. A higher portion of the premium is needed for the larger amount at risk under this design.

3-14.	Most universal life policies credit current interest rates on the cash value as long as there are no outstanding policy loans. Once the policyowner borrows funds from the cash value, the insurance company usually credits a lower interest rate or earnings rate to the portion of the cash value associated with the policy loan. Many universal life policies sold today credit the cash value with the current rate for non-borrowed funds and a lower rate, which is often 2 percentage points lower than the current rate, for borrowed funds. Any outstanding debt will reduce any death benefit proceeds or cash value proceeds otherwise payable under a universal life policy.

3-15.	Universal life policies cover expenses through front-end loads and/or back-end loads (surrender charges). Most of the early universal life policies were heavily front-end-loaded products. They took a significant proportion of each premium dollar as administrative expenses, and the remaining portion was then credited to the policy cash value account. As the universal life insurance policies evolved, more of them moved to a back-end loading design. They lowered or eliminated the up-front charge levied against incoming premium amounts and instead imposed new or increased surrender charges applicable to the cash value of a policy surrendered during the contract's first 7 to 15 years. Surrender charges are highest during the first policy year and decrease on a straight-line basis over the remaining years until the year in which the insurance company expects to have amortized all excess first-year expenses. At that point, the surrender charge is reduced to zero and will not be applicable at later policy durations. After the premiums (less any front-end load) reach the policy cash value account, they are subject to charges for current death benefits in the form of a mortality charge based on the amount at risk. The current mortality rate actually charged is often considerably less than the guaranteed maximum mortality rate set forth in the policy contract for each attained age of the insured. After deductions for expenses and mortality, the universal life cash value account is then increased at the current crediting rate to reflect investment earnings on that cash value. These are the dollars at work for the policyowner to help reduce his or her current and future out-of-pocket premium expenses. The actual rate credited is a discretionary decision on the part of the insurance company, and it tends to fluctuate freely, reflecting current economic conditions. Competitive pressures have caused insurance companies to minimize front-end loading in order to emphasize that nearly all premium dollars go directly into the cash value account. The actual expenses are still being deducted internally, but the manner in which they are handled is not easily discernible by the consuming public. For example, expenses can be embedded in the spread between actual mortality costs and actual mortality charges or in the spread between investment earnings and the interest rate credited to the cash value accounts.

3-16. A current assumption whole life policy has a guaranteed death benefit and at any point in time, a premium that must be paid by the end of the grace period or the policy will lapse. Premiums paid are charged for mortality and expense and credited with interest to produce the policy cash value. In low premium plans, premiums are guaranteed for several years and then *redetermined* periodically (every 2 or 5 years). Depending upon current assumptions and the amount already accumulated in the cash value, premiums for the next period may go up or down. In the high-premium version of current assumption whole life, favorable experience may increase the cash value to a level where the policy becomes self-supporting. There is, however, no guarantee that premiums will ever vanish, or if they do, that they will not have to be paid again in the future if experience worsens. There are still quite a few guaranteed elements in current assumption whole life policies. There is a guaranteed death benefit and a minimum guaranteed interest rate to be credited on policy cash values. Beyond this, there are design variations that lead to different names in the marketplace. Some companies guarantee the mortality charge and the expense charges. When mortality and expense charges are guaranteed, the policy is often referred to as an *interest-sensitive whole life* policy, because excess interest (credited interest minus guaranteed interest) credited to the cash value becomes the only non-guaranteed element in the contract. Most current assumption whole life policies have some degree of flexibility in the expense elements. Because many of these designs periodically recast the premium amount based on recent experience, some of these policies are referred to as *indeterminate premium whole life* policies. There is a guaranteed maximum premium that can be charged, but the actual mortality, interest, and expenses result in lower premium amounts being charged if there is favorable experience under the policy. The high premium version of current assumption whole life insurance uses favorable experience to increase the cash value and as a result, the policy may become self-supporting.

3-17. In low-premium plans, premiums are guaranteed for several years and then periodically redetermined (recalculated). The level of premiums influences the frequency of redetermination.

The lower the premium design, the more frequent the policy's redetermination dates. In some of the more recent policy designs, redetermination can be every year; more often the redetermined frequency is every 2 years or every 5 years. On policy anniversaries when redetermination is applicable, the insurance company looks at its actual experience for the block of policies since the previous redetermination date and decides what adjustments, if any, are necessary, based on the assumption that past experiences are indicative of what to expect in the period before the next redetermination. The policyowner generally selects the method he or she prefers to adjust the policy from an available group of options when redetermination occurs. For example, if the redetermination results in a potentially lower premium, the policyowner has the option of continuing the past level of premiums and having the favorable results applied to enhance the policy's cash value, or increasing the death benefit (assuming the insured can provide satisfactory evidence of insurability). The policyowner also may choose to pay the lower policy premium amount. When past experience is less favorable than expectations, the policyowner again has a range of options, including lowering the death benefit, increasing the premium amount, or maintaining the status quo and allowing the policy accumulation account to decrease as the mortality and expense charges exceed the investment earnings on the accumulated fund. This last choice, if available, may have restrictions on its use.

3-18. Variable universal life insurance (VUL) incorporates all of the premium flexibility and policy adjustment features of the universal life policy with the policyowner-directed investment aspects of variable life insurance.

a. VUL differs from universal life in providing no minimum interest rate guarantee. Premium net of mortality and expense charges are invested in separate accounts chosen by the policyowner and the VUL cash value depends solely on the investment results achieved. Like variable life insurance, variable universal life insurance policies are classified as securities and are subject to regulation by the SEC. The SEC requires registration of agents marketing the product, the separate accounts supporting the contracts, and the contracts themselves. Policies must conform with the SEC requirements that the investment funds be separate accounts that are segregated from the insurance company's general investment portfolio and, therefore, not subject to creditors' claims applicable to the insurer's general portfolio in times of financial difficulty. Because variable universal life is a registered investment product, policies must be accompanied by a prospectus, which is governed by the same rules applicable to prospectuses for variable life policies.

b. VUL discards the fixed-premium features of the variable life insurance contract and also, unlike variable life insurance, offers a choice of level or increasing death benefits.

Answers to Self-Test Questions

3-1. D
3-2. A
3-3. B
3-4. A
3-5. C
3-6. B
3-7. B
3-8. A
3-9. B
3-10. D

Chapter 4

Answers to Review Questions

4-1. Expenses commonly associated with a breadwinner's death include bills for uninsured medical treatments as well as deductibles and co-pay portions; convalescent care; funeral, burial or other disposition of the body; managing and settling the estate; and, in large estates, taxes; and emergencies that cause death sometimes create the need for immediate repairs or replacement of property.

4-2 Common ongoing needs include food, clothing, shelter, education, transportation, utilities, taxes, lifetime support for disabled dependents, support until self-dependency of young children, dependent parents, and debt repayment (mortgages, loans, and so on).

4-3. Sometimes a trust is used to provide professional management of the finances. Trusts can be used to control assets after the death of a parent and, in some cases, disabled dependents, and prevent the squandering of funds by beneficiaries who cannot manage money.

4-4. Social Security, corporate pensions, IRAs, qualified and non-qualified retirement plans, investments, life insurance proceeds, life insurance surrenders, life insurance cash withdrawals and policy loans are all sources of retirement/supplemental income. Life insurance can protect the survivor in the event of death in the pre-retirement period as well as the retirement period. Permanent life insurance surrenders, withdrawals or loans can provide cash that can supplement retirement income.

4-5. Life insurance policy proceeds may be directed to a charity or a person by making them the beneficiary. The policy itself may be given to the intended party. Cash can be obtained from permanent life insurance policies either as withdrawals or policy loans. Policies can also be surrendered (terminating coverage) for their cash value. Life insurance can be used to fund a trust that has the desired recipient named as trust beneficiary.

4-6. Attaining credit through collateral assignment of a policy or enhancing credit through cash value policies, employee benefits such as group term life insurance, qualified pension plans and key employee compensation benefits such as executive bonus, split dollar, group carve-out, non-qualified and qualified deferred compensation, key employee life insurance, and funding for buy-sell agreements are some examples of business uses of life insurance.

4-7. The business can take a business expense deduction for premium paid for group term (Sec. 79) plans. If the plan is nondiscriminatory, the first $50,000 of coverage is tax free to all plan participants. Taxable amounts of coverage (above $50,000) are taxed at Table 1 rates. With groups of 10 or more employees, the coverage tests requires the plan to do one of the following: cover at least 70 employees, have no more than 15 percent in the key employee group, or benefit a reasonable classification of participants. Participants with less than 3 years of service, part-time, or subject to collective bargaining may be excluded. The benefits test requires a flat amount or a uniform percentage of compensation.

4-8. One advantage to executive bonus is the ability to avoid the nondiscrimination rules applicable to other fringe benefits. In a Sec. 162 plan, shareholder-employees and executives who participate in the plan apply for, own, and name the beneficiary on permanent life insurance policies covering their lives. The premiums for such policies are provided through a bonus payment by the employer-corporation. The corporation either pays the premium directly to the insurer or bonuses the premium to the employee. The income taxation of the plan is simple. The premium amount paid directly to the insurer (or bonused to the employee) is treated as gross compensation income to the employee. This compensation is treated as ordinary income subject to the employee's individual income tax rate. If the bonus along with the employee's other compensation represents reasonable compensation, the corporation deducts the amount of the bonus as an ordinary business expense under Sec. 162.

4-9. Split-dollar splits the premium, death benefits and cash value between an employer and an employee, under a number of different arrangements, to satisfy the goals of those parties. For example the executive may need life insurance for family protection or estate liquidity, or needs assistance in affording the premiums. Perhaps the employer wishes to reward the employee and provide tax-advantaged benefits or additional compensation. Policy ownership is very important. In the endorsement method the employer owns the policy and an endorsement is attached, indicating that after the premiums paid by the employer are reimbursed, the employee's beneficiary receives the balance of any death proceeds. With the collateral assignment method, the employee owns the policy, which is collaterally assigned to the employer to the extent of indebtedness on employer contributions to the policy. The taxation under the new regulations follows two mutually exclusive regimes determined by policy ownership. Under the economic benefit regime, the participant reports income based on the value of pure insurance coverage under Table 2001 or equivalent. Under the loan regime, the non-owner (employer) is treated as loaning premium payments to the owner. Loan interest must be paid, or the interest will be treated as compensation and taxed accordingly.

4-10. A qualified plan must generally purchase life insurance in order to provide any substantial pre-retirement death benefit. This gives the plan significant funds at a participant's death, which is particularly important in the early years of his or her employment when the amount contributed on the participant's behalf is still relatively small. An insured pre-retirement death benefit can be provided in either a defined-benefit or defined-contribution plan. Contributions to the plan by the employer may be used to pay life insurance premiums as long as the amount qualifies under the tests for *incidental benefits*. In general the IRS considers that non-retirement benefits—life, medical, or disability insurance, for example—in a qualified plan will be incidental and therefore permissible as long as the cost of providing these benefits is less than 25 percent of the cost of providing all the benefits under the plan. The 25 percent rule is applied to the portion of any life insurance premium that is used to provide current life insurance protection. Any portion of the premium that is used to increase the cash value of the policy is considered to be a contribution to the plan fund that is available to pay retirement benefits, and it is not considered in the 25 percent limitation.

4-11. Deferred-compensation plans can be categorized as either *qualified* or *nonqualified*. Qualified plans must meet federal nondiscrimination and administrative compliance standards. These standards increase the cost of such plans. A broad base of employees must be included and significant administrative fees must be paid. The corporation gets an immediate income tax deduction for contributions to the plan while the employee's tax on plan benefits is deferred until the benefits are received. Qualified plans will include pension plans, IRAs, profit-sharing plans, and Sec. 403(b) plans. Nonqualified plans provide a similar deferral of the employee's receipt of ordinary income. Nonqualified plans also cause a deferral of the employer's tax deduction until such benefits are paid. Because closely held corporations often want to maximize the benefits for shareholder-employees, the goal of their retirement plans is to discriminate in favor of shareholder-employees and key executives to the fullest extent of the nondiscrimination rules. Since discrimination is permitted in nonqualified arrangements, these plans are often more favorable to the closely held corporation. The employer can finance its obligation in a nonqualified plan through corporate-owned life insurance. This type of financing is attractive since life insurance as a corporate asset is a good match for the type of liabilities created by nonqualified arrangements. The accumulation in an ordinary life insurance policy can be useful in the participant's retirement years to provide for any salary continuation benefits offered by the plan. The primary benefit of the life insurance financing is its ability to meet the employer's death benefit obligation should the participant die prematurely. The life insurance financing is particularly appropriate to provide benefits in a DBO (Death Benefit Only) plan. Nonqualified plan policies are owned by and payable to the employer. As such, they avoid the constructive-receipt or economic-benefit problems because the general creditors have access to the funding policies. The premiums are nondeductible. The cash surrender value builds up tax free, and the proceeds will be nontaxable when received. The corporation receives a deduction when the benefits are actually paid to the participant.

4-12.   Key Employee Life Insurance indemnifies a business concern for the loss of earnings caused by the death of a key officer or employee. In many business concerns, there is one person whose capital, technical knowledge, experience, or business connections make him or her a valuable asset of the organization and a necessity to its successful operation. Insurance is purchased on the life of the key employee by the business and is made payable to the business as beneficiary. In most cases, some form of permanent insurance, usually ordinary life, is purchased, and the accumulating cash values are reflected as an asset on the business's books. If key person protection is needed for only a temporary period, term insurance is normally used. Premiums paid for key person insurance are not deductible as a business expense, but in the event of death, the proceeds are received free of federal income tax.

4-13.   A buy-sell agreement binds the surviving parties to purchase the business interest of the first owner to die at a price set forth in the agreement and obligates the deceased owner's estate to sell his or her interest to the surviving owners. The various interests are valued at the time the agreement is drawn up and revised from time to time thereafter. Each owner is insured for the amount of his or her interest, and either the business or the other owners own the insurance. Upon the first death among the owners, the life insurance proceeds are used by the survivor(s) to purchase the deceased's interest. Thus, the business continues in operation for the benefit of the surviving owners, and the deceased's heirs receive the going value of his or her business interest in cash. Under a stock-redemption agreement the corporation is the "purchaser" of the stock at the death of a shareholder. Each shareholder subject to the agreement binds his or her estate to transfer the stock to the corporation in exchange for the required purchase price. The cross-purchase agreement is where each shareholder agrees to purchase a specified percentage of the shares of stock held by a deceased shareholder at the time of death. Each shareholder must also agree to bind his or her estate to sell the stock owned at his or her death.

Answers to Self-Test Questions

4-1.   B
4-2.   B
4-3.   D

4-4. A
4-5. C
4-6. C
4-7. C
4-8. A
4-9. B
4-10. D

Chapter 5

Answers to Review Questions

5-1. The net cost method is a flawed method of comparing policies. It looks at a period of coverage, takes the aggregated net premiums paid under the policy, subtracts any cash value accumulated at the end of the period and all dividends paid over the period. It does not consider time value of money (interest and timing of payments) so it is therefore misleading because it does not take into account when the money was paid or received, and the opportunity cost, or alternative use value for the money.

5-2. There are two interest-adjusted cost indexes: the *surrender cost index* and the *payment cost index*. The logic of using interest-adjusted indexes is similar to that of the traditional net cost approach with the exception that interest-adjusted indexes explicitly take into account the time value of money. Essentially the interest-adjusted methods take all payments for premiums and treat them as if they had been put into interest-bearing accounts to accumulate interest (usually assumed to be 5 percent) until the end of the interval for evaluation (usually 20 years). Similarly, all dividend payments are carried as if they are deposited in an interest-bearing account, and that account balance is calculated for the end of the interval of evaluation. For the surrender cost index, the policy cash value at the end of the evaluation period and the amount of accumulated dividends are subtracted from the accumulated value of all the premiums paid and the result is divided by the future value of an annuity due of $1 for the length of the evaluation period at the assumed rate of interest. Determining the payment cost index is similar to calculating the surrender cost index except that there is no recognition of the end-of-period cash value.

5-3. The cash accumulation comparison method involves accumulating the premium differences between the policies being compared, while holding the death benefits of both policies constant and equal. For example, to compare a cash value contract with a term contract, set the death benefits equal at the beginning of the period, and use the yearly premium difference between the cash value contract and the term policy to determine the amount to deposit into a side fund to accumulate at interest. The calculation is basically a buy-term-and-invest-the-difference approach to comparing the policies. At the end of the interval being evaluated the side fund accumulation amount can be compared to the cash value in the whole life or other form of cash value insurance policy. The policy with the greater accumulation at the end of the comparison interval is considered the preferable of the two contracts. One of the strengths of the cash accumulation method is that it is acceptable to compare permanent insurance policies with term policies. It can also be used for evaluation of replacement proposals. The method has several weaknesses: The cash accumulation comparison method is much more complex than the net cost and interest-adjusted methods and requires a computer to make the calculations. A significant amount of data must be entered into the computer program in order to calculate the results accurately.

5-4. The equal outlay method is somewhat similar to the cash accumulation method. Again, the same amount of premium dollars is expended, on the one hand for a cash value contract and on the other for a term policy. The amount by which the cash value contract premiums exceed the term premiums is deposited into a side fund, and the difference in premium amounts is accumulated at specified interest rates. Then the death benefit of the term insurance plus the accumulated side fund amounts are compared with the death benefit under the cash value contract in which dividends, if any, have been used to purchase paid-up additions. Under this type of comparison the policy producing the greater death benefit is considered the preferable contract.

5-5. The comparative interest rate method is really a modification of the cash accumulation method, whereby we are calculating the interest rate that would make a term insurance policy side fund exactly equal to the cash value policy's cash surrender value at the end of the evaluation period. The comparative interest rate method looks for the interest rate that would make the buy-term-and-invest-the-difference comparison exactly equivalent in the death benefits provided. Its primary drawback is the complexity of the calculation, which requires not only a computer program to accurately calculate the interest rate desired but also a large amount of policy information that must be entered into the program before it can be run.

5-6. Under the Belth yearly rate of return approach, only one year of the policy is considered in making an individual calculation. Such a calculation can be made for each and every year of coverage over the given interval. The objective is to identify the benefits provided by the policy during that year (the end-of-year cash value plus the dividends paid during the year and the net death benefit for the policy year) and the investments in the policy necessary to derive those benefits (a combination of the beginning-of-the-year cash value and the premium paid for that year of the policy). The yearly rate of return formula divides the sum of the benefits by the sum of the investments and then subtracts the number 1 from that amount. This process is repeated for each year over the comparison interval. The policy with the highest rates of yearly return in the largest number of years over the observation interval is considered the preferable policy.

Two key differences between the two methods are:

- The comparative interest rate method produces an average interest rate (rate of return) for the evaluation period, while Belth's method computes a yearly interest rate (rate of return).
- The comparative interest rate method requires a computer to make the calculation, whereas Belth's method can be executed with or even without a calculator.

Under the Belth yearly price approach we must assume an investment or interest rate and thereby calculate the cost of protection. The calculations are made one year at a time for each of the years in the comparison interval (usually 10 or 20 years as in most other comparison methods). Using this method, the beginning cash value plus the current premium are accumulated at the assumed rate of interest to derive a theoretical year-end surrender value. After computing the theoretical end-of-year value from the beginning cash value and the premium plus interest, we subtract the actual end-of-year cash value plus dividends paid during the year. This is the difference assumed to have been available to pay mortality charges. The next step is to divide the difference between theoretical year-end values and actual year-end values plus dividends by the amount at risk per $1,000 of coverage. After making a yearly price-of-protection calculation for each policy being compared for each year in the comparison interval, identifying the policy with the lowest cost of protection for the largest number of years over that interval. In most cases that policy would be the preferable one of those under consideration.

5-7.   There is an inverse relationship between the interest rate and the accumulated values in policy illustrations. That is, higher interest rates result in lower present values, and lower interest rates produce higher present-value amounts.

5-8.   Ledger statements and policy illustrations that do not include interest adjustments are really based on an implicit assumption that the interest rate is zero and the inflation rate is zero.

5-9.   The *Professional Practice Guideline* is a checklist of guidelines for sales material and presentations. This *Professional Practice Guideline* is intended to serve as a checklist of information for members of the Society of Financial Service Professionals to be evaluated before a prospect or client is asked to make a buying decision. This document can be used to ensure that all relevant questions have been explained to a prospect. The Life Insurance Illustration Questionnaire (IQ) was intended to stimulate agents to question and more thoroughly understand the intricacies of illustrations so they could better explain them to purchasers and prospects. The IQ questions are directed to the insurance company regarding the assumptions and methodology underlying the responding insurer's illustrations.

5-10.   The IQ elicits answers to the following questions about mortality:

- Do mortality rates underlying the scale used in the illustration differ from actual recent historical experience and what was the latter?
- Does the illustration assume mortality improvements in the future and, if so, what are they?
- Do the mortality or cost of insurance charges used in the illustration include some expense charge (if so, describe)?
- Do the underlying mortality rates vary by product (for example, whole life, universal life, survivorship life), policy size or by any other feature (for example, term riders)? If so, specify.
- What is the approximate duration, if any, when all underlying mortality rates vary only by attained age (for example, when does select become ultimate?).

5-11. The IQ elicits the following type of information about interest or crediting rates:

- The interest rate used in the dividend scale or credited in the illustration is a portfolio rate or other (describe), is a gross rate or net rate (net of what?), and does include realized, unrealized or no capital gains.
- Do the interest rate(s) reflect the earnings on all invested assets; a portion of the assets; new investments over certain number of years (If so, specify number of years); an index (If so, briefly describe.)?
- At any policy duration, do the company investment earnings rates required to support the scale used in the illustration exceed the company's actual recent historical earnings rate on the investment segment backing that block of policies?
- Does the interest rate used in the underlying scale reflected in the illustration vary between new and existing policies? Describe.
- Except for any impact of using an investment generation approach, do the interest rates used in the scale reflected in the illustration vary by policy duration? Describe.
- Do the illustrated interest rates vary by product, class or otherwise? Describe.
- How does individual policy loan activity affect the illustrated interest rates? Describe.

5-12. The IQ elicits answers to the following questions about expenses:

- Do the expense factors used in the scale reflected in the illustration represent actual recent historical company experience? If so, what is the experience period? If not, describe the basis under which the experience factors are determined.
- Are the expense factors based on a fully allocated, marginal, or generally recognized approach, as defined in the NAIC Model Regulations?
- Are the expense charges used in the underlying scale reflected in the illustration adequate to cover the expenses incurred in sales and administration? If not, how are remaining expenses covered (for example, charges against interest rate, increased mortality charges)?
- How are investment expenses and all taxes assessed?

- Are expense factors used in the scale reflected in the illustration different for new and existing policies? If so, describe.
- Do the expense factors underlying the scale reflected in the illustration vary by product, class or otherwise? If so, describe.
- Do the expense charges used in the dividend scale or charged in the illustration vary by duration after the initial expenses are amortized? If so, describe.

5-13. The IQ elicits the following type of information about persistency:

- If the actual persistency is better than that assumed, would that negatively affect illustrated values?
- Persistency bonuses are generally amounts illustrated as being paid or credited to all policyholders who pay premiums for a specified number of years. Does the illustration involve such a bonus?
  - If so, is it guaranteed?
  - Is there any limitation on company discretion in deciding whether to pay or credit the bonus?
  - What conditions must be met to pay or credit the bonus?
  - What is its form (for example, cash amount, additional interest credit, refund of mortality and/or loading charges)?
  - Does the company set aside any reserve or other liability earmarked for future bonuses?

5-14. The major elements of the NAIC Life Insurance Illustrations Model Regulation are:

- The regulation applies to all nonvariable group and individual *life insurance* policies and certificates for more than $10,000 of death benefit.
- The regulation requires the insurance company to declare to the state insurance department for each policy form whether or not it intends to use illustrations to market that form of coverage. A copy of each illustration the insurer intends to use must be forwarded to the state insurance department.
- Each illustration used in the sale of a life insurance policy covered by the regulation must be clearly labeled "life insurance illustration" and must include certain specified pieces of information about the company, the agent, the proposed insured, the policy and its benefit features.
- The NAIC Model Regulation prohibits insurers and their agents from misrepresenting various specified types of information to the client.
- The illustration must clearly indicate what elements are guaranteed and what elements are nonguaranteed.
- Any amount illustrated as being available upon surrender will be the amount after deduction of surrender charges.

- Each illustration must be accompanied by a narrative summary that describes the policy premiums and features and defines column headings used in the illustration.
- The summary should also state that actual results may be more or less favorable than those shown in the illustration.
- The regulation states that illustrations for universal life policies must comply with the regulation requirements, that the insurance company must issue annual reports to policyowners after the policy is issued, and specifies the content of those annual reports.
- The regulation further stipulates that policyowners have the right to request an in-force illustration annually without charge.
- Each insurer's board of directors must appoint at least one illustration actuary, who will certify that the illustrations are in compliance with the illustration regulation and are insurer-authorized. The regulation states the qualifications of an illustration actuary, including membership in good standing of the American Academy of Actuaries.
- The model regulation sets forth limits on the methodology for calculating illustrations.

5-15. The illustration actuary must certify that the illustrations are in compliance with the illustration regulation and are insurer-authorized. The illustration actuary must annually certify the method used to allocate overhead and expenses for all illustrations and file such certification with the insurance commissioner and with the insurer's board of directions. Further, the illustration actuary is required to report any mistakes found in previous certifications to both the commissioner and the board of directions.

Answers to Self-Test Questions

5-1. A
5-2. C
5-3. C
5-4. B
5-5. A
5-6. C
5-7. C
5-8. D
5-9. A
5-10. C

Chapter 6

Answers to Review Questions

6-1. The function of the selection process is to determine whether an applicant's degree of risk for insurance is commensurate with the premium established for people in the same classification being considered.

6-2. Even though they would be in the same age group and are the same sex, differences stemming from physical condition, occupation, avocations, smoking, and other factors might result in them being placed in different rate categories and, thus, paying different premiums for the same policy.

6-3. Irrespective of the underwriting procedures used by a company, if each risk classification is overbalanced with risks whose longevity prospects are less favorable than the assumed average for the classification, the company will end up with excessive mortality costs and—unless it enjoys offsetting advantages in other areas of operations—will have difficulty in maintaining its competitive position.

6-4. If a company's underwriting standards are not at least as effective as those utilized by the companies that supplied the data for the mortality table, its actual mortality experience will likely be worse than that assumed in calculating its premium rates, and unless it enjoys offsetting advantages in other areas of operations, it will suffer an underwriting loss.

6-5. The applicant's age is the most important single factor on individual mortality expectations. Except for the first few years of life, resistance to disease and injury weakens with age, and the probability of death increases with age. Age is the starting point in classifying applicants for insurance. Each applicant is placed within the proper age classification and is then compared to the norm for that age to determine insurability. All companies have upper-age limits beyond which they will not write insurance on any basis and somewhat lower limits for writing certain types of policies, such as term insurance. The absolute limit may be as low as 60 or as high as 75 or more; the age of the applicant may bar acceptability to the company on any basis.

   The applicant's build—the relationship between height, weight, and girth—is one of the basic determinants of mortality expectation. Build tables containing debits for various combinations of height and weight are used to determine an applicant's debit (if any) for purposes of the numerical rating system. In evaluating an application for insurance, the company wishes to know whether there are any impairments of body or mind that would tend to shorten the life expectancy of the applicant. In the short run, the applicant's physical condition may outweigh all other factors in importance. Questions designed to elicit information on the applicant's physical status are included in the application. If a sizable amount of insurance is involved, the information is also confirmed and supplemented by a medical examination and laboratory testing. The primary purpose of the medical examination is to detect any malfunctioning of vital organs.

6-6. Enlargement of the heart is a condition of underwriting significance, because it is nature's way of compensating for damage to the valves or other sections of the heart mechanism. High blood pressure may be a symptom of a condition that impairs longevity. It is particularly associated with kidney ailments. A combination of excess weight and hypertension is always regarded seriously. The condition of the circulatory system can also be evaluated by the pulse rate, normally 60 to 80 beats per minute. A rapid pulse is unfavorable, because it indicates that the heart has to work harder than usual to meet the body's needs. Blood profile tests have gained added importance with the discovery of Acquired Immune Deficiency Syndrome (AIDS). The availability of this additional information has facilitated the proliferation of products that offer preferred-premium classifications. Urinalysis has a three-fold purpose: (1) to measure the functional capacity of the kidneys, (2) to detect infections or other abnormal conditions of the kidneys, and (3) to discover impairments of other vital organs of the body.

6-7. The applicant's personal history provides information about previous illnesses, injuries, and operations that can indicate the necessity for special additional tests or examinations. The company also wants to know whether the applicant has even been addicted to drugs or alcohol, because it is always possible that the "cure" will be only temporary. Past abuse may have caused irrevocable damage to one or more body systems. The personal history may reveal that the applicant has only recently left a hazardous or unhealthful occupation; he or she may retain ill effects from the job or return to the job in the future. It may also disclose that the applicant has changed residence to improve his or her health or has had intimate association with a person who has a contagious disease such as tuberculosis. Finally, the company wants to know whether the applicant has even been refused insurance by any other company or offered insurance on rated terms. That may indicate a prior impairment that may still be present. Information about existing insurance also enables the company to judge whether the amount of insurance (existing and proposed) bears a reasonable relationship to the applicant's needs and financial resources.

6-8. Family history is considered significant because certain characteristics are hereditary. Build follows family lines, and to some extent, so do structural qualities of the heart and other organs.

6-9. a. All people working with machinery are exposed to some accident hazard. Construction workers are exposed to the hazard of falling, Underground miners—in addition to the hazard of machinery—run the risk of explosions, rock falls, fire, and lung disease. Some electrical workers are exposed to high voltages and some to the danger of falling from high places. Laborers handling heavy materials run the risk of having the materials fall on them. Railroad workers, particularly those around heavy rolling equipment, are subject to a high accident rate. Other groups subject to a higher-than-normal accident rate include fishermen, lumbermen, and farmers.

b. The socio-economic hazard is associated with occupations that employ unskilled and semi-skilled labor and pay commensurately low wages. The extra mortality that occurs among such people is attributable primarily to their unsatisfactory living and working conditions and to inadequate medical care. Their low economic status may reflect substandard physical or mental capacity. There are some occupations that are thought to have a socio-economic hazard not because of low wages but because of the environment in which the people work. Bartenders, liquor salespeople, and cab drivers, for example, are believed to represent a hazard purely because of environment.

6-10.   The applicant's residence is important because mortality rates vary throughout different geographical regions of the world. If the applicant is contemplating foreign travel or residence, the insurance company wants to know about it. It also wants to know whether the applicant has recently traveled or resided in a foreign country, particularly in the tropics. Differences among countries as to climate, living standards, sanitary conditions, medical care, political stability, and terrorist risk can be expected to have a decided effect on mortality. Generally policies are not issued to applicants whose permanent residence is in a foreign country, even though that country may have a climate and living conditions similar to those of the United States. Policies are freely issued to persons who plan to be abroad temporarily, provided they do not contemplate visiting crises areas or making an extended stay in tropical countries.

An insurance company is interested in the moral fiber of the applicant because it has been established that departures from the commonly accepted standards of ethical and moral conduct involve extra mortality risks. Marital infidelity and other kinds of behavior that are considered immoral are regarded seriously because they are frequently found in combination with other types of risky behavior, such as overindulgence in alcoholic beverages, gambling, and the drug use. The hazards to longevity are the impairment of health and the possibility of violence. Unethical business conduct is another form of moral hazard. Companies do not care to insure persons who have a record of numerous bankruptcies, operate businesses that are just within the law, or have a general reputation for dishonesty. The companies fear the applicant's misrepresentation and concealment of material underwriting facts on the application. A person who is dishonest in general business dealings is not likely to make an exception for insurance companies, which have always been prime targets for unscrupulous schemes.

6-11.   The treatment of private pilots depends on the person's age, experience, training, and amount of flying, with an extra premium charged or credits allowed based on these factors. The underwriting treatment of a crew member of a military aircraft depends on the applicant's age and type of duty. Service with combat aircraft is regarded the least favorably, as one would naturally suppose. Accidental death benefit riders often exclude aviation deaths if the insured was the pilot or crew member of any type of aircraft. Flying ultra-light aircraft that are dangerous and not nearly as regulated as regular aircraft may require an extra premium.

6-12. a. American life insurance companies have taken special underwriting scrutiny of the extra mortality risk associated with applicants engaged in or facing military service during a period of armed conflict. Underwriting action has taken three principal forms: outright rejection of the applicant, limitation on the face amount of insurance issued, or the attachment of a *war clause* that limits the insurer's obligation to return of premiums, less dividends, with interest, if the insured dies under circumstances as defined in the war clause.

b. A *status clause* limits the insurer's obligation to return of premium if the insured should die while in military service outside the territorial boundaries of the United States, whether or not the cause of death can be attributed to military service. A *results war clause* limits the insurer's obligation only if the insured's death is the result of military service. While regarded as more liberal to the insured than the status clause, the results provision limits liability even though the insured is no longer in a war zone at the time of death.

6-13. a. A company's field force is the foundation of the selection process. The other parts of the selection mechanism can go into operation only after the field force has acted. The home office can exercise its underwriting judgment only on the risks submitted by the agents and brokers. Most companies give their agents explicit instructions about the types of risks that will or will not be acceptable, and they instruct the agents to solicit only those risks they believe to be eligible under the company's underwriting rules. The agent is asked to supply a variety of information in the agent's report, typically including the following information:

- how long and how well the agent has known the applicant
- an estimate of the applicant's net worth and annual income
- the applicant's existing and pending insurance, including any plans for the lapse or surrender of existing insurance
- whether the applicant sought the insurance or was solicited by the agent
- whether the application came through another agent or broker

The degree of selection exercised at the field level depends on the integrity and reliability of the agents and brokers. There is clearly some selection involved, since self-interest would cause the agent not to solicit insurance from persons who, because of obvious physical impairments, moral deficiencies, or unacceptable occupations, could not meet the underwriting standards of the company. Beyond that, the amount of selection practiced by the agent is rather limited. The agent is usually the only company representative to see an applicant face-to-face and make a visual assessment. If there is anything unusual about the applicant that requires an explanation, it is up to the agent to convey that information to the home office. The agent can include this information with the agent's report that accompanies the application. Experienced agents know what types of additional information the home office underwriters are likely to request when the application reveals specific health problems. These agents can expedite the process by asking for the supplemental reports at the same time the application is completed. Some experienced agents have a reputation with the home office underwriters for thoroughness, accuracy, and attention to detail in furnishing applications and supporting documents. This reputation can benefit applicants who are on the borderline between classifications and can be rated either way. They may get the benefit of the lower premium class because of their agent's reputation. Borderline cases from agents who always argue with the home office evaluation and send applications with less than complete information are more likely to be classified under the higher premium category when it is strictly a judgment call.

b. Applications vary in their content and design, but they usually consist of two parts: the first contains informational questions and the second has questions about medical history. Statements made by the applicant in the first part of the application cover the particulars of identification, such as name, address, former and prospective places of residence, and place and date of birth. If the applicant has recently moved, including previous places of residence enable the company, through reporting services, to interview the applicant's former acquaintances. A question in the first part of the application asks the applicant's occupation, including any changes within the last 5 years or any contemplated changes of occupation; aviation activities other than passenger travel on regularly scheduled airlines (unusual aviation hazard details must be provided in a supplementary form); and the possibility of foreign residence. The application also elicits information about the applicant's insurance history: details of all insurance already in force, declinations and other insurance company actions of underwriting significance. This information, with the amount of insurance applied for, the plan of insurance, the names of the policy beneficiary and policyowner, and the respective rights of the insured, beneficiary, and policyowner as to control of the policy, completes the first part of the application. The answers to questions in the second part of the application normally must be recorded in the medical examiner's handwriting, and the applicant must sign the form to attest to the completeness and accuracy of its contents. This part of the application asks several groups of related questions. The first group seeks the details of the applicant's health record, including illnesses, injuries, and surgical operations, usually within the last 10 years. The applicant is also required to give the name of every physician or practitioner consulted within a specified period of time (usually the last 5 years) in connection with any ailment whatsoever. The second group of questions elicits information about the applicant's present physical condition, the applicant's use of alcohol and drugs, and questions concerning the applicant's family history.

c. The purpose of the medical examiner's report is to transmit the findings of the physical examination. In addition to recording the answers to part two of the application, the medical examiner files a separate report, which accompanies the application but is not seen by the applicant. The first portion of the report contains a description of the applicant's physical characteristics, which provides useful underwriting information and guards against substituting a healthy person for an unhealthy applicant in the medical examination. Some companies ask the examiner to review the applicant's identification to establish conclusive identification. The medical examiner's comments are required regarding any abnormalities of the applicant's arteries or veins, heart, respiratory system, nervous system, abdomen, genitourinary system, ears, eyes, and skin. The examiner also reports the urinalysis result, certifies that the urine examined is authentic, describes the applicant's build, and indicates the applicant's blood pressure. The examiner may be requested to indicate any knowledge or suspicion that the applicant abuses alcohol or narcotics or has any moral deficiencies that would affect his or her insurability.

d. The Medical Information Bureau (MIB) is a clearinghouse for confidential medical data on applicants for life insurance. The information is reported and maintained in code symbols to help preserve its confidentiality. Companies that are members of the Bureau are expected to report any impairments designated on the official list. All impairments must be reported whether the company accepts, postpones, or declines the risk, or offers a modified plan of insurance. In no event does the company report its underwriting decision to the Bureau. A company normally screens all of its applicants against the MIB file of reported impairments. If the company finds an impairment and wants further details, it must submit its request through the MIB, but only after it first conducts its own complete investigation from all known sources. The company that reported the impairment is not obligated to supply further information, but if it agrees to do so, it provides the requested information through the MIB. The rules of the MIB stipulate that a company cannot take unfavorable underwriting action *solely* on the basis of the information in the MIB files. In other words, the company must be in possession of other unfavorable underwriting facts or else determine through its own channels of investigation that the condition of impairment recorded in the MIB files is substantial enough to warrant an unfavorable decision.

6-14. Ideally, the evaluation and classification system used by a company should (1) accurately measure the effect of each of the factors, favorable and unfavorable, that can be expected to influence an applicant's longevity; (2) assess the combined impact of multiple factors, including the situations in which the factors are conflicting; (3) produce consistently equitable results; and (4) be simple and relatively inexpensive to operate.

6-15. The judgment method of rating functions very effectively when there is only one unfavorable factor to consider or when the decision is simply one of accepting the applicant at standard rates or rejecting the application altogether.

6-16. The numerical rating system is based on the principle that a large number of factors enter into the composition of a risk and that the impact of each of these factors on the longevity of the risk can be determined by a statistical study of lives possessing that factor. Among the criticisms leveled against the numerical rating system are (1) the system is too arbitrary, (2) there are many impairments for which knowledge is too limited to permit the assignment of numerical values, (3) the interrelated factors are non-additive in so many cases that it nullifies the value of the numerical process, and (4) too many minor debits and credits are taken into account in evaluating risk.

6-17.   In practice, weights are generally assigned to the following 10 factors when the numerical rating system is used to evaluate and classify risks: (1) build, (2) physical condition, (3) medical history, (4) family history, (5) occupation, (6) aviation and avocation, (7) residence, (8) habits, (9) morals, and (10) plan of insurance. The values assigned to these factors are derived from mortality studies among groups of people possessing those characteristics or, in some cases, from estimates of what such mortality studies might be expected to show.

6-18.   a.   Perhaps the most important safeguard in the issuance of nonmedical insurance is a limit on the amount made available to any one applicant. The limit is determined by the extra mortality that can be expected from eliminating the medical examination and the savings in selection expenses that will be available to absorb the extra mortality costs. Today, most companies will provide up to $100,000 on a nonmedical basis, subject to appropriate age restrictions, while many will issue up to $250,000 or more on that basis. The limit generally varies by age groups; the largest amounts are available to the younger age groups.

b.   A second safeguard companies impose is a limit on the ages at which insurance will be issued. Studies have shown that the extra mortality resulting from waiving the medical examination increases with age and after a point, will exceed any savings in selection expense. The point at which the extra mortality costs will exceed the expense savings is obviously a function of the underwriting age limit; most companies offer nonmedical insurance down to age zero.

c.   A third safeguard is the general limitation of nonmedical insurance to standard risks. Substandard risks must typically submit to medical examinations, but exceptions are commonly made for risks that are substandard because of an occupational, aviation, or avocational hazard.

d.   A final safeguard is the cultivation of sources of underwriting information other than the medical examiner. Insurance companies place a heavier burden on the applicant, agent, and inspector to offset in some measure the absence of a medical examiner's findings. The application form used in connection with nonmedical insurance is elaborate, containing all the questions usually contained in an application, as well as those normally asked by a medical examiner. A urine specimen and blood profile may be required. If the applicant has recently been under the care of a physician, a statement may be necessary from the attending physician (at the expense of the company). If any adverse medical information is revealed by the applicant's statement, the inspection report, or other source, the company may demand a complete medical examination. Responsibility is placed on the agent, with great reliance on the agent's judgment and integrity. Agents may submit nonmedical applications only from applicants who meet the company's underwriting requirements from a physical, medical, occupational, and moral standpoint. The agent must elicit from the applicant, and accurately record, most of the information that a medical examination would seek. A detailed agent's report that records the agent's underwriting impressions of the applicant is also required. Inspection reports are sometimes ordered to supplement the larger nonmedical insurance applications, even though such information would not be requested for medically underwritten cases for the same or larger amounts of coverage.

6-19. Nonmedical insurance is subject to a higher rate of mortality than medically examined business. This extra mortality is believed to stem from (1) impairments known to the applicant but deliberately concealed and (2) impairments not known to the applicant that could have been discovered by a medical examination.

6-20. Insurers writing insurance on the lives of very young children attempt to cope with the lack of insurable interest in three ways: (1) by limiting the coverage to amounts much smaller than those available to adults, particularly at the early ages, (2) by seeing that the insurance on the child bears a reasonable relationship to the amounts in force on the other members of the family, especially the breadwinner, and (3) by seeking a large volume of juvenile insurance applications to minimize adverse selection. At the older ages, the lack of insurable interest is only one of the complicating factors. In the first place, the volume of insurance issued at ages above 70 or 75 is not large enough to yield predictable mortality results. The restricted demand for insurance at those ages reflects the high cost of the insurance, the general inability to satisfy the medical requirements, and the limited need for new insurance. Secondly, a high degree of adverse selection is associated with applications received at those ages. Low volume in itself is suggestive of adverse selection, but when it is accompanied by burdensome premium payments, the environment is even more conducive to adverse selection. This antiselection may be exercised by the insureds themselves aware of a serious impairment, or by a third party, perhaps a relative, who seeks insurance on the life of an elderly person for speculative reasons. A third factor is the relative ineffectiveness of the medical examination for elderly people, which does not reveal many conditions of a degenerative nature that can materially shorten the life of the elderly applicant.

6-21. If 1,000 persons, each of whom is suffering from a particular physical impairment, are granted insurance, it is certain that the death rate among them will be greater than the death rate among a group of people the same age who are free from any discernible impairments. To allow for the higher death rates that will certainly occur within the substandard group, the company must collect an extra premium from—or impose special terms on—all who are subject to the extra risk because it is not known what members of the group will be responsible for the extra mortality. It is not expected that every member of the group will be responsible for the extra mortality. It is not expected that every member of the group will survive for a shorter period than the normal life expectancy. In fact, it is a certainty that this will not be the case; it is known merely that a larger proportion of people in a normal group will attain normal life expectancy. The fact that certain members of the impaired group reach old age is, therefore, no indication that an error was made in their cases. If they had paid no extra premium, a still higher premium would have been required from the others. Generally speaking, nothing could or should be refunded to members of a substandard group who live beyond the normal life expectancy, provided that the extra premiums charged (or other special terms imposed) were a true measure of the degree of extra hazard represented by the group.

6-22.   The majority of companies proceed on the assumption that each substandard risk falls into one of three broad groups:

1.   The additional hazard increases with age (for example, high blood pressure)
2.   In the second group, the additional hazard remains roughly constant at all ages (for example, occupational hazards)
3.   In the third group, the additional hazard decreases with age (for example, many impairments attributable to past illnesses and surgical operations).

6-23.   a.   Under the increase-in-age method, the applicant is assumed to be a number of years older than his or her real age, and the policy is written accordingly. The number of years older is usually determined by adding the amount estimated as necessary to provide for the extra mortality to the net premium for the applicant's actual age, and then finding the premium in the standard table that most closely matches that total, and deriving the rate-up from the standard age in the table. The policy would contain the same surrender and loan values and would be entitled to the same dividends, if any, as any contract of that type issued at the increased age.

b.   This method of dealing with substandard risks is suitable only when the extra risk is a decidedly increasing one and will continue to increase indefinitely at a greater rate. Although few impairments give rise to such a consistent and rapid increase in the rate of mortality as provided in the rated-up age method, the method is considered to be appropriate for all types of substandard risks where the extra mortality, in general, increases with age

c.   The chief appeal of the method for the insurance company is its simplicity. Policies can be dealt with for all purposes as standard policies issued at the assumed age. No separate set of records is required; no special calculations of premium rates, cash and other surrender values, reserves, and dividends are involved. For the applicant, the method is attractive because the higher premium is accompanied by higher surrender values and dividends (if participating).

6-24. a. The extra-percentage-tables method classifies risks into groups based on the expected percentage of standard mortality and charges premiums that reflect the appropriate increase in mortality. The number of substandard classifications may vary from three to 12, depending on the degree of extra mortality the company is willing to underwrite. A special mortality table reflecting the appropriate degree of extra mortality is prepared for each substandard classification, and a complete set of gross premium rates is computed for each classification.

b. This is the most common method of dealing with risks that present an increasing hazard.

c. The most notable feature of the extra-percentage-table premiums is that they do not increase in proportion to the degree of extra mortality involved. There is a twofold explanation of this result: 1) the rates charged the policyowner are gross premium rates, and the amount of loading does not increase from one rate classification to the other, except for commissions and premium taxes but remains constant (with minor exceptions); 2) the percentage of extra mortality is computed on the basis of actual—rather than tabular—mortality. The premiums for standard risks are calculated on the basis of the 1980 CSO Table, which contains a considerable overstatement of mortality at the young and middle ages, but additions to standard premiums to arrive at the substandard rates reflect only the excess mortality for the substandard classifications over the actual mortality. Hence, the rates for the substandard classifications are not proportionally greater than even the net premiums for the standard risks.

d. The reserves under policies issued in accordance with extra-percentages tables must be calculated on the basis of the mortality assumptions underlying the premium, which requires separate classification records and tabulations. Depending on company practice and state law, surrender values may be based on the special mortality table or may be the same as surrender values under policies issued to standard risks. Many companies do not make the extended term insurance nonforfeiture option available under extra-percentage-table policies, especially at the higher percentages, and those that do compute the period on the basis of the higher mortality rate even when only the normal surrender value is allowed.

6-25. a. Under the flat extra-premium method, the standard premium for the policy in question is increased by a specified number of dollars per $1,000 of insurance. Assessed as a measure of the extra mortality involved, the flat extra premium does not vary with the age of the applicant. It may be paid throughout the premium-paying period of the policy (permanent), or it may be terminated after a period of years when the extra hazard has presumably disappeared (temporary).

b. The flat extra-premium method is normally used when the hazard is thought to be constant (deafness or partial blindness, for example) or decreasing (as with a family history of tuberculosis or the aftermath of a serious illness or surgical operation, in which case the flat extra is usually temporary in duration). The flat extra premium is widely used to cover the extra risk associated with certain occupations and avocations. Unless a permanent impairment is involved, the extra premium is generally removed if the insured leaves the hazardous occupation or avocation.

c. When the extra risk is constant, the extra premium for a cash value contract should diminish each year in the proportion that the amount at risk decreases. To avoid the labor and expense that would be involved in such an annual adjustment, and in recognition of the fact that the flat extra premium is an approximation, most companies compute the flat extra addition on the basis of the average amount at risk. Some companies vary the extra premium with the plan of insurance, charging less for high cash value policies than for policies with lower reserve elements.

d. The flat extra premium is not reflected in policy values and dividends. It is assumed that the entire amount of the extra premium is needed each year to pay additional claims and expenses. The dividends and guaranteed values are identical to those of a comparable policy without the flat extra premium.

6-26. Theoretically, the substandard rating should not be removed unless the impairment on which it was based was known to be temporary or was due to occupation or residence. At the time the policy was originally issued, the insured was placed in a special classification of risks whose members were presumably impaired to approximately the same degree. It was known by the company that some of the members of the group would die within a short period, while others would survive far beyond their normal expectancy. By the time the insured under consideration is in normal health, the health of many others in the original group has undoubtedly worsened. If the company reduces the premiums for those whose health has improved, it should be permitted to increase the premiums of those whose death has deteriorated. Because the premiums of those in the latter category cannot be adjusted upward, the premiums of those in the former category should not be reduced. As a practical matter, however, the company is virtually forced to remove the substandard rating of a person who can demonstrate current insurability at standard rates. If it does not do so, the policyowner will almost surely surrender the extra-rate insurance and replace it with insurance at standard rates in another company. Where an extra premium has been imposed because of occupation, residence, or a temporary risk, it is proper to discontinue the extra premium upon termination of the condition that created the extra hazard. It is necessary to exercise care in these cases, however, particularly when the source of the rating was occupation or residence.

Answers to Self-Test Questions

6-1. C
6-2. C
6-3. A
6-4. B
6-5. B
6-6. D
6-7. A
6-8. D
6-9. B
6-10. D

Chapter 7

Answers to Review Questions

7-1. The prospective policyowner performs only these two functions in the creation of a life insurance contract:

- He or she applies for the policy (the contract) by filling out the application and supplying any medical information required by the insurer.
- The applicant is then asked to accept or reject the contract as offered by the insurer. The applicant accepts the offer by paying the initial premium. If a partial premium is paid and the insurer's agent issues a premium (conditional) receipt, only temporary coverage under the terms of the receipt is in effect. The contract is accepted by the applicant and binding on the insurer under the particular terms of the receipt and the policy. Even after the applicant accepts the insurer's offer of coverage and a contract is binding on the insurer, the policyowner may, in effect, reject the contract and get a full refund based on the 10-day free look provision.

7-2. Because the prospective policyowner can only accept or reject the contract offered by the insurer, the contract of adhesion rules provide that all ambiguities in the contract of insurance will be resolved in favor of the policyowner and against the insurer.

7-3. The face page of the contract usually has the following information:

- the name of the insurance company
- some specific details for that policy
- a general description of the type of insurance provided by that policy contract
- a statement about the policy's free look provision
- the insurer's promise to pay
- the signatures of the officers (usually the president and the secretary) of the company, which binds the company to the terms of the contract

7-4. The standard policy provisions laws of the various states require that life insurance policies include certain provisions but allow the insurance companies to select the actual wording. However, the wording must be submitted to and approved by the state insurance department. The state insurance codes generally impose a requirement that unless specifically exempted from the law, all life insurance policies delivered or issued for delivery in the state must contain language substantially the same as certain specified provisions. Insurers are also generally given the option to insert different provisions than those specified in the statute if the language in the insurer's provisions is more favorable to policyowners. The insurance department determines whether an alternative provision is more favorable to consumers.

7-5. Because of the provision, a policy that would have lapsed for nonpayment of premiums continues in force during the grace period. The premium remains due, however, and if the insured dies during the grace period, the insurer may deduct one month's premium from the death benefit.

7-6. There is usually no provision in the contract concerning late remittance offers. Such offers are made solely at the insurer's option. The late remittance offer is not a right of the policyowner or an obligation of the insurer that is included in the insurance contract under the requirements of the law. With a late remittance offer, coverage is not continued as a result of the offer. Late remittance offers are intended to encourage the policyowner to reinstate the policy; they do *not* extend coverage. The inducement from the insurer is that coverage can be reinstated without having to provide evidence of insurability.

7-7. The policyowner is expected to pay interest on the "loan" because he or she has withdrawn assets from the insurer that were intended to support the level premium concept. If the policyowner withdraws those assets, it is fair to expect him or her to pay an interest rate that would approximate what the insurer would earn if the money were left with the insurer to invest.

7-8. The goals of the entire contract statutes are

- to assure that the policyowner is given a copy of all documents that constitute the contract
- to preclude any changes in the contract after it has been issued

7-9. The typical requirements that must be met for a policyowner to reinstate a life insurance policy are as follows:

- Normally, insurers do not permit reinstatement of a policy that has been surrendered for its cash value.
- The reinstatement must occur within a specified period of time from the date of lapse—for example, 3 or 5 years.
- The policyowner must provide evidence of insurability satisfactory to the insurer.
- The policyowner must pay or reinstate any other policy indebtedness with interest at a specified rate. This includes back premium due and policy loans if required by the insurer.

7-10. Rather than voiding the contract based on misrepresentation of age, the practice after discovering the inaccuracy is to adjust the policy's premium or benefits to reflect the truth. Because Jim is already dead, the benefits would be adjusted. Adjustments in the policy's premiums or benefits based on misstatements of age or sex are not precluded by the incontestable clause. This is because incontestability clauses preclude contests of the *validity* of the policy. The typical policy provides that if the age of the insured has been misstated, the insurer will adjust all benefits payable under this policy to that which the premium paid would have purchased at the correct age or sex. In this case, the death benefit would be reduced from $100,000 to approximately $90,000 (that is, $100,000 x [$1,500/$1,667]).

7-11. The Standard Nonforfeiture Law does not require specific surrender values. Rather it requires the following:

- surrender values must be at least as large as those that would be produced by the method the law prescribes
- each policy must contain a statement of the method used to find the surrender values and benefits provided under the policy at durations not specifically shown
- after a cash value policy has been in effect for a minimum number of years (usually 3) the insurer must use part of the reserved excess premium to create a guaranteed minimum cash value
- the insurer must give the policyowner a choice of two additional nonforfeiture options: (1) extended term insurance for the net face amount of the policy or (2) paid-up insurance at a reduced death benefit amount
- if the policyowner has not elected between them, the policy must provide that one of these two options will be effective automatically if the policy lapses.

7-12. $10,000   loan
       + 800   first-year interest ($10,000 x 0.08)
       + 864   second-year interest ($10,800 x 0.08)
       $11,664   policy indebtedness

       $60,000   cash value
       –11,664   indebtedness
       $48,336   cash upon surrender

7-13. Normally, there are no reinstatement rights available to a policyowner after surrendering a policy for its cash value.

7-14. When the reduced paid-up option is elected, the policyowner receives a reduced amount of paid-up cash value insurance, payable upon the same conditions as the original policy. The amount of paid-up insurance provided under the reduced paid-up option is the sum that can be purchased at the insured's attained age by the net surrender value (cash value, less any policy indebtedness, plus the cash value of any dividend additions or deposits) applied as a net single premium computed on the mortality and interest bases specified in the policy for the calculation of the surrender value.

7-15. The reduced paid-up option is provided by a benefit provision in a whole life policy and is a guaranteed option upon lapse. For a variable universal life policy or universal life policy, there is no option providing for reduced paid-up insurance. The policyowner has to explicitly request a death benefit reduction to create the equivalent of a reduced paid-up surrender option. Moreover, because the policyowner bears the investment risk with variable universal life insurance, further adjustments may be needed if the earnings on the cash value drop below the level anticipated when the policy benefit was reduced.

7-16. The extended term insurance option provides paid-up term insurance in an amount equal to the original face of the policy, increased by any dividend additions or deposits and decreased by any policy indebtedness. The length of the term is that which can be purchased at the insured's attained age by the application of the net surrender value as a net single premium.

7-17. a. $90,000 of extended term ($100,000 – $10,000)
       b. $20,000 as a net single premium purchase ($30,000 – $10,000)

7-18. From the standpoint of the companies, extended term insurance is a more attractive surrender benefit than paid-up whole life insurance. Companies consider the favorable features of extended term insurance to be (1) relatively large amount of insurance involved, with the correspondingly low expense *rate*; (2) the definite date of expiry, which limits the maintenance expenses and minimizes the problem of tracing policyowners; (3) the uninterrupted continuation of the original amount of coverage, as modified by dividend additions and policy loans, for those persons who contemplate eventual reinstatement; and (4) its adaptability to liberal reinstatement requirements, which stems from the fact that the amount at risk is normally decreased by reinstatement, in contrast to the increase in the amount at risk that occurs on the reinstatement of reduced paid-up insurance. The only real disadvantage of extended term insurance from the insurer's standpoint is the adverse mortality selection encountered, and this can be hedged through the use of the higher mortality assumptions authorized by law or minimized through making the extended term option the *automatic* paid-up benefit.

7-19. The automatic premium loan clause provides that any defaulted premium will be automatically paid and charged against the cash value without request from the policyowner unless he or she elects to surrender the policy for cash or one of the paid-up insurance options. The effect of the automatic premium loan clause is to extend the original plan of insurance for the original face amount decreased by the amount of premiums loaned with interest. Such extension will continue as long as the cash value at each premium due date is sufficient to cover another premium.

7-20. Certain policy provisions are prohibited because they violate public policy.

7-21. The five generally prohibited policy provisions are as follows:

- The insurance producer, who is the agent of the insurance company, cannot be made the agent of the insured for purposes of filling out the application for insurance.
- Nonpayment of a loan cannot cause forfeiture.
- Less-value statutes preclude an insurer from promising something on the face of the policy and taking it away in the fine print.
- Insurers may not contractually reduce the period for filing a lawsuit against them to a period shorter than that specified in the statute.
- No lengthy backdating to save age is allowed.

7-22. Insurers are protected because the laws allow them to impose shorter limitation periods than otherwise permitted in the state. This benefits insurers because it requires plaintiffs to sue while information relevant to the insurance policy is still easy to obtain. The public is protected because the statutes do not allow insurers to shorten the limitation period so much that the public does not have sufficient time to determine whether a lawsuit is worthwhile.

7-23. The advantage of backdating is that the insured will pay lower annual premiums for each increment of the policy because the premium will be based on the younger age. The disadvantage is that the insured must pay the premium applicable to the length of the backdating. This means that the insured will have paid for insurance protection during a period of time before the policy was issued when no coverage was provided.

7-24. a. If Sally committed suicide during the first year of coverage, the company would pay the amount described in the suicide provision (typically, only the premiums paid less any unpaid policy loans).

      b. If Sally committed suicide during the fifth year of coverage, the company would pay the $250,000 (less any unpaid policy loans).

7-25. The following limitations are typically found in accidental death benefit coverage:

- This benefit is payable only in the event of the insured's *accidental* death; not if the cause of death is disease.
- There is a standard practice of putting a time limit in the accidental death benefit provision—most commonly, the death must occur within 90 days of the accident that is said to have caused the injury.
- Basic definitions preclude coverage for any death that is the natural and probable result of a voluntary act.
- Most accidental death benefit clauses do not provide coverage in the event of the insured's death by suicide.

7-26. There are two types of accidental death clauses: (1) the *accidental result* type and (2) the *accidental means* type. Under an accidental means clause, both the cause (means) of the death and the result must be unintentional. Under an accidental result clause, only the result must be unintentional. The accidental result clause is more favorable to the consumer. Most courts have recognized that the difference between the two clauses is too difficult for many consumers to understand and therefore ceased to recognize a distinction between the two types of clauses.

7-27. Under the typical provision, the policyowner receives the right to acquire additional insurance in specified amounts at specified times or ages. Typically, this provision allows additional purchases every 3 years and after marriage or the birth of a child, provided the events occur before the insured reaches the specified maximum age (often 45). This right to purchase additional insurance may be very valuable because the insured does not have to provide evidence of insurability in order to exercise the option.

7-28. If a policy is sold in a state but does not include a required provision or has not been filed with the state for approval, the courts will treat the policy as if it did include all the required provisions under the law of that jurisdiction. The policyowner or beneficiary will be permitted to enforce the policy against the insurer as if it complied in all respects with the applicable state law. If an insurer issues a policy that has not been approved by the insurance department, the policyowner may seek a refund of premiums paid or seek to enforce the policy. If suit is brought, the courts will enforce the unapproved contract against the insurer on behalf of the beneficiary. If the unapproved policy does not include a provision that would have been required for approval, the courts will treat the policy as if it does contain such a provision. Furthermore, if a required provision is more favorable to the policyowner than one actually included in the contract, the courts will treat the contract as if it included the more favorable provision. The insurer that violates the laws requiring filing of the policy and approval of its provisions by the state will also be subject to fines or other penalties (such as revocation of the insurer's right to do business in that state).

Answers to Self-Test Questions

7-1. C
7-2. D
7-3. B
7-4. C
7-5. B
7-6. C
7-7. B
7-8. C
7-9. D
7-10. C

Chapter 8

Answers to Review Questions

8-1. When the proceeds of a life insurance policy are payable in a lump sum, the company's liability under the policy is fully discharged with the payment of such sum. If, however, the company retains the proceeds under one of the optional methods of settlement, its liability continues beyond the maturity of the policy and must be evidenced by some sort of legal document. That document (called the *settlement agreement*) contains the designation of the various classes of beneficiaries and a detailed description of the manner in which the proceeds are to be distributed.

8-2. When either the policyowner or beneficiary elects the settlement option, and the settlement option is to benefit the party who elected it, a spendthrift clause (if included in the settlement agreement) will not be enforced. A spendthrift clause is generally enforceable when the party procures the life insurance policy or settlement agreement for the benefit of someone else.

8-3. If the applicant's request for the particular settlement option is granted, a specified rate of income per $1,000 is guaranteed in the policy. These rates are referred to as contract rates. This means that the issuing company cannot later modify the actuarial assumptions underlying the benefits provided under this optional mode of settlement.

8-4. The right of withdrawal may be limited as to the following: the frequency with which it can be invoked, the minimum amount that can be withdrawn at any one time, the maximum amount that can be withdrawn at any one time, in any one year, or in the aggregate. The first two types of limitations are imposed by the insurers to control the cost of administration, while the last three are imposed by the policyowner (often a parent of the beneficiary) to prevent dissipation or too rapid exhaustion of the proceeds by the beneficiary. The right of withdrawal can usually be invoked only on dates when regular interest or liquidation payments are due.

8-5. A cumulative right of withdrawal means that if any or all of withdrawable amounts are not withdrawn during a particular year, they can be withdrawn in a later year along with any other amounts withdrawable that (later) year. A noncumulative right of withdrawal means that at the end of the time period allowed for withdrawal, the right to withdraw that time period's amounts ends and is not carried over into later periods.

8-6. Cathy can withdraw a maximum of $20,000 (5 x $4,000) during the 5-year period. Because she withdrew $6,000 during that time, she has a maximum amount of $18,000 that she can withdraw in year 6. This is the cumulative sum, less the withdrawals over the 5 years, plus the $4,000 right-of-withdrawal amount attributed to year 6.

8-7. Life insurance settlement options, as a group, embody these three basic concepts: retention of proceeds without liquidation of principal, systematic liquidation of the proceeds without reference to life contingencies (that is, without reference to how long the primary beneficiaries live), systematic liquidation of the proceeds with reference to one or more life contingencies (that is, with reference to how long the primary beneficiaries live)

8-8. The four fundamental settlement options are: the interest option, the installment time option or fixed-period option, the installment amount option or fixed-amount option, and the life income option.

8-9. The interest option is a simple option because the insurance company maintains the proceeds intact until a stated period of time has expired or a stated occurrence has taken place. Afterwards, a method of ultimate disposition of the proceeds commences. The interest option is flexible because of the varying degrees of control over proceeds held by the company that a primary beneficiary can be given. For example, if a policyowner wants the beneficiary to have access to money for emergencies, he or she may give the primary beneficiary a limited right of withdrawal.

The policyowner may also give the primary beneficiary the right to elect a liquidating option if additional flexibility is desired.

8-10. The fixed-period option provides payments over a stipulated period of time, while the fixed-amount option provides payments of a stipulated amount. The two options are based on the same mathematical principles and differ only as to whether emphasis is attached to the *duration* of the payments or to the *level* of payments.

8-11. When the fixed-period option, the amount of each payment during the liquidation period depends on several factors: the size of the fund, the rate of interest assumed to be earned, the time when the first payment is to be made, and the interval between payments. If the amount of each payment is fixed in advance, the period over which the liquidation is to take place depends on these same factors.

8-12. Additional proceeds payable because of the accidental death benefits, dividend accumulations, paid-up additions, increased investment earnings during the payout period, or prepaid or discounted premiums that are considered to be part of the proceeds can increase the amount of proceeds available. Outstanding policy loans at the insured's death may decrease the proceeds available and reduce the size of the monthly benefits.

8-13. The fixed-amount option offers a great deal of flexibility. The beneficiary can be given the right to indicate when the liquidation payments are to begin. In the meantime, the proceeds will be held at interest, with the interest payments going to the primary beneficiary. Unlike the fixed-period option, the beneficiary can be given either a limited or an unlimited right of withdrawal. Under this option, withdrawals will merely shorten the period of installment payments and will not necessitate re-computing benefit payments. The beneficiary can also be given the right to accelerate or retard the rate of liquidation. That is, he or she can be given the privilege of varying the amount of the monthly payments, subject to any limitations the insured might wish to impose. Furthermore, the beneficiary can be given the privilege of discontinuing payments during particular months of the year or from time to time. Finally, this option can include a provision for transferring the remaining proceeds to another liquidating option.

8-14. The principle underlying a life income option is identical to that underlying an annuity. A life income option is simply the annuity principle applied to the liquidation of insurance proceeds. At a minimum, all life income options guarantee benefit payments as long as the primary beneficiary (or beneficiaries) lives. Other guarantees can be added such as a minimum number of benefit payments (payments for at least a specified period of time) or return of at least the amount of proceeds placed under the option. In the case of a life income option, the annuity principle works as follows: If the primary beneficiary is willing to pool his or her death proceeds with those of other people in the same situation, the insurer, relying on the laws of probability and large numbers, can provide each of the participants with an income of a specified amount as long as he or she lives, regardless of longevity. No one would outlive his or her income. Such an arrangement, however, implies a willingness on each participant's part to have all or a portion of his or her unliquidated principal and/or interest at the time of death used to supplement the exhausted principal of those who live beyond their expectancy.

8-15. There are several life income options available in a life insurance policy:

a. The straight life income option is equivalent to a pure immediate annuity. The first payment is due one payment period (usually, one month) after maturity of the policy or after election of the option, whichever is later. The monthly income provided per $1,000 of proceeds depends on the age and sex of the beneficiary and the insurer's assumptions as to mortality and interest. The monthly income benefit is paid as long as the primary beneficiary lives, but ceases upon his or her death.

b. The life income option with a specified period of guaranteed payments is mathematically a combination of a fixed-period installment option of appropriate duration and a pure deferred life annuity. For example, a life income option that promises to provide payments of a specified amount to a beneficiary aged 45 throughout his or her remaining lifetime, and in any event for 20 years, is a combination of a fixed-period installment option running for 20 years and a pure life annuity deferred to the beneficiary's age 65. If the beneficiary does not survive to age 65, the portion of the proceeds allocated to the deferred life annuity is retained by the insurance company without further obligation. The primary beneficiary receives a monthly income benefit as long as he or she lives, but if the primary beneficiary were to die during the 20-year period certain, the monthly income benefit would be to due during the 20-year period certain, the monthly income benefit would be continued to the contingent beneficiary for the remainder of the period certain.

c. The installment refund option is a combination of a pure immediate life annuity and decreasing term insurance in an amount sufficient to continue payments until the proceeds, without interest, have been paid out in full. (In addition to promising monthly benefit payments as long as the primary beneficiary lives, this option promises to continue the monthly payments beyond the primary beneficiary's death until the proceeds of the life insurance policy have been returned.) At the inception, the term insurance is in an amount equal to the proceeds, less the first payment due immediately, but it decreases with each periodic payment and expires altogether when the cumulative benefit payments equal or exceed the life insurance proceeds committed to the installment-refund option.

d. Like the installment refund option, the cash-refund option is a combination of a pure immediate life annuity and decreasing term insurance. Because the refund is payable in cash rather than payable in installments, however, a slightly larger amount of term insurance is required.

8-16. Because benefits are calculated according to the primary beneficiary's age and gender, there are no substitutions allowed after the payments have started. Rights of withdrawal and commutation are not available.

8-17. When life insurance proceeds are payable to an irrevocable life insurance trust, funds can be made indirectly available to the insured's estate for liquidity purposes, either by the trustee's purchase of non-cash assets from the estate or by loans of money to the estate. If the insurance proceeds are more than sufficient to meet the insured's estate liquidity needs, the excess may be made available for the insured's dependents without the delay and expense associated with probate.

8-18. If the mortgage has no prepayment privilege or can be prepaid only with a heavy penalty, an income settlement can be arranged to provide funds in the required amount and frequency for the mortgage payments. Either the fixed-period option or the fixed-amount option is generally satisfactory.

8-19. The actual dependency period is considered to be the period of time from the end of the readjustment period following Hal's death until the youngest child's (Joanie's) 18th birthday, assuming Joanie remains in generally good health. If Social Security survivorship benefits in conjunction with the interest on retained life insurance proceeds are inadequate during this period, additional income can be provided through the fixed-period or fixed-amount options. If the fixed-amount option is elected, Greta can also be granted the right of withdrawal for even greater flexibility in meeting family needs.

8-20. The basic ethical rule can be summarized: pursue your interests fairly and unselfishly. Selfish behavior is behavior in which the pursuit of self-interest is without regard for the interests of, or at the expense of, others. Reflecting on the principle of fairness helps us see the unethical nature of selfishness. By "selfishness" we do not mean just the pursuit of self-interest. The pursuit of self-interest is a perfectly natural and acceptable activity. Selfishness is the pursuit of self-interest *at the expense of another* when one is not entitled to the good pursued. When a person is being selfish, he or she puts their own interest first in a situation where pursuing that interest will hurt another.

8-21. Most people would agree that the advisor should follow the Golden Rule and treat clients as the advisor would like to be treated. This rule exists and needs to be followed because insurance advisors, like everyone else, are subject to the conflict between self-interest and the interests of others. Advisors should make recommendations based on their client's needs. It is unethical to sell a client an unnecessary insurance policy. The attempt to sell a client an unnecessary policy would tend to involve lying and/or deception, practices universally considered unethical. It is an obligation of the advisor to keep personal and private information confidential. The advisor is responsible for delivering the insurance policy to the insured and explaining all the policy provisions. The advisor is also responsible for handling client clients and providing good service.

8-22. Misrepresenting the benefits or terms of a policy; misrepresenting dividends as guaranteed when they are not; misrepresenting the financial condition of the insurer; misrepresenting a life insurance policy as other than what it is; or, finally, misrepresenting oneself by perhaps claiming to be a financial planner when one is not. Coercion that restricts free choice of products is also unethical. Twisting occurs when a policyowner is induced to discontinue and replace a policy through advisor or insurer distortion or misrepresentation of the facts. When a policy is replaced unnecessarily it is known as churning. These practices are obviously unethical to the extent they exemplify the advisor pursuing self-interest at the expense of the client. Rebating is defined as any inducement in the sale of insurance that is not specified in the insurance contract. An offer to share a commission with an applicant is an example of such an inducement, and is illegal in most states except California and Florida. Rebating is generally considered wrong because it gives one advisor an unfair advantage over other advisors, or is seen as unfair to those clients who are not given a rebate. Company bashing is telling lies or misrepresenting the strengths and weaknesses of another advisor or another company. Unethical discrimination is exclusion committed on the basis of some unjustified bias or hatred toward a person or group.

Answers to Self-Test Questions

8-1. C
8-2. B
8-3. C
8-4. D
8-5. A
8-6. C
8-7. A
8-8. A
8-9. D
8-10. A

Index

A

Accelerated benefits, 7-28
Accidental death benefit rider, 7-30
Accumulation of whole life insurance, 2-21
Adjustable life insurance, 3-7
Adverse selection (Antiselection), 1-7, 2-5
Age
    extremes of, 6-28
    limiting for nonmedical insurance issue, 6-24
    misstatement of, 7-12
    rating up of, 6-31
    risk and, 6-7
Advisor/client relationship, 8-32
Advisor/insurer relationship, 8-39
Advisors, xiii
Alcohol consumption, 6-12
Amount at risk, 1-12
Annuity due, 5-6
Applicant information, 6-18
Assignment provision, 7-27
Attained-age method, 2-6
Automatic premium loans, 7-37
Average annual earnings, estimation of, 1-22
Aviation activities, risk and, 6-14
Avocation, risk and, 6-15

B

Backdating, 7-26
Belth, Joseph, 5-13
    benchmark prices of insurance of, 5-15
    yearly cost method of, 5-4
    yearly price of protection method, 5-14
    yearly rate of return method, 5-13
Blackout period, 8-27
Blood pressure levels, 6-9
Blood tests, 6-9
Build, 6-7
    table for adults, 6-8

Burial expenses, 1-28
Business, 4-19
    Buy-sell funding with joint-life policy, 4-53
    continuation of, 4-53
    life insurance uses for, 4-19
Business partners, joint-life policy for, 2-26
Buy-sell agreements, 4-53
    entity plan, 4-59
    cross-purchase plan, 4-59
    stock redemption, 4-60

C

Capital needs, 1-37
Capital needs analysis, 1-37
Capitalized value, 1-20
Cash accumulation comparison method, 5-11
Cash needs, 1-35, 8-27
Cash surender value, 7-14
Caveat emptor, 8-43
Caveat vendor, 8-43
Churning, 8-35
Cleanup fund, 1-28
Commissioners Standard Ordinary (CSO) Mortality Tables, 1-4
Commutation, 8-8
Comparative interest rate method, 5-13
Contestability, 7-9
Contract of adhesion, 7-3
Contract rates, 8-5
Conversions of ordinary life contract, 2-6
Convertibility,
    retroactive, 2-6
    time limit for, 2-8
Corridor test, 3-6
Cost-of-insurance charge, 3-13
Credit enhancement, 4-19
Crediting rates, in *Life Insurance Illustration Questionnaire*, 5-32

CSO (Commissioners Standard Ordinary) Mortality Tables, 1-4
Current assumption whole life insurance, 3-27
   cash value in, 3-29
   low premium/high premium designs of, 3-30
   redetermination of, 3-31
   uses of, 3-32
Current cash value, 3-23
Current interest assumptions, 3-23
Current rates, 8-5

D

Daily living needs, 4-4
Death
   lump-sum needs at, 1-35
   income needs at, 1-35
Death benefits
   choice of in universal life insurance, 3-19
   of endowment policy, 3-3
   increasing, 3-20
   level or increasing, 3-19
   of whole life policy, 2-20
Death taxes
   life insurance to repay, 1-28, 2-26
Deaths, number of in sample population, 6-6
Debts
   life insurance to repay, 1-28
Deceptive sales practices, 5-25
Decreasing term, 2-11
Deferred (life) annuity, 8-17
Delay clause, 2-24
Dependency period income, 1-29, 8-26
Direct recognition, 3-23
Disability waiver-of-premium rider, 7-33
Discrimination, 4-22
Divisible surplus, 7-10
Drug addiction, 6-12

E

Economic security, preservation of, 1-18
Economic value
   diminishing nature of, 1-25
   five-step procedure for estimating, 1-22
   source of, 1-18
Educational needs, 1-30

Emergency needs, 1-31, 4-13
Employee Retirement Income Security Act of 1972 (ERISA), 4-38
Endowment insurance, 3-3
Entire contract statutes, 7-10
Equal outlay comparison method, 5-12
Equity among policyowners, 6-5
ERISA (Employee Retirement Income Security Act of 1972), 4-38
Estate clearance fund, 1-28
Estoppel, 7-28
Ethical behavior, 8-29
   of market conduct, 8-31
   of risk classification, 8-44
Evidence of insurability, 1-4
Executive bonus, 4-23
Executor costs, 1-28
Expenses
   in *Life Insurance Illustration Questionnaire*, 5-32
   in pricing performance comparisons, 5-32
Extended term insurance, 7-14, 7-19
   disadvantage of, 7-22
Extra percentage tables, 6-32

F

Family
   charitable donations of, 4-15
   death tax funds for, 4-12
   debt repayment funds for, 4-11
   income needs after death , 4-3
   moral obligation to protect, 1-19
   settlement options adapted to needs of, 8-23
   sources of immediate funds for, 4-3
   uses of life insurance by, 1-17
Family history, risk and, 6-10
Financial needs analysis, 1-37
Fixed amount option, 8-13
Fixed period option, 8-12
Flat extra premium, 6-35
Free look provision, 7-4
Future income
   estimating needs for, 1-31
   estimating payments of, 1-31

G

Gender
   misstatement of, 7-12
   risk and, 6-13
Gifts
   funding with life insurance, 4-16

future interest, 4-38
   taxes, 4-38
Grace period, 7-6
   late remittance offers and, 7-6
Group life insurance, 4-21
   Group term life insurance, 4-21
   danger of sole reliance on, 2-14
Guaranteed cash value, 3-11
Guaranteed purchase option, 7-37

H

Habits, risk and, 6-12
Human life value, 1-17
   approach, 1-20
   bases for insurance of, 1-26
   calculating present value of, 1-23
   diminishing nature of economic
      value of, 1-25
   estimating economic value of, 1-20

I

Illustrated scale, 5-39
Illustration actuaries, 5-38
Immediate annuity, 8-16
   cash refund, 8-17
   installment refund, 8-17
   life with guaranteed installments,
      8-17
   straight life annuity, 8-16
Income
   computing present value of
      payments, 1-23
   during dependency period, 1-29
   readjustment, 1-29, 8-26
   for surviving dependent spouse, 1-
      29, 8-27
Income needs
   ongoing, 1-27
   settlement options adapted to, 8-23
Income producer, death of, 1-18
Income stock funds, 3-10
Income tax
   for early depletion in variable
      universal life policy, 3-36
Incontestable clause, 7-9
Increase-in-age method, 6-31
Increasing term, 2-12
Indeterminate premium whole life
      policies, 3-28
Inflation, effects of, 1-36
Information
   from Advisor, 6-16
   from applicant, 6-18

from attending physicians, 6-19
from inspection report, 6-19
from medical examiner, 6-18
from Medical Information Bureau,
     6-20
sources of
   for nonmedical insurance, 6-24
   for risk classification, 6-21
Inspection reports, 6-19
   Information from for nonmedical
      insurance, 6-24
Installment options, 8-11
   fixed-amount option, 8-13
   fixed-period option, 8-12
   refund option, 8-17
Insurability option, 7-35
Insurance
   amount of, 1-33
   basic principles of, 1-3
   cost of, 3-10, 3-13
   expenses of
      level premium technique effect
         on, 1-12
Insurance policies. *See also* Life
      insurance policies; specific
      policies
   costs of, 3-10, 3-13
   provisions of, 7-3
Insured/insurer relationship, 8-42
Interest
   crediting rates, 3-23
   on proceeds, retention of, 8-10
Interest income, 8-10
   principal needed to provide, 1-37
Interest option, 8-10
   for readjustment period, 8-26
Interest rates
   cost comparisons that isolate, 5-12
   in illustrative dividend
      computation, 5-33
   in *Life Insurance Illustration*
      Questionnaire, 5-32
Interest-adjusted cost indexes, 5-4
Interest-only option, 8-16
   in estate clearance, 8-23
   for life income for surviving
      spouse, 8-27
Interest-sensitive whole life policy,
      3-28
Internal Revenue Code (IRC)
   Sec. 79, 4-22
   Sec. 101, 3-5
   Sec. 162, 4-23
   Sec. 7702, 3-5

Investment funds
    switching in variable universal life
        policy, 3-10
    with variable life insurance, 3-10
Investment portfolio
    sample characteristics of, 3-35
    in variable life policy, 3-10
    objectives of, 2-16
    performance of, 3-13

J

Joint-life insurance, 2-26
Judgment method of rating, 6-21

K

Key person indemnification, 4-50

L

Late remittance offer, 7-6
Legal reserve, 1-19
Level premium concept, 1-8, 2-20
    effect on cost of insurance, 1-12
Level premium insurance, 1-8
    ordinary life policies, 1-10
    overcharging of policyholders in,
        1-12
    significance of, 1-8
    term policies, 2-11
    whole life policies, 2-19
Life income option, 8-16
    monthly income provided by, 8-19
    principal amount to provide $1- per
        month, 8-19
    with specified period of guaranteed
        payments, 8-17
    straight, 8-16
Life insurance
    analysis of needs for, 1-27
    bases for, 1-26
    basic principles of, 1-3
    basic types of, 1-5, 2-3, 3-3, *See
        also* Endowment life
        insurance; Term insurance;
        Universal life insurance;
        Whole life insurance
    for business continuation, 4-53
    business purposes of, 4-19
    charitable donations, 4-15
    comparing policy costs for, 5-29
    credit purposes of, 4-19
    debt repayment funds, 1-28
    dependent educational funds from,
        1-30

    economic bases of, 1-18
    in employee benefit plans, 4-20
    ethical basis of, 1-19
    family purposes of, 1-29
    family survivor income, 1-29
    family uses of, 1-17
    function of, 1-17
    funding home health care or
        nursing home care, 4-17
    funding individual gifts, 4-16
    group, 4-21
    risk pooling in, 1-3
    savings vs. protection, 1-11
    supplementing retirement income,
        4-17
    term, 2-3
    transferring assets to younger
        generation, 4-16
Life insurance companies, 1-4
    mutual, 1-4
    stock, 1-4
*Life Insurance Illustration
    Questionnaire*, 5-32
Life insurance policies
    illustrations of, 5-17
    regulations for illustrations, 5-34
Limited-payment (whole) life
    insurance, 2-24
Linton yield method, 5-13
Liquidation
    systematic, with reference to life
      contingencies, 8-10
    systematic, without reference to
      life contingencies, 8-11
    fixed-amount option, 8-13
    fixed-period option, 8-12
Loans, 7-7, *See also* Policy loans
Lump-sum cash needs, 8-23
Lump-sum needs, 1-35

M

Market conduct
    deceptive sales practices, 5-25
    ethics of, 8-34
Marketing
    ethical, 8-32, 8-43
Medical Information Bureau (MIB), 6-20
Military service
    risk and, 6-15
Misstatement of age and gender, 7-12
Modified endowment contract (MEC),
    3-37
Morals, risk and, 6-12

Mortality
    select, ultimate, 2-9
Mortality assumptions, 6-3
    compatibility with, 6-3
    establishing range of, 6-4
    at various age groups, 6-28
Mortality rates
    in illustrations, 5-33
    in *Life Insurance Illustration
        Questionnaire*, 5-32
Mortality risk, at extremes of age, 6-28
Mortgage
    as need, 1-30
    redemption needs, 1-30
Mortgage cancellation fund, 1-30, 8-25
Mutual life insurance companies, 1-4

N

National Association of Insurance
        Commissioners (NAIC),
        5-4
    model illustration, 5-34
    life insurance policy illustrations
        standards of, 5-17
Needs
    determining, 1-27
    insurance to meet, 1-26
    monetary evaluation of, 1-20
    special, 1-30
Needs analysis, 1-27
    liquidating and nonliquidating
        approaches, 1-37
Net cost method, 5-3
Net level premium, 1-8
Net payment cost index, interest-
        adjusted, 5-6
Net single premium, 2-20, 7-17
Net surrender cost index,
        interest-adjusted, 5-5
Nonforfeiture options, 7-13, *See also*
        Surrender options
Nonlevel term insurance, 2-11
Nonmedical insurance, 6-24
    economics of, 6-25
    paramedical examination, 6-27
    underwriting safeguards of, 6-24
Nonparticipating policies, 2-23
Nonqualified deferred compensation,
        4-47
Numerical method of rating, 6-21

O

Occupational risk, 6-11

Ongoing income needs, 1-31
Ordinary life insurance, 2-19
    cash-value or accumulation
        element of, 2-21
    level annual premium for, 1-8, 2-20
    lowest premium outlay in, 2-20
    permanent protection under, 2-20
    policy loans, 2-21
    proportion of protection and
        savings elements in, 1-10
    reduced paid-up insurance for, 7-16
    surrender options of, 7-14
Original age method, *See* Retroactive
        conversion
Ownership provision, 7-26

P

Paramedical examination, 6-27
Participating policies, 2-23
Payment cost index, 5-6
Pension plans, 4-44
Permanent insurance, 2-20
Persistency
    in *Life Insurance Illustration
        Questionnaire*, 5-34
Personal history, risk and, 6-10
Physical condition, risk and, 6-8
Physician information, 6-19
Pilots, risk of, 6-14
Plan change provision, 7-29
Policy
    cost comparison methods, 5-3
    face page of, 7-4
    illustrations, 5-17
    provisions of, 7-5
        common, 7-30
        optional, 7-26
        prohibited, 7-24
        required, 7-6
        standard, 7-5
        waiver and estoppel, 7-28
    summary, 5-5
Policy loans, 7-7
    interest rate for, 7-8
Policy proceeds left at interest, 8-10
Policyowner
    rights, 7-27
    risks to, 3-14
Prefunding, 1-12
Premium, 2-20, *See also* Net level
        premium; Net single
        premium
    calculation, 1-5, 2-20

determining in yearly renewable
term insurance, 1-5
fixed, 2-19
flat extra, 6-35
flexibility of universal life policies,
3-15, 3-26
level, 1-8, 2-20
levels of and redetermination
frequency, 3-31
lowest outlay for, 2-20
rates, 1-5, 2-9
target, 3-17
waiver of, 7-33
of whole life vs. yearly term, 2-12
Present value, 1-21
of $1 per annum, 1-22
of annual payments, 1-23
Price indexes, 5-4
Professional Practice Guidelines,
Society of Financial
Service Professionals, 5-29
Prohibited provisions, 7-24
Prospectus, variable life policy, 3-12
Protection
versus cash value in ordinary life
contract, 2-19
moral obligation to provide, 1-19
permanent, 2-20
temporary need for, 2-13
of whole life policy, 2-20

Q

Qualified retirement plans, 4-43
Qualified terminal interest property
trust (QTIP), 4-11
Qualifying medical conditions,
accelerated benefits for,
7-28

R

Readjustment income, 1-29, 8-26
Rebating, 8-34
Re-entry term insurance, 2-9
Redetermination, 3-31
Reduced paid-up insurance, 7-16
Refund option, 8-17
cash, 8-17
installment, 8-17
Reinstatement, 7-11
Renewability, 2-4
of term insurance, 2-4
period, limiting, 1-7
Reserve, 1-8

Retirement needs- 1-31
Retroactive conversion, 2-6
Revocable contingent beneficiary, 8-5
Right to assign, 7-27
Risk, 6-3
age and, 6-7
aviation activities and, 6-14
avocation and, 6-15
build, 6-7
categories of balance within, 6-5
classification of, 6-21
ethical issues of, 8-42
economic status and, 6-14
factors affecting, 6-3
family history and, 6-10
gender and, 6-13
guiding principles of selection and,
6-5
habits and, 6-12
information on, 6-16
sources of, 6-16
of insurance at extremes of age,
6-28
insurance plan and, 6-13
investment, 3-12
limiting in nonmedical insurance,
6-24
measurement of, 6-21
military service and, 6-15
morals and, 6-12
for nonmedical insurance, 6-24
numerical rating of, 6-21
occupation and, 6-11
personal history and, 6-10
physical condition and, 6-8
rating of, 6-21
judgment method of, 6-21
numerical system of, 6-21
residence and, 6-11
selection of, 6-3
substandard insurance, 6-29
removal of rating, 6-36
treatment of, 6-31
Risk pooling, 1-3, 6-5
illustration of, 1-4
Risky behaviors, 6-12

S

Sarbanes-Oxley Act, 4-38
Select term insurance, 2-9
Selection, costs of, 6-3
Self-interest, 8-28
Selfishness, 8-28
Settlement agreements, 8-3

Settlement options, 8-9. *See also*
        Structured settlements
    income needs, 8-26
    contract vs. current rates in, 8-5
    right of commutation in, 8-8
    right of withdrawal in, 8-7
    use of options for, 8-23
Sex, *See* Gender
Single-life insurance, 2-26
Single-premium whole life policy, 2-25
Social Security benefits, 1-32
    for ongoing income needs of
        survivors, 1-32
Society of Financial Service
        Professionals
    *Life Insurance Illustration
        Questionnaire*, 5-32
    Professional Practice Guidelines,
        5-29
Socio-economic hazards, 6-11
Spendthrift clause, 8-4
Split-dollar life insurance plans, 4-25
    collateral assignment method, 4-28
    econonmic benefit regime, 4-32
    endorsement method, 4-27
    equity split-dollar, 4-31
    loan regime, 4-32
    PS 58, 4-33
    split-dollar rollout 4-34
    Table 2001, 4-33
Standard group, predominance of, 6-5
Stock fund options, 3-10
Stock insurance companies, 1-4
Substandard classifications, 6-31
Substandard risk, 6-31
    incidence of, 6-30
    removal of rating, 6-36
    treatment of, 6-31
Suicide provision, 7-26
Surrender cost index, 5-5
Surrender options, 7-14
    cash, 7-14
    extended term-up insurance, 7-13
    surviving spouse, life income for,
        8-27
Survivor benefits, life income, 8-27
Survivor needs, ongoing income, 1-27
Survivorship benefits
    of whole life policy, 2-26

T

Target premium amount, 3-17
    additional premium payments, 3-15
Tax Code

modified endowment contract
        (MEC) provisions, 3-37
Taxes, gift, 4-38
Term life insurance, 2-3
    areas of usefulness, 2-13
    convertibility, 2-6
    critique of, 2-12
    decreasing, 2-11
    fallacious arguments for, 2-14
    group, 4-21
        danger of sole reliance on, 2-14
    guarding against contestability of,
        2-11
    increasing, 2-12
    level annual premium for, 2-20
    long-term contracts, 2-11
    nature of, 2-3
    nonlevel, 2-11
    re-entry, 2-9
    renewability, 2-4
    select, 2-9
    versus whole life, 2-14
    yearly renewable, 1-5
        determining premium of, 1-5
        limiting period of renewability
            in, 1-7
Time limit, for conversion, 1-7
Time value of money, 5-3
Transfer-for-value, 4-37
Twenty-payment life policy, 2-24
Twisting, 8-34

U

Ultimate term insurance, 2-9
Underwriting, 6-16
    ethical, 8-42
    safeguards for nonmedical
        insurance, 6-24
Unethical business conduct, 8-34
Universal life insurance, 3-32
    death benefits in, 3-19
    extended term, 7-13, 7-20
    flexibility to last lifetime, 3-26
    flexible premiums of, 3-15
    internal funds flow, 3-23
    NAIC regulation of, 3-5
    policy illustrations for, 5-25
    prefunding, 3-16
    target premium amount in, 3-17
    Type I, A, 3-21
    Type II, B, 3-21
    variable, 3-32
Urinalysis, 6-9

V

Variable life insurance, 3-8
    adjustable, 3-14
    cash values of, 3-11
    fixed premium in, 3-8
    investment choices of, 3-10
    linkage of death benefits with
        investment performance,
        3-10
    policyowner risks in, 3-14
    prospectus, 3-12
    SEC objections to, 3-9
    universal, 3-32
        death benefit and investment
            performance in, 3-34
        extended term, 7-13, 7-20
        income tax burdens for early
            depletion in, 3-36
        ultimate flexibility of, 3-34

W

Waiver, 7-29
Waiver-of-premium provision, 7-33
War exclusion clauses, 6-15
Weight/height measurements, 6-7
Whole life insurance, 2-19
    adjustable life, 3-7
    annual premiums of versus yearly
        term premiums, 1-11
    automatic premium loan effects on,
        7-39
    current assumption, 3-27
    with fixed premiums, 2-19
    functions of, 2-28
    joint-life, 2-26
    limited-payment, 2-24
    participating vs. nonparticipating
        basis, 2-23
    principal types of, 3-3
    versus term insurance, 2-14
    universal life, 3-32
    variable adjustable life, 3-14
    variable life, 3-8
    variable universal, 3-32
    variations of, 3--3
Withdrawals
    cumulative, 8-8
    limitations on, 3-17, 8-7
    right of, 3-17, 8-7
    in universal life policies, 3-17

Y

Yearly price of protection method, 5-14

Yearly rate of return method, 5-13
Yearly renewable term insurance, 1-5,
    See also Term insurance